Aw, Shucks!

Aw, Shucks!

The Dictionary of Country Jawing

Anne Bertram

Printed on recyclable paper

NTC Publishing Group
Lincolnwood, Illinois USA

TECHNICAL COLLEGE OF THE LOWCOUNTRY
LEARNING RESOURCES CENTER
POST OFFICE BOX 1288
BEAUFORT, SOUTH CAROLINA 29901-1288

Library of Congress Cataloging-in-Publication Data

Bertram, Anne.

Aw, shucks! : the dictionary of country jawing / Anne Bertram.

p. cm. — (Artful Wordsmith series)

ISBN 0-8442-0906-6 (pbk.)

1. English language—Dialects—United States—Dictionaries.
2. Country life—United States—Terminology—Dictionaries.
3. Figures of speech—Dictionaries. 4. Americanisms—Dictionaries.
I. Title. II. Series.

PE2839.B.B468 1996

427'.973—dc20 96-26179

CIP

Manufactured in the United States of America.

6 7 8 9 0 VP 9 8 7 6 5 4 3 2 1

Contents

Introduction

In many parts of America a surprising number of folksy, regional, and rural expressions have developed through the years and, even today, are heard and used by many American speakers of English. A large number of these colorful sayings also live in the memories of today's citified adults who can remember hearing their grandparents use these sayings frequently. Even in areas where they are not heard as part of the colloquial language, American movies and novels bring many of these expressions to a wide audience. Often these expressions demonstrate a wry sense of humor and keen understanding of human nature lurking in the speech of country folks, hillbillies, and cowboys. Not many of these sayings are welcome in proper writing. In fact, quite a few of them are considered downright illiterate. While this is not completely flattering to some social groups, these expressions remain an important part of American culture and language. As such, they are a source of fascination and intrigue to tourists, foreigners, and native speakers alike.

This dictionary is a selection of folksy and homespun expressions representing many parts of the country and three centuries of American life. Among its entries are sayings that continue to spice up American movies and television, and this volume is an excellent resource for deciphering these expressions. Browsers will be rewarded and entertained by the directness and self-effacing tone of these backwoods sayings.

No claims are made as to where these expressions were used or who used them—only that they are part of the American experience. Familiarity with these sayings will give the reader greater insight into Americans—where they have been and where they are going as well as an idea of the types of cultural messages available in these expressions.

Included with each expression are two example sentences showing how the saying is typically used. A Phrase-Finder Index at the end of the book will help the reader locate any entry by looking up any major word in the entry.

Guide to the Use of the Dictionary

1. Entry heads are alphabetized according to an alphabetical order that ignores punctuation and hyphens.
2. Entry heads appear in **boldface type**. When words or expressions that are not entries in this dictionary are cited, they appear in *italics*.
3. An entry head may have one or more alternative forms. The alternatives are printed in **boldface type** and are preceded by AND.
4. Definitions and paraphrases are in roman type. Alternative or closely related definitions and paraphrases are separated by semicolons.
5. A definition or paraphrase may be followed by comments in parentheses. These comments give additional information about the expression, including pronunciation when necessary.
6. If you cannot find the expression you want, or if you cannot decide on the exact form of the expression, look up any major word in the expression in the Phrase-Finder Index, which begins on page 313. Pick out the expression you want—or the closest thing to it—and look it up in the dictionary.

Terms and Symbols

□ (a box) marks the beginning of an example.

[T] (a box containing a "T") marks the beginning of an example in which two elements of the phrase, usually a particle and an object, are transposed.

AND indicates that an entry head has variant forms that are the same or similar in meaning to the entry head. One or more variant forms are preceded by AND.

Aw, Shucks!

A

a-tall at all. (Used in negative expressions.) □ *I don't like that a-tall.* □ *John is of no help a-tall.*

a ways a distance. (Often used in the expressions *up a ways; down a ways*.) □ *The picture's not level. Move the left side up a ways.* □ *You want to get to Springfield? That's quite a ways from here.*

(a)back of behind. □ *They built a new barn aback of the house.* □ *There was a hidden threat back of Mary's friendly words.*

abide to tolerate someone or something; to stand someone or something. (Usually negative.) □ *I cannot abide grits every damn morning.* □ *Maw cannot abide your constant fussing.*

above one's bend AND **above one's huckleberry** beyond one's ability. □ *Fixing them new cars with computers in 'em is above my bend.* □ *Joe's a good cook, but fancy desserts are above his huckleberry.*

above one's huckleberry See *above one's bend.*

ace in the hole a hidden shoulder holster with a gun in it. (Used mostly in Western movies and novels.) □ *Deadeye thought that Black Bart was unarmed, but Black Bart had an ace in the hole.* □ *When that varmint tried to steal my winnings, I had to use my ace in the hole.*

acequia an irrigation ditch. (Spanish. Pronounced *uh-SAKE-uh*.) □ *In the rainy season, the children were not allowed to play in the acequia, for fear of flash floods.* □ *The workers dug an acequia through the middle of the field.*

ackempucky AND **ackenpucky** gooey food; a gooey mess. (Sometimes jocular food-dirtying.) □ *Here, put some of this ackempucky on your potatoes.* □ *I ain't gonna eat a whole plate of ackenpucky!*

ackenpucky See *ackempucky.*

acknowledge the corn to admit a fault or wrongdoing. □ *I told Jane I thought she wasn't honest with me. She acknowledged the corn.* □ *If you've made a mistake, acknowledge the corn and ask pardon.*

across lots by using shortcuts. □ *There's a better way to get to the store across lots.* □ *Take time to do this job right. Don't try to do it across lots.*

acrost across. □ *The guard put a chain acrost the doorway to keep folks from coming in.* □ *She drew a line acrost the page.*

addled confused. □ *Gramps usually thinks pretty clearly, but he gets addled now and then.* □ *The more she tried to explain, the more addled I got.*

adios "Good-bye." (Spanish. Pronounced *ah-dee-OSE.*) □ *I'll see you later. Adios!* □ *We all gathered around Mary to say adios.*

admire to do something to want to do something; to be happy to do something. □ *I would surely admire to have those boots.* □ *He asked her to the dance. She said she would admire to go with him.*

adobe **1.** a kind of brick made of clay and straw. (Spanish.) □ *The walls of adobe shone golden in the late afternoon sun.* □ *The dirt in these hills makes good adobe.* **2.** a house made from adobe. □ *Joe lives in a little adobe over on Second Street.* □ *Mary bought a one-hundred-year-old adobe.*

afeard AND **scairt; ascairt** afraid. □ *Something's wrong with Tom, I'm afeard.* □ *What's the matter, you scairt of snakes?* □ *Joe won't climb the ladder 'cause he's ascairt of heights.*

afore AND **afore'n; afore's** before. □ *You got to heat up the oven afore you put the cake in.* □ *Joe could drive a truck afore he was thirteen years old.*

afore'n See *afore.*

afore's See *afore.*

aggravate someone or something to bother or upset someone or something, such as a situation, condition, or group. □ *Them noisy kids are allus aggravatin' me.* □ *Don't ask for a raise. It only aggravates the management.*

agin' against. □ *I leaned the planks up agin' the wall.* □ *Ma thinks Jane and I should get married, but Pa is agin' it.*

aguardiente hard liquor. (Spanish.) □ *The cowboy always carried a flask full of aguardiente.* □ *Joe had a little too much aguardiente and passed out right there on the floor of the saloon.*

(Ah) shoot! See *(Ah) shucks!*

(Ah) shucks! AND **(Ah) shoot!** "Darn!" (A mild oath.) □ *Ah, shucks! I forgot to call Grandma.* □ TOM: *We can't get chocolate ice cream. The store's all out.* JANE: *Shucks.* □ *Ah, shoot! I missed my favorite TV show.* □ *What should we do now? Shoot, I don't know.*

ail someone to hurt someone or some creature; to afflict someone or some creature. □ TOM: *Joe's at home in bed today.* JANE: *What ails him?* □ *What ails you? How come you're acting so rude?*

ailing sick. □ *Granny appears to be ailing. What's wrong?* □ *How long have you been ailing with this cold?*

aim to do something to intend to do something. □ *Mary aims to be a doctor when she grows up.* □ *I didn't aim to hurt your feelin's, sugar, you know I didn't.*

ain't am not, are not, or is not. (Contraction. Typical of country talk.) □ *I ain't gonna do it.* □ *Joe ain't such a bad fella, once you get to know him.* □ *We ain't rich, but we do all right.*

ain't fittin' is not right; is inappropriate. □ *It ain't fittin' for the bridegroom to see his bride before the ceremony.* □ *Young folks shouldn't talk back to their elders. It ain't fittin'.*

ain't fittin' to roll with a pig is or are uncouth and disgusting. □ *No child of mine is going to hang around with that Williams boy. He ain't fittin' to roll with a pig.* □ *Sally ain't fittin' to roll with a pig. She ain't had a bath in her whole life.*

ain't got a grain of sense AND **ain't got a lick of sense** is or are foolish. (See also *ain't got the sense God gave a squirrel.*) □ *Mary spends money like there's no tomorrow. She sure ain't got a grain of sense.* □ *I wouldn't trust Jim to take care of my kids. He ain't got a lick of sense.*

ain't got a lick of sense See *ain't got a grain of sense.*

ain't got no call (to do something) not to have a reason to do something. □ *Jane's only half an hour late getting home. You ain't got no call to worry yet.* □ JANE: *Why won't you give Mary a ride home?* TOM: *Ain't got no call. She don't have that far to go.*

ain't got the brains God gave a squirrel AND **ain't got the sense God gave geese** is or are very foolish. (See also *ain't got a grain of sense.*) □ *There goes John, running around barefooted in the snow. He ain't got the brains God gave a squirrel.* □ *No use trying to explain anything to Jane. She ain't got the sense God gave geese.*

ain't got the sense God gave geese See also *ain't got the brains God gave a squirrel.*

Ain't it the truth? "That is true." (Used to agree with a statement someone has made.) □ TOM: *Kids can be a hassle sometimes.* MARY: *Ain't it the truth?* □ JANE: *I swear, life can be a trial sometimes.* BILL: *Yes, Lordy. Ain't it the truth?*

ain't particular **1.** doesn't or don't care. □ TOM: *Would you rather have ice cream or cheese on your apple pie?* MARY: *Whatever you're having. I ain't particular.* □ *Joe sure ain't particular about* *what he wears. Why, half the time, he goes around in rags!* **2.** doesn't or don't have a preference. □ *Jane ain't particular. She'll use any old brand of tools.* □ *I ain't particular about who I sit next to at the table, so long as we don't bump elbows.*

air one's lungs **1.** to swear. □ *Don't pay those old cowboys no mind. They're just airin' their lungs.* □ *I could tell John was working on his old car 'cause I could hear him out in the garage, airin' his lungs.* **2.** to talk or brag. □ *The ladies just love to air their lungs whenever they get together.* □ *Here comes that braggart, airing his lungs again.*

air one's paunch to vomit. □ *He got so drunk he had to go out and air his paunch.* □ *Something in that meal had me airing my paunch all night.*

airish cool. □ *Mighty airish today, ain't it?* □ *Come on inside. It's too airish out on the porch.*

airy See *ary.*

Alabam' AND **Bama; Bamy** Alabama. □ *Jane grew up in Alabam'.* □ TOM: *Where you from?* BILL: *Birmingham, Alabama.* TOM: *No kidding? My dad was from Bama.* □ *Ain't nothin' like them warm summer nights in Bamy.*

alive and kicking alive and active. □ JANE: *How's your grandma?* MARY: *Still alive and kicking.* □ *John dropped me a note to let me know he was still alive and kicking.*

alkalied sick from drinking water that contains alkali, such as dissolved sodium sulfate or carbonate. □ *Bill knew his horse was alkalied from drinking that water.* □ *Don't drink water from that desert spring. You'll get alkalied.*

all and sundry everyone; all. □ *Jane sent out an invitation to all and sundry.* □ *This is a secret. Don't go telling it to all and sundry.*

all beat out exhausted. □ *They played basketball till they were all beat out.* □ *You go on ahead without me. I'm all beat out.*

all by one's lonesome all alone. □ *Mary's folks went out and left her all by her lonesome.* □ *Come on in. I'm all by my lonesome and could use some company.*

all-fired excitably; extremely. □ *What are you so all-fired mad about?* □ *He gets so all-fired cross with me, I hate to talk to him.*

all gurgle and no guts lots of threatening talk but no courage; making idle threats. □ *Don't let Joe frighten you. He's all gurgle and no guts.* □ *Bill made lots of patriotic speeches, but when it came time to fight, he was all gurgle and no guts.*

all hands and the cook absolutely everyone. □ *At the auto plant, all hands and the cook were working overtime that week.* □ *All hands and the cook pitched in to clean up the mess.*

all hat and no cattle all show and no substance. (See also *all vine and no taters.*) □ *He acted like a millionaire, but he was all hat and no cattle.* □ *She wanted us to think she was some fine society lady, but we figured out she was all hat and no cattle.*

(all) het up very angry or upset. □ *The boss got all het up when I said my project would be late.* □ *Jane gets real het up when folks tease her about her freckles.*

all horns and rattles showing great anger; having a temper tantrum. □ *Mary was all horns and rattles when I told her I lost her money.* □ *Tom's a moody fellow. One minute he's sweet and smiling, the next minute he's all horns and rattles.*

(all) in a dither upset and not sure what to do. □ *We were all in a dither, trying to fix things up for our unexpected guest.* □ *Mary gets in a dither every time she has to make a decision.*

all oak and iron bound AND **(as) sound as a barrel** in good health; feeling good. □ TOM: *How are you today?* BILL: *All oak and iron bound, thank you.* □ *Jane made a wonderful recovery from her surgery, and now she's as sound as a barrel.*

all of a size of the same size. □ *I tried to pick out the biggest tomato, but they were pretty much all of a size.* □ *The houses in that neighborhood are all of a size.*

all over creation AND **all over hell and half of Georgia; all over hell and gone; to hell and gone** everywhere. □ *Little Billy had his toys spread out all over creation. It took forever to clean up after him.* □ *They're looking all over creation, trying to find the missing man.* □ *Tom has traveled all over hell and half of Georgia trying to find the man who done him wrong.* □ *Jane went all over hell and gone looking for a decent job.* □ *I've been to hell and gone trying to get the toy my kid wanted for his birthday, but no luck.*

all over hell and gone See *all over creation.*

all over hell and half of Georgia See *all over creation.*

all-overs a nervous, uneasy feeling. (Always used with the definite article *the*.) □ *Walking around in that empty house gave me the all-overs.* □ *The way that man was staring at me gave me a case of the all-overs.*

all righty all right; OK. □ TOM: *Let's go to the state fair.* BILL: *All righty, let's do that.* □ *Everybody ready? All righty, then, let's get started.*

all show and no go all good looks and no action. (Used to describe someone or something that looks good but does not do what it is supposed to.) □ *That shiny car of Jim's is all show and no go.* □ *He's mighty handsome, but I hear he's all show and no go.*

all the farther as far as; the farthest. □ *The old hoss had gone all the farther he could.* □ *This is all the farther the highway goes.*

all the faster as fast as; the fastest. □ *This is all the faster I can walk, anymore.* □ *Sixty miles an hour is all the faster this poor little car can go.*

(all the) fixin's the side dishes that are usually served with a main dish. □ *For Thanksgiving, we had turkey with all the fixin's.* □ *The cook was busy making the fixin's for the barbecue.*

all the higher as high as; the highest. □ *That's all the higher Tom can climb.* □ *Is that all the higher you can bid?*

all the livelong day all day long. □ *Well, of course you get to feeling stiff, sitting in front of a computer all the livelong day.* □ *I'd go crazy if I had to stay at home all the livelong day.*

all the more as much as; the most. □ *That's all the more I can give you. I ain't got no more than that.* □ *Fred told me all the more he knew.*

all thumbs awkward with one's hands. (See also *one's fingers are all thumbs.*) □ *I can't help you. I'm all thumbs.* □ *Tom is all thumbs and is no good with fine work.*

all tore up about something very upset and sorry about something. □ *When Jim's dog was lost, he was all tore up about it.* □ *I'm all tore up about denting your car like that. I'd be more than happy to pay for fixing it.*

all vine and no taters all display and no real value. (See also *all hat and no cattle.*) □ *She's a good-looking woman, but really she's all vine and no taters.* □ *Don't be fooled by Jim's flowery promises. They're all vine and no taters.*

all wool and a yard wide trustworthy and genuinely good. (A description of good quality wool cloth. See also *all wool and no shoddy; full sixteen hands high.*) □ *Mary's a fine human being —all wool and a yard wide.* □ *I won't hear a word against Bill. He's all wool and a yard wide.*

all wool and no shoddy one hundred percent good quality. (See also *all wool and a yard wide; full sixteen hands high.*) □ *Everything Mary sells is the best there is, all wool and no shoddy.* □ *John's a good man through and through—all wool and no shoddy.*

allow to ackowledge or admit that someone or something is something. ☐ *He allowed as how he knew Mary.* ☐ *I'll allow that Bill's a smart man, but I still say there's a lot he doesn't know.*

allus always. ☐ *The train is allus on time.* ☐ *You are allus complaining about suthin.*

almighty very. ☐ *It's an almighty hot day.* ☐ *John's got an almighty high opinion of himself.*

(a)long about near a particular time. ☐ *We arrived in town long about midnight and went right to the hotel.* ☐ *Along about his thirteenth birthday, Tom decided he was old enough to leave home.*

ambeer tobacco spittle. ☐ *The brass spittoon was full of ambeer.* ☐ *He spat ambeer into the yard.*

amen corner AND **amen pew** a place in a church where enthusiastic worshipers sit. ☐ *Daddy's over in the amen corner, hollerin' "Praise the Lord!"* ☐ *Everything the preacher said got a hearty response from the amen pew.*

amen pew See *amen corner.*

amount to much See *amount to something.*

amount to something AND **amount to much** to be as good as something; to be any good. ☐ *His fine plans don't amount to a hill of beans, since he won't work for 'em.* ☐ *She's a nice girl, but she'll never amount to much.*

Anadama bread a kind of bread made of cornmeal, flour, and molasses. ☐ *Aunt Sue sent me her recipe for Anadama bread.* ☐ *We cooked up some Anadama bread to go with our greens.*

and that's a fact "and that is true." (Used to emphasize a statement.) ☐ *John ain't no friend of mine, and that's a fact.* ☐ *I'll be glad when this day is over, and that's a fact.*

and them See *and those.*

and then some indeed; very much so. (Used to emphasize a statement.) □ MARY: *Jim sure is good-looking.* JANE: *And then some!* □ *Bill is a smart man and then some.*

and this and that and so on. □ *Mom sent me some pillowcases, some sheets, a couple of blankets, and this and that.* □ *The repairman tightened some screws, fiddled with some bolts, and this and that.*

and those AND **and them** and some others. □ *But if we invite Jill, Mary and them will want to come.* □ *Jim and those was sayin' nasty things about me.*

Andale! "Get moving!"; "Hurry up!" (Spanish. Pronounced *AHN-duh-lay.)* □ *Andale! We're late already!* □ *Quit dragging your heels! Andale!*

Anglo someone of English or Northern European ancestry. (Spanish.) □ *The first Anglos came to the area in the nineteenth century.* □ *The villagers regarded the Anglo tourist with suspicion.*

animule animal. (Now in jocular use.) □ *Would you kindly get your animule offen my yard?* □ *What sort of animule is that you got there?*

answer for something to be responsible for something. □ *If he stole that money, he'll have to answer for it.* □ *On Judgment Day, you'll have to answer for your sins.*

answer (someone) back to make a disrespectful or rude reply. □ *Don't you answer me back, girl!* □ *Every time the teacher scolded him, Jimmy would answer back.*

anti-fogmatic an alcoholic drink. □ *Let's stop by the saloon for an anti-fogmatic.* □ *The old drunk needed an anti-fogmatic just to get out of bed in the morning.*

anti-godlin AND **si-godlin; anti-sigodlin** crooked. (See also *catabias; catawampus; slaunchways; whopper-jawed.*) □ *The table legs were nailed on anti-godlin, so the table doesn't sit straight.* □

Joe was a sight, with his hair mussed up and his necktie done up si-godlin. □ *The gate's on anti-sigodlin and it won't shut right.*

anti-sigodlin See *anti-godlin.*

anty-over a children's game in which two teams toss a ball back and forth over a roof. □ *The kids played anty-over till suppertime.* □ *The old toolshed was a favorite place for games of anty-over.*

anxious seat a seat in a church where people who are supposedly worried about their spiritual condition sit. (See also *mourners' bench.*) □ *Jim sat in the anxious seat with other poor sinners.* □ *The whole congregation prayed for the folks in the anxious seat.*

any fool thing any ridiculous or insignificant thing. (See also *every fool thing.*) □ *He'll buy his wife any fool thing she wants.* □ *Bill can get distracted by any fool thing.*

anymore nowadays; these days. □ *You meet a lot of folks who've had face-lifts, anymore.* □ *To get good furniture, you have to go to garage sales, anymore.*

Appaloosa a horse whose coat is marked with large spots, usually on the rump. (Possibly an Amerindian word. See also *bay; chestnut; paint; palomino; piebald; roan.*) □ *Pete rode an Appaloosa mare.* □ *Jane breeds Appaloosas out at her ranch.*

apple of someone's eye the most precious person or thing to someone. □ *Mary's grandson is the apple of her eye.* □ *How can I tell Joe that I put a dent in his car? That car is the apple of his eye!*

apple pandowdy a dessert made of apples baked with a biscuit crust. □ *For dessert, we each had a big bowl of apple pandowdy.* □ *Bill likes apple pandowdy with vanilla ice cream.*

applejack hard liquor made from apples. □ *The Joneses make their own applejack. It's mighty tasty but it's sure got a kick to it.* □ *We passed around a jug of applejack, and everybody soon got drunk as a boiled owl.*

applesauce nonsense. □ BILL: *Joe says he saw aliens from outer space on the courthouse lawn.* TOM: *Applesauce. He's been drinking again.* □ *The mayor said that all those stories about him taking bribes were pure applesauce.*

Arbuckle('s) coffee. (Mostly used in Western novels and movies.) □ *When the cowboys got back to the camp, the cook had a pot of Arbuckle's waiting for them.* □ *Let's have another cup of that Arbuckle.*

argufy (with someone) to argue or debate (with someone). □ *Bill will argufy with anybody on any subject.* □ *I heard the folks next door argufyin' all night long.*

Arizona strawberries AND **prairie strawberries** dried red beans. □ *We had just a sack full of Arizona strawberries to last us till spring.* □ *Sally got awful sick of prairie strawberries for breakfast, lunch, and dinner.*

Arizona tenor someone with tuberculosis. (People with tuberculosis often went to Arizona because the dry air supposedly helped cure the disease.) □ *What's wrong with Mary? She's been coughing like an Arizona tenor.* □ *The health spa was filled with drunks and Arizona tenors.*

Arkansas toothpick a bowie knife. □ *Joe took out his Arkansas toothpick and peeled an apple with it.* □ *In the middle of the fight, one of the men pulled an Arkansas toothpick and stabbed the other guy.*

Arkansas wedding cake cornbread. □ *I'll have a little of that Arkansas wedding cake to sop up the gravy, if you don't mind.* □ *We were poor in them days. We thought a pan full of Arkansas wedding cake was a real feast.*

Arkansawyer AND **Arkie** someone from Arkansas. (*Arkie* may be considered insulting.) □ TOM: *Where do you hail from?* MARY: *Little Rock.* TOM: *So you're an Arkansawyer, huh?* □ *The teacher was prejudiced. "All Arkies are ignorant," he said.*

Arkie See *Arkansawyer.*

arm baby AND **breast baby; floor baby; knee baby; lap child; waist baby** a newborn baby that must be held in the arms. (A *breast baby* is a nursing baby; a *floor baby* is a baby that can crawl around on the floor; a *knee baby* is a baby tall enough to reach the knees; a *lap child* can be held on the lap; a *waist baby* is tall enough to reach the waist.) □ *She can't crawl yet. She's just an arm baby.* □ *You sure have grown! I ain't seen you since you was a waist baby!* □ *Sue's got three kids, the oldest five years old, the other two just a knee baby and a breast baby.*

armed to the teeth carrying plenty of weapons. □ *Don't try to fight with him. He's armed to the teeth.* □ *All the police officers in that neighborhood are armed to the teeth.*

armful a great deal to hold on to or control. □ *Mary's twins are an armful, let me tell you.* □ *Jim only has one little boy, but he's an armful.*

arroyo a deep, usually dry riverbed. (Spanish.) □ *In the springtime, melted snow from the mountains runs down the arroyos.* □ *We climbed down the steep side of the arroyo.*

arter See *atter.*

ary AND **airy** any. (Compare to *nary.*) □ *The sheriff asked if ary of the townsfolk would join his posse.* □ *Is airy of y'all ready to join me?*

(as) awkward as a cow on a crutch AND **(as) awkward as a cow on roller skates** very awkward. □ *When Lulu was pregnant, she was awkward as a cow on a crutch.* □ *Tom will never be a gymnast. He's as awkward as a cow on roller skates!*

(as) awkward as a cow on roller skates See *(as) awkward as a cow on a crutch.*

(as) baleful as death promising evil; very threatening. □ *The wind's moan was as baleful as death.* □ *His voice sounded baleful as death.*

(as) big around as a molasses barrel very big around. □ *He ate till he was as big around as a molasses barrel.* □ *The athlete's chest was big around as a molasses barrel.*

(as) big as a house very big. (Used to describe people.) □ *Sally's seven months' pregnant and big as a house.* □ *That quarterback is as big as a house!*

(as) big as all outdoors very big. □ *He had a smile as big as all outdoors.* □ *The Johnson ranch was big as all outdoors.*

(as) big as life, and twice as natural See *(as) big as life, and twice as ugly.*

(as) big as life, and twice as ugly AND **(as) big as life, and twice as natural** real and identifiable. □ *What did I see on the front page of today's paper, but a picture of Tom, big as life, and twice as ugly.* □ *I opened my front door, and there stood Uncle Lou, as big as life, and twice as natural.*

(as) black as a skillet black. □ *I don't want to go down to the cellar. It's as black as a skillet down there.* □ *The bruise turned black as a skillet.*

(as) black as a stack of black cats very black. (See also *(as) black as the ace of spades.*) □ *I'm ascairt to go into that closet. It's as black as a stack of black cats in there.* □ *Her hair was black as a stack of black cats.*

(as) black as the ace of spades very black. (See also *(as) black as a stack of black cats.*) □ *The car was long and shiny and black as the ace of spades.* □ *Jill's shoes are black as the ace of spades.*

(as) broad as a barn door very broad. □ *Jim's backside is as broad as a barn door.* □ *The weight-lifter's chest was broad as a barn door.*

(as) busy as a beaver (building a new dam) very busy. □ *Sorry I can't go to lunch with you. I'm as busy as a beaver building a new dam.* □ *In springtime, the farmer was busy as a beaver.*

(as) busy as a cranberry merchant very busy. (See also *(as) busy as a fish peddler in Lent.*) ☐ *Sorry I can't go to lunch with you today, but I'm busy as a cranberry merchant.* ☐ *Bill was as busy as a cranberry merchant, holding down three jobs at once.*

(as) busy as a fish peddler in Lent very busy. (See also *(as) busy as a cranberry merchant.*) ☐ *Taking care of the kids keeps me busy as a fish peddler in Lent.* ☐ *The roofers were as busy as a fish peddler in Lent, repairing all the houses after the big storm.*

(as) busy as a hibernating bear not busy at all. ☐ TOM: *I can't go with you. I'm busy.* JANE: *Yeah. You're as busy as a hibernating bear.* ☐ *He lounged on the sofa all day, busy as a hibernating bear.*

(as) busy as a one-armed paperhanger very busy. ☐ *My boss keeps me as busy as a one-armed paperhanger.* ☐ *I've got plenty of work. I'm busy as a one-armed paperhanger.*

(as) busy as popcorn on a skillet very active. ☐ *She rushed around, as busy as popcorn on a skillet.* ☐ *Prying into other folks' business kept him busy as popcorn on a skillet.*

(as) calm as a toad in the sun very calm and content. ☐ *She smiled, as calm as a toad in the sun.* ☐ *Nothing ruffles him. He's calm as a toad in the sun.*

(as) clear as a bell very clear. ☐ *I fixed the radio, so now all the stations come in clear as a bell.* ☐ *Through the wall, I could hear the neighbors talking, just as clear as a bell.*

(as) close as two coats of paint close and intimate. ☐ *When Tom and Mary were kids, they were as close as two coats of paint.* ☐ *All their lives, the cousins were close as two coats of paint.*

(as) cocky as the king of spades boastful; overly proud. ☐ *He'd challenge anyone to a fight. He's as cocky as the king of spades.* ☐ *She strutted in, cocky as the king of spades.*

(as) cold as a welldigger's ass (in January) AND **(as) cold as a welldigger's feet (in January); (as) cold as a welldigger's ears (in January)** very, very cold. (Use caution with *ass.*) ☐ BILL:

How's the weather where you are? TOM: *Cold as a welldigger's ass in January.* □ *By the time I got in from the storm, I was as cold as a welldigger's feet.* □ *The car's heater broke, so it's as cold as a welldigger's ears to ride around in it.*

(as) cold as a welldigger's ears (in January) See *(as) cold as a welldigger's ass (in January).*

(as) cold as a welldigger's feet (in January) See *(as) cold as a welldigger's ass (in January).*

(as) cold as a witch's caress AND **(as) cold as a witch's tit** very cold; chilling. (Use caution with *tit*.) □ *The wind was as cold as a witch's caress.* □ *She gave me a look as cold as a witch's caress.*

(as) cold as a witch's tit See *(as) cold as a witch's caress.*

(as) common as an old shoe low class; uncouth. □ *That trashy girl is just as common as an old shoe.* □ *Jim may have money, but he's common as an old shoe.*

(as) conceited as a barber's cat very conceited; vain. □ *Ever since he won that award, he's been as conceited as a barber's cat.* □ *She's stuck up all right—conceited as a barber's cat.*

(as) crazy as a betsy bug loony. □ TOM: *Susan says she's really the Queen of England.* BILL: *She's crazy as a betsy bug.* □ *Ever since his wife left him, Joe's been acting as crazy as a betsy bug.*

(as) crazy as a peach-orchard boar loony. □ *What's wrong with Jim? He's acting as crazy as a peach-orchard boar.* □ *Mary's been standing out on the street corner, telling everybody the world's about to end. Poor thing—she's crazy as a peach-orchard boar.*

(as) crooked as a barrel of fish hooks AND **(as) crooked as a fish hook** dishonest. □ *Don't play cards with him. He's as crooked as a barrel of fish hooks.* □ *After Brenda cheated a few folks, word got around that she was crooked as a fish hook.*

(as) crooked as a dog's hind leg dishonest. (See also *(as) crooked as a rail fence.*) □ *Don't trust John. He's as crooked as a dog's hind leg.* □ *Mary says all politicians are crooked as a dog's hind leg.*

(as) crooked as a fish hook See *(as) crooked as a barrel of fish hooks.*

(as) crooked as a rail fence **1.** crooked. (A rail fence is built in a zigzag pattern.) □ *Joe's writing is crooked as a rail fence.* □ *That child's teeth are as crooked as a rail fence. She should have braces to straighten them out.* **2.** dishonest. (See also *(as) crooked as a dog's hind leg.*) □ *Mary is honest most of the time, but when it comes to playing poker, she's crooked as a rail fence.* □ *That shopkeeper would cheat his own grandmother. He's as crooked as a rail fence!*

(as) crooked as a rattler in a cactus patch **1.** very crooked; bent. □ *The fence was as crooked as a rattler in a cactus patch.* □ *Her smile was crooked as a rattler in a cactus patch.* **2.** very dishonest. □ *This card game is as crooked as a rattler in a cactus patch.* □ *The politician was crooked as a rattler in a cactus patch.*

(as) cute as a bug's ear very cute. □ *Have you seen Lulu's baby? He's just as cute as a bug's ear.* □ *Jill is cute as a bug's ear with that ribbon in her hair.*

(as) daft as a brush stupid. □ *That puppy's as daft as a brush. You'll never teach him anything.* □ *Henry never learned the multiplication tables because he's daft as a brush.*

(as) dark as the inside of a cow's belly AND **darker than the inside of a cow's belly** very dark. □ *The cellar was as dark as the inside of a cow's belly.* □ *There was no moon out. It was darker than the inside of a cow's belly.*

(as) dead as a beef dead. □ *I found the poor old dog lying in the yard, as dead as a beef.* □ *When they found the body, he had been dead as a beef for a week.*

(as) dead as a tin of corned beef dead. □ TOM: *Is that snake dead?* JANE: *As dead as a tin of corned beef.* □ *The dog got bit by a snake, and the next day, he was dead as a tin of corned beef.*

(as) drunk as a biled owl See *(as) drunk as a boiled owl.*

(as) drunk as a boiled owl AND **(as) drunk as a biled owl** very drunk. (See also the following two entries.) □ *When Tom came home from the bar, he was as drunk as a boiled owl.* □ *Jane got drunk as a biled owl every Saturday night.*

(as) drunk as a coot AND **(as) drunk as Cooter Brown** very drunk. (See also the preceding and following entries.) □ *After only one beer, Mary was as drunk as a coot.* □ *At John's bachelor party, they got him drunk as Cooter Brown.*

(as) drunk as Cooter Brown See *(as) drunk as a coot.*

(as) drunk as who shot John AND **drunker than who shot John** very drunk. (See also the preceding two entries.) □ *"You're as drunk as who shot John!" Bill's wife accused him.* □ *You shouldn't drive. You're drunker than who shot John.*

(as) dull as a meat axe **1.** not sharp. □ *Better sharpen that knife. It's dull as a meat axe.* □ *The hoe was as dull as a meat axe and not much use.* **2.** stupid. (See also *(as) dumb as a shovel; (as) daft as a brush.*) □ *I tried to explain things to Tom, but he sat there looking as dull as a meat axe.* □ *Susan's pretty smart, but her sister's dull as a meat axe.*

(as) dumb as a shovel stupid. (See also *(as) dull as a meat axe; (as) daft as a brush.*) □ *He's a beautiful horse, but dumb as a shovel.* □ *This kid I'm tutoring is as dumb as a shovel.*

(as) easy as lickin' butter off(en) a knife simple; very easy. □ *Getting Mary to agree was as easy as lickin' butter offen a knife.* □ MARY: *Was it a difficult job?* JANE: *No. It was easy as lickin' butter off a knife.*

(as) fine as frog hair very fine. (Sometimes humorously used as an answer to "How are you?") □ *The spines on that cactus are as fine as frog hair.* □ CHARLIE: *How are you this evening?* TOM: *Fine as frog hair.*

(as) freckled as a turkey egg covered with freckles. □ *Susan's face is as freckled as a turkey egg.* □ *When I sit out in the sun, I get freckled as a turkey egg.*

(as) full as a tick **1.** well-fed; very full of food. □ BILL: *Care for some more potato salad?* MARY: *No thank you, I'm as full as a tick.* □ *The puppy drank till she was full as a tick.* **2.** drunk. □ *No use reasoning with him. He's full as a tick.* □ *To celebrate the victory, we went out and got as full as ticks.*

(as) funny as a crutch not funny at all. □ *Tom's jokes are generally as funny as a crutch.* □ BILL: *It sure was funny when I pulled that chair out from under you.* TOM: *Yeah. Funny as a crutch.*

as good as common as well as usual. □ TOM: *How's your mother doing?* JANE: *As good as common, thank you.* □ SALLY: *How are you feeling today?* BILL: *As good as common.*

(as) green as a gourd innocent and ignorant. □ *Everyone takes advantage of Joe. They know he's as green as a gourd.* □ *When I first came to the city, I was green as a gourd.*

(as) handy as a pocket in a shirt very useful. □ *These kitchen towels are as handy as a pocket in a shirt.* □ *I'm glad I took my jackknife on the camping trip. It came in handy as a pocket in a shirt.*

(as) happy as a clam very happy and content. □ *Jim's been as happy as a clam in his new job.* □ *Some folks get lonely when all their kids leave home, but I'm happy as a clam since the last one left.*

(as) happy as a flea in a doghouse very happy. □ *The kids were as happy as a flea in a doghouse, playing out in the sun.* □ *Three* *of my favorite movies are on TV tonight. I'm happy as a flea in a doghouse.*

(as) happy as a fly in a pie very happy. □ *She loved cooking. The afternoon before the dinner party, she was as happy as a fly in a pie.* □ *He danced with all the pretty girls, happy as a fly in a pie.*

(as) happy as a pig in mud AND **(as) happy as pigs in mud** happy and content. □ *As long as I have a TV to watch, I'm as happy as a pig in mud.* □ *The kids played under the sprinkler all afternoon, happy as pigs in mud.*

(as) happy as ducks in Arizona very unhappy; discontent. □ *Jane's pay was cut, so she's just as happy as ducks in Arizona.* □ *Ma was happy as ducks in Arizona when she saw the mess we made in the kitchen.*

(as) happy as pigs in mud See *(as) happy as a pig in mud.*

(as) harmless as a pet rabbit harmless; gentle. □ *Don't be afraid of Bill. He's as harmless as a pet rabbit.* □ *She may look strict, but she's harmless as a pet rabbit.*

(as) helpless as a turtle on his back completely helpless. □ *With my arm in a cast, I feel helpless as a turtle on his back.* □ *The fever left Jane as helpless as a turtle on his back.*

(as) high as a Georgia pine very drunk. □ *Tom took a bottle of blackberry brandy and got high as a Georgia pine.* □ *Jane felt like celebrating, so she got as high as a Georgia pine.*

(as) high as the hair on a cat's back very expensive. □ *Did you see that fancy wedding gown? That was as high as the hair on a cat's back, you can be sure!* □ *I can't go visit Aunt Velma. Plane tickets are high as the hair on a cat's back.*

(as) homely as a boil ugly. □ *That kid is as homely as a boil.* □ *She's good-hearted, but homely as a boil.*

(as) homely as a mud fence ugly. ☐ *She's a nice girl, but homely as a mud fence.* ☐ *Jane's boyfriend is as homely as a mud fence.*

(as) honest as (old) Abe honest. (*Abe* refers to Abraham Lincoln. There are many popular stories about Lincoln's honesty.) ☐ *The car dealer tried to convince us that he was honest as Abe.* ☐ *He's a good fellow, as honest as old Abe.*

(as) hot as the hobs of hell very hot. (A *hob* is a *hobgoblin.* See also *(as) hot as the seven brass hinges of hell.*) ☐ TOM: *How's the weather where you are?* MARY: *As hot as the hobs of hell.* ☐ *The desert sand was hot as the hobs of hell.*

(as) hot as the seven brass hinges of hell extremely hot. (See also *(as) hot as the hobs of hell.*) ☐ *Texas in August is as hot as the seven brass hinges of hell.* ☐ *Even in the shade, it was hot as the seven brass hinges of hell.*

as how that. (A subordinating conjunction.) ☐ *He allowed as how he might have seen me before.* ☐ *I can't say as how I approve of what you're doing.*

(as) hungry as a bear very hungry. ☐ *What's for dinner? I'm as hungry as a bear!* ☐ *When Mary got back from the volleyball game, she was hungry as a bear.*

(as) like as two peas (in a pod) very similar. ☐ *The two brothers were as like as two peas.* ☐ *The puppies were like as two peas in a pod.*

(as) limp as a rag exhausted. ☐ *Housework leaves me as limp as a rag.* ☐ *After Mary runs a marathon, she's limp as a rag for the rest of the week.*

(as) low as a snake's belly dishonest, tricky, and cruel. ☐ *Fred is as low as a snake's belly. He kicked his aged mother out of her own house.* ☐ *You're low as a snake's belly for playing that trick on me.*

(as) low-down as a snake in a wagon track very mean and dishonest. □ *Her friends all thought her husband was as low-down as a snake in a wagon track, and they told her so.* □ *Anyone who would treat his daddy that way is low-down as a snake in a wagon track.*

(as) mad as a (blind) hornet very angry. (See also *mad enough to bite off a drawbar; mad enough to kick a cat.*) □ *Jane's as mad as a blind hornet because they canceled her favorite TV show.* □ *Bill's mad as a hornet, but I don't know why.*

(as) mad as a stunned gopher very angry. (See also *(as) mad as a wet hen.*) □ *Mary was mad as a stunned gopher when she found out she'd been tricked.* □ *Tom came in yellin' and screamin', mad as a stunned gopher.*

(as) mad as a wet hen AND **madder than a wet hen** very angry. (See also *(as) mad as a stunned gopher.*) □ *When he found that scratch on his new car, John was as mad as a wet hen.* □ *The teacher gets madder than a wet hen when the students act up in class.*

(as) mean as a stuck snake cruel and angry. □ *Bill is as mean as a stuck snake. I once saw him kick a poor helpless puppy.* □ *Old Man Jones, mean as a stuck snake, sat on his porch and cursed everyone who came by.*

as much chance (of something) as a wax cat in hell no chance at all. □ TOM: *Does Joe have any chance of winning the race?* JANE: *As much chance as a wax cat in hell.* □ *That store has as much chance of succeeding as a wax cat in hell.*

(as) naked as a jaybird naked. □ *After his bath, the little boy ran into the living room, naked as a jaybird.* □ *That crazy Nelly likes to sit out in her garden as naked as a jaybird.*

(as) nervous as a long-tailed cat in a room full of rocking chairs very nervous. (Jocular.) □ *Will you quit drumming your fingers like that? You make me as nervous as a long-tailed cat in a room* *full of rocking chairs.* □ *What makes you so jumpy? You're nervous as a long-tailed cat in a room full of rocking chairs!*

as often as a goose goes barefoot all the time. □ JANE: *Do you get to see Jim very often?* MARY: *As often as a goose goes barefoot.* □ TOM: *How often do you run short of money?* CHARLIE: *As often as a goose goes barefoot.*

(as) old as the courthouse very old. (Used to describe old people.) □ *If you want to know anything about the town's history, ask Mrs. Johnson. She's as old as the courthouse and remembers everything.* □ *The two men playing checkers looked to be old as the courthouse.*

(as) plain as the hump on a camel **1.** obvious; easy to see or understand. □ *The answer is easy. It's as plain as the hump on a camel.* □ *I can see the car in the distance, plain as the hump on a camel.* **2.** not good-looking. □ *The baby was as plain as the hump on a camel.* □ *No matter how she did her hair or her makeup, she was plain as the hump on a camel.*

(as) poor as Job's turkey very poor. □ *The family was poor as Job's turkey. They couldn't even afford new shoes for their little boy.* □ *It doesn't seem fair. Tom works real hard, but he's still as poor as Job's turkey.*

(as) pretty as a picture very pretty. □ *With her hair all combed and her good dress on, she's just as pretty as a picture.* □ *Joe and Mary decorated the table with fresh flowers and their best china. It was pretty as a picture.*

(as) pretty as a speckled pup very pretty. (Usually used to describe girls and women.) □ *Tom's youngest girl is pretty as a speckled pup.* □ *You may not think Lulu is much to look at, but to me she's as pretty as a speckled pup.*

(as) proud as a pup with a new collar very proud. □ *Look at Joe with his new baby. He's as proud as a pup with a new collar.* □ *She's been showing off her diploma, proud as a pup with a new collar.*

(as) proud as Lucifer See *(as) proud as Satan.*

(as) proud as Satan AND **(as) proud as sin; (as) proud as Lucifer** overly proud. □ *Bill is as proud as Satan and won't ask help from anybody.* □ *That whole family is just as proud as sin. They don't mix with the rest of us.* □ *Mary, being proud as Lucifer, never let her friends see how humiliated she felt.*

(as) proud as sin See *(as) proud as Satan.*

(as) quick as a dog can lick a dish fast; very quickly. □ *I'll get it done as quick as a dog can lick a dish.* □ *With everyone working together, they got the room clean, quick as a dog can lick a dish.*

(as) red as a beet very red. (Usually used to describe someone's face.) □ *You could tell he was embarrassed because his face turned red as a beet.* □ *I was out in the sun all day and came in as red as a beet.*

(as) rough as a corncob very rough. □ *That washcloth felt as rough as a corncob!* □ *The wooden bench was rough as a corncob and very uncomfortable to sit on.*

(as) sad as a hound dog's eye very sad; pitiful. □ *The song was as sad as a hound dog's eye.* □ *The look on her face was sad as a hound dog's eye.*

(as) safe as in God's pocket very safe; secure. □ *When they saw the blizzard coming, they burrowed into a haystack, where they were as safe as in God's pocket.* □ *With Joe to take care of you, you'll be safe as in God's pocket.*

(as) sensitive as an eyeball very sensitive. □ *Jane's as sensitive as an eyeball when it comes to her looks.* □ *Tom was sensitive as an eyeball about being a woods colt.*

(as) sharp as a briar very clever. □ *That kid's as sharp as a briar. He'll probably be a lawyer when he grows up.* □ *She may be quiet, but she's sharp as a briar.*

(as) sharp as a tack very intelligent. □ *She's a sweet girl and sharp as a tack.* □ *He may act like an old fool, but he's as sharp as a tack.*

(as) shy as a ring-necked pheasant very shy. □ *She was a modest young lady and as shy as a ring-necked pheasant.* □ *He hated to meet new people. He was shy as a ring-necked pheasant.*

(as) sick as a dog very sick; nauseated. □ *I think I got food poisoning at the restaurant. I was as sick as a dog last night.* □ *Jim got the flu and was sick as a dog for five days.*

(as) simple as mutton very simple; uncomplicated. □ *Why can't you understand this? It's as simple as mutton!* □ TOM: *I'll need help fixing my shirt.* JANE: *Why? It's simple as mutton.*

(as) skinny as a (bean)pole AND **(as) skinny as a rail** overly thin. □ *Tom was skinny as a beanpole when he was a kid.* □ *You should eat more. You're as skinny as a rail!*

(as) skinny as a rail See *(as) skinny as a beanpole.*

(as) slack as fiddle strings very loose. □ *His muscles were as slack as fiddle strings.* □ *The springs on that chair are slack as fiddle strings.*

(as) slick as a baby's bottom bald. □ *His head is as slick as a baby's bottom.* □ *Under the wig, her head's slick as a baby's bottom.*

(as) slick as a peeled onion **1.** very slick and slippery. □ *The road was icy and as slick as a peeled onion.* □ *Be careful walking on that marble floor. It's slick as a peeled onion.* **2.** shrewd; clever; suave. □ *The salesman was slick as a peeled onion, but I wouldn't buy.* □ *The preacher was as slick as a peeled onion, but I didn't give him none of my money.*

(as) slick as bear grease See *(as) slick as owl grease.*

(as) slick as goose grease See *(as) slick as owl grease.*

(as) slick as owl grease AND **(as) slick as bear grease; (as) slick as goose grease; (as) slick as snot** very slick and smooth. (Use caution with *snot*. See also *slicker than calf slobbers.*) □ *Joe puts hair tonic on his hair till it's slick as owl grease.* □ *We oiled up the hinge just as slick as bear grease.* □ *The finish on that oak table is shiny and slick as goose grease.* □ *The soles of his new boots were slick as snot, so he slipped on the kitchen floor.*

(as) slick as snot See *(as) slick as owl grease.*

(as) slow as coal tar running uphill backwards very slow. □ *Spring was slow in coming that year, as slow as coal tar running uphill backwards.* □ *It took him forever to get home. He was slow as coal tar running uphill backwards.*

(as) slow as molasses in January very slow or sluggish. □ *Can't you get dressed any faster? I declare, you're as slow as molasses in January.* □ TOM: *I sent Joe a postcard a week ago, and he still hasn't got it!* JANE: *Well, you know the Post Office—slow as molasses in January.*

(as) slow as wet gunpowder very slow. □ *I've been waiting for you for half an hour! I declare, you're as slow as wet gunpowder.* □ *The police never get here on time. They're slow as wet gunpowder.*

(as) smart as a box of rocks AND **(as) smart as a rock** very stupid. □ *He's a sweet old dog, but about as smart as a box of rocks.* □ *The guy we got to fix the sink was smart as a rock. Just look how he ruined the plumbing.*

(as) smart as a rock See *(as) smart as a box of rocks.*

(as) smart as a tree full of owls very smart. □ *They all say that Jill is as smart as a tree full of owls. She'll solve this problem for sure.* □ *The wily outlaw was smart as a tree full of owls. He made sure the law never caught up with him.*

(as) smart as a whip very intelligent. □ *He's a funny-looking old horse, but as smart as a whip.* □ *The little girl was smart as a whip and generally asked questions her folks couldn't answer.*

(as) solemn as soap very solemn and serious. □ *He can tell the most outrageous jokes with a face as solemn as soap.* □ *Reading the letter, Bill looked as solemn as soap.*

as someone damn well pleases just as someone wants. □ *Jane will listen to your advice, and then she'll do as she damn well pleases.* □ *I've always done as I damn well please, and I'm not going to change my ways now.*

as something as all get-out as something as can be. □ *Look out. Ma's coming, and she's as mad as all get-out!* □ *Liz can afford anything. Her family's as rich as all get-out.*

(as) something as you please very something. □ *Bill walked in as cool as you please, even with a whole roomful of folks glaring at him.* □ *"What can I do for y'all?" Jane asked, sweet as you please.*

(as) sorry as owl bait worthless. □ *That son of mine is as sorry as owl bait. He doesn't do a blamed thing to help.* □ *His first wife was sorry as owl bait, but his second one's a prize.*

(as) sound as a barrel See *all oak and iron bound.*

(as) sound as a dollar dependable; stable; healthy. □ *The doctor says my lungs are as sound as a dollar.* □ *It's a good investment —sound as a dollar.*

(as) steady as a rock very steady. □ *The surgeon's hands were steady as a rock as she began the difficult operation.* □ *You can depend on Jane. She's as steady as a rock.*

(as) steep as a cow's face AND **steeper than a cow's face** extremely steep. □ *That road is as steep as a cow's face. We could hardly get the car up it.* □ *The side of that hill is steeper than a cow's face.*

(as) still as time in a grave very still and quiet. □ *The night was still as time in a grave.* □ *After we heard the awful news, we all sat as still as time in a grave.*

(as) straight as a yard of pump water straight. □ *Mary's long hair hung as straight as a yard of pump water.* □ *The aspen tree was straight as a yard of pump water.*

(as) strong as Annie Christmas very strong. □ *She's a skinny little thing, but strong as Annie Christmas.* □ *All of the kids in that family are big and broad and strong as Annie Christmas.*

(as) sure as God made little green apples certainly; without a doubt. □ *As sure as God made little green apples, we're going to get in trouble for what we did.* □ TOM: *Is it really going to rain today?* JANE: *Sure as God made little green apples. Just look at them clouds on the horizon.*

(as) sure as I'm sitting here AND **(as) sure as I'm standing here** without a doubt; certainly. □ *Cover up your head when you go out in that rain, or sure as I'm sitting here, you'll catch cold.* □ TOM: *Mark moved to Alaska.* JANE: *Are you sure?* TOM: *As sure as I'm standing here.*

(as) sure as I'm standing here See *(as) sure as I'm sitting here.*

(as) sure as shootin' for certain. □ *Don't mess with Tom, or sure as shootin', you'll make him mad.* □ *It's going to rain tonight, as sure as shootin'.*

as the crow flies in a straight line. (Used to describe distances.) □ *It's about five miles as the crow flies, but eight miles if you follow the road.* □ *Washington is thirty miles from here, as the crow flies.*

(as) thick as hops thick; dense. □ *Kudzu vines were growing as thick as hops in my front yard.* □ *After John got out of school, he had job offers coming in thick as hops.*

(as) tough as puttin' socks on a rooster very difficult. □ *Getting those kids into bed at night is tough as puttin' socks on a rooster.* □ *Schoolwork is easy for Jane, but for Mary it's as tough as puttin' socks on a rooster.*

(as) ugly as a tar-bucket very ugly. □ *The baby was as ugly as a tar-bucket, but I told his mother he was beautiful.* □ *I felt ugly as a tar-bucket after looking at the beautiful women in the magazine.*

(as) ugly as home-made soap very ugly. □ *When she frowns, her face is as ugly as home-made soap.* □ *He's strong and kind and hard-working, but ugly as home-made soap.*

(as) useless as tits on a boar See *(as) useless as tits on a bull.*

(as) useless as tits on a bull AND **(as) useless as tits on a boar** completely useless. (Use with caution.) □ *Now that his kids are grown and do all the farm work, John feels as useless as tits on a bull.* □ *My daughter sent me some newfangled kitchen gadget that's useless as tits on a boar.*

(as) weak as a cat AND **(as) weak as a kitten** very weak. □ *The fever left me as weak as a cat.* □ *I laughed till I was weak as a kitten.*

(as) weak as a kitten See *(as) weak as a cat.*

(as) weak as pond water weak and watery. □ *This whiskey is as weak as pond water!* □ *The coffee they serve there is weak as pond water.*

(as) yeller as mustard but without the bite cowardly. (*Yeller* means *yellow.*) □ *He backed down from the fight. He's as yeller as mustard but without the bite.* □ *You'll never take me on. You're yeller as mustard but without the bite.*

ascairt See *afeard.*

ash-barrel baby an illegitimate child. (See also *blackberry baby; brush colt; outsider; volunteer; woods colt.*) □ *Folks used to make fun of Jim on account of he was an ash-barrel baby.* □ *Nelly acts so prim and proper now, but she had an ash-barrel baby when she was just sixteen.*

asleep at the switch not paying attention to one's job. □ *I can't believe the referee missed that foul! He must have been asleep at the switch!* □ *How come no one's answering the phone? I think the secretary's asleep at the switch!*

ass-over-teakettle AND **ass-over-tit** head over heels; turning over and over. (Use with caution.) □ *Bill knocked Joe ass-over-teakettle.* □ *I scrambled ass-over-tit to finish the job.*

ass-over-tit See *ass-over-teakettle.*

ast ask or asked. (Dialect or error for *ask*. Eye-dialect for *asked.*) □ *Ast your ma if you can come out and play.* □ *He ast me where I was from.*

at someone's beck and call at someone's command. □ *Jane has her son at her beck and call.* □ *I worked as a housekeeper awhile, but I hated being at someone else's beck and call.*

atter AND **arter** after. □ *The bear took out atter your pappy and like to caught him too.* □ *What you doing arter dinner tonight?*

ax to ask. (A very old pronunciation.) □ *My neighbor axed to borrow a cup of flour.* □ *If you want to know where he's from, just ax him!*

B

back and forth discussing something; talking back and forth about something; arguing. □ *We went back and forth about the dispute for a long time.* □ *It was back and forth, back and forth. We never got nothin' done.*

back door trots diarrhea. (The privy was usually in the backyard.) □ *She had the stomach flu. It gave her the back door trots for two days.* □ *I don't know what I ate, but it sure gave me the back door trots.*

back East in the East; to the East. □ *When Jane moved to Colorado, her folks stayed back East.* □ *John failed as a Texas rancher and went back East.*

backhouse an outdoor toilet, usually located in back of the house. □ *Jim excused himself and went to the backhouse.* □ *Mary spent so long in the backhouse, we thought she must have fallen in.*

backset a setback; a disappointment. □ *Don't get discouraged just because you've had a couple of backsets.* □ *There were too many backsets along the way. We had to give up.*

backside someone's bottom. □ *When the kids misbehave, I just swat 'em on the backside.* □ *After I sat on that cactus, my backside was sore for a week.*

backtalk disrespectful talk, especially a disrespectful answer. □ *Sit right back down in that seat and don't give me any backtalk.* □ *Jane's backtalk to the teacher got her in trouble.*

backwoods coming from or having to do with remote parts of the country. □ *The tiny little backwoods community was the last place in the state to have indoor plumbing in every house.* □ *Sally was embarrassed by her family and their backwoods ways.*

bad as I hate to do it even though I hate to do it. □ *Bad as I hate to do it, I'm going to have to have my old dog put to sleep.* □ *I've got to tell Mary a lie, bad as I hate to do it.*

bad blood bad feelings. (Usually in the expression *bad blood between them*, meaning bad feelings between them.) □ *There was some bad blood between the two brothers that kept them from speaking to one another for ten years.* □ *They used to be partners, but there's bad blood between them.*

bad man the devil. (Used with the definite article *the*.) □ *If you go into the woods after dark, the bad man will get you!* □ *The bad man tempted me, but I stayed away from the liquor.*

bad medicine dangerous; powerful. □ *Word got around that Colorado Slim was bad medicine. No one wanted to fight with him.* □ *Rattlesnakes are real bad medicine. Don't mess with 'em.*

bad-mouth someone to say bad things about someone. □ *Joe has been bad-mouthing me behind my back.* □ *Jim's always bad-mouthing his mother, blaming her for all his problems.*

bad off doing badly. (Usually refers to either health or money.) □ *Jim's real bad off. They don't know if he'll live till spring.* □ *The family sold the farm at a pretty good profit, so they're not too bad off.*

bad place hell. (Used with the definite article *the*.) □ *If you keep up your sinful ways, you'll go to the bad place.* □ *The preacher is always threatening me with the bad place.*

bad time (of the month) a menstrual period. (See also *Grandma's come; visit from Flo; have one's lady's time; monthlies*.) □ *I don't feel like doing much. It's my bad time of the month.* □ *Her* *bad time doesn't bother her any. She'll hike around and play tennis like she always does.*

badlands a dry, barren region. □ *The wagon train had to make it through the badlands to get to the settlement.* □ *The bandits lived in the badlands and robbed any traveler who came along.*

baker's dozen thirteen. (Used with the indefinite article *a*). □ *At the donut shop, you always get a baker's dozen when you pay for twelve.* □ *The hen had thirteen chicks—a baker's dozen.*

ball the jack to go very fast. □ *There's a deadline coming up at work, so we're really ballin' the jack.* □ *If you want to get there on time, you better ball the jack.*

Bama See *Alabam'*.

Bamy See *Alabam'*.

bandido a bandit. (Spanish.) □ *Three masked bandidos ambushed the stagecoach.* □ *The desperate bandido shot the lawman.*

bangtail a horse. □ *I keep a couple of bangtails for riding on the weekend.* □ *He hitched up his bangtail to the buggy.*

banquette a sidewalk. (Used mostly in Louisiana.) □ *He drove his car up onto the banquette.* □ *I wish they'd build a banquette on our side of the street.*

bar-dog a bartender. □ *Tell the bar-dog I want another whiskey.* □ *The bar-dog got used to hearing the cowboys tell their troubles.*

bar none with no exceptions. □ *Arizona Slim was the best cattle-roper I ever seen, bar none.* □ *It was our best Fourth of July picnic, bar none.*

barb(ed) wire AND **bobwire** wire with small barbs attached, used as fencing. □ *Joe tried to climb the barbed wire fence. All he did was get his clothes tore up.* □ *We fenced the pasture around with barb wire.* □ *I got a good bobwire fence around my property.*

bare-faced lie a shocking lie. □ MARY: *Jim says you're going out with him on Saturday night.* JANE: *That's a bare-faced lie!* □ MARY: *Jill told me she won a million dollars in the lottery.* TOM: *I never heard such a bare-faced lie in all my life.*

bark up the wrong tree to pursue the wrong person, thing, or idea. □ *If you think I stole your wristwatch, you're barking up the wrong tree.* □ *Joe is barking up the wrong tree, trying to sell fancy gourmet foods in this little town.*

barkeep a bartender. □ *Gimme some of that there red-eye, barkeep.* □ *The barkeep polished the glasses while the piano player played a sad tune.*

barn-burner a fast and lively person or thing. □ *That old dance tune is a real barn-burner.* □ *When Jim gets to work shelling peas, he's a barn-burner. None of us can keep up with him.*

barranca a deep ravine. (Spanish.) □ *The sides of the barranca were too steep for our horses.* □ *The trail wound down into the barranca.*

batter bread See *spoon bread.*

battle-axe a tough older woman. (Somewhat insulting.) □ *I feel sorry for Jim, married to such an old battle-axe.* □ *Have you ever met my Aunt Edna? She's a real battle-axe!*

battlin' board a board used for beating laundry. □ *Grandma used to do laundry with a battlin' board. I'm glad I have a washing machine!* □ *She still uses her battlin' board to beat out the toughest stains.*

battlin' stick a stick used for beating laundry. □ *I'm pretty good with the battlin' stick. No stains in my wash.* □ *When Grandma was too old to swing the battlin' stick, she bought an old worsher.*

bay a horse with a bright reddish-brown coat and a black mane and tail. (See also *Appaloosa; chestnut; paint; palomino; piebald; roan.*) □ *My horse Star was a bay with a white splash on the forehead.* □ *Arizona Slim rode a big, glossy bay.*

bayou a marshy, slow-moving stream or lake. □ *Joe lives down on the bayou.* □ *Tree branches draped with Spanish moss hung down over the bayou.*

be a fool about something AND **be a fool for something** to like something a great deal. □ *Mary is a fool about the color yellow. Everything she owns is yellow, almost.* □ *James is a fool for my blackberry dumplings.*

be a fool for something See *be a fool about something.*

be (back) in harness to be (back) at work. □ *I'd rather be in harness than sit idle all the time.* □ *The school year has started. The teachers and students are back in harness.*

be fixing to do something to be about to do something; to be getting ready to do something. □ *Are you fixing to go to town anytime soon?* □ *I'm fixing to write Jim a letter.*

be gettin' on (in years) to be elderly. □ *Lulu's gettin' on in years. She can't take care of that big ol' house by herself.* □ *Grampa's gettin' on. He won't be with us too much longer.*

be (just) shy of something See *run (just) shy of something.*

be on someone like a duck on a June bug **1.** to confront someone swiftly. □ *Every time I tried to pull a prank in class, the teacher was on me like a duck on a June bug.* □ *Whenever Joe made the tiniest mistake, his boss was on him like a duck on a June bug.* **2.** to monitor someone or something carefully and watchfully. □ *After the first mistake, she was on him like a duck on a June bug.* □ *The candy story clerk was on all the kids like a duck on a June bug.*

be on someone like white on rice AND **stick (to someone) like white on rice** **1.** to punish someone swiftly. □ *You slap your sister one more time, boy, and I'll be on you like white on rice.* □ *The minute the fugitive showed his face, the police were on him like white on rice.* **2.** to stick very close to someone. □ *The dirt stuck to us like white on rice.* □ *Don't let that cat rub against you. You'll have cat hair on you like white on rice.*

be up a tree to be in a very difficult situation. □ *If I can't get two hundred dollars by the end of the month, I'll really be up a tree.* □ *Charlie will be up a tree for sure if his wife finds out he got fired.*

be worth one's salt to be worth what one is paid. □ *That carpenter isn't worth his salt. Just look at the rotten job he did on my front steps!* □ *That dang weather forecaster ain't worth her salt. She said it wasn't going to rain today!*

bealing a boil. □ *You ought to see the doctor about that bealing under your arm.* □ *He had a big, red bealing over one eye.*

beans that talk behind your back beans that give you intestinal gas. □ *Someone in this room must have had beans that talk behind your back.* □ *The beans he had for dinner were talking behind his back.*

bear a difficult thing or person. □ *This assignment sure is a bear!* □ *Rumor has it that our new boss is a bear.*

bear grass a kind of coarse grass. □ *We looked around for something for the horses to eat, but there was nothing but bear grass as far as the eye could see.* □ *We used dried bear grass to start a fire.*

beat bobtail to be extraordinary. (See also *Don't that (just) beat all?; If that don't beat a pig a-pecking!; that beats something all to pieces.*) □ *Don't that beat bobtail! The plum tree's blooming in February!* □ *If that don't beat bobtail! I was just thinking about Joe, and now he calls me up on the phone!*

beat someone or something all hollow to be much better than the person or thing named. □ *I thought I made good flapjacks, but yours beat mine all hollow!* □ TOM: *This sure is a fine Thanksgiving Day parade.* MARY: *Yes, it sure beats last year's all hollow.*

beat someone till his hide won't hold shucks to beat someone severely. □ *They got in a fight, and Bill beat Joe till his hide won't hold shucks.* □ *If I ever see him making eyes at my sister, I'll beat him till his hide won't hold shucks.*

beat the bejeebers out of someone or something AND **beat the bejesus out of someone or something** to beat someone or something severely. (See also *stomp the bejeebers out of someone or something; knock the bejeebers out of someone or something.*) □ *He didn't just slap him around. He beat the bejeebers out of him.* □ *When I was a kid, my dad would beat the bejesus out of me for nothing at all.*

beat the bejesus out of someone or something See *beat the bejeebers out of someone or something.*

beat the daylights out of someone or something to beat someone or something severely; to spank someone. □ *Jim doesn't just spank his kids. He beats the daylights out of 'em.* □ *You can beat the daylights out of that poor horse if you want, but you can't make him go any faster.*

beat the devil and carry a rail to be the best by far. □ *Jane can beat the devil and carry a rail when it comes to fixing cars.* □ *At the All-State competition, our school band beat the devil and carried a rail.*

beat the devil around the stump AND **whip the devil around the stump** to avoid something. □ *He was supposed to cut the grass, but he beat the devil around the stump by saying that the lawn mower was broken and taking it over to Joe's to fix it.* □ *Say what you've come to say. Quit whipping the devil around the stump.*

beat the (natural) stuffing out of someone See *kick the (natural) stuffing out of someone.*

beat the tar out of someone to beat someone severely. □ *Mr. Jones'll beat the tar out of you if he catches you stealing from his cherry tree.* □ *Big Jim can beat the tar out of anybody in the whole school.*

beaten biscuit a biscuit made by beating the dough with a stick or mallet. □ *Her beaten biscuits are the best I ever et.* □ *I make beaten biscuits for special occasions.*

beatin'est the very best; the most astonishing. □ *Mary is the beatin'est fiddle player in the whole county.* □ *That tiny little kid ridin' that big ol' horse is the beatin'est thing I ever did see.*

beau a suitor. (From French. The French plural is *beaux*; the English plural is *beaus*.) □ *Tom is Jane's beau.* □ *Mary had six beaux the year she was eighteen.*

bed down to make one's bed; to prepare a place to sleep. □ *They bedded down in a haystack.* □ *The farmer let us bed down in his barn.*

bed someone down to kill someone. □ *If I ever get him in my sights, I'll bed him down.* 🅃 *The outlaw swore he'd bed down the sheriff.*

bedbug a kind of small, biting insect that often lives in beds. (*Good night, don't let the bedbugs bite* is a cute way of saying, "Good night.") □ *I don't like to stay over at Tom's. The beds there are so filthy I'm sure they're full of bedbugs.* □ BILL: *I'm going up to bed now.* MARY: *Good night. Don't let the bedbugs bite.*

bedroll a roll of blankets and a tarpaulin, used for sleeping on the ground. □ *Everything the cowboy owned was rolled up in his bedroll.* □ *The hikers found a sheltered place to put their bedrolls.*

bee-gum beeswax; a beehive. □ *Jed was chewing on a wad of bee-gum and could hardly talk.* □ *The bear pulled out a big chunk of bee-gum and stuffed it in his mouth.*

beggar-lice a kind of burr. □ *When we came back from our hike, our socks were covered with beggar-lice.* □ *I tried to pull off the beggar-lice, but they stuck to my fingers.*

behaps maybe. (Probably a combination of *maybe* and *perhaps*.) □ TOM: *Are you going to the fair?* JANE: *Behaps.* □ *Behaps I'll give Mary a call.*

behind the door when the brains were passed out stupid. □ *Jim's a sweet kid, but he musta been behind the door when the brains* *were passed out.* □ *It took Sally three years to get through first grade. She sure was behind the door when the brains were passed out.*

beholden (to someone) in someone's debt. □ *Thank you very much. I'm beholden to you for the loan.* □ *Jane never borrowed. She hated being beholden to anybody.*

believe you me believe me. (Emphatic.) □ *Believe you me, I'm not going to give up without a fight.* □ *That boyfriend of hers is nothing but trouble, believe you me.*

bell-tail a rattlesnake. □ *She was a smart kid. She knew what to do if a bell-tail bit her.* □ *I went for a walk up the hill and almost stepped on a bell-tail.*

beller to bellow. □ *"Get out here!" he bellered.* □ *The ox bellered.*

bellow like an ox to yell loudly. □ *He bellowed like an ox when they tried to get that splinter out of his foot.* □ *What's Sue mad about? I can hear her bellowing like an ox!*

belly-ache to complain; to whine. □ *Quit belly-aching.* □ *No matter what I serve him for dinner, Jim belly-aches about the food.*

belly-buster AND **belly-flop** a dive in which the diver's belly hits the water flat. □ *I tried to dive, but it just turned into a belly-buster. It really hurt!* □ *The kids were clowning around, doing belly-flops into the swimming pool.*

belly button the navel. □ *The baby laughs when you tickle his belly button.* □ *I don't like those bathing suits that show your belly button.*

belly-flop See *belly-buster.*

belly up dead. (Fish often turn belly upward when they die. Also literal.) □ *All the fish in my fish tank were belly up this morning.* □ *We found a deer lying belly up in our front yard.*

belly up to something to come stand up close to something. (Often *belly up to the bar*, meaning come up to the bar.) □ *At five o'clock, all the regulars bellied up to the bar and ordered the usual.* □ *We bellied up to the lunch counter and asked to see the menu.*

belt and suspenders having two people or things do the same job. □ *Jane wears a wristwatch and also has a clock on her desk at work. That's belt and suspenders, I think.* □ *I fastened the picture to the wall with both nails and glue. You may think that's belt and suspenders, but I call it being secure.*

bent out of shape upset; agitated. □ *Don't get all bent out of shape. They was just teasing you.* □ *He got all bent out of shape over something they printed about him in the paper.*

bet one's bottom dollar to be sure. □ *I'd bet my bottom dollar that Bill's seeing a girl on the side.* □ *You can bet your bottom dollar that Mary won't apologize.*

better had (do something) ought to do something; had better do something. (See also *(had) best do something.*) □ *He better had fix that stove by the time I get back.* □ TOM: *Do you think Jim will apologize?* JANE: *He better had!*

better than a poke in the eye with a sharp stick preferable; not so bad. □ *It's not a great job, but it's better than a poke in the eye with a sharp stick.* □ TOM: *All I got for my birthday was some dumb book.* MARY: *Well, that's better than a poke in the eye with a sharp stick.*

Better the gravy than no grease at all. It is better to have something, even if it is not the best, than to have nothing at all. □ *I'm almost ashamed to go out in this shabby old coat, but it does keep me warm. Better the gravy than no grease at all, I suppose.* □ MARY: *I'm sick of canned peaches for dessert. Don't give me any.* TOM: *But it's all we have.* MARY: *Well, all right. Better the gravy than no grease at all.*

between a rock and a hard place **1.** having no money at all. □ *Can you loan me five dollars till payday? I'm between a rock and* *a hard place.* □ *By the end of the month, me and all my friends were between a rock and a hard place.* **2.** between two unpleasant alternatives. □ *I'm between a rock and a hard place—if I don't sell my car, I can't pay the rent, but if I do sell my car, I won't be able to get to work.* □ *Mary was between a rock and a hard place. She felt she couldn't carry her baby any further, but on the other hand, she could hardly leave the tiny child by the side of the road while she searched for help.*

between hay and grass between childhood and adulthood. (Usually used to describe young men.) □ *Joe's at that time of life between hay and grass, when nothing seems to satisfy him.* □ *The boy was between hay and grass, and just beginning to learn about love.*

between whiles between other activities. □ *I shovel snow in the winter, cut grass in the summer, and sell newspapers between whiles.* □ *Jane came out to set on the stoop and talk with us between whiles.*

Beulah land Paradise. (The *Land of Beulah* is a peaceful land in Bunyan's *Pilgrim's Progress.*) □ *When I first saw this part of the country, it seemed like Beulah land to me.* □ *One day, I shall see my dear departed father again, when we are all together in Beulah land.*

Bible-banger See *Bible-thumper.*

Bible-thumper AND **Bible-banger** an evangelical Christian who frequently quotes the Bible. □ *Our last minister was very quiet and learned, but now we got a real Bible-banger.* □ *After she got religion, she turned into a right down Bible-thumper.*

bidness business. □ *Joe's going to work in his pa's bidness.* □ TOM: *Whatcha got in that sack?* MARY: *None of your bidness!*

big pregnant. □ *Sally's big, due in about five months.* □ *Nancy was big five times in the first five years she was married.*

big dog AND **big dude** an important person. □ *Joe's runnin' around in that new car of his, acting like he's some kind of big dog.* □

Jimmy's a big dude in this here town. If you want anything done, just go to him.

big-doins a big event. □ *There's big-doins down to the picnic grounds tonight.* □ *We're having some big-doins at our house when my sister gets married.*

big drink of water AND **(long) tall drink of water** a very tall or skinny person. □ *Wally shore is a big drink of water.* □ *The basketball player was a long tall drink of water with a six-and-a-half-foot reach.*

big dude See *big dog.*

big enough to choke a cow AND **big enough to choke a hog** very big. □ *No wonder the baby couldn't swallow that pill. It's big enough to choke a cow!* □ *The apples were big enough to choke a hog.*

big enough to choke a hog See *big enough to choke a cow.*

big enough to shade an elephant very big. □ *He was a big man—big enough to shade an elephant.* □ *The tree was two hundred years old and big enough to shade an elephant.*

big-eye(d) greedy; envious. □ *John's so big-eye, everything he sees, he wants.* □ *Them big-eyed kids ate all three of the pies I made for the church social.*

big honker a big thing or animal. □ *Out of the bush came a buck, a big honker.* □ *Mark's new tractor is a big honker.*

Big Muddy See *Old Muddy.*

big time **1.** an exciting time. □ *I'm gonna go into the city on Saturday, have me a big time.* □ *The crooks had a big time with the money they stole.* **2.** to a large degree. (Used to emphasize a statement.) □ *They cheated me big time.* □ *Joe won big time in the lottery. He'll never have to work again.*

biggest duck in the puddle AND **biggest frog in the pond** the most important person in some small group. □ *Tom got elected class president. I guess that makes him the biggest duck in the puddle.* □ *Jane wanted that promotion more than anything. She had her heart set on being the biggest frog in the pond.*

biggest frog in the pond See *biggest duck in the puddle.*

biggity acting very important. □ *After they won the championship, all the football players got mighty biggity.* □ *"Some assistance, if you please," she said, in that biggity way she has.*

bighorn (sheep) a kind of mountain sheep with big horns. □ *The two bighorns butted heads, and the sound echoed through the valley.* □ *A bighorn sheep stood on the crag, sniffing the breeze.*

bile to boil. □ *She biled a few eggs and we ate them with salt.* □ *It's hot enough to bile turnips out there.*

bimeby See *by and by.*

bird dog someone's buttocks. □ *If you don't quit that, I'm gonna swat you right across the bird dog.* □ *Jim slipped on the ice and fell right down on his bird dog.*

bird-dog someone or something to pursue someone or something. □ *You quit bird-doggin' that poor girl. She already told you she don't want to go out with you.* □ *The sheriff bird-dogged the outlaw all across the county.*

birthing the process of giving birth. □ *Lulu's ma came to help with the birthing.* □ *It was a difficult birthing, but mother and baby are doing fine.*

biscuit-bread a kind of bread made from wheat flour. □ *For dinner we had stew and biscuit-bread.* □ *How do you get your biscuit-bread so nice and fluffy?*

bite to eat something to eat. (Used with the indefinite article *a*.) □ *Won't you sit down and have a bite to eat?* □ *We can stop at the diner and have a bite to eat on the way home.*

bitter pill (to swallow) an unpleasant thing to have to endure. (Used with the indefinite article *a*.) □ *My son's divorce was a bitter pill for me to swallow, I can tell you.* □ *To Jim, losing the contest was a bitter pill indeed.*

black-eyed Susan a revolver with six chambers. (Mostly used in Western movies and novels. From the name of the common flower.) □ *As long as I got my black-eyed Susan, I ain't afraid of nobody.* □ *Arizona Slim had a rifle across his saddle and a black-eyed Susan in his belt.*

black sheep (of the family) the most troublesome member of the family; the unaccepted member of the family. □ *George was the black sheep of the family. He gambled all of Ma's savings away.* □ *I'm the black sheep because I can't hold down a job.*

blackberry baby an illegitimate child. (A baby found under a blackberry bush. See also *ash-barrel baby; brush colt; outsider; volunteer; woods colt.*) □ *John was a blackberry baby, but we don't hold it against him.* □ *Three girls in my high school class had blackberry babies that year.*

black-eyed pea a kind of bean with a black spot in the middle. (See also *cowpea; crowder pea.*) □ *On New Year's Day, our family always eats black-eyed peas for luck.* □ *Gramma cooked up some black-eyed peas with bacon.*

blackjack **1.** a card game in which the winner is the first person to get twenty-one points. □ *I lost two hundred dollars at blackjack.* □ *Whenever Joe goes to Las Vegas, he plays blackjack till all his money is gone.* **2.** an alcoholic drink made of rum and molasses. □ *This here blackjack's got a kick to it.* □ *Gimme a shot of blackjack, barkeep.*

blackstrap crude molasses. □ *How can you put that blackstrap on your pancakes? It's so bitter!* □ *Jane uses blackstrap in her gingerbread.*

blankety-blank damned. (A mild expletive used to suggest that a stronger expletive is being deleted.) □ *I turned the key, and the* *blankety-blank car wouldn't start.* □ *Joe cussed up a storm, going on about his blankety-blank job and his blankety-blank boss.*

blaze a white stripe down the center of a horse's face. □ *Arizona Slim's horse was black with a white blaze.* □ *The foal had a blaze, just like its mother.*

bleed like a stuck pig to bleed very freely. (See also *squeal like a stuck pig.*) □ *It was just a shallow cut, but I bled like a stuck pig.* □ *Can't you help me, Doc? I'm bleeding like a stuck pig!*

bless my soul My goodness! (Used to express surprise. See also *bless my time of day.*) □ *Why, bless my soul! Someone mowed my lawn while I was away.* □ *When she saw who was at the door, Mary said, "Bless my soul, it's Tom! I haven't seen you in years!"*

bless my time of day My goodness! (Used to express surprise. See also *bless my soul.*) □ *Bless my time of day! All my tulips are blooming.* □ *When Joe saw all the birthday presents we had put on his desk, he said, "Bless my time of day, what's this?"*

Bless your heart. "Thank you."; "What a wonderful thing you have done." (Compare to *Bless your little black heart.*) □ JANE: *I made dinner for you. I figured you'd be tired.* TOM: *Bless your heart.*

Bless your little black heart. "What a terrible thing you have done." (Often said in sarcastic admiration of a mischevious or evil deed. Compare to *Bless your heart.*) □ *"Well, bless your little black heart!" Mary said when she heard about the practical joke played on John.* □ *Jimmy got finger paints all over the wall, but his mama just laughed and said, "Bless your little black heart!"*

blessed damned. (Always pronounced with two syllables. A mild expletive.) □ *Why is it that every blessed thing is going wrong today?* □ *I asked all my kinfolks for help, and every blessed one of 'em turned me down.*

blind pig a place to buy illicit liquor. □ *Iffen you want some white lightning, I know where there's a blind pig.* □ *There's a blind pig in the woods out back of Johnson's place.*

blind staggers extreme drunkenness. □ *He came home from the saloon with a bad case of the blind staggers.* □ *Don't let her drive, for goodness' sake. She's got the blind staggers.*

blinky sour. (Used to describe milk.) □ *Don't drink that milk. It's blinky.* □ *Gramma uses blinky milk to make biscuits.*

blood one's own family. (Short for *blood relatives.*) □ *How could you go telling the Joneses all our business? They ain't even blood!* □ *We'll do anything to help Jim, if we can. He's blood.*

bloody flux dysentery. □ *It's no joke when little kids get the bloody flux.* □ *Something in the water gave him the bloody flux.*

blow a fuse to become extremely angry; to throw a temper tantrum. □ *When Joe heard that I had messed up his car, he blew a fuse.* □ *Mary is awfully touchy. She'll blow a fuse about the least little thing.*

blow to boast. □ *There goes Jim, blowing about how he won the football game single-handed.* □ *I'm tired of hearing Jane blow about the great job she has.*

blow one's own horn AND **toot one's own horn** to praise oneself or tell others about one's accomplishments. □ *Jane tries to impress people by blowing her own horn.* □ *If you want to succeed in business, you'll have to toot your own horn a little bit.*

blow over to pass. □ TOM: *Mary and Bill had a big fight today.* JANE: *I'm sure it will blow over.* □ *His bad moods always blow over.*

blown up like a toad unpleasantly swollen or puffed up. □ *Tom got so many bee stings he's blown up like a toad.* □ *Mary has hives and is blown up like a toad.*

blowout a big celebration. □ *The kids had a blowout at the end of the school year.* □ *Joe put on a big blowout for his daughter's wedding.*

blue devils feelings of depression. □ *I'm glad you called. I've been having an attack of the blue devils all morning, and talking to you is sure to cheer me up.* □ *When Jane gets the blue devils, it lasts for days.*

blue john skim milk. (Skim milk has a bluish tint.) □ *Tom's doctor told him to lose weight, so he's drinking blue john instead of regular milk.* □ *I bought a quart of blue john to go with my breakfast cereal.*

blue-tick hound a hunting dog with blue speckles on its coat. □ *Grampa had a blue-tick hound that could hunt quail like nobody's business.* □ *I've got one red dog and one blue-tick hound.*

bluebelly someone from the Northern United States; a Yankee. (Insulting.) □ *I could tell by the way he talked he was a no-good bluebelly.* □ *After the War, we had to sell the farm to a bluebelly speculator.*

bluegrass (music) country music played on acoustic instruments, such as banjos, guitars, and violins. □ *We tapped our toes and sang along to that good ol' bluegrass music.* □ *Jim's band plays bluegrass.*

boardinghouse reach reaching across the table to get something you want rather than asking someone to pass it to you. □ *"Pardon my boardinghouse reach," said Mary, reaching for the butter.* □ *The family never talked at the dinner table. In fact, they'd rather do a boardinghouse reach than say, "Pass the salt."*

bobble a small mistake. □ *The teacher caught the bobble in my solution to the math problem.* □ *He made a bobble when he copied out the recipe for me.*

bobwire See *barb(ed) wire.*

bodacious extremely good. □ *Mary cooked up a bodacious welcome-home dinner for the travelers.* □ *Jane is one bodacious fiddle-player.*

bodaciously completely. □ *When they got home from the shindig, they was bodaciously drunk.* □ *I'm bodaciously wore out.*

body a person. (Used with the indefinite article *a*.) □ *All this walking sure wears a body out.* □ *A beautiful sunset like that can make a body glad to be alive.*

boiled shirt a starched dress shirt. □ *Joe put on a boiled shirt and went a'courtin' Mary.* □ *I hate these fancy dinners where I have to wear a boiled shirt.*

boiling corn corn that is good to eat boiled. (See also *boiling ear.*) □ *I'm growing some boiling corn in the vegetable garden out back.* □ *Bring some of that good boiling corn and we'll have it at the picnic.*

boiling ear an ear of corn that is good to eat boiled. (See also *boiling corn.*) □ *Mary picked some boiling ears to have with supper.* □ *This kind of corn makes good boiling ears.*

boll weevil an insect that eats cotton. □ *The cotton crop that year was full of boll weevils.* □ *Boll weevils got to all my cotton shirts, and now they're full of holes.*

bollixed up messed up; ruined. □ *My knitting got all bollixed up. I'll have to unravel it.* □ *My boss blamed me because the project was bollixed up.*

bomgilly short for Balm of Gilead, an evergreen tree whose leaves can be used for medicine. □ *Grandma cured me with bomgilly tea.* □ *There was a stand of bomgilly in the woods.*

bonanza a very great deal of something. □ TOM: *Were there lots of things on sale?* MARY: *Yes, indeed. It was a regular bonanza.* □ *Jane's garden yielded a bonanza of fresh vegetables.*

bone orchard AND **marble orchard** a graveyard. □ *I'm afeard of walking through that bone orchard at night.* □ *There's a marble orchard out back of the church.*

boneyard **1.** a graveyard. □ *They buried him in the boneyard.* □ *The boneyard looked spooky in the moonlight.* **2.** a bony, worn-out horse. (Slang.) □ *You ought to put that boneyard out to pasture.* □ *He bought an old boneyard to pull his plow.*

Bonny Blue Flag the state flag of South Carolina during the U.S. Civil War (1861–1865), a symbol of Confederate patriotism. □ *Great-Uncle Bill still flies the Bonny Blue Flag, to show his loyalty to the South.* □ *The sons of the family both died defending the Bonny Blue Flag.*

boocoo very; a great deal. (From the French *beaucoup*.) □ *She was boocoo smart and good-looking, too.* □ *Don't cross Bill. He'll mess you up boocoo.*

book-learning information from books, as opposed to real-life experience. □ *Tom's got plenty of book-learning, but not much good sense.* □ *The teacher was respected for her book-learning.*

boondoggle a trick; a swindle. □ *The con men pulled off the biggest boondoggle this town has ever seen.* □ *I sent money to that charity, and then I found out it was just a boondoggle.*

booze blind very drunk. □ *He says all kinds of fool things when he's booze blind.* □ *She wanted to drink till she was booze blind.*

born on crazy creek crazy; loony. □ MARY: *Jim says he can talk to the man in the moon.* TOM: *Yeah, but you know he was born on crazy creek.* □ *Because Jane had such wild ideas, her neighbors said she was born on crazy creek.*

born short and slapped down flat short of stature. (Jocular.) □ *No, he's not a tall man. He was born short and slapped down flat.* □ *Her parents were both tall, but she's born short and slapped down flat.*

born tired and raised lazy lazy and shiftless. □ *Joe ain't never gonna amount to anything. He was born tired and raised lazy!* □ *You'll never get Mary to help you out. She's born tired and raised lazy.*

born with a silver spoon in one's mouth born into a rich family; well-to-do. □ *Jane will never understand how ordinary folks live, because she was born with a silver spoon in her mouth.* □ *Tom was born with a silver spoon in his mouth, so he ain't worked a day in his life.*

borned born. □ *Me and all my brothers and sisters was borned at home.* □ *What year was she borned?*

bosque a woods. □ *The outlaw was hiding out in the bosque.* □ *I have a little cabin in the bosque where I go when I want to be alone.*

bossy AND **bossie** a cow. (Often used as a name for a cow.) □ *"Hey there, bossy," Jim said, patting the cow on her side.* □ *She was a nice old bossie, never kicked nobody.*

botheration **1.** "Darn it!"(A mild oath.) □ *Botheration! I left my wallet at home.* □ *Jane hit her thumb with the hammer. "Botheration!" she yelled.* **2.** a fuss. □ *The restaurant almost closed when they had that botheration with the health department.* □ *I don't want no kind of botheration about my birthday, you hear?*

bottle fever delerium tremens; hallucinations from drinking too much. □ *He's raving. He's got the bottle fever.* □ *He drank all weekend and had bottle fever all of Monday.*

bottom(land) a lowland area; low-lying land near a river or stream. □ *The whole bottom was flooded when we had them heavy rains.* □ *The poor folks lived down in the bottomland, while the rich folks lived up in the hills.*

boughten bought from a store, instead of made at home. □ *Joe got himself a boughten shirt for the special occasion.* □ *Our garden failed, so we ate boughten vegetables that summer.*

bound and determined very determined. □ *Mary's bound and determined to paint the house this summer.* □ *Joe was bound and determined he was going to go to the rodeo, whether or not his folks approved.*

bound to do something certain to do something. □ *Joe's bound to be upset if he finds out we broke his window.* □ *Keep up with your studies and you're bound to do well.*

bounden duty a promise; an obligation. □ *Jane feels it's her bounden duty to take care of her mother at home.* □ *As club president, it is my bounden duty to attend every meeting.*

bowie knife a heavy, long-bladed hunting knife. □ *The two cowhands drew their bowie knives and commenced to fighting.* □ *All I need to survive in the wilderness is my canteen and my bowie knife.*

Boy, howdy! "Wow!"; "I am certainly surprised!" (An exclamation.) □ *We sure did have a good time, boy, howdy!* □ *Boy, howdy! That's the biggest hoss I ever did see!*

braces See *galluses.*

brag someone or something up to brag about someone or something; to make someone or something sound impressive by bragging about it. □ *We like to brag our town up to show folks we're proud of it.* 🅃 *Jane's always bragging up her father, talking about all his college degrees.*

Brains in the head saves blisters on the feet. Careful thinking ahead will save you from having to go back and forth to get what you need. □ *I always take all my tools with me when I go outside to fix something. Brains in the head saves blisters on the feet.* □ *It might get cold later, so take your sweater with you now. Brains in the head saves blisters on the feet.*

branch a brook or creek that is a branch of a larger stream. □ *We can fill our water bottles at the next branch.* □ *The kids waded in the branch, catching minnows.*

branch water pure water from a natural stream. □ *They make that beer with branch water. That's why it's so good.* □ *They're selling bottled branch water for two dollars a bottle, down in the city.*

brand-spanking new as new as can be. □ *Have you seen Tom's new house? Everything in it is brand-spanking new. Where did he get the money?* □ *The car is old, but the tires are brand-spanking new.*

break a horse to tame a horse so it can be ridden. □ *He started breaking that horse when it was one year old.* □ *Mary found out how tough it is to break a wild horse.*

break bread (with someone) to eat a meal with someone; to eat together with someone. □ *The family was glad to be able to break bread with one another again after their long separation.* □ *In the unwritten law of the frontier, you couldn't kill a man after you broke bread with him.*

break one's arm patting oneself on the back See *have callouses from patting one's own back.*

break someone of something to make someone stop doing something. □ *I am trying to break little Jimmy of hollering so loud.* □ *How can I break them boys of getting so dirty?*

breast baby See *arm baby.*

breathe one's horse to give one's horse a rest. □ *We'd better stop and breathe our horses.* □ *At the top of the hill, she stopped to breathe her horse.*

breeze off to boast at great length. □ *I wish Bill would quit breezing off about his new tractor.* □ *She loves to breeze off about her grandchildren.*

breezeway a passageway between buildings. □ *On hot summer evenings, we sat out in the breezeway, drinking lemonade.* □ *There was a breezeway between the old outdoor kitchen and the main house.*

bright-eyed having to do with eggs fried with the yolks uncooked on top. (See also *sunny-side up.*) □ TOM: *How do you want your eggs?* BILL: *Bright-eyed.* □ *I had bright-eyed eggs and toast.*

bright-eyed and bushy-tailed eager and alert. □ *I'm not exactly bright-eyed and bushy-tailed first thing in the morning.* □ *Our pup is always bright-eyed and bushy-tailed.*

bring-'em close glass a magnifying glass. □ *She looked at the bug through her bring-'em close glass.* □ *You'd need a bring-'em close glass to read that tiny print.*

bring home the bacon to bring back money or food, especially to provide for one's family. □ *Joe is a good husband. He's kind and considerate, and he brings home the bacon.* □ *In the Johnson family, Tom stays home to take care of the kids, while Mary brings home the bacon.*

bring someone's saddle home to do to someone that which someone has done to you. □ *The students decided to bring the teacher's saddle home by giving him a grade at the end of the year.* □ *Mary got tired of Bill staying out all night, so she stayed out all night herself. I guess that brought his saddle home!*

bringin'-up someone's upbringing; the way someone was raised. □ *I don't know why Bill turned out so rotten. He had a decent bringin'-up.* □ *Jane is always trying to interfere in her grandson's bringin'-up.*

britches pants; trousers. □ *I tore a hole in my britches trying to get over the barbed wire fence.* □ *Joe uses suspenders to hold his britches up.*

bronc(o) a wild horse. □ *I bet you fifty dollars you can't ride that bronc.* □ *Arizona Slim could tame any bronco you could catch.*

bronco buster someone who breaks wild horses so they can be ridden. □ *Arizona Slim is the best bronco buster west of the Mississippi.* □ *The bronco buster was no good with people, but he sure did understand horses.*

broomtail a horse. (Slang. See also *shavetail.*) □ *She came riding into town on a sorry-looking broomtail.* □ *Joe let me bed my broomtail in his barn for the night.*

brung brought. (Past tense of *bring.*) □ *Look what I brung you!* □ *When I was in the hospital, all the kids brung flowers.*

brush colt an illegitimate child. (Said of a colt found in the wild. See also *ash-barrel baby; blackberry baby; outsider; volunteer; woods colt.*) □ *If Sally don't get married soon, her baby'll be a brush colt.* □ *Jim was ashamed of being a brush colt.*

buck at something to resist something; to object to something. □ *The boss bucked at the new proposal.* □ *You know how Sally is—she bucks at any change in her routine.*

buck naked AND **butt naked** naked. (Use caution with *butt.*) □ *When we've got company, you can't go walking through the house buck naked.* □ *There's a guy standing by the river butt naked!*

buck nun a bachelor; a celibate male. □ *One or two of the cowhands was married, but most of 'em was buck nuns.* □ *He had been a buck nun for a lot of years and was kinda shy around women.*

buckaroo a cowboy. (Often used as a form of address, as in the second example.) □ *They was a rowdy bunch of buckaroos. They'd as soon fight you as look at you.* □ *Why, howdy there, buckaroo! Long time no see!*

Buckeye State Ohio. (A *Buckeye* is someone from Ohio.) □ *I'm from the Buckeye State, born and raised in Cincinnati.* □ *We'll be passing through the Buckeye State on our way to Pennsylvania.* □ *My neighbor is an old Buckeye who thinks Ohio is the most beautiful place on earth.*

bucking at the halter rebelling. □ *Joe's bucking at the halter, can't wait to get out of his folks' house and be out on his own.* □ *It was the last day of the school year, and all the students were bucking at the halter.*

buckle down (to something) to get seriously to work at something. □ *If we buckle down, we can get this finished today.* □ *Tom buckled down to his studying, determined to pass the test.*

buckra a white person, especially a poor white person. (Derogatory. Often with *poor*.) □ *Daddy didn't want his children to mix with no poor buckras.* □ *I thought he was an ignorant buckra from out in the country.*

buffalo chip a piece of buffalo manure. (See also *cow chip*.) □ *We made a fire out of dried buffalo chips.* □ *Mom! Billy threw a buffalo chip at me!*

buffalo grass a coarse grass eaten by buffalo. □ *As far as the eye could see, there was nothing for the horses to eat, just buffalo grass.* □ *The farmer wrestled the plow through the tough buffalo grass.*

buffaloed completely fooled and confused. □ *The salesman had me so buffaloed that I wound up buying two sets of encyclopedias.* □ *The audience was completely buffaloed by the performer's tricks.*

bugger someone or something up to make a mess of someone or something. (Now usually considered British.) □ *Whenever Bill tries to do something perfectly, he buggers it up.* 🅃 *By getting drunk in public, Jim buggered up his chances of being made a deacon.*

built like a brick outhouse See *built like a brick shithouse.*

built like a brick shithouse AND **built like a brick outhouse; built like a depot stove** **1.** having a good figure. (Used to describe people. Use caution with *shithouse*.) □ *The new girl on the block was built like a brick shithouse. All the guys wanted to go out with her.* □ *She was skinny when she was a kid, but now that she's grown up, she's built like a depot stove.* **2.** stout, strongly built. □ *Every last one of the piano movers was built like a brick outhouse.* □ *Susan was big and tall and built like a depot stove.*

built like a depot stove See *built like a brick shithouse.*

bullwhip a long, braided leather whip used to whip teams of oxen. □ *Bill cracked his bullwhip, and the oxen began to move along.* □ *He was so good with that bullwhip, he could whisk the fly out of a bull's eye at ten paces.*

bull(y)-rag someone to tease someone. □ *Quit bull-raggin' your brother.* □ *Everyone bully-ragged me about my new glasses.*

bumbershoot AND **bumpershoot** an umbrella. □ *Best take a bumbershoot. Looks like rain.* □ *I put the bumpershoot in the bathtub to dry.*

bumfuzzle someone to confuse someone. □ *The lawyer's fancy talk bumfuzzled me completely.* □ *Them crazy road signs bumfuzzled me, and I took a wrong turn.*

bumpershoot See *bumbershoot.*

bumptious easily angered. □ *She's a bumptious youngun, ain't she?* □ *Now, Sam, don't be getting bumptious on me!*

bung someone or something up to damage someone or something by blows. (See also *bunged up.*) □ *Don't let the watermelon rattle around in the trunk of your car. You don't want to bung it up.* 🅃 *Last time I put up the storm windows, I really bunged up my hands.*

bunged up battered or bruised. (See also *bung someone or something up.*) □ *It used to be a nice table, but it got all bunged up.* □ *What happened to Jane? Her face was bunged up.*

bunk to settle down for the night; to lie down in a bed. □ *You'll have to bunk with Joe tonight.* □ *We bunked in Sally's spare room.*

buñuelo a piece of sweet, fried dough. (From Mexican Spanish.) □ *We had buñuelos and coffee for breakfast.* □ *My grandmother makes buñuelos according to an old family recipe.*

burgoo a spicy meat and vegetable stew. □ *Jane's making burgoo for the Fourth of July picnic.* □ *We had a regular feast at the family reunion, with barbecue, cornbread, beans, rice, and burgoo.*

bury the hatchet to make peace. □ *You've been quarrelling for two years. It's time to bury the hatchet.* □ *I know we've had our differences, but I'd like to bury the hatchet.*

buryin' a funeral. □ *Not many folks came to the buryin'.* □ *I was so sorry I couldn't make it to Aunt Nelly's buryin'.*

bush bacon a rabbit. □ *John brought in some bush bacon this morning.* □ *Pappy and I went out for some bush bacon and got some, too.*

bush-whacker someone who ambushes and attacks people. □ *The stagecoach was attacked by bush-whackers.* □ *The bandit was a cowardly bush-whacker.*

bushel and a peck (and some in a gourd) a great deal. (Usually used to answer the question, "How much do you love me?") □ MARY: *How much do you love me?* TOM: *A bushel and a peck and some in a gourd.* □ *We knew that Grandpa loved us a bushel and a peck.*

bust a bronco to break a wild horse so that it can be ridden. □ *In them days, I made my livin' bustin' broncos.* □ *That was the meanest bronco I ever seen. Nobody could bust 'im.*

bust to break. (See also *bust something.*) □ *My garbage disposer busted.* □ *I barely touched that china plate, and it busted.*

bust out laughing to start laughing suddenly. □ *I busted out laughing when I saw him in that get-up.* □ *The bridegroom was so nervous, it was all he could do not to bust out laughing.*

bust someone wide open to beat someone severely. □ *If you ever take a step onto my property, I'll bust you wide open.* □ *Jim threatened to bust Bill wide open.*

bust something to break something. (See also *bust.*) □ *Somebody busted my car window.* □ *I busted my leg when I went skiing.*

but good severely; thoroughly. (Emphatic.) □ *She told him off but good.* □ *Joe whupped Bill but good.*

butt naked See *buck naked.*

butte a steep hill with a flat top. □ *We climbed to the top of the butte so as to get a good look around.* □ *Mary built her house atop a butte.*

(butter and) egg money money that a farm woman earns. (Farm women would often sell butter and eggs for extra money that would be stashed away for an emergency.) □ *Jane was saving her butter and egg money for a new TV.* □ *I've got my egg money. Let's go shopping.*

butter bean a Lima bean. □ *I made a succotash of butter beans and corn.* □ *I ordered the fish with a side dish of butter beans.*

butterball a fat person or animal. □ *Sally was a butterball when she was a girl, but she grew up tall and slim.* □ *What a cute puppy! He's such a butterball!*

buy a pig in a poke to buy something without looking at it first. □ *If you don't get a good look at the engine of a used car before you buy it, you'll wind up buying a pig in a poke.* □ *I just took the salesman's word that this camera worked. I guess I bought a pig in a poke.*

buy something on time to buy something on credit. □ TOM: *That's an awful fancy TV. Are you sure you can afford it?* JANE: *I'm buying it on time.* □ *I bought the sofa on time, but I paid cash for the chairs.*

buzzard a vulture. □ *Tom knew he was in trouble when he saw the buzzards start to circle overhead.* □ *The buzzards picked at the horse carcass.*

buzzard bait a dying or worthless animal or person. (See also *crow bait.*) □ *That old horse of yours is buzzard bait. Why don't you just shoot him?* □ *Jim does nothing all day long but drink whiskey and cuss at his wife. He's nothing but buzzard bait.*

by a hair See *by a whisker.*

by a whisker AND **by a hair** by a very narrow margin. □ *Tom is taller than Joe, but just by a whisker.* □ *My horse won the race by a hair.*

by and by AND **bimeby** at some time in the future. □ *The weather's sure to clear up by and by.* □ *You may think your heart is broken, but you'll feel better bimeby.*

by ankle express on foot. (See also *shank's mare; ride shank's ponies.*) □ *After my horse was stolen, I had to go by ankle express.* □ *It's a five-minute drive, forty minutes by ankle express.*

by cracky "By God." (A mild oath, often used to express surprise or approval. See also *by gum; by jingo; by godfrey.*) □ *Jim said he'd get the whole house painted this weekend, and by cracky, that's just what he did.* □ *By cracky! That thunder sure was loud.*

by godfrey "By God." (A mild oath. See also *by gum; by jingo; by cracky.*) □ *By godfrey, Jim's brother is a big man!* □ *Those cats sure do make a lot of noise, by godfrey.*

by guess and by golly See *by guess and by gosh.*

by guess and by gosh AND **by guess and by golly** by estimating; without expert knowledge or careful planning. □ JANE: *Did you have a plan for putting up that toolshed?* TOM: *Nope, we just sort of did it by guess and by gosh.* □ *Gramma always made dresses by guess and by golly, without using a pattern, and they always turned out just fine.*

by gum "By God." (A euphemism. See also *by cracky; by godfrey;* and the following entry.) □ *If Mary says she'll do something,* *then by gum, she'll do it.* □ TOM: *That girl in the blue dress sure is pretty.* BILL: *Why don't you ask her to dance?* TOM: *By gum, I will!*

by jingo "By Jesus." (A euphemism. See also *by cracky; by godfrey; by gum.*) □ *By jingo, that hired man can work!* □ *I never thought our team could win that game, but by jingo, they did.*

by main strength and awkwardness by force or brute strength. □ TOM: *How did you get that piano up the stairs?* MARY: *By main strength and awkwardness.* □ *By main strength and awkwardness, we got all the luggage crammed into the car.*

C

caballero a gentleman. (Spanish. Pronounced *kah-bah(l)-YER-oh.*) □ *Tom's a real caballero. He has excellent manners and is always kind to women and children.* □ *Come on in, caballeros. The party is just starting.*

cabin fever anxiety caused by being confined to a place. (See also *shack whacky.*) □ *The blizzard lasted for two weeks, and we all got cabin fever.* □ *Cabin fever made the two brothers so jumpy that they fought nearly all the time.*

cackleberry an egg. □ *We fried up some cackleberries for breakfast.* □ *It was Mary's chore to go out to the henhouse and collect all the cackleberries.*

cain't cannot. □ *I cain't even begin to see what you mean.* □ *I cain't for the life of me get there on time.*

cakewalk **1.** a very easy task. □ *The football game was a cakewalk for our team.* □ *Jim's been fixing cars since he was thirteen, so he thinks changing the oil is a regular cakewalk.* **2.** a type of dance contest in which first prize was a cake. □ *Ma and Pa always won the cakewalk on Saturday nights when they was young.* □ *John and Jane fell in love doing the cakewalk.*

calaboose a jail. (From Spanish *calabozo.*) □ *Dave's bad behavior landed him in the calaboose.* □ *The sheriff wanted to put the outlaw in the calaboose for good and all.*

calculate to think or figure. □ *I calculate I'll need about two cups of sugar to make lemonade for all these people.* □ *How do you calculate to make that worn-out coat last another year?*

calf slobber(s) meringue. (Jocular.) □ *The cook made a fancy pie with calf slobbers all over the top.* □ *Do you want a slice of this apple pie, or the chocolate kind with the calf slobber?*

call hogs to snore. □ *I couldn't sleep at all last night, with Cousin Joe calling hogs in the next room.* □ *Joe calls hogs so loud the windows rattle.*

call on someone to court someone. □ *Jim's calling on the hired girl over at the Browns'.* □ *In the old days, a boy had to ask a girl's father for permission to come call on her.*

call something to mind to remember something. □ *I used to know that man's name, but just now I can't call it to mind.* □ *Mary tried to call to mind where she had seen the red car before.*

call the dog to compete in order to see who can tell the biggest lie. □ *The old gents would sit out in front of the general store, calling the dog.* □ *Don't believe the stories your uncles tell. They're just calling the dog.*

called to straw brought or sent into labor. □ *Susan was called to straw when she was only seven months along.* □ *Nancy's nine months pregnant and could be called to straw any day now.*

camp meeting a religious revival meeting held outdoors, often in a tent. □ *Reverend Jones came to town to preach at the camp meeting.* □ *When there's a camp meeting going on in the hollow, you can hear the cries of "Praise Jesus!" all the way up to town.*

can (just) whistle for something can just forget about having something. □ *The last time Mary came over for dinner, she was downright rude. If she wants dinner at my house again, she can just whistle for it!* □ *I asked the boss for a promotion. He told me I could whistle for it.*

can see dawn. □ *I was up and at work before can see.* □ *I didn't get to bed nearly till can see.*

candidate for a pair of wings someone who is likely to die; someone who is close to death. □ *Whenever Jane wants to cross the street, she just walks out into traffic without looking. She's a candidate for a pair of wings, I say.* □ TOM: *How's Bill doing? I heard he was sick.* JANE: *Not good, I'm afraid. He's a candidate for a pair of wings.*

can't call one's soul one's own working for other people all the time. □ *Jane has to take care of both her aging parents. She can't call her soul her own.* □ *Between supporting his family and working off his brother's bad debts, Bob really can't call his soul his own.*

can't carry a tune in a bucket See *can't carry a tune in a bushel basket.*

can't carry a tune in a bushel basket AND **can't carry a tune in a bucket; can't carry a tune in a paper sack** unable to sing or hum a melody. □ *I declare to goodness, I don't know why Mary's in the choir. She can't carry a tune in a bushel basket.* □ *Joe likes to sing in the shower, though he can't carry a tune in a bucket.* □ *I'd try to hum the song for you, but I can't carry a tune in a paper sack.*

can't carry a tune in a paper sack See *can't carry a tune in a bushel basket.*

can't find one's butt with both hands (in broad daylight) is stupid or incompetent. (Use caution with *butt*.) □ *Why did they put Jim in charge? He can't find his butt with both hands!* □ TOM: *Jane seems like a bright girl.* BILL: *You've got to be kidding! She couldn't find her butt with both hands in broad daylight!*

can't hack it unable to do the job. □ *I thought delivering papers would be an easy job, but I just can't hack it.* □ *If you can't hack it, let me know, and I'll help you out.*

can't hold a candle to someone or something not as good as someone or something. □ *As far as Joe is concerned, no other girl can hold a candle to Mary.* □ *She's a good doctor, but she can't hold a candle to old Dr. Blaine.*

can't hold a light for someone cannot be compared to someone. □ *Jim's a dear man, but he can't hold a light for my first husband.* □ *Mr. Gunnison just can't hold a light for our last year's teacher.*

can't say (a)s I do, (can't say (a)s I don't) "I am not sure." □ TOM: *Do you know Mr. Smith?* MARY: *Well, I can't say as I do, can't say as I don't.* □ JANE: *What do you think of my cousin? Do you like him?* MARY: *Can't say's I do, can't say's I don't.*

can't say boo to a goose shy and not talkative. □ *I was surprised to see Joe so talkative at the party. Usually he can't say boo to a goose.* □ *She's a mousy little kid. Can't say boo to a goose.*

can't say for sure uncertain. □ *I can't say for sure, but I think I saw Mary go into the barbershop.* □ JANE: *How much gas does that stove burn in a year?* TOM: *Can't say for sure, but I'll tell you one thing—it costs less than electric.*

can't say, not knowing "I do not know." □ MARY: *Who's that girl walking with Jim?* JANE: *Can't say, not knowing.* □ BILL: *What time is it?* TOM: *Can't say, not knowing.*

can't see a hole in a ladder stupid or drunk. □ *No use asking her questions. She can't see a hole in a ladder.* □ *After the big party, Joe needed someone to drive him home. He couldn't see a hole in a ladder.*

can't-see time twilight. □ *Around can't-see time, everyone's out on their front porches, enjoying the cool breeze.* □ *We'd best make camp before can't-see time.*

cantankerous bad-tempered; disagreeable. □ *That cantankerous old woman yells at anyone who comes into her yard.* □ *Mary's horse is a downright cantankerous beast.*

cantina a saloon or small restaurant. (Spanish.) □ *Miguel and his wife ran a little cantina on the edge of town.* □ *I know a cantina where the food is cheap and really good.*

carcass the human body. □ *Park your carcass on that chair and put your feet up.* □ *"This old carcass is about worn out," sighed Grampa.*

carpetbagger a Northerner coming to the South in order to make money, especially during the Reconstruction period after the U.S. Civil War (1861–1865). □ *After the War, our family plantation was auctioned off to some no-'count carpetbagger.* □ *When Mary came down from New York to start her business here in South Carolina, folks thought she was some kind of carpetbagger.*

carry on (so) to be overly dramatic. (See also *take on (so).*) □ *When Bill finally came home, his wife cried and carried on.* □ *Calm down. There's no need to carry on so.*

carry someone somewhere to take or escort someone somewhere. □ *Friday nights, Joe always carries his wife to town.* □ *"May I carry you home?" the young man asked Jane.*

carry weight (with someone) to be worth thinking about (to someone); to be credible (with someone). □ *Nothing I say carries weight with Bill. He thinks I'm foolish.* □ *Everyone respects Jane, so her words carry weight.*

case-knife a knife kept in a sheath. □ *Jane always carries a little case-knife hanging off her belt.* □ *All the hired hands brought their own case-knives to use at the dinner table.*

case of the stiff neck a hanging. □ *When we catch that cattle rustler, we'll give him a case of the stiff neck.* □ *The outlaw died of a case of the stiff neck.*

cash in one's chips to die. □ *When my car swerved like that, I thought I was gonna cash in my chips for sure.* □ *Mark was sick for fourteen years before he finally cashed in his chips.*

cash money money in bills and coins. □ *You could make cash money selling your quilts, you really could.* □ *Joe wants cash money for his old TV set. He won't let me have it on credit.*

cash on the barrelhead cash at the time of purchase. □ *Jonson's store doesn't give credit. Everything is cash on the barrelhead.* □ *They offered me fifty thousand dollars cash on the barrelhead for Aunt Nancy's old house.*

catabias crooked. (See also *anti-godlin; catawampus; slaunchways; whopper-jawed.*) □ *I just can't sew. All my seams come out catabias.* □ *That gate's hung catabias. It won't never shut right.*

catalpa a type of tree with broad, heart-shaped leaves and long seed pods. (They are often trimmed into a neat ball-shape.) □ *Our house is easy to spot. We've got two big catalpas in the front yard.* □ *The children played in the shade of the catalpa trees.*

catamount a cougar or lynx. (From *catamountain.*) □ *When the brick fell on her toe, Jane howled like a catamount.* □ *A catamount got into the henhouse and killed all our chickens.*

catawampus crooked; askew. (See also *anti-godlin; catabias; slaunchways; whopper-jawed.*) □ *That picture's hung up all catawampus. Put it straight.* □ *Bill isn't a very careful carpenter. All his bookshelves come out catawampus.*

catch hell (about someone or something) to be scolded (about someone or something). □ *This isn't the first time Bill's caught hell about his drinking.* □ *We knew we were gonna catch hell when Ma saw how we'd ruined her garden.*

catch one's death (of cold) to catch a cold. □ *Put on a hat and scarf before you go out! You'll catch your death going out bareheaded.* □ *Make sure Joe has a warm coat for the winter. I don't want him to catch his death of cold.*

catching flies having an open mouth. □ *Well, don't just stand there catching flies. Come say hello to me!* □ *"Catching flies?" Joe teased, seeing my open-mouthed expression.*

catfish hole a small pond where catfish can be caught. (See also *crawdad hole*.) □ *Bill's got a secret catfish hole. He manages to catch at least three fish every day.* □ *The boys were all down at the catfish hole, fishin'.*

cathead biscuit a large wheat biscuit. □ *We had cathead biscuits and chicken soup for dinner.* □ *How do you get your cathead biscuits so light?*

cattle guard a grid of metal bars or pipes in the road, to keep cattle from crossing. □ *The bars of the cattle guard went rumble, rumble under the wheels of the car.* □ *Too many of our cattle were wandering off, so we put up a cattle guard toward the end of the road.*

caught short pregnant and unmarried. □ *Both of Jane's sisters got caught short before they graduated high school.* □ *Susan's parents let on that she had pneumonia, but we all knew she'd been caught short.*

caution a very amusing person. (Used with the indefinite article *a*.) □ *Seems everything John says sets us to laughing. He's a caution, all right!* □ *Mary's such a caution, always pulling practical jokes.*

cayuse a wild horse or an Indian horse. □ *After that spotted cayuse was gentled, it was the best riding horse I ever had.* □ *That little cayuse ain't good for much.*

certain sure very sure. □ TOM: *Are you sure you saw Bill at work today?* MARY: *Certain sure.* □ *If you keep hanging around with them no-good kids, you'll get in a heap of trouble for certain sure.*

change one's tune to change one's opinion, story, or statement. □ *She changed her tune when she saw that I was right.* □ *The townsfolk scorned him till they found out he was rich. Then they changed their tune.*

chaparral an area full of scrub oak. (From Spanish.) □ *The cowboys had to drive the cattle through two hundred miles of chaparral.* □ *A faint trail wound its way through the dense chaparral.*

chaps leg coverings made of leather and used to protect someone riding a horse from being hurt by thorny plants. (From Spanish *chaparajos*. Sometimes pronounced *shaps*.) □ *Arizona Slim was never without his cowhide chaps.* □ *Put on your chaps. We'll be riding through rough country today.*

charge it to the dust and let the rain settle it Do not expect to be paid for this. (A humorous answer to a question like, "Who is going to pay for this?") □ SALES CLERK: *Will this be cash or charge?* CUSTOMER: *Oh, charge it to the dust and let the rain settle it!* □ TOM: *Who's going to pay me all that money you owe?* MARY: *Charge it to the dust and let the rain settle it!*

chaw (of tobacco) AND **tobacco chaw** a piece of chewing tobacco. □ *Joe offered the stranger a chaw. "No thanks. I smoke, I don't chew," said the stranger.* □ *Uncle Bob always kept a chaw of tobacco in the pocket of his shirt.* □ *Bill always seems to have a big ol' tobacco chaw parked in one cheek.*

chaw (something) to chew something. (Literal and figurative uses.) □ *You've been chawing on that same mouthful for two minutes!* □ *He chawed it over in his mind.*

chayote a green squash. □ *Mary fried the chayotes with garlic and a little bit of lime.* □ *Stuffed chayotes are one of my favorite dishes.*

checkerbacker a woodpecker. □ *All day long, I heard that checkerbacker pecking away at the tree trunk.* □ *The tree was full of checkerbacker holes.*

cheesehead someone from Wisconsin. (Mildly derogatory.) □ *On weekends, all the cheeseheads come across the border into Minnesota to play.* □ *I'm a cheesehead born and bred.*

chess pie a pie with a filling made of butter, eggs, spices, and fruit or nuts. □ *This chess pie is so rich, I can only eat a small slice.* □ *Confederate women made a special kind of chess pie called "Jefferson Davis pie."*

chestnut a horse with a reddish-brown coat. (See also *Appaloosa; bay; paint; palomino; piebald; roan.*) □ *She had a pair of chestnuts hitched to her buggy.* □ *His saddle horse is a chestnut.*

chew one's own tobacco to mind one's own business. (See also *hoe one's own row.*) □ SALLY: *You seem awfully happy all of a sudden. How come?* TOM: *Chew your own tobacco.* □ *I'm just sitting here chewing my own tobacco, not bothering anybody.*

chew the fat to talk, often idly. □ *Every so often, I like to call up my sister and chew the fat for a while.* □ *The men were on the front porch chewing the fat while the women washed the dishes.*

Chick Sale (barn) an outhouse; a privy. (From the pen name of Charles Partlow, who wrote a humorous sketch on outhouses.) □ *Granpappy is out to the Chick Sale.* □ *Some bad boys tip over our Chick Sale barn every Halloween.*

chicken bog a stew made of chicken, rice, and spices. □ *I cooked up a big dish of chicken bog.* □ *Chicken bog was our usual Sunday dinner.*

chickenfeed a very small amount of money. □ *I like this job, but the pay is chickenfeed.* □ *Your handicrafts are worth a lot more than the chickenfeed you're getting for them now.*

chiffarobe a piece of furniture that has a chest of drawers as well as a cabinet for hanging clothes. (Based on the French word *chiffonnière.*) □ *That's an antique chiffarobe, cost three hundred dollars.* □ *Jane painted her chiffarobe bright yellow, to match her bedroom curtains.*

chigger a small, bloodsucking insect. □ *When we came back from our walk, our bare ankles were covered with chigger bites.* □ *I got a lot of chigger bites from playing outside all day.*

chimbley a chimney. □ *The room's full of smoke. The chimbley must be blocked.* □ *Joe's house has a big, tall brick chimbley.*

chin music talk; conversation. (See also *wag one's chin.*) □ *Whenever those two get together, you can be sure there'll be plenty of chin music.* □ *Bill just loves to hear hisself talk. He'll make chin music for hours at a time.*

chinook a warm, wet spring wind. □ *Spring's coming. The chinook's starting to blow.* □ *The chinook blew in from the ocean and melted the snow in the mountains.*

chippy a prostitute; a promiscuous woman. □ MARY: *Susan says she'd like to come over and see you.* JANE: *I won't have that chippy in my house!* □ *She may act like a chippy, but she's really a good girl.*

chitlins fried hog intestines. □ *Joe cooked up a big mess of chitlins.* □ *We eat a lot of chitlins at pig-killing time.*

choke-rag a necktie. □ *He's got a job in the city where he has to wear a choke-rag every day.* □ *I bought me a choke-rag to wear to the wedding.*

cholla a kind of cactus with many branches and long spines. (Spanish. Pronounced *CHOY-ya*.) □ *She grew a cholla outside her window to keep burglars out.* □ *It was rough country. Only chollas grew there.*

chompers teeth or dentures. □ *If you've got trouble with your chompers, you'd better go see the dentist.* □ *At bedtime, Grampa takes his chompers out and puts them in a glass on the bedside table.*

choose to want. □ *Joe never chooses to dance at parties.* □ *Mary likes that blue car, but I choose a red one.*

choppin' block a board, stump, or block of wood on which wood, meat, or vegetables are chopped. □ *He put the chicken's head on the choppin' block and cut it off with one blow.* □ *I've got a choppin' block out back for splitting logs.*

chuck wagon a wagon equipped to carry food, supplies, and a stove to where people are camped. □ *The cowboys were sure happy to see the chuck wagon coming up the trail.* □ *Mary's car was our chuck wagon during the hiking trip.*

chuckle-head a foolish person. (Mildly insulting. See also *chuckle-headed.*) □ *Ms. Davis probably thinks I'm a chuckle-head after I said that stupid thing to her.* □ *Here comes Bill with that chuckle-head.*

chuckle-headed foolish. (See also *chuckle-head.*) □ *John got to acting a little chuckle-headed when he was courting Mary.* □ *"Where'd ya get a chuckle-headed idea like that?" Jane hollered.*

chuffy short and stout. □ *He's blond and chuffy, just like his daddy.* □ *She's chuffy, but she sure can run.*

chunk something to throw something. □ *The kids were out chunking rocks into the lake.* □ *Somebody chunked a snowball at me!*

Church ain't out till they quit singing. Things have not yet reached the end. □ TOM: *I guess Bill and Mary are split up for good.* JANE: *Well, now, church ain't out till they quit singing. They ain't got a divorce yet.* □ CHARLIE: *No way our team can win now.* MARY: *Church ain't out till they quit singing. There's another inning to go.*

church key a combination can-opener and bottle-opener. □ *I'm looking for the church key so's I can open this beer.* □ *She opened the can of tomato juice with the church key.*

cicada a kind of insect that makes a high, buzzing sound. (Also called *locust.*) □ *At twilight, we heard the cicadas buzzing in the trees.* □ *I found a dead cicada that was as big as my thumb.*

citified accustomed to city living; sophisticated. (Mildly insulting.) □ *Joe is awful snooty, with his citified ways.* □ *When Jane came back from New York, she had all sorts of citified notions about how to cook.*

(city) slicker someone from the city who is not familiar with country ways. □ *Them city slickers think we're stupid just because we talk different.* □ *The slicker didn't know the first thing about fishing for trout.*

clabber thickened and curdled sour milk. □ *Uncle Earl always had a plate of clabber for lunch.* □ *Aunt Jane put clabber on her cornbread.*

claimjumper someone who takes someone or something claimed by someone else. (See also *jump a claim.*) □ *That dirty, rotten claimjumper! He stole my girl!* □ *A claimjumper stole my mining claim.*

clap-hand a round of applause. □ *All the proud parents gave a big clap-hand after the schoolchildren sang their song.* □ *Jane got a big clap-hand for her fiddle solo.*

clean someone's plow to beat someone up. □ *If Joe crosses me one more time, I'll clean his plow for sure.* □ *Somebody must have really cleaned Bill's plow last night. He had two black eyes this morning!*

clean up one's duty to finish what one is supposed to do. □ *Clean up your duty before you go out to play.* □ *Johnny's a good kid. He always cleans up his duty without havin' to be told.*

close chewer and a tight spitter someone who hates to spend money; a cheapskate. □ *He's a close chewer and a tight spitter. Everything about him looks run-down, but he's probably the richest man in the county.* □ *No use asking her for a loan. She's a close chewer and a tight spitter.*

close enough to use the same toothpick very close. (Used to describe close friends.) □ *We've been friends since we were five years old. We're close enough to use the same toothpick.* □ *They tell each other everything. They're close enough to use the same toothpick.*

close only counts in horseshoes (and hand grenades) coming close but not succeeding is not good enough. (The *hand grenades* version is jocular.) □ *I came close to winning the election, but close only counts in horseshoes.* □ TOM: *So maybe my arrow didn't hit the target. At least it was close!* MARY: *Close only counts in horseshoes and hand grenades.*

close shave a narrow escape. (Used with the indefinite article *a*.) □ TOM: *That car would have hit me if I hadn't jumped onto the sidewalk!* JANE: *You had a close shave, all right.* □ *The police almost caught up with us! That was a close shave!*

cobbler a dessert made of fruit baked with a biscuit crust on top. □ *Would you like some ice cream with your blueberry cobbler?* □ *Joe makes a delicious peach cobbler.*

cock-and-bull story an untrue story. □ *When I asked Bill how he got that black eye, he gave me some cock-and-bull story about running into the barn door.* □ *I want the truth, not one of your cock-and-bull stories!*

cockamamie foolish; ridiculous; no-good. □ *As usual, Jim gave me some cockamamie excuse for getting home so late.* □ *They came up with this cockamamie idea for turning the old house into a shopping center.*

cocola the cola brand Coca Cola. (Southern.) □ *I sure could use a nice cold cocola.* □ *No root beer for me. I want cocola.*

coffin nail a cigarette. □ *Can I borrow a coffin nail off you?* □ *I ought to give up smoking these here coffin nails, but I just can't seem to.*

coffin varnish whiskey. □ *He went into the bar for a bottle of coffin varnish.* □ *Pour me a little of that there coffin varnish.*

coke a generic term for any soft drink, as well as the cola brand Coca Cola. (See also *dope*.) □ TOM: *Would you like a coke?*

MARY: *Why yes, thank you.* TOM: *What kind? Sprite, Coca-Cola, or Dr. Pepper?* □ *We generally have a couple kinds of coke in the fridge.*

cold cock someone to knock someone unconscious. □ *He hit him once and durned if he didn't cold cock him.* □ *She cold cocked him with her walking stick.*

cold feet a cowardly feeling. □ *Jim had cold feet on his wedding day, but he went through with it anyway.* □ *They dared me to climb up the water tower, but I got cold feet.*

colder than a mother-in-law's kiss AND **colder than a pawn broker's smile** very cold. □ *It's cold outside—colder than a mother-in-law's kiss.* □ *The look in her eye was colder than a mother-in-law's kiss.* □ *There was no fire in the cabin. It was colder than a pawn broker's smile.* □ *His greeting was colder than a pawn broker's smile.*

colder than a pawnbroker's smile See *colder than a mother-in-law's kiss.*

collar-and-tie men businessmen who wear suits and ties. □ *After Jim graduated from college, he went off to join the collar-and-tie men.* □ *Us working folks at the plant have an awful time getting the collar-and-tie men to see our point of view.*

collard (green)s the leaves of the collard plant, used as food. □ *When I boil my collard greens, I usually toss in a little bacon, for the flavor.* □ *We had a quick lunch of cornbread and collards.*

Colt the trademark name of a revolver. □ *The sherriff whipped out his Colt and shot the outlaw dead.* □ TOM: *You armed?* BILL: *I got my Colt in a shoulder holster.*

combine a machine used to harvest crops. (Pronounced with the accent on the first syllable.) □ *The harvest went much quicker this year with the new combine.* □ *The farmers worked late into the night, driving their combines back and forth across the fields.*

Come again? "Please repeat what you just said." (Sometimes used as an expression of surprise or disbelief, as in the second example.) ☐ *Mrs. Johnson is hard of hearing, and often has to say, "Come again?"* ☐ TOM: *Mary just dyed her hair purple.* JANE: *Come again?*

come Monday When Monday comes. (Can be used with other expressions for time, as in *come next week, come December, come five o'clock.* See the second example.) ☐ *Joe plays so hard on the weekend that come Monday, he's all worn out.* ☐ *You may think that putting up storm windows is a bother, but come December, you'll be glad you did it.*

Come 'n get it! Food is ready, come and eat it. ☐ *"Come 'n get it!" Mama yelled from the porch.* ☐ TOM: *Is dinner ready yet?* BILL: *Yep! Come 'n get it!*

come out the little end of the horn to lose a great deal; to end with less than one started with. ☐ *He thought he would make a pile of money with his barbershop, but instead he came out the little end of the horn.* ☐ *After the stock market crash, plenty of folks came out the little end of the horn.*

come to a pretty pass to encounter a difficult situation. ☐ *This project has come to a pretty pass. I don't know how we can possibly finish on time.* ☐ *Mary had come to a pretty pass. She quit her job to be with her husband, and then he left her. She had no money at all.*

come up a storm to become stormy. ☐ *Look at them clouds. It'll come up a storm today for sure.* ☐ *It came up a storm as I was on my way home, and I got soaked to the skin.*

comeback a witty or disrespectful reply. ☐ *Jimmy got in trouble for that smart comeback he gave the teacher.* ☐ *The comedian had a comeback for every remark the heckler made.*

comfort a comforter; a thick blanket. ☐ *I gave Mary and Joe a flannel comfort for a wedding present.* ☐ *When I was sick, my* *mamma wrapped me up in a soft old comfort and gave me hot tea to drink.*

coming up a cloud getting ready to rain. □ *Look at that sky! It's comin' up a cloud!* □ *Is it getting dark or is it jest coming up a cloud?*

commence (something) to start (something). □ *When she saw me, she commenced to cryin'.* □ *They all commenced talking at once.*

common low class; no good. □ *I don't know where Susan got those fine manners of hers. Her family is as common as can be.* □ *Daddy objected to my associating with such common folks.*

compañero a companion; a friend. (Spanish.) □ *Good to see you, compañero!* □ *The cowboy brought all his compañeros to the dance at Miss Kitty's.*

complected complexioned; having a certain skin color. □ *He was very fair complected, and his skin burned easily.* □ *The menfolks all admired the beauty of the dark-complected woman.*

conch a white person from the Florida Keys. (Pronounced *conk*. Possibly derogatory.) □ *I'm just a conch from Key West.* □ *How come you're hanging out with them conchs?*

Conestoga a covered wagon. (Named for Conestoga, PA.) □ *The family came out west in a Conestoga.* □ *There were thirty Conestogas in the wagon train.*

Confederate coffee a coffee substitute made from rye, cornmeal, or chicory. □ *During the War, the best we had to drink was Confederate coffee.* □ *I can't have caffeine, so I drink Confederate coffee.*

Consarn it! "Damn it!" (A mild oath.) □ *Consarn it! I can't find my keys.* □ *That's the second batch of muffins I've burned today, consarn it!*

considerable greatly; a great deal. □ *She perked up considerable when she saw who was at the door.* □ *It surprised folks considerable when Joe married Susan.*

contraption a device. (See also *doodad; thingamajig; whatchamacallit.*) □ *This little contraption cuts up vegetables at the touch of a button.* □ *Mary has some kind of contraption that tells her how many miles she walks.*

cookie a camp cook. (A term of address.) □ *Hey, cookie! Give us some more of these dough gods!* □ *All the cookie knew how to make was pork and beans.*

Coon my dogs! "My goodness!"; "I am amazed!" □ *Coon my dogs! Did you ever see such a thing?* □ *Well, coon my dogs! That little boy carried my big ol' suitcase up three flights of stairs!*

cooter a turtle. □ *That little pond is just full of cooters.* □ *You oughta taste Aunt Jessie's cooter stew.*

cooter around to lounge; to be lazy. □ *How come you're cootering around at this hour of the morning? Get to work!* □ *He don't do anything but fish and cooter around.*

cootie a louse. □ *The kid sitting next to me in class had cooties.* □ *They gave Joe some ointment to kill the cooties on his scalp.*

cork high and bottle deep very drunk. □ *By the time the party was over, he was cork high and bottle deep.* □ *I've only been drunk once in my life, but that time I was cork high and bottle deep.*

corn dodgers corn bread cooked in small cakes. □ *We had fresh, hot corn dodgers with lots of honey.* □ *Mary makes the best corn dodgers in town.*

corn juice corn liquor. □ *Pappy likes his corn juice straight.* □ *Granny never touches corn juice, 'ceptin' when she is awake.*

(corn) squeezings whisky; *moonshine.* □ *Where did I put my jug of corn squeezings?* □ *Jed has a jar of squeezings hid in the floorboards.*

cornpone **1.** corn bread. (See also *pone.*) □ *I fry my cornpone in bacon grease.* □ *He cut off a hunk of cornpone and ate it.* **2.** well-known, silly, "corny" jokes. □ *The comedian's act was pure cornpone.* □ *The movie was full of cornpone and sight gags.*

cornrows a hair style of rows of small braids. □ *She put her daughter's hair in cornrows and put pretty beads on the ends of the braids.* □ *She went to the beauty parlor to have her hair put in cornrows.*

corral a fenced area in which animals are kept. □ *We got all the horses back into the corral.* □ *The corral was barely big enough to hold all the cattle.*

corral someone or something to herd someone or something into a corral or other enclosed space. □ *It took the cowboys two hours to corral the mustangs.* □ *The nursery school teacher herded the kids off the playground and corraled them in the classroom.*

cost a pretty penny to be expensive; to cost a lot of money. □ *Mary's dress is real silk. It must have cost a pretty penny.* □ *Taking care of a fancy car like that can cost a pretty penny, let me tell you.*

cottage fries See *home fries.*

cotton-picking damned. (A mild expletive.) □ *Can't you make up your cotton-picking mind?* □ *If one more thing goes wrong with this cotton-picking car, I'm gonna push it off a cliff.*

cotton to someone or something to like someone or something. □ *I don't cotton to that new teacher a-tall.* □ *Folks cotton to him because he's a good listener.*

cougar a type of large wildcat. □ *Take your gun in case you meet a cougar.* □ *Something's killing all our calves. I think it's a cougar.*

could fight a circle-saw (and it a-runnin') eager to fight. ☐ *He was so mad he could fight a circle-saw and it a-runnin'.* ☐ *She's a good watchdog. She could fight a circle-saw.*

couldn't boil water without burning it See *couldn't boil water (without scorching it).*

couldn't boil water (without scorching it) AND **couldn't boil water (without burning it)** unable to cook. ☐ *How is Jane going to make lunch for her in-laws? She couldn't boil water!* ☐ *When I first got married, I couldn't boil water without scorching it. Now I'm a fairly good cook.*

couldn't hit a bull in the ass with a bass fiddle unable to aim; very clumsy. (Jocular. Use with caution.) ☐ *I don't want Bill on our ball team. He couldn't hit a bull in the ass with a bass fiddle.* ☐ TOM: *Is Jane a good shot?* CHARLIE: *She couldn't hit a bull in the ass with a bass fiddle.*

couldn't pour water out of a boot (if there was instructions on the heel) stupid. ☐ *I won't say Jim is dumb, but he couldn't pour water out of a boot.* ☐ *Jane couldn't pour water out of a boot if there was instructions on the heel—and she's the smartest one in her family!*

couldn't see straight could not function. ☐ *I was so mad I couldn't see straight.* ☐ *She left me so frustrated that I couldn't see straight.*

country mile a great distance. ☐ *The batter knocked that ball a country mile.* ☐ *I had to walk a country mile to the next gas station.*

courtin'-apple AND **skunk egg** an onion. ☐ *I fried up some courtin'-apples to go with my steak.* ☐ *Put some skunk eggs in with the tomato soup.*

Cousin Jack a Cornishman. ☐ *The mine owner hired a couple of Cousin Jacks as engineers.* ☐ *Mr. Llewellyn was a Cousin Jack and the nicest man you'd ever hope to meet.*

cow chip AND **cow pie; cow patty; cow flop** a pile of cow manure. (See also *buffalo chip; meadow muffin.*) □ *The pioneers didn't have much wood, so they burned dried cow chips.* □ *How did that big ol' cow pie get in the middle of my flower bed?* □ *Tom stepped on a cow patty. It made him slip and fall.* □ *You can tell somebody's cattle have been grazing here. Look at all them cow flops.*

cow-critter a cow, bull, or steer. □ *I'm no big rancher. I just keep a few cow-critters in the barn.* □ *The cowboy made sure all the cow-critters was settled for the night.*

cow flop See *cow chip.*

cow juice milk. (Jocular.) □ *How'd you like a tall glass of cow juice?* □ *Here's a little cow juice to pour on your cereal.*

cow paste butter. (See also *slickem.*) □ *Would you kindly pass the cow paste?* □ *Corn bread ain't nothing without cow paste.*

cow patty See *cow chip.*

cow pie See *cow chip.*

cow poke AND **cow puncher** someone who drives cattle; a *cowboy.* □ *I'm just an old cow poke, don't know much about manners and such.* □ *The cow puncher laughed at the city slicker's shiny clean cowboy boots.*

cow puncher See *cow poke.*

cowboy a man who herds cattle. (See also *cow poke.*) □ *Dozens of cowboys came to the rodeo to show off their skills.* □ *Early in the morning, the cowboy hit the trail again.*

cowboy pencil a stick used to draw in the dirt. □ *He got a cowboy pencil and sketched a map on the dirt road.* □ *They sat around the campfire and drew pictures with a cowboy pencil.*

cowcumber a cucumber. □ *My garden's doing so well, I've got more cowcumbers than I know what to do with.* □ *I don't like cowcumbers in my green salad.*

cowlick a patch or whirl of hair that grows in a certain direction and cannot be combed the other way. (Like a tuft of grass left after a cow has wrapped its tongue around it and bitten it off.) □ *I have to part my hair on the left side. I have a cowlick.* □ *Jim has a stubborn cowlick, so he greases his hair before he combs it.*

cowpea a kind of bean with a black spot in the middle. (See also *black-eyed pea; crowder pea.*) □ *We was so poor, all we had to eat was cowpeas and turnip greens.* □ *Tom makes a nice dish with cowpeas and rice.*

cowtown a city or town where the main business is raising or selling cattle. □ *Fort Worth started out as a cowtown, but now it's a city full of industry and culture.* □ *It was just a little cowtown, but it seemed like a metropolis to the country girl.*

coyote a wild animal related to wolves and dogs. (From an Amerindian language via Spanish. Pronounced *KIE-ote* or *kie-O-tee.*) □ *At night, we heard the coyotes howling.* □ *Coyotes were killing the rancher's sheep.*

coyote round to sneak around. □ *I caught him coyotin' round our barn.* □ *Someone's been coyoting round our front yard.*

crack a smile to grin; to smile. □ *I was tellin' my best jokes, but Jim never cracked a smile.* □ *She looked surprised, and then cracked a big, beautiful smile.*

crack of dawn sunrise; the very earliest part of the day. □ *We'll have to get up at the crack of dawn if we want to get to Montgomery by noon.* □ *The rooster crowed at the crack of dawn.*

crack one's sides to laugh hard. □ *That sure was a funny movie. I really cracked my sides.* □ *We cracked our sides at Tom's crazy jokes.*

crack (open) the door AND **crack (open) the window** to open the door or window a very little way. □ *Just crack the door to let some air inside.* □ *I cracked open the door to peek out.* □ *If you crack open the car window, the air-conditioning will work better.* □ *The nurse cracked the window so the patient could get a breeze.*

crack (open) the window See *crack (open) the door.*

cracker **1.** a poor, ignorant country person from the Southern U.S. (Insulting.) □ *On the weekends, the crackers come into town in their pickup trucks.* □ *My family may live way out in the country, but we ain't crackers!* **2.** someone from Georgia. (Often used in the phrase *Georgia cracker.*) □ *I'm a Georgia cracker and proud to say it.* □ TOM: *How come you've got a Southern accent? You were born in Ohio.* JANE: *Yes, but my mama was a Georgia cracker.*

cracker-jack excellent. □ *You did a cracker-jack job of setting the table!* □ *He had a cracker-jack record in school.*

cracklin' bread cornbread made with *cracklin's,* the crispened fat left over from rendering lard. □ *After she rendered the lard, Mama made cracklin' bread as a treat for us.* □ *Cracklin' bread is my favorite kind of corn bread.*

cracklin's crisp pieces of animal tissue from which the fat has been cooked out. □ *We nibbled on cracklin's and drank soda pop.* □ *There's always plenty of cracklin's at hog-killin' time.*

crave to do something to want to do something. □ *I don't crave to ride the roller coaster, thank you.* □ TOM: *Would you like to go to the movies with me?* JANE: *I'm craving to!*

crawdad hole a pond or deep, still place in a river where crawfish can be caught. (See also *catfish hole.*) □ *We got some bait and went to the crawdad hole.* □ *They fished that crawdad hole till there were no crawdads left.*

crawdad(dy) a crayfish, a type of shellfish related to shrimp and lobsters. □ *Let's go down to the pond and catch crawdads.* □ *Mary brought home a big bucket of crawdaddies, so that's what we had for dinner.*

crazy bone See *funny bone.*

crazy in the head crazy. □ *Be quiet, Jed. You are just crazy in the head.* □ *Am I crazy in the head, or did Tom McCoy just go by in a big black car?*

creeping Charlie ground ivy. □ *They had creeping Charlie 'stead of grass in their front yard.* □ *Creeping Charlie took over my flower garden this year.*

Creole **1.** a Southern person with French or Spanish ancestry. □ *She married a Creole from Baton Rouge.* □ *I learned some Creole recipes from my Louisiana friend.* **2.** of or relating to someone or something with Spanish and French ancestry. □ *Chef Bob is known for his fabulous Creole cooking.* □ *The housekepper taught the children some Creole words.*

critter an animal; a creature. □ *You've got some kind of little critter crawling down your arm, there. Looks like a daddy longlegs.* □ *That dog is the orneriest critter I ever had to live with.*

crocus sack See *croker sack.*

croker sack AND **crocus sack** a burlap sack. (See also *gunny sack.*) □ *She put all her clothes into an old croker sack and ran away from home that night.* □ *We dug up the sapling and wrapped the roots in a crocus sack to protect them.*

crope creeped; crept. (The past tense and past participle of *creep.*) □ *Cousin Sue crope up on me and pinched my behind.* □ *The fox crope along the ground, a-waiting for me to turn my back so's he could grab a chicken.*

cross over to die. (A euphemism.) □ *She ain't been the same since her husband crossed over.* □ *My mama crossed over when I was just a youngun.*

cross someone to oppose someone. □ *You best not cross Jim. He'll have your hide.* □ *This is the last time you cross me, you hear?*

crow bait someone or thing that is likely to die. (Derogatory. See also *buzzard bait.*) □ *That old dog used to hunt good, but now he's just crow bait.* □ *No one tried to help the old drunk. They all figured he was crow bait.*

crowder pea a kind of bean with a black spot in the middle. (See also *black-eyed pea; cowpea.*) □ *I bought a few cans of crowder peas.* □ *Eat your crowder peas. They're full of protein.*

cruller a sweet, fried, twisted doughnut. □ *Saturday morning, Dad always had fresh, hot crullers waiting for us when we woke up.* □ *We sat on the porch eating crullers and drinking coffee.*

cry calf rope to admit defeat. (See also *holler uncle.*) □ *He twisted Jimmy's arm, but Jimmy wouldn't cry calf rope.* □ *This lawsuit against me has gone on so long, I'm about ready to cry calf rope.*

cry uncle See *holler uncle.*

curandero a folk healer. (Spanish.) □ *I'd rather go to the curandero than one of them fancy town doctors, any day.* □ *The curandero gave Nancy some tea to drink and said it would make Jim fall in love with her.*

curly dirt AND **house moss; sluts wool; snorf** puffs of dirt and dust. (See also *dust bunny.*) □ *How long has it been since you swept under this bed? There's a mountain of curly dirt under here!* □ *No one's been in this room for an age. Look at all the cobwebs and curly dirt.* □ *She was a terrible housekeeper. House moss collected in all the corners of her rooms.* □ *I cleaned the sluts wool from under the davenport.* □ *There was a big bunch of snorf behind the bookcase.*

cuss a blue streak to curse a great deal. (See also *talk a blue streak.*) □ *When she dropped the brick on her toe, she cussed a blue streak.* □ *Bill could cuss a blue streak by the time he was eight years old.*

cuss **1.** a difficult person. □ *Jim's a pretty stubborn cuss.* □ *Grampa can be hard to live with, but I love the old cuss.* **2.** to curse. □ *Can't you say two words without cussin'?* □ *No need to cuss at me.*

cuss someone out to curse at someone. □ *Dad cussed me out for losing the money he gave me.* □ *They sound like they're cussing each other out, but they're just playing.*

cussed stubborn. (Pronounced with two syllables.) □ *Jane will forgive you—just forget your cussed pride and ask her to!* □ *I can't get this cussed door to open!*

cussedness stubbornness. □ *Joe's inborn cussedness helped him survive his injuries.* □ TOM: *Why won't she admit that she's wrong?* MARY: *Pure cussedness.*

cussfight a fight in which the opponents curse at each other. □ *The cussfight turned into a fistfight.* □ *Out in the playground, two kids had started a cussfight.*

cut a rusty to do something extraordinary, such as doing a trick, playing a prank, or making a foolish mistake. □ *Joe is always cutting a rusty. Last night he put six hairbrushes in my bed.* □ *Once when Jim was drunk, he tried to milk a steer. He sure cut a rusty that time!*

cut capers to perform antics. □ *At night, after the work was done, they gathered around the fire and cut capers.* □ *We cut all sorts of capers when we were teenaged kids.*

cut dog has no pups I do not want to cut the cards. (Used in poker games.) □ TOM: *Your turn to cut.* JANE: *Cut dog has no pups.* □ *"Cut dog has no pups," said Joe, handing the cards to the next player.*

cut one's eyes at someone or something to glance at someone or something. □ *He cut his eyes at me to see if I was looking.* □ *She cut her eyes at the TV for a second.*

cut one's eyeteeth on something to have a lot of experience with something. □ *Do I know how to fix a Ford car? Child, I cut my eyeteeth on Ford motors!* □ *She was a newspaper reporter from the git-go. She cut her eyeteeth on police reporting.*

cut out for something suited for something. □ *She was bright and she loved to read. Her folks thought she was cut out for being a schoolteacher.* □ *He did his best, but he just wasn't cut out for farming.*

cut out for somewhere to leave quickly for somewhere. □ *After he robbed the bank, he cut out for his hideout in the mountains.* □ *She cut out for home right quick.*

cut the blood out of someone to beat someone severely. □ *The next time you go bad-mouthing me, I'm gonna cut the blood out of you.* □ *They had a real bad fight. Jim cut the blood out of his cousin.*

cut the mustard be successful. (Survives in *too old to cut the mustard.*) □ *With a little practice, I think I can cut the mustard.* □ *He can't do it. He's too young to cut the mustard.*

cut up to play tricks or perform antics. □ *He was always cutting up in class.* □ *The two girls cut up in Sunday school once too often.*

cut your peaches go on with what you were doing. □ *Stop gawking and cut your peaches.* □ *There's no need for you to follow me around. Go cut your peaches.*

cymlin head a fool. (From *cymling,* a kind of squash.) □ *She's such a cymlin head, she left the cat to look after the chickens.* □ *He can't learn anything. He's a cymlin head.*

D

dad fetch my buttons "What a surprise!"; "Goodness me!" □ *Dad fetch my buttons! It's a letter from Aunt Rita!* □ *Dad fetch my buttons, I never was so happy in all my life!*

dadburned damned. (A mild expletive.) □ *I'd like to have a flower bed, but the dadburned kids keep stepping on all my flowers.* □ *I don't know what I'll do if the dadburned boss doesn't give me a raise.*

dadgum it See *dadgummit.*

dadgummit AND **dadgum it; dadratit; dagnab it** damn it. □ *Dadgummit! The hot water heater's broke.* □ *Dadgum it, Nancy, that's the third time you've interrupted me.* □ *Dadratit! I just can't seem to make this checkbook balance!* □ *"Dagnab it!" Mary hollered when she stubbed her toe.*

dadratit See *dadgummit.*

dagnab it See *dadgummit.*

Damn it to blue blazes! "Damn it." (An oath.) □ *Damn it to blue blazes, I told you I can't lend you any more money!* □ *"Damn it to blue blazes! I give up!" Joe shouted, flinging his tools aside.*

(damn) sight better much better. (Used with the indefinite article *a*.) □ *Mary can sing a damn sight better than Tom can.* □ *You look a sight better with your hair cut short.*

damnfool **1.** a fool; an idiot. (Disparaging.) □ *Joe's mother left him five thousand dollars when she died, and the damnfool gambled it all away.* □ *If you don't apologize to that boy right away, you're a bigger damnfool than I thought.* **2.** foolish; idiotic. □ *I'd like to go to Washington and tell them damnfool politicians a thing or two.* □ *Spray-painting cuss words on the school building was a damnfool thing to do.*

dancehall a building where people can gather to dance. □ *Are you goin' down to the dancehall on Saturday night?* □ *Biddy's is the best dancehall in town.*

dandy a fine or noteworthy thing. □ *Jane went fishing and caught a real dandy!* □ *You've made a lot of mistakes in your time, but this one sure is a dandy.*

darker than the inside of a cow's belly See *(as) dark as the inside of a cow's belly.*

darnedest most amazing. □ *When I put the music on the stereo, my cat started dancing around to the beat. It was the darnedest thing!* □ *That was the darnedest campaign speech I ever did hear —the candidate promised to* raise *taxes!*

da'st to dare. □ *Nobody da'st bother Uncle Jim when he's napping.* □ *If you da'st steal Miss Jane's apples, she'll be after you with a stick.*

da'stn't to dare not. □ *I da'stn't go near that old dog. He'll bite me for sure.* □ TOM: *I'm gonna break a window in that old building.* MARY: *You da'stn't!*

dauncy fussy about eating. □ *The way Tom eats now, you'd never guess he was such a dauncy child.* □ *My dauncy Cousin Jane won't hardly eat Ma's good cooking.*

dead cat on the line [for something to be] wrong. □ *I'm afraid there's a dead cat on the line over to Martha's place. I haven't heard from them for days.* □ *Bill has a kind of sixth sense. He can tell a dead cat on the line before anybody knows there's something wrong.*

dead certain very sure. (*Dead* means *absolutely.*) □ *I'm dead certain that horse will win. I bet two hundred on it myself.* □ *I didn't believe the rumor at first, but Bill's dead certain that it's true.*

(dead) cinch a very easy task. (*Dead* means *absolutely.*) □ TOM: *Did you figure out how to change the tire?* JANE: *Yep! It was a cinch.* □ *Altering clothes patterns is difficult for me, but for Mary, it's a dead cinch.*

dead duck someone or something that is certain to die or fail. (See also *gone gosling.*) □ *If I fail that test, I'm a dead duck.* □ *When the outlaw drew his pistol, the sheriff knew he was a dead duck.*

dead-eye someone who shoots very accurately. □ *Jane's a real dead-eye. She once shot a fly off a cow's back.* □ *Everything Bill aims at, he hits. He's a dead-eye, all right.*

dead man's hand [in poker] two aces and two eights. □ *I ain't much superstitious, but it gave me the shivers when I saw I'd been dealt a dead man's hand.* □ *When Wild Bill Hickok was shot at the poker table, they found he was holding the dead man's hand.*

dead serious serious; not joking. □ TOM: *You're funning me.* BILL: *No, I'm dead serious.* □ *Mary has threatened divorce a hundred times, but this time she says she's dead serious.*

dead set against something firmly opposed to something. □ *My boy wants to go into the Army, but I'm dead set against it.* □ *They know their parents are dead set against their marriage, but they're bound and determined to go ahead with it.*

deadbeat **1.** someone who does not work or help out in any way. □ *Ever since Joe came home from school, he's been a real deadbeat, lying around on the sofa watching TV.* □ *Martha has to support her whole family because her husband is a deadbeat.* **2.** unwilling to work or help out. □ *The law's going after deadbeat fathers who don't pay their child support.* □ *How did such hard-working people raise such a deadbeat kid?*

deal from the bottom (of the deck) to cheat; to do something dishonest. □ *I suspect he's dealing from the bottom of the deck.*

□ *She had a shifty look in her eyes. She looked like the kind who would deal from the bottom.*

decent clothed, groomed, or ready to be seen in public. □ *When I knocked on Mary's door, she called, "Don't come in! I'm not decent!"* □ *Bill thinks he's not decent unless he's got his coat and necktie on.*

deringer See *derringer.*

derringer AND **deringer** a small pistol. (Named for its inventor, Henry Deringer.) □ *She pulled a derringer out of her pocket and said, "Hold it right there."* □ *The gunman had a pistol in each holster and a deringer in his boot.*

desert rat a prospector who travels through the desert. □ *Somewhere in Utah, we ran into a desert rat who showed us the trail to Salt Lake City.* □ *They say the old desert rat had ten thousand dollars worth of gold in the sacks he carried around on his mule.*

devilment evil doings; deviltry. □ TOM: *What's Joe doing?* SALLY: *Oh, he's up to some devilment, no doubt.* □ *Just that one girl was responsible for an awful lot of devilment.*

diamond in the rough someone who could be very impressive if properly trained, groomed, or prepared. □ *My boyfriend may not look like much, but he's a diamond in the rough.* □ *That singer is a diamond in the rough. If she gets some good voice lessons, she could be a star.*

did everything he could 'cept eat us acted very hostilely. □ *We went to see the banker about a loan and, lawsamercy, he did everything he could 'cept eat us.* □ *When it came time to pass sentence on the criminal, the judge did everything he could 'cept eat him.*

diddly(-squat) AND **doodly(-squat); squat** nothing. □ *Nelly may have a good education, but she knows diddly-squat about real life.* □ *You can't sell that old chair. It ain't worth diddly.* □ *I don't know doodly-squat about electrical wiring.* □ *I did a lot of hard work and got paid squat for it.*

didey a diaper. □ *The baby's crying. I think she needs her didey changed.* □ *The neighbors must have a baby. Look at all them dideys hangin' on the line.*

didn't care a whit didn't care at all. □ *Sally thought Joe liked her, but he didn't care a whit about her.* □ *I don't care a whit what you do with my old clothes.*

didn't care too hard didn't mind. □ *Dad said he didn't care too hard if I took the dog out with me.* □ *If you don't care too hard, I'll shut this window.*

didn't invent gunpowder did not do anything terribly important. □ *He may be the class president, but he didn't invent gunpowder.* □ *What's all this fuss about a movie star? She didn't invent gunpowder!*

die of throat trouble to be hanged. □ *He died of throat trouble after the posse caught up with him.* □ *The cattle rustler died of throat trouble.*

dig up one's tommyhawk to get angry. □ *When Joe saw the mess we made, he dug up his tommyhawk and went looking for us.* □ *Now don't go digging up your tommyhawk. Everybody makes mistakes.*

diggings a place where someone lives. □ *His diggings are upstairs from the saloon.* □ *Come around to my diggings.*

dinero money. (Spanish.) □ *Loan me a little dinero.* □ *How much dinero do you have?*

dip a pinch of snuff. (See also *dip snuff.*) □ *He offered me a dip from his tin of tobacco.* □ *She took a dip and put it up under her lip.*

dip snuff to take snuff; to chew or inhale tobacco. (See also *dip.*) □ TOM: *Does he smoke?* JANE: *No, he dips snuff.* □ *The saloon has a spittoon for those who dip snuff.*

directly right away; very soon. □ *I'll get to it directly.* □ *When we heard you was sick, we came over directly.*

dirty someone or something up to make someone or something dirty. □ *The day after I washed my car, the rain came and dirtied it up.* Ⓣ *Those kids sure can dirty up a house.*

disfurnish someone to inconvenience someone. □ TOM: *Come on in and set a spell.* JANE: *Well, I will, if it won't disfurnish you.* □ *Will it disfurnish you if I borrow a cup of sugar?*

disremember (someone or something) to forget (someone or something). □ *I disremember that young man's name.* □ *I used to know Mary's address, but just now I disremember.*

ditties miscellaneous things. □ *We packed up all our ditties and left the campsite.* □ *What are all these little ditties in your desk drawer?*

ditty See *thingamajig.*

divan See *settee.*

Dixie See *Dixieland.*

Dixieland **1.** AND **Dixie** the Southern United States. □ *We took a trip through Dixieland last summer.* □ *What part of Dixie do you all hail from?* **2.** a special type of jazz from the South. □ *He just can't get enough of that Dixieland.* □ *She can listen to Dixieland for hours on end.*

do-fotchet See *thingamajig.*

do someone a power of good to be very good for someone. □ *You should take a vacation. It'd do you a power of good.* □ *Just hearing your voice does me a power of good.*

do someone dirt(y) to do something bad or dishonest to someone. □ *He sure did his wife dirty, leaving her like that.* □ *She did me dirt when we divided up the things mother left us.*

do someone (down) to treat someone badly. □ *I ain't speaking to Mary. Not after the way she did me.* □ *I think it's awful how Joe does his parents.* □ *He did his own partner down.*

do someone proud to make someone proud. □ *Bill's kids sure did him proud at the boat race.* □ *Mary resolved she would do her friends proud.*

do something up brown to do something to the highest possible degree. □ *Whenever they put on a party, they do it up brown.* □ *He was determined to cause a scandal, and he really did it up brown.*

Do what? "What did you say?"; "You want me to do what?" □ CHARLIE: *My mama's coming to visit, so I want you to cook a fancy dinner.* MARY: *Do what?* □ TOM: *Let's perambulate.* BILL: *Do what?* TOM: *Take a walk.*

Doc a form of address for a doctor or an educated person. □ *You gotta come over to my house, Doc. My wife's real sick.* □ *Everyone missed Doc Jones when he retired.* □ BILL: *Tell me, my good man, where can I find lodgings in this vicinity?* TOM: *Say, Doc, you sure know a lot of fancy words.*

doesn't care who knows it does not try to conceal something. □ *Jane dyes her hair, and she doesn't care who knows it.* □ *Yeah, my old man's in jail. I don't care who knows it!*

doesn't have enough sense to bell a cat acts foolish. □ *I should've known Mary would mess things up completely. She doesn't have enough sense to bell a cat.* □ *Look after Joe and make sure he doesn't get into trouble. You know he doesn't have enough sense to bell a cat.*

doesn't have enough sense to come in out of the rain acts foolish. □ *I ain't surprised that Jim spends a hundred dollars a week on the lottery. Everyone knows he doesn't have enough sense to come in out of the rain.* □ *Mary's sensible now, but when she was a girl, she didn't have enough sense to come in out of the rain.*

doesn't know B from bull's foot acts ignorant. □ *Bill has a high-school diploma?! But he doesn't know B from bull's foot!* □ *That clerk at Carrol's Dry Goods doesn't know B from bull's foot.*

doesn't know beans does not know anything. □ *Bill doesn't know beans about car engines.* □ *Don't ask your daddy for advice about child rearing. He doesn't know beans.*

doesn't know his ass from a hole in the ground acts ignorant. (Use with caution.) □ *That teacher doesn't know his ass from a hole in the ground.* □ *She's supposed to be an expert, but she doesn't know her ass from a hole in the ground.*

doesn't know whether to shit or go blind acts indecisively. (Use with caution.) □ *Jim got two job offers in one week, and he doesn't know whether to shit or go blind.* □ *Tom and Bill told Jane she has to decide once and for all which one of them she's going to go out with, and the poor thing doesn't know whether to shit or go blind.*

dofunnies knickknacks; small decorative objects. □ *Mary's mantelpiece is covered with dofunnies from all the places she's been.* □ *Once a week, I dust all them dofunnies in the front room.*

dog days the hottest days of summer, usually during July and August. □ *Bill spent the dog days lying out in his hammock.* □ *I hate doing yard work in the dog days.*

dog drunk very drunk. □ *I was so depressed, I went out and got dog drunk.* □ *He staggered in, dog drunk.*

dog-faced liar a terrible liar. □ *Suzy said Jimmy was a dog-faced liar.* □ *If Joe says that, he's a dog-faced liar.*

Dog my cats! "My goodness!"; "What do you know!" (An exclamation of surprise.) □ *Dog my cats! Somebody painted my house green!* □ *Well, dog my cats—a Democrat won the election!*

dog trot an narrow, open passageway between two parts of a house or two houses. □ *She sat on her rocking chair in the dog* *trot, enjoying the evening breeze.* □ *That part of the house used to be the kitchen, and the servants would bring the food through the dog trot to the dining room.*

doggone AND **doggonedest** damned; damnedest. (A mild expletive.) □ *Doggone car wouldn't start this morning.* □ *That hoss is the doggonedest animal I ever knowed.*

doggonedest See *doggone.*

dogie a motherless calf. □ *Mary gave the dogie milk from a bottle.* □ *Look after them dogies. Don't let coyotes get to 'em.*

dogleg a sharp turn. □ *Walnut Street makes a dogleg about a mile past Twelfth.* □ *There's a dogleg in the hallway there where the new addition was put on the building.*

doin's goings-on; happenings. □ *I could tell by the noise there was some doin's over at my neighbor's.* □ *There'll be plenty of doin's for the Fourth of July.*

doll baby a doll. □ *Put your doll baby to bed, now, honey, and get your nightie on.* □ *He brought home a brand new doll baby for his little girl.*

done has or have. (Used as an auxiliary verb.) □ TOM: *Sally still here?* MARY: *No. She done gone.* □ *I done seen that yesterday.*

done and gone gone. □ *She's not here. She's done and gone.* □ *Jed was done and gone before dawn.*

done in exhausted. □ *I been working in the garden all day. I'm done in.* □ *They were done in after their long hike.*

done 'n' did already did. □ TOM: *Guess I better take the garbage out.* BILL: *No need. I done 'n' did it.* □ *Mary done 'n' did the chores for you.*

done told you have already told you something. □ *I done told you not to touch that pan, and you went and did it anyhow.* □ *Sally done told you to leave that dog alone.*

doney(-gal) sweetheart; girlfriend. □ *Slim's got a doney-gal up at Pine Creek.* □ *All the young fellers was dancing with their doneys.*

don't amount to a bucket of spit is not worth anything. □ *Joe's a shiftless cuss. He don't amount to a bucket of spit.* □ *All your pretty promises don't amount to a bucket of spit.*

don't bother me none "Doesn't bother me at all." □ *Let the kids play their music. It don't bother me none.* □ TOM: *Mind if I smoke?* CHARLIE: *Don't bother me none.*

don't care if I do AND **don't mind if I do** "Thank you."; "I will." □ TOM: *Have some more grits.* JANE: *Don't care if I do.* □ CHARLIE: *Come on in and set a spell.* MARY: *Don't mind if I do.*

don't cut no ice (with someone) AND **don't cut no squares (with someone)** doesn't influence me. □ *That excuse don't cut no ice with me.* □ *I'm tired of you coming home drunk. Your fancy apologies don't cut no squares.*

don't cut no squares (with someone) See *don't cut no ice (with someone).*

don't give a continental does not care at all. □ *I don't give a continental if I never see him again.* □ *Mary's kids can do whatever they want. She doesn't give a continental.*

don't give a hoot in hell's hollow does not care. □ MARY: *Joe left town. Are you sorry to see him go?* TOM: *No! I don't give a hoot in hell's hollow.* □ *She's a devil-may-care young woman, doesn't give a hoot in hell's hollow about anything.*

don't have a pot to piss in (or a window to throw it out of) doesn't have anything of value. (Use with caution.) □ *When Ed was a young man, he didn't have a pot to piss in.* □ *Jane's folks don't have a pot to piss in or a window to throw it out of.*

don't kiss by the garden gate; love is blind but neighbors ain't See *don't make love by the garden gate; love is blind but neighbors ain't.*

don't know whether to eat it or rub it on do not know what to do with something. (Used to describe food.) □ *That sure was a fancy dessert Mary served. I didn't know whether to eat it or rub it on.* □ *What kind of sauce is this? I don't know whether to eat it or rub it on!*

don't make love by the garden gate; love is blind but neighbors ain't AND **don't kiss by the garden gate; love is blind but neighbors ain't** Do not kiss or cuddle in public. □ *Come on inside if you want to kiss me. Don't make love by the garden gate; love is blind but neighbors ain't!* □ *They were so in love that they forgot the old rule, "Don't kiss by the garden gate; love is blind but neighbors ain't."*

don't make two bites of a cherry Do not leave a job half-done. □ TOM: *I washed the dishes and left them in the rack. I'll put them away tomorrow.* MARY: *Oh, come on. Don't make two bites of a cherry.* □ *You sewed all the rest of the dress, now finish the hem. Don't make two bites of a cherry.*

don't mind if I do See *don't care if I do.*

don't rush the cattle **1.** "Do not hurry." □ *Slow down! Don't rush the cattle.* □ *Take some time to think what you're doing. Don't rush the cattle.* **2.** "Do not hurry me." □ TOM: *Come on! We're going to be late!* BILL: *Don't rush the cattle.* □ *I'm going as fast as I can. Don't rush the cattle.*

Don't take any wooden nickels. Be careful and do not let anyone cheat you. (Often used as a way of saying good-bye.) □ TOM: *So long.* BILL: *Don't take any wooden nickels.* □ *Good luck in college. Don't take any wooden nickels.*

Don't that (just) beat all? AND **If that don't beat all!** "Isn't that the most amazing thing!"(See also *beat bobtail; If that don't beat a pig a-pecking!; that beats something all to pieces.*) □ *That tiny little kid won the footrace! Don't that beat all?* □ *I needed twenty dollars to pay the gas bill, and then I found a twenty in the street. If that don't beat all!*

don't worry your (pretty little) head about it "Do not worry about it." (See also *trouble one's (little) head about something.*) □ MARY: *How are you going to get another job if you don't start looking for one?* TOM: *Now don't worry your pretty little head about it. Just leave it to me.* □ TOM: *What are we going to do if we can't find an apartment?* SALLY: *Don't worry your head about it. We'll find one, one way or another.*

dood did; done. (A past tense and past participle from of *do.* Often jocular.) □ *I dood it! I dood it!* □ *Who done dood this?*

doodad a small device or thing. (See also *contraption; thingamajig; whatchamacallit.*) □ *Mary's got a nice blue dress with little sparkly doodads hanging off the hem.* □ *I bought a birdfeeder with lots of fancy doodads to keep the squirrels out of it.*

doodle bug a type of insect that curls into a ball when threatened. □ *The kids was out in the yard pokin' at some doodle bugs.* □ *My tomato plants are just covered with doodle bugs.*

doodly(-squat) See *diddly(-squat).*

doohickey See *thingamajig.*

doorinckus See *thingamajig.*

doozy a remarkable person or thing. (Used with the indefinite article *a.*) □ *They only ever had one fight, but it was a doozy.* □ *A giant hailstone put a dent in my car—a real doozy.*

dope a soft drink. (See also *coke.*) □ *Tom sat down at the soda fountain and said, "Gimme a dope."* □ *We've got some dopes in the cooler if you'd like one.*

double saw buck a twenty-dollar bill; twenty dollars. (See also *saw buck.*) □ *They wanted a double saw buck for the ticket.* □ *Jim found a double saw buck in the street!*

doublin's double-distilled corn whiskey. (See also *singlin's.*) □ *Bill's got a mighty good batch of doublin's all ready for us to enjoy.* □ *They sat out in the barn and passed around a jug of doublin's.*

dough-god a biscuit. □ *The cook's dough-gods were as hard as rocks.* □ *For two months all we had to eat was beans and dough-gods.*

doughbeater a wife. □ *What you need is a doughbeater to make this place nice and homey-like.* □ *She's his doughbeater, but he treats her like his slave.*

down-home homelike; in the way things are done at home. □ *That restaurant has real down-home cookin'.* □ *Thanksgiving at Jim's house is a down-home celebration, with lots of food and folks, and games for the little ones.*

down the road a piece AND **down the road a pike; down the road a stretch** a short distance down the road. □ *Smith's Dry Goods Store? It's down the road a piece, on the left-hand side.* □ *Go down the road a pike till you see a yellow barn on your right.* □ *I'm not sure we're lost. Let's go on down the road a stretch and see if we recognize anything.*

down the road a pike See *down the road a piece.*

down the road a stretch See *down the road a piece.*

down to a gnat's eyebrow down to the smallest detail. □ *He described what the thief was wearing down to a gnat's eyebrow.* □ *No use trying to sneak anything out of the refrigerator. Ma knows what's in there, down to a gnat's eyebrow.*

down to chili and beans very poor; down to one's last penny. □ *Mary and Tom aren't doing too well. They're down to chili and beans.* □ *Many's the time I was down to chili and beans, but I always pulled through.*

downright very. □ CHARLIE: *Can I give you a lift into town?* TOM: *Thanks. That's downright nice of you.* □ *Sally was downright rude to me, the last time we met.*

draw a bead on someone or something to take aim at someone or something. □ *I drew a bead on the quail, fired, and missed.* □ *The sniper drew a bead on the soldier in the street.*

draw 1. a ditch or riverbed that is often dried up. □ *She built her house down in the draw and got flooded out the very first spring.* □ *The ranchers all water their cattle at the draw.* **2.** welfare; the government dole. □ *After he lost his job, he was on the draw for two months.* □ *She was determined to do anything to keep her family off the draw.*

draw in one's horns AND **pull in one's horns** to back down from a fight. □ *For a minute it looked like they was gonna start sluggin' each other, but then they drew in their horns.* □ *We tried to calm him down and get him to pull in his horns.*

draw up to shrink. □ *Don't wash that shirt in hot water. It'll draw up.* □ *These cheap clothes always draw up when they get wet.*

drawers underwear. □ *When she was little, Mary used to love to run around without any drawers on.* □ *You got enough clean drawers to last the week?*

dressed eggs deviled eggs with parsley on top. □ *I made dressed eggs for the picnic.* □ *She snacked on some dressed eggs and celery sticks.*

dressed (up) fit to kill dressed very stylishly. (See also *fit to kill.*) □ *When Joe came to pick Mary up for the movie, he was dressed up fit to kill and carrying a dozen roses.* □ *Jane always comes to the office dressed fit to kill.*

drop off to die. □ *He's real sick. He could drop off any day now.* □ *My mama dropped off when I was three.*

drop one's candy to make a serious mistake. □ *The politician dropped his candy when he let the press catch him having an affair.* □ *Mary sure dropped her candy when she sassed Joe like that. Now he'll never help her.*

drunker than who shot John See *(as) drunk as who shot John.*

druv drived; drove. (The past tense and past participle of *drive.*) □ *We druv over to the picnic ground, but the rains came and druv us back again.* □ *I druv a buggy since I was a youngun.*

dry gulch someone to ambush someone. □ *The outlaw dry gulched the traveler and took everything he had.* □ *The posse planned to dry gulch the outlaw by waiting outside his favorite saloon.*

dry spell a period with no rain. □ *The dry spell killed the crops.* □ *We ain't had such a long dry spell since 1988.*

dude an Easterner, someone who is not familiar with life on a ranch. (Derogatory.) □ *Look at that dude in his fancy city clothes.* □ *A dude came into the saloon, and the cowboys all glared at him.*

dude ranch a ranch where Easterners or city people can spend a vacation. □ *I'm working up at the dude ranch, teaching them city folks how to ride horseback.* □ *Every summer, our family went to a dude ranch in Montana.*

duded up dressed up. □ *She got all duded up in her fanciest two-steppin' costume.* □ *He hates fancy clothes. He didn't even get duded up for his own wedding.*

duds clothes. □ *Get your duds on and let's hit the trail.* □ *Where'd you get them fancy duds?*

dust bunny AND **dust kitten; turkey's nest** a clump of dust and lint. (See also *curly dirt.*) □ *She swept the dust bunnies out from under the bed.* □ *There's a huge dust kitten behind the chiffarobe.* □ *He hasn't cleaned in weeks. There are turkey's nests in every corner.*

dust devil a whirlwind that carries dust. □ *A dust devil came up right in front of me. I couldn't see more than a foot ahead of me, and the dust stung my face.* □ *Dust devils flickered across the barren landscape.*

dust kitten See *dust bunny.*

Dutch oven a large pot with a tight-fitting lid. □ *I boiled the potatoes in the Dutch oven.* □ *The cook set the Dutch oven in the coals to cook the stew.*

duz does. (Eye-dialect.) □ *I duz the best I can.* □ *She never duz what she's told.*

E

eager beaver someone who is very eager to do something. □ *Jane is so hard-working! I never saw such an eager beaver.* □ *Bill can't wait to get up in the morning and get going. He's an eager beaver, all right.*

earbobs earrings. □ *Mary's got a pair of gold earbobs.* □ *Oh, no! I lost one of my earbobs!*

earful a great deal to hear. □ *If you ask Joe's opinion about the Republican Party, he'll give you an earful.* □ *Mary gave me an earful of the latest gossip.*

earn one's spurs to prove oneself. □ *After that rodeo, all the cowboys agreed that Sally had earned her spurs.* □ *He felt that he had earned his spurs when he received his Ph.D.*

Easy, there! Calm down! □ *"Easy, there!" said Arizona Slim, patting his horse's neck.* □ *Easy, there! Before you start yellin', tell me what you're yellin' about.*

eat crow to be shamed; to admit that one was wrong. □ *When it became clear that they had arrested the wrong person, the police had to eat crow.* □ *Mary talked to Joe as if he was an uneducated idiot, till she found out he was a college professor. That made her eat crow.*

eat good to taste good. □ *This beef stew sure eats good.* □ *The pie looked purty, but it didn't eat good.*

eat someone out of house and home to eat a great deal of someone's food. □ *Their guests are eating them out of house and home.* □ *What an appetite that boy has! He's eating his parents out of house and home.*

eat someone's salt to be someone's guest. □ *The least you can do when you're eating someone's salt is to help them out around the house.* □ *That good-for-nothing Jim was sparking with Bill's wife at the same time he was eating Bill's salt.*

eat(en) up with something consumed with something, such as jealously. □ *Jed was so eat up with hatred that he couldn't see straight.* □ *Effie was eaten up with jealously.*

eating high off the hog See *living high off the hog.*

eats food. □ *They got good eats at that restaurant.* □ *Jane always fixes me some eats when I get home.*

eejit See *ijit.*

effen See *iffen.*

egg bread AND **egg toast** French toast. □ *Our favorite is egg bread and long sweetening.* □ *Jimmy wants egg toast for breakfast.*

egg toast See *egg bread.*

elbow grease hard scrubbing. □ TOM: *What did you use to get your car so shiny?* MARY: *Just regular wax and some elbow grease.* □ *Joe put a lot of elbow grease into cleaning the kitchen.*

elegant sufficiency See *gracious plenty.*

elsewise otherwise. □ *Lemme borrow your pencil, elsewise I'll have to go out and buy one of my own.* □ *Mind your own business, elsewise I'll slap you up the side of the head.*

emmet (ant) a black ant. □ *The back porch is just covered with emmets.* □ *There is a little emmet ant on your knee.*

emptier than a banker's heart completely empty. □ *My wallet was emptier than a banker's heart.* □ *His pockets were emptier than a banker's heart.*

enough and some to spare plenty. □ *Would you like some more pie? We've got enough and some to spare.* □ MARY: *Can I borrow a cup of milk?* TOM: *Don't worry about borrowing. Take it. I have enough and some to spare.*

enough of something to plague a saint enough of the thing named to annoy anybody. □ *That little boy has enough curiosity to plague a saint!* □ *Sally's a well-meaning woman, but her endless gossiping is enough to plague a saint.*

epizootic an epidemic; a cold. (The name of an epidemic for animals.) □ *Pappy is down with the epizootic.* □ *Why are you sneezing? You got the epizootic?*

equalizer a revolver. □ *I carry an equalizer with me, just in case I run into trouble.* □ *In them days, every man kept his equalizer handy, even in bed.*

'er See *she*.

et ate. □ *We et all the ham and started on the chicken soon after.* □ *I et and et till I thought I would bust open.*

ever every. □ *Ever time Jim comes over, we have a good time.* □ *The coyote killed ever last one of my chickens.*

everlasting tremendous; incredible. □ *Jim makes such an everlasting fuss every time one of his kids gets a good report card.* □ *Old Red was one everlasting fine horse.*

every fool thing every ridiculous or insignificant thing. (See also *any fool thing*.) □ *Every fool thing seems to go wrong with this car.* □ *I don't want to hear about every fool thing you did on your vacation.*

every little bit helps "Even the smallest amount is helpful." □ TOM: *I can only give a dollar to your charity.* MARY: *That's OK. Every little bit helps.* □ *Jane gave me a pair of booties for my new baby. It's not much, but every little bit helps.*

every mother's son of them every one of them. □ *The scout leader said that unless the scouts told him who had stolen the money, he would punish every mother's son of them.* □ *When the football team won the championship, they were all crying, every mother's son of them.*

ever(y) which way in all directions. □ *When they heard me yell, the kittens ran off every which way.* □ *That mountain road kind of turns you ever which way before it finally gets you to the top.*

everybody and his brother AND **everybody and his uncle** everybody; lots of people. □ *The state fair was packed. Everybody and his brother was there.* □ *Everybody and his uncle was asking me where you was today.*

everybody and his uncle See *everybody and his brother.*

everything an' all everything. □ *The thieves broke into Mary's house and took the television, the silver, her jewelry, everything an' all.* □ *I had to write a report about my trip to Memphis, what I did, what I ate, what I saw, and everything an' all.*

(ex)ceptin' except. □ *Everyone in the family came to the wedding, exceptin' Uncle Bill, who was feeling poorly.* □ *It's real peaceful around here, 'ceptin' in the summer when the tourists come.*

excuse me ma'am a bump in the road. (See also *wham bam thank you ma'am.*) □ *There's a real excuse me ma'am at the bottom of that hill!* □ *Our heads hit the ceiling as the car flew over that excuse me ma'am.*

exercised about something upset about something. □ MARY: *You lost a hundred dollars playing poker!?* BILL: *Now don't get exercised about it.* □ *I can't tell Ma I'm failing English class. She gets exercised about every dumb thing I do.*

eyeful an astonishing thing to see. (See also *get an eyeful.*) □ *The children saw an eyeful of stars through the telescope.* □ *That X-rated movie sure was an eyeful.*

eyes like two burnt holes in a blanket eyes with dark circles around them. □ *I can tell you ain't slept. You got eyes like two burnt holes in a blanket.* □ *Joe came downstairs with his eyes like two burnt holes in a blanket.*

eyewash nonsense. □ TOM: *Joe says you're planning to leave town.* MARY: *That's eyewash! Why would I want to do that?* □ *Bill's crazy conspiracy theories are pure eyewash.*

F

fair to middlin' mediocre; not bad but not good. ☐ TOM: *How are you feeling today?* BILL: *Fair to middlin'.* ☐ *My sewing is excellent, but my cooking is only fair to middlin'.*

fair up [for weather] to clear up. ☐ *We sat in the barn during the rainstorm, waiting for it to fair up.* ☐ *Weatherman says it should fair up by afternoon.*

fall off **1.** to lose weight. ☐ *Jim's fallen off so much these last few weeks. Do you think he's sick?* **2.** [for business] to decline. ☐ *I'm afraid my business will fall off if I leave it to take a vacation.* ☐ *John's business fell off after he was arrested.*

fall out to faint. ☐ *I heard my blood rushing through my head. I was sure I was going to fall out.* ☐ *The bride fell out, right there in front of the altar.*

fancy woman a prostitute or mistress. ☐ *Don't hang out with them fancy women. They'll cause you nothin' but grief.* ☐ *They say she's his fancy woman.*

fat and sassy in good health and spirits. ☐ *She came back from her vacation all fat and sassy.* ☐ *Under Joe's care, the runt of the litter grew up fat and sassy.*

fatback fat from a pig's back. ☐ *We don't have no bacon, just fatback.* ☐ *He fried up some fatback.*

fault someone to blame someone. ☐ *I can't fault him. He didn't know any better.* ☐ *Joe faults me for everything that goes wrong.*

faunch to be angry; to express anger. □ *Stop faunching and do what you are told!* □ *The youngun faunched for a while and finally ate her turnips.*

faunch around to fuss and complain. □ *Stop faunching around about your problems and go to sleep.* □ *Aunt Bess is always faunching around about something.*

favor someone to look like someone. □ *She sure favors her mama, don't she?* □ *I think the baby favors my daddy.*

feather into someone to attack someone. □ *All I did was say good morning, and he feathered into me!* □ *He jumped off the bar stool and feathered into the stranger.*

federal building an outhouse. (Humorous. See also *gardenhouse; necessary.*) □ *Can you show me where to find your federal building?* □ *Excuse me while I retire to the federal building.*

feed lot a lot where a large number of animals are fed to get them ready for market. □ *You can sure smell the feed lot when you drive by it.* □ *The steer had spent his whole life in the feed lot.*

feed off someone's range to pry into someone's business. □ *Sally is always feeding off my range. I don't like it.* □ *It was easy for the mailman to feed off everybody's range. He just opened all our letters.*

feed one's face to eat; to feed oneself. □ *Will you stop feeding your face long enough to say hello?* □ *Jed is out on the porch, feeding his face.*

feel for someone to have sympathy for someone. □ *I really feel for Bill. He's had such a hard time since his folks died.* □ *Her neighbors felt for her and did everything they could to help.*

feel one's oats to be very lively. □ *Careful with that horse. He's feeling his oats today.* □ *Mary was feeling her oats and decided to go out dancing.*

feeling puny feeling ill. □ *I'm feeling puny. Think I might be coming down with a cold.* □ *Bill had to skip football practice on account of he was feeling puny.*

feisty spirited and eager to fight. □ *The feisty puppy pounced on the sock, growling.* □ *She's a feisty kid. She stands up for her rights.*

fence-lifter a very heavy rain. (See also *goose-drownder; gully washer.*) □ *It's coming down out there. A real fence-lifter.* □ *The fence-lifter washed away all the seeds out of my garden.*

fer why why. □ *I know you stole the shirt. What I want to know is, fer why?* □ BILL: *Let's go downtown.* CHARLIE: *Fer why?*

fernenst See *fernent.*

fernent AND **fernenst** across from. □ *He built his son and daughter-in-law a house fernent his.* □ *The train station is over there fernenst the bank.*

fess up to confess. □ *Whoever did this, better fess up!* □ *My conscience wouldn't let me sleep till I fessed up.*

fetch to give. □ *She fetched a deep sigh.* □ *He fetched me a slap across the face.*

few bricks short of a load lacking in intellectual ability. □ TOM: *Joe thinks he can build a car out of old milk jugs.* MARY: *I think Joe's a few bricks short of a load.* □ *Ever since she fell and hit her head, Jane's been a few bricks short of a load, if you know what I'm saying.*

F.F.V. the First Families of Virginia; aristocratic Virginia families. □ *They were one of the F.F.V., though they had fallen on hard times.* □ *I was just a white trash country girl, but my roommate was an F.F.V.*

fifth wheel an unwelcome or extra person. □ *I don't like living with my son and daughter-in-law. I feel like a fifth wheel.* □ *Bill* *always begs to come on camping trips with us, but really, he's a fifth wheel.*

figger to figure. □ *Figger the total, and we'll pay the bill.* □ *I figger I can get two dollars a head for them chickens.*

figger something up to add something up; to total something. □ *It took John half an hour to figger his checkbook up.* 🅃 *The waitress figgered up our bill and we left.*

fighting mad angry enough to fight. □ *When I saw that the grocery store charged me too much, I was fighting mad.* □ *Jane's been fighting mad ever since Bill dumped her for another girl.*

fill someone full of lead to shoot someone. □ *The shopkeeper bought a gun and swore the next time someone broke into the shop, he'd fill him full of lead.* □ *Don't move, or I'll fill you full of lead.*

fill the bill to be acceptable. □ JANE: *I need some string.* TOM: *Here's some twine. Will it fill the bill?* □ *I need cloth to make a shirt. This muslin ought to fill the bill.*

fine and dandy very good. □ TOM: *Morning, Mary! How are you? How's Bill?* MARY: *Fine and dandy.* □ CHARLIE: *I'll send you a check on Saturday.* MARY: *That will be fine and dandy.*

fine how do you do an unpleasant situation. (Used with the indefinite article *a*.) □ *This is a fine how do you do! Someone left a big puddle of motor oil in my driveway.* □ *John saw his girlfriend out with another young man. He walked up to her and said, "Well, isn't this a fine how do you do!"*

fire-eater a passionate believer in a cause. □ *I'd hate to be a Republican in this town. The Democrats are all fire-eaters.* □ *When it comes to women's rights, Sally's a real fire-eater.*

firewater hard liquor. □ *Bill had a little too much of that firewater on Saturday night.* □ *I took a couple swallows of firewater and started feeling brave.*

fish fry an occasion when meals, including fried fish, are sold to the public. □ *Every Friday night, I go down to the fish fry at the Veterans' Hall.* □ *The church had a fish fry as a fundraiser.*

fit to be tied angry and agitated. (As if needing to be restrained.) □ *Joe was fit to be tied when his wife told him she was leaving.* □ *I was fit to be tied when Mary walked in the door, after three years of not speaking to me.*

fit to kill a great deal; to the highest possible degree. (See also *dressed (up) fit to kill.*) □ *We laughed fit to kill when we saw the expression on Jim's face.* □ *I had my car gussied up fit to kill.*

fitsy temperamental; subject to bursts of temper. □ *Effie was always a fitsy child.* □ *What is making you so fitsy lately?*

fix trouble. (See also *in a fix.*) □ *We were in a terrible fix, and no mistake.* □ *Jim's hot temper got him in fix after fix.*

fixins **1.** clothes. □ *It takes Molly most of an hour to get all her fixins on.* □ *I got up and put on my fixins.* **2.** equipment. □ *Have you got the fixins for me to roll a cigarette?* □ *Best get all your fixins packed up.* **3.** accompanying foods and garnishes. □ *She made turkey dinner with all the fixins.* □ *I don't care none for meat, but the fixins is mighty fine.*

flannelmouth a smooth talker; a flatterer. □ *If that flannelmouth don't shut up, I'll shut his mouth for him.* □ *Mr. Anderson, the flannelmouth, talked me into buying a new tractor.*

flap one's gums AND **flap one's jaws** to talk aimlessly. □ *They're still out on the porch, flapping their gums.* □ *Well, I can't sit here flapping my jaws all day. Gotta get back to work.*

flap one's jaws See *flap one's gums.*

flapjack a pancake. (See also *griddle cake.*) □ *When we camp out, we always have flapjacks for breakfast.* □ *Would you like some syrup for your flapjacks?*

flash in the pan someone or something that is very famous or popular for only a brief time. □ *The singer was a flash in the pan. He only had one big hit.* □ *Mark my words, this fad for pierced noses will be just a flash in the pan.*

flat busted broke; having no money at all. □ *I'd like to loan you some, but I'm flat busted.* □ *Mary was flat busted, and it was two more weeks before she was due to get paid.*

flat-out definitely; directly. □ *She flat-out disobeyed me.* □ *I don't care how much money you offer me. This house is flat-out not for sale.*

flatlander someone from the plains, rather than the mountains. (Mildly derogatory.) □ *Lots of them flatlanders come up here to the mountains for their vacation.* □ *I'm a flatlander, don't know the first thing about mountain climbing.*

flinders pieces. □ *She picked up an axe and chopped that log to flinders.* □ *I dropped the jar and it busted into flinders.*

float someone a raft of shit to make a lot of trouble for someone; to tease someone. (Use with caution.) □ *My boss floated me a raft of shit after I messed up on the big project.* □ *They floated him a raft of shit when they found out he had a girlfriend.*

floor baby See *arm baby.*

flunky a subordinate. □ *He's a big honcho in that company. He's got a flunky just to shine his shoes.* □ *I don't want to be anybody's flunky. I want to be the boss!*

foam at the mouth to talk crazily; to act out of control. □ *That preacher's always foaming at the mouth about women who wear short skirts.* □ *Mary was so mad about Bill getting home late, she practically foamed at the mouth.*

folderol nonsense; foolishness. (See also *foolishness.*) □ *The senator's campaign speech sounded like folderol to me.* □ *When we were growing up, we never had time for movies and dating and all that folderol.*

folding money bills of various dollar denominations. □ *I don't want no check. Give me folding money!* □ *You got any folding money with you?*

foolishness nonsense; frivolity. (See also *folderol.*) □ *If you want a two-hundred-dollar prom dress, earn the money for it yourself. I don't have any money to spare for such foolishness.* □ *Tom spends his spare time writing poetry, or some such foolishness.*

footlog a log used as a footbridge. □ *I slipped on the footlog and fell in the creek.* □ *That footlog's not safe. We should build a real bridge.*

for crying out loud for goodness' sake. (A mild oath, used to express irritation.) □ *Oh, for crying out loud! How many times do I have to tell you to wipe your feet before you come in?* □ MARY: *Jim's on the phone. He wants to know if he can borrow some more money.* TOM: *Oh, for crying out loud.*

for my money "in my opinion." □ *That's the best brand of tools there is, for my money.* □ *For my money, you can't go wrong with a pure wool sweater.*

for pity('s) sake(s) "For goodness' sake." (A mild oath, used to express irritation.) □ *Oh, for pity's sakes. I got a run in my nylons.* □ *For pity's sake, will you shut up about your gol dern kidney stones!*

for the life of me at all; even one little bit. □ *For the life of me, I can't figure this out.* □ *I can't for the life of me climb up no mountain.*

fork to sit astride a horse. □ *She was used to riding sidesaddle. She didn't know how to fork.* □ *The roan's chest was so broad that it was tough to fork.*

fork something over to hand something over; to surrender something. □ *The robber demanded my wallet. I forked it over.* 🅃 *She had to fork over three thousand dollars in back taxes.*

forty-niner someone who came West during the 1849 California gold rush. □ *My granddaddy was a forty-niner.* □ *The book was written by a forty-niner who settled on a ranch in Oregon.*

foxfire a luminescent fungus that grows on decaying wood. □ *They say it's ghosts out in the swamp, but I say it's just foxfire.* □ *We saw foxfire flickering in the woods ahead of us.*

frail someone to beat someone; to flail someone. □ *He frailed the boy till he could hardly stand.* □ *If you sass me again, I'll frail you but good.*

Freeze! "Do not move!" □ *The police officer shouted "Freeze!" to the fleeing suspect.* □ *"Freeze!" said the bandit, drawing his gun.*

freeze one's tail off to freeze; to get very cold. □ *Don't stand out there in the cold wind! You'll freeze your tail off!* □ *It's as cold as a welldigger's nose today. I about froze my tail off walking to work.*

fresh out (of something) just run out (of something). □ CUSTOMER: *Do you have any blackstrap molasses?* STORE CLERK: *Nope. We're fresh out of it.* □ *The farmers' market was fresh out of blueberries.*

fret to worry. □ *Now, don't you fret. Everything will be all right.* □ *Jim will fret over the least little thing.*

frijoles beans. (Spanish.) □ *I don't need no fancy food. Just some frijoles and tortillas, and I'm happy.* □ *He ordered a bowl of chili with another bowl of frijoles to boot.*

fritter a cake of fried dough. □ *Jane makes the best corn fritters in the county.* □ *I've got a nice recipe for zucchini fritters.*

fritter something away to waste something. T *He inherited a lot of money, but he frittered away the greater part of it.* □ *They frittered the time away.*

frogsticker AND **toadsticker** a short knife. □ *I don't have much of a weapon on me, just this frogsticker.* □ *She pulled out a toad-sticker and carved her initials on the tree.*

from Dan to Beersheba from one end of the earth to the other; everywhere. (*Dan* and *Beersheba* were two distant towns in ancient Palestine. See also *from hell to breakfast.*) □ *The sheriff vowed he would chase the outlaw from Dan to Beersheba.* □ *The drought killed the crops from Dan to Beersheba. No one had a harvest that year.*

from hell to breakfast from one end of the earth to the other; all over; everywhere. (See also *from Dan to Beersheba.*) □ *We searched from hell to breakfast, but never did find the runaway kid.* □ *I tracked that deer from hell to breakfast, but never got a shot at it.*

from here till next Tuesday for a great distance; for a long time. □ *If you try that again, I'll knock you from here till next Tuesday.* □ *You can lecture him from here till next Tuesday, but he won't listen.*

from off alien; not from this location. □ *Miss Johnson is from off and can't be expected to know our ways.* □ *I'm not from off! I was born right in this very town!*

from pillar to post from one place to another. □ *He dragged his poor wife from pillar to post, looking for a job that suited him.* □ *For ten years we went from pillar to post, never settling down anywhere.*

(from) so far south they call people from Georgia Yankees very far south (in the U.S.). (Jocular. In the South, a *Yankee* is a Northerner.) □ *Is he a Southerner? My dear, he's from so far south they call people from Georgia Yankees.* □ *I come from a little town so far south they call people from Georgia Yankees.*

front name a first name; a given name. □ *That's Miz Brown. Don't know her front name.* □ *His front name was Andrews, his mother's maiden name.*

fudge to cheat; to make a dishonest change. □ *He fudged with the figures in his checkbook to keep his wife from finding out how much money he had lost.* □ *There was a scandal when it was found that the famous scientist had fudged his data.*

full of beans See *full of prunes.*

full of prunes AND **full of beans** full of nonsense. (Both beans and prunes produce intestinal gas.) □ *That's silly. You're just full of beans.* □ *Suzy's a fast talker, but always full of beans.*

full sixteen hands high the full quantity. (See also *all wool and a yard wide; all wool and no shoddy.*) □ TOM: *What do you think of Mary?* CHARLIE: *She's a good woman all right, full sixteen hands high.* □ *Everything they sell at Johnson's store is the best there is, full sixteen hands high.*

full up full. □ *I ate till I was full up.* □ *I can't get any more gas in the tank. It's full up.*

funnies AND **funny paper** the comics section of a newspaper. □ *Did you read the funnies on Sunday? Snuffy Smith had a real good joke.* □ *Hand me the funny paper. You can have the sports section.*

funny bone AND **crazy bone** the elbow bone. □ *Ouch, I hit my funny bone.* □ *Effie bumped her crazy bone and made a horrendous face.*

funny paper See *funnies.*

fur piece a long distance. (Used with the indefinite article *a*.) □ *It's a fur piece to the library. You'd best take the bus instead of walking.* □ *It's a pretty fur piece to the nearest big town.*

furrin foreign. □ *Do you speak any furrin languages?* □ *I don't buy any of them furrin goods. It's Made in the USA for me.*

furriner a foreigner. □ *Lots of furriners come to our town to see the sights.* □ *He was a furriner. He didn't know how we do things here.*

fuss **1.** to move around or make noise restlessly. □ *The baby fussed all day.* □ *Now, don't fuss, little one.* **2.** to complain. (Often with *about.*) □ *You are always fussing about something!* □ *Quit fussing about my clothes. They're all right.*

fuss and feathers fancy, troublesome things. □ *A truly elegant dress doesn't have a lot of fuss and feathers.* □ *They ruined a nice room with all that fuss and feathers.*

fussbudget a fussy person. □ *Jimmy has been a fussbudget all day today. I think he is cutting a tooth.* □ *Effie is such a fussbudget. She is never happy.*

fustest first. □ *I was the fustest one at school and the onliest one with shoes.* □ *Whoever is fustest gets the most grits.*

G

gad about See *gad around.*

gad around AND **gad about** to go from place to place, having fun. □ *I'm too old to gad around like that.* □ *She wasted too much time gadding about with her friends.*

gal a girl or woman. □ *She's a nice gal, all right.* □ *Charlie met a gal at the library and asked her out.*

galackin' gathering greens. □ *We'll have to go galackin' if we want any greens for supper.* □ *My old lady's out galackin' this morning.*

gallery a porch. □ *The house has a gallery all along the front.* □ *We sat out in the gallery, enjoying the cool evening breeze.*

gallin' courting a girl or woman. □ *Every since he turned fifteen, Joe spends all his time gallin'.* □ *Charlie's gallin' up at the O'Connor place.*

gallivant (around) to go around having fun. □ *He spent his time gallivanting around when he should have been studying.* □ *I'm too old to gallivant all night.*

galluses AND **braces** suspenders. □ *Jones always wears a pair of bright red galluses.* □ *I'm gettin' too fat for a belt. Guess I'll have to wear braces.*

garden-sass vegetables from the garden. □ *I'm gonna go out and get some garden-sass for a salad.* □ *I'm a meat and potatoes man. No garden-sass for me.*

gardenhouse an outhouse. (See also *federal building; necessary.*) ☐ *He excused himself to go to the gardenhouse.* ☐ *They didn't have flush toilets at camp, just a gardenhouse.*

'gator an alligator. ☐ *There was a big ol' 'gator lying in the road.* ☐ *Tom stays away from the swamp because he's afraid of 'gators.*

geechee a black person from the rural South. (Usually derogatory. Originally referred to blacks in communities that retained many African cultural features.) ☐ *Joe claimed to be church-goin' man, but he was allus talking about "them geechees."* ☐ *A lot of the geechees out this way own their own farms.*

gentle someone or something to make someone or something tame. (Usually used in the expression *gentle a horse.*) ☐ *Arizona Slim could gentle a mustang in no time flat.* ☐ *He was a pretty rough customer, but his little wife gentled him.*

get a rise from someone or something AND **get a rise out of someone or something** to make someone or something react, usually angrily. ☐ *Tease Joe about his girlfriend. That generally gets a rise from him.* ☐ *I pestered Mary for half the afternoon, but didn't get a rise out of her.*

get a rise out of someone or something See *get a rise from someone or something.*

get a skinful to drink a great deal of liquor. ☐ *He went to the saloon and got a skinful.* ☐ *Anyplace in this town where a man can go to get a skinful?*

get about AND **get around** to manage to move around. ☐ *I broke my hip last year, but I can still get about.* ☐ *Dad can't get around too much anymore, so I go over to help him.*

get an eyeful to see something astonishing. (See also *eyeful.*) ☐ *When the kids peeped into Miss Nelly's bedroom, they got an eyeful.* ☐ *John got an eyeful when he read Mary's journal.*

get around See *get about.*

get cracking to get to work. □ *If you want to finish that quilt by Labor Day, you best get cracking.* □ *Sit down to your homework and get cracking!*

get down to brass tacks to reach the important part of the matter. □ *Let's get down to brass tacks. How much do you want for the boat?* □ *We swapped small talk for half an hour before we finally got down to brass tacks.*

get euchred out of something to get cheated out of something. □ *Joe's dad left him a farm, but he got euchred out of it by some city slicker real estate agent.* □ *I got euchred out of ten bucks by a con artist with a hard-luck story.*

get on with your rat-killin' Do not waste time.; Carry on with what you are doing. □ *Get on with your rat-killin', now. We can't stand here gossiping all day.* □ *You ain't got time to watch TV. Get on with your rat-killin'.*

get one's comeuppance to get a deserved punishment. □ *I can't wait till that snobbish girl gets her comeuppance.* □ *Joe got his comeuppance when the teacher caught him making fun of her.*

get one's ears set out to get a haircut. □ *Well, I see you got your ears set out!* □ *Better get my ears set out because I'm getting a little shaggy.*

get one's wires crossed to fail to communicate; to get a wrong message. □ *I thought I was supposed to meet you at one o'clock, not two. I guess we got our wires crossed.* □ *Bill and Mary got their wires crossed, and he didn't meet her at the airport like she thought he would.*

get oneself up to dress oneself up. □ *I got myself up in my Sunday best.* □ *Jane got herself up as if she was a movie star.*

get religion to be dramatically converted to religious faith (or other belief). □ *Jim got religion at the camp meeting last year.* □ *I quit drinking when I got religion.*

get shed of someone or something See *get shut of someone or something.*

get shet of someone or something See *get shut of someone or something.*

get shut of someone or something AND **get shed of someone or something; get shet of someone or something** to get rid of someone or something. □ *I can't wait to get shut of that old refrigerator.* □ *Tom followed me around for months, but I finally got shed of him.*

get someone's dander up to make someone angry. (*Someone* includes *oneself.*) □ *That smart remark really got your daddy's dander up.* □ *It really gets my dander up when you don't clean up after yourself.*

get someone's goat to irritate someone; to anger someone. □ *It really gets my goat, the way grocery prices seem to go up every week.* □ *Bill's prank got the teacher's goat.*

get sore to get angry. □ *When Mary hears what you said about her, she'll get sore for sure.* □ *Please don't get sore at me.*

get the draw on someone to be faster than one's opponent in a fight. □ *The sheriff got the draw on Arizona Slim and shot him in the arm.* □ *Bill's competitor got the draw on him. She was the first one in town to start selling those popular new shoes.*

get the drop on someone to ambush someone in a fight. □ *It looked like the outlaw might win, but then the sheriff got the drop on him.* □ *Bob got the drop on Jim and pounded him to within an inch of his life.*

get the kinks (ironed) out to fix a problem associated with something. □ *The actors had to get the kinks out before they were ready to present the play to an audience.* □ *That'll be a right nice car, when you get the kinks ironed out in the engine.*

get-up an elaborate outfit of clothes. □ *How am I supposed to dance in this formal get-up?* □ *That was some get-up Mary had on. Did you see the pink feathers and rhinestones on her hat?*

get wind of something to hear about something. □ *When I got wind of their plans for a party, I was upset that they hadn't invited me.* □ TOM: *How did Jim know I was going to move?* JANE: *He must have gotten wind of it somehow.*

ghost town an abandoned town. □ *We walked through the main street of the ghost town, hearing the wind whistle through the broken windows.* □ *After the mine was played out, the little mining village became a ghost town.*

gimcracks small, useless, decorative objects. □ *The room would look bigger if you didn't have them gimcracks on every surface that'll hold 'em.* □ *I built Jane a little cabinet to keep her gimcracks in.*

gimp someone who limps. (Mildly insulting.) □ *One of my legs is shorter than the other, so I'll be a gimp all my life.* □ *The other kids called Billy a gimp and teased him because he couldn't run fast.*

ginger liveliness; spirit. □ *She was a good mare and full of ginger.* □ *There was a heap of ginger in that kid. No one could keep up with him.*

Git! Go away! □ *"Git!" Nelly said to the dog in her flower bed.* □ *Git! Go on! Get away from here!*

give out something to say something; to tell someone something. □ *Mary gave out that she was going to Chicago for a business trip.* □ *Bill's giving out that he won a hundred bucks in the lottery.*

give someone a leg up to give someone a boost; to help someone up. (See also *have a leg up on someone else.*) □ *I was having trouble getting onto the horse, so Joe gave me a leg up.* □ *Give me a leg up so I can get over this fence.*

give someone down the road to scold someone. (See also *give someone Hail Columbia; give someone what-for.*) □ *Mary gave Bill down the road when she found out he'd been drinking again.* □ *If your ma finds out, she'll give you down the road!*

give someone fits to upset someone a great deal. □ *It gives Jim fits when I go out with another man.* □ *Dirty dishes in the sink just give me fits. I can't rest till I've washed them.*

give someone Hail Columbia to scold someone severely. (See also *give someone down the road; give someone what-for.*) □ *The teacher gave her students Hail Columbia over their poor test scores.* □ *If Miss Ellen finds out I broke her window, she'll give me Hail Columbia for sure!*

give someone some lip to speak rudely or disrespectfully to someone; to sass someone. (Also slang.) □ *Billy gave me some lip, so I whupped him.* □ *Jane is always giving the teacher some lip.*

give someone some sugar to give someone a kiss. □ *Come here, honey, and give me some sugar.* □ *"Give me some sugar!" Gramma said when she saw me.*

give someone the big eye **1.** to look at someone flirtatiously. □ *Lookathere—that pretty girl is giving you the big eye.* □ *I thought she was cute, so I gave her the big eye.* **2.** to make eye contact with someone. □ *Tom gave me the big eye to let me know he wanted to talk to me.* □ *I tried to give her the big eye, but she never looked my way.*

give someone the go-by to reject someone; to ignore someone. □ TOM: *Did you get that job?* MARY: *No, they gave me the go-by.* □ *Jane had been going out with Jim for two years, then all of a sudden she gave him the go-by.*

give someone the high sign to signal to someone. □ *Don't come in till I give you the high sign.* □ *Jim gave me the high sign, so I knew everything was all right.*

give someone what-for to scold someone severely. (See also *give someone Hail Columbia; give someone down the road.*) □ *The* *angry customer gave the waiter what-for.* □ *Mom gave us what-for when she saw how we'd wrecked her good dress.*

gizzards internal organs; insides; innards. □ *Doc says the X-ray shows something wrong with my gizzards.* □ *Have some of this hot soup to warm your gizzards.*

glutton for punishment someone who does something painful or difficult again and again. (Sometimes used humorously, as in the second example.) □ MARY: *How come Jane went back to that no-good husband of hers?* SALLY: *I guess she's a glutton for punishment.* □ *Say, this is the second time this week you've come over to visit. You must be a glutton for punishment!*

go at something like a boy killing snakes to do something with a great deal of energy. □ *Once Mary decided to take that test, she went at her books like a boy killing snakes.* □ *I hired Joe to weed my garden, and he went at it like a boy killing snakes.*

go belly up See *turn belly up.*

go for wool and come back shorn to lose everything trying to make a profit. □ TOM: *Jim's business failed right quick, didn't it?* CHARLIE: *Yessir. He went for wool and came back shorn.* □ *The gambler went for wool and came back shorn.*

go great guns to make progress fast, working enthusiastically. □ *It took Joe awhile to get started on his history project, but now he's going great guns.* □ *Business at the store is going great guns this summer.*

go haywire to go wrong. □ *The gol dern computer at the bank went haywire, and now the bank thinks I owe them a thousand bucks!* □ *Our plan went haywire. Nothing came out the way we wanted it to.*

go off half-cocked to go into action without thinking. □ *Don't go off half-cocked. Plan out what you're going to do.* □ *Bill went off half-cocked and told everybody he was running for the state legislature.*

go shares in something to divide something up; to share something. ☐ *We'll go shares in the profits.* ☐ *The sisters went shares in everything—clothes, money, and chores.*

go south **1.** to leave secretly. ☐ *He went south before his partners discovered the money he had taken.* ☐ *If you know what's good for you, you'll go south in a hurry.* **2.** to fail; to decline. ☐ *The price of cotton went south last week. We'll lose a bundle.* ☐ *Our whole crop went south last year.*

go to bed with the chickens to go to bed early. (See also *go to bed with the sun.*) ☐ *We'd better go to bed with the chickens. We have to get up early in the morning.* ☐ *I keep my good health by eating what I should and going to bed with the chickens.*

go to bed with the sun to go to bed early, at sunset. (See also *go to bed with the chickens.*) ☐ *The campers went to bed with the sun.* ☐ *The children had to go to bed with the sun. The grown-ups stayed up a little later.*

go to do something to start to do something. ☐ *He went to running the store after his pa got so sick.* ☐ *She got her tools and went to fixing the bathroom plumbing.*

go to grass (and eat hay) "Go away." (Used to express contempt.) ☐ BILL: *But, honey, can't I make it up to you somehow?* MARY: *Go to grass and eat hay!* ☐ *Anyone who thinks I can't do the job can go to grass!*

go to hell in a bucket AND **go to hell in a handbasket** to get rapidly worse and worse. ☐ *The school system in this district is going to hell in a bucket, and no mistake.* ☐ *His health is going to hell in a handbasket ever since he started drinking again.*

go to hell in a handbasket See *go to hell in a bucket.*

go to one's (just) reward to die. (A euphemism.) ☐ *Let us pray for our departed sister, who has gone to her just reward.* ☐ BILL: *How's your grandma these days?* TOM: *She went to her reward last winter, may she rest in peace.*

go to pot to become ruined; to deteriorate physically. □ *Mary has really gone to pot since her husband died.* □ *He's letting that fine old house go to pot. He doesn't maintain it at all.*

go to see a man about a dog to go to use the toilet. □ *Excuse me. I have to go to see a man about a dog.* □ BILL: *Where's Charlie?* TOM: *He went to see a man about a dog.*

go to the bushes to go to the bathroom. □ *Can we stop somewheres? I need to go to the bushes.* □ *He stopped by the side of the trail to go to the bushes.*

go-way sack a suitcase. □ *He folded his shirts and put them in his go-way sack.* □ *She kept her go-way sack in the attic. She didn't do much traveling.*

go whole hog to do something to the highest possible degree. □ *When Jill gives a party, she goes whole hog—makes tons of food, decorates the whole house, and invites everyone she knows.* □ *Bob's mother bought him a new suit for his wedding. She went whole hog and got everything from underwear on out.*

God willing and the creek don't rise AND **Lord willing and the creek don't rise** "If all goes well." □ TOM: *Will you be able to get the house painted before the cold weather sets in?* JANE: *Yes, God willing and the creek don't rise.* □ *We'll be able to visit our daughter for Christmas, Lord willing and the creek don't rise.*

God's gift (to women) a perfect man. □ *Tom thinks he's God's gift to women, but if the truth were known, they laugh at him behind his back.* □ *He acted like he was God's gift and I should be real grateful to be going out with him.*

God's honest truth See *gospel truth.*

God's nightgown! "For goodness' sake!" (A mild oath.) □ *God's nightgown! Aren't you dressed yet?* □ *God's nightgown! Can't you see I'm busy?*

gol dang See *gol dern.*

gol dern AND **gol dang** "God damn."; "God-damned." (A euphemism and a mild expletive.) □ *Gol dern it, Mary, shut the screen door! Them bugs is gettin' in here in droves.* □ *The gol dang car's in the shop again.*

goldarned See *goldurned.*

goldurned AND **goldarned** God-damned. (A partial disguise.) □ *Get your goldurned feet off'n the table!* □ *Sam is a goldarned pantywaist!*

gollywhopper a very large thing. □ *Look at that storm cloud a-comin'. It's a gollywhopper!* □ *The prize pumpkin at the state fair sure was a gollywhopper.*

gone fishin' away from work; away enjoying oneself. □ *You won't find Bill at the shop this week. He's gone fishin'.* □ *A sign on the gas station said, "Gone fishin'."*

gone gosling someone or some creature that is certain to die. (See also *dead duck.*) □ *I'm a gone gosling if Joe finds out I spent all the money he gave me.* □ MARY: *Your horse looks awful sick.* TOM: *Yep, she's a gone gosling, I'm afraid.*

gone to Texas gone away to escape something. □ BILL: *Seen Bob lately?* JANE: *He's gone to Texas. He shot a man, you know.* □ *All my old friends from the ranch are gone to Texas, for one reason or another.*

gone where the woodbine twineth **1.** dead. (Jocular.) □ *I'm afraid our old compadre is gone where the woodbine twineth.* □ *Suzy is in mourning for her goldfish, who has gone where the woodbine twineth.* **2.** run away. □ *If anybody asks after me, just tell them I'm gone where the woodbine twineth.* □ *When the police came looking for the criminal, they discovered she had gone where the woodbine twineth.*

goner someone who is certain to die. □ *I figured I was a goner for sure when the doc told me I had cancer.* □ *Bill got hit by a car, and we thought he was a goner.*

goober AND **guber** a peanut. □ *We bought a bag of roasted goobers at the ballpark.* □ *We had boiled gubers for a snack.*

good and something very or completely something. (*Something* is a state of being.) □ *Joe never does anything till he's good and ready.* □ *Mary's good and mad, all right.*

good feed a large and tasty meal. (Used with the indefinite article *a*.) □ *John always makes sure everybody has a good feed when we go to his house for dinner.* □ *We had a good feed at the new Italian restaurant.*

good for what ails you able to cure any problem or illness. (Usually used to describe food or liquor.) □ *Have a sip of this whiskey. It's good for what ails you.* □ *Sally's beef broth is good for what ails you.*

Good grief! See *Goodnight!*

good many quite a few. (Used with the indefinite article *a*.) □ *I have a good many kinfolk in Texas.* □ *Mary owns a good many acres of land.*

good ole boy a man with country ways. □ *None of that fancy city stuff for me. I'm just a good ole boy.* □ *Joe's a good ole boy, likes huntin' and fishin', drinkin' and gamblin'.*

Goodnight! AND **Good grief!** "Isn't that a surprise!" □ *Goodnight! We're late again!* □ *Good grief! Is that all I get?*

goose bumps See *turkey bumps.*

goose-drownder a very heavy rain. (See also *fence-lifter; gully washer.*) □ *Look at it come down out there! What a goose-drownder!* □ *From the look of them clouds, I'd say we're in for a goose-drownder before nightfall.*

goose hangs high AND **goose honks high** "Everything is good." □ *Looks like we'll have a good harvest this year. The goose hangs high.* □ MARY: *How are you these days? How's your family?* TOM: *The goose honks high, thank you.*

goose honks high See *goose hangs high.*

goosy ticklish. □ *Jane's so goosy, you just have to wiggle your fingers to get her to scream.* □ *My girlfriend's awful goosy. Everything I do seems to tickle her.*

goozlum syrup; molasses. □ *Could you pass me a bit more of that goozlum?* □ *Why do you put so much goozlum on your egg bread?*

gopher to mine or prospect. □ *He had been gophering in the hills to the east.* □ *He gophered away at his claim all week, then came into town to spend what he found.*

gorm something to dirty something. □ *He gormed his new clothes playing football with his buddies.* □ *She gormed my clean rug, dragging her dirty shoes all acrost it.*

gospel truth AND **God's honest truth** the absolute truth. □ *I didn't take the money. It's the gospel truth.* □ *Tell me the God's honest truth. Are you really in love with him?*

gossip-trot someone who goes around gossiping. □ *Mrs. Johnson is an old gossip-trot who loves to get into other people's business.* □ *Don't tell Sally anything you don't want the whole town to know. She's a gossip-trot.*

got the dry grins has a nervous smile. □ *"Did you eat all the pie in the refrigerator?" I asked Joe. Joe suddenly got the dry grins.* □ *Mary got the dry grins and couldn't look me in the eye.*

gotta get up pretty early in the morning to do something it would be difficult to do something. □ *You gotta get up pretty early in the morning to cheat Bill Johnson. He's a sharp businessman for sure.* □ *You gotta get up pretty early in the morning to know your Bible better than Preacher Harris.*

gouge someone to cheat someone. □ *I wouldn't shop at that store, not with the way they gouge folks.* □ *Jim would gouge his own mother for a nickel.*

grab a root to do the best you can with what you have. □ *I got no money, but the kids got to have good clothes for school. I'll have to grab a root and figure out how to make some out of my old clothes.* □ MARY: *How am I gonna get to town with the car broke?* TOM: *Grab a root and figure something out.*

gracious plenty AND **elegant sufficiency** enough (food). □ *No more, thanks. I have a gracious plenty on my plate.* □ *At Thanksgiving, we always have an elegant sufficiency and are mighty thankful for it.*

gran(d)-baby a young grandchild. □ *Come on over to my daughter's house and see my new grand-baby.* □ *Jane had pictures of her two gran-babies.*

granddaddy grandfather. □ *You sure got your granddaddy's eyes.* □ *My granddaddy farmed this land.*

(grand)daddy longlegs a kind of insect with long, thin legs. □ *There's a big ol' granddaddy longlegs hangin' on the ceiling.* □ *I found a daddy longlegs climbing on my rosebush.*

Grandma's come a woman's menstrual period has begun. (See also *visit from Flo; have one's lady's time; monthlies; bad time (of the month).*) □ *Grandma's come, so I don't feel like doing much today.* □ *Jane's going to go rest for a while. Grandma's come.*

gran(d)pappy a grandfather. (Also a term of address.) □ *Grandpappy, why don't you set a spell?* □ *Granpappy has been gone for a week now.*

granny woman a midwife; a female folk healer. □ *Joe went to get the granny woman when his wife went into labor.* □ *You were born at home, and with a granny woman, not a doctor.*

grass-roots populist; led by or having to do with ordinary people. □ *There's grass-roots opposition to the new power plant.* □ *She's not a well-known candidate, but she has grass-roots support.*

grass widow a woman abandoned by her husband. (See also *graveyard widow.*) □ *Jane's husband isn't dead, but she's a widow just the same—a grass widow.* □ *Bill ran off and left Mary a grass widow.*

grave rock a tombstone. □ *We all clubbed together to get a grave rock with Grandpa's name inscribed.* □ *The grave rocks looked white and eerie in the moonlight.*

graveyard widow a woman whose husband is dead. (See also *grass widow.*) □ *Bill died twenty years after he ran out on Mary. So instead of a grass widow, Mary's a graveyard widow now.* □ *When my husband disappeared, I was afraid I was a graveyard widow.*

Great balls of fire! "Good heavens!"; "Wow!" □ *Mary got up to play the fiddle, and great balls of fire! That girl can play!* □ TOM: *Will you marry me?* JANE: *Yes, I will.* TOM: *Great balls of fire! I'm the happiest man on earth.*

Great day (in the morning)! "My goodness!" (An exclamation of surprise.) □ *Great day in the morning! I didn't expect to see you here.* □ *Great day! That thunder sure is loud!*

Great Rebellion the U.S. Civil War (1861–1865). (From the Southern point of view.) □ *One of my great-granddads fought for the South in the Great Rebellion, and one of them fought for the North.* □ *The town courthouse burned at the time of the Great Rebellion.*

great unwashed the general public; the lower middle class. □ *The Simpsons had a big fence around their house—put there to discourage the great unwashed from wandering up to the door by mistake, I suppose.* □ *Maw says the great unwashed don't know enough to come in out of the rain.*

greatest thing since indoor plumbing AND **greatest thing since sliced bread** the most wonderful thing in the world. (Usually with *the*.) □ *As far as I'm concerned, this new food processor is the greatest thing since indoor plumbing.* □ *Joe thinks Sally is the* *greatest thing since sliced bread. You can tell just by the way he looks at her.*

greatest thing since sliced bread See *greatest thing since indoor plumbing.*

green inexperienced. (See also *greenhorn; pea-green.*) □ *The new camp cook was awful green. Got all in a swivet when we teased him about his biscuits.* □ *The cowboy was so green, he couldn't tell a cow from a steer.*

green around the gills pale and sick-looking. □ *Jim looked green around the gills after our ride down the twisty mountain road.* □ *Are you OK? You're a little green around the gills.*

greenback a piece of paper money. (Only the back side of a U.S. bill is printed completely in green.) □ *Mary's wallet was full of greenbacks.* □ *He won a big stack of greenbacks at the poker table.*

greenhorn an ignorant, inexperienced person. (See also *green; pea-green.*) □ *That cowboy's a greenhorn. He can't even rope a calf.* □ *I get to train all the greenhorns, teach them how to pitch a tent and lay a fire.*

greens leafy vegetables, usually boiled. □ *We had turnip greens and fried chicken for dinner.* □ *Eat your greens. They're full of vitamins.*

griddle cake a pancake. (See also *flapjack.*) □ *The restaurant serves griddle cakes just like Grandma used to make.* □ *I could smell the griddle cakes frying all the way upstairs.*

grin like a barrel of possum heads AND **grin like a mule eating briars** to grin very wide. □ *She came in the door, grinning like a barrel of possum heads.* □ *He's got something up his sleeve. He's been grinning like a mule eating briars.*

grin like a mule eating briars See *grin like a barrel of possum heads.*

gringo someone of European ancestry. (Insulting or jocular. Probably from the Spanish word for *Greek*, here meaning foreigner.) □ *"What do you want here, gringo?" the police officer asked.* □ WAITER: *The customer sent these enchiladas back. He said they're too spicy.* COOK: *Stupid gringo! He doesn't know good cooking when he tastes it.*

groundnut a peanut. (See also *pinder.*) □ *Jane makes a nice stew with chicken and groundnuts.* □ *We lived on groundnuts that winter.*

grow like Topsy to grow very rapidly. (*Topsy* is a character in Harriet Beecher Stowe's novel, *Uncle Tom's Cabin.*) □ *I declare, those children are growing like Topsy.* □ *The squash vines are growing like Topsy. We'll have a right smart crop of squashes this year.*

grub food. □ *I'll cook us up some grub.* □ *We'll have to carry our own grub on the trail.*

grub-slinger a cook. □ *They got a pretty good grub-slinger at Harrison's ranch.* □ *The grub-slinger burned the damn biscuits again. I say we kill him.*

grubstake the amount of money necessary to start an undertaking. □ *Curly's trying to raise a grubstake to go out prospecting in the Rockies.* □ *I'll sell the house and use the money as a grubstake to start my own business.*

guber See *goober.*

guff nonsense; bragging. □ *He gave me a lot of guff about what an important person he was.* □ *I never heard such guff in all my life!*

gulch a ravine or deep riverbed. □ *We rode down to the bottom of the gulch so we couldn't be seen.* □ *In the wet season, that dry gulch is a rushing river.*

gully washer a heavy rain. (See also *fence-lifter; goose-drownder.*) □ *The rain came down in sheets. It was the biggest gully washer* *we'd had all year.* □ *All the houses in the bottom got flooded in that gully washer.*

gumbo a spicy stew usually including tomatoes, okra, seafood, and peppers. □ *Dish me up some of that gumbo.* □ *Mary makes the best gumbo in Louisiana.*

gumption spirit; energy. □ *Jane will do well. She's got lots of smarts and plenty of gumption.* □ *It took a lot of gumption to stand up to your boss like that.*

gun-shy **1.** afraid of guns and shooting. □ *I've been gun-shy since my hunting accident.* □ *When he came home from the war, Bill was gun-shy.* **2.** afraid of something that has caused pain or trouble in the past. □ *Jane doesn't date anymore. She's been gun-shy ever since Joe rejected her.* □ *Jim used to give speeches all the time, but he got gun-shy after the crowd booed him at the Fourth of July last year.*

gunning for someone looking for and intending to shoot or punish someone. □ *The posse was gunning for the cattle thief.* □ *Dad's gunning for Billy. He found out Billy was the one who broke his hacksaw.*

gunny sack a sack made of burlap. (See also *croker sack.*) □ *She carried the chickens to market in a gunny sack.* □ *I made curtains out of an old gunny sack.*

gunslinger someone who often shoots people. □ *Billy the Kid was a notorious gunslinger in the old West.* □ *The two gunslingers met at high noon to shoot it out.*

gussied up dressed up fancy. □ *All the girls got gussied up for the dance, but the guys wore their regular clothes.* □ *Mary really got gussied up. She even curled her hair.*

H

hacienda **1.** a large ranch. (Spanish.) □ *Alvarez owns a big hacienda north of here.* □ *They've got thirty men working on that hacienda.* **2.** a large ranch house. (Spanish.) □ *It's a beautiful old house. Used to be the hacienda on this estate.* □ *They turned the old adobe hacienda into a hotel.*

hack someone to annoy someone; to embarrass someone. □ *Ma is always hacking me by showing my baby pictures to my friends.* □ *It really hacks me when you drum your fingers like that.*

(had) best do something ought to do something, had better do something. (See also *better had (do something)*.) □ *Mary had best learn to mind her manners.* □ *You best listen to what I say.*

hadn't oughta should not have. □ *You hadn't oughta teased me like that.* □ *I know I hadn't oughta stolen that candy.*

hail from somewhere to come from somewhere. □ *Where do you all hail from?* □ *I hail from Memphis, Tennessee.*

haint See *ha'nt.*

hair and hide(, horns and tallow) every last thing; every part. □ *They took everything Mary had, hair and hide, horns and tallow.* □ *Joe never threw anything away. He found a use for everything, hair and hide.*

hair of the dog (that bit you) a small alcoholic drink taken to cure a hangover. □ TOM: *Sure wish I hadn't had all that to drink last* *night. My head hurts like fury today.* MARY: *Here. Drink this. The hair of the dog that bit you.* □ *I was seeing double when I woke up, so I stumbled to the liquor cabinet for a little hair of the dog.*

half-baked not well thought-out; incomplete. □ *Joe's got some half-baked idea about turning the old warehouse into a restaurant.* □ *Mary's always trying to sell us some half-baked scheme for making money.*

half-breed **1.** someone of racially mixed parentage, usually Amerindian and European descent. (Originally disparaging, now offensive and derogatory.) □ *Who is that half-breed who just came into the bar?* □ *The young half-breed by the fence is looking for work.* **2.** of racially mixed parentage, usually Amerindian and European descent. (Originally disparaging, now offensive and derogatory.) □ *Who is that half-breed cowboy who just came into the bar?* □ *Joe married a squaw and had a bunch of half-breed kids.*

half the time sometimes. □ *I like that TV show, but half the time I forget to watch it when it's on.* □ *She says she's my friend, but she can't remember my name, half the time.*

hammer and tongs very energetically; animatedly. □ *They were still arguing when I left. Going at it hammer and tongs, as a matter of fact.* □ *He was whalin' on that guitar hammer and tongs.*

hand over fist in large quantities. (Often used in the expression *to make money hand over fist.*) □ *The store made money hand over fist the first year, then went bust the second.* □ *She makes money hand over fist, raising and selling them purebred pups.*

handle a name or nickname. (This old expression reappeared in the citizens band radio slang of the 1970s.) □ *I'm the Coca-Cola Kid. What's your handle?* □ *His handle was Roadrunner, and he hailed from Tennessee.*

hangin' judge a judge who often sentences criminals to death. □ *I didn't have much chance of getting a light sentence. Judge Jones was a well-known hangin' judge.* □ *The hangin' judge was elected because he promised to get criminals off the streets.*

hanker after someone or something to want someone or something very much. ☐ *She's been hankering after that country music album for I don't know how long.* ☐ *He hankers after Sally something awful.*

hankering a desire. ☐ *She had a strange hankering for kiwi fruit.* ☐ *I've got a hankering for a nice hot bowl of greens.*

ha'nt AND **haint** a ghost. (Something that *haunts*.) ☐ *They say there's a ha'nt in the top story of the old courthouse.* ☐ *I saw a haint when I was walking home through the slough.*

happy hunting ground heaven; the afterlife. (Originally used to describe the afterlife for American Indians.) ☐ *The two Indians breathed their last and headed for the happy hunting ground.* ☐ *My old hound dog died and went to the happy hunting ground.*

hard-favored ugly. ☐ *It's too bad she's so hard-favored. She'd make some lucky man a good wife, otherwise.* ☐ *He was hard-favored, but he had a good heart.*

hard put having a difficult time. ☐ *I was hard put to know how to feed six people on two cups of cornmeal and a handful of greens.* ☐ *The teacher was hard put to answer the curious student's questions.*

hard sledding AND **tough sledding** a very difficult time. ☐ *They had some hard sledding when they were first married.* ☐ *It was tough sledding for sure when our crops failed that year.*

hard tail a mule. (See also *shavetail*.) ☐ *The prospector's best friend was Jenny, a two-year-old hard tail.* ☐ *We don't have any horses, just one old hard tail.*

harder than the back of God's head very hard. ☐ *The soil was harder than the back of God's head. We had a hard time digging it.* ☐ *The wood was solid and dense and harder than the back of God's head.*

hardshell Baptist a very conservative Baptist. ☐ *My daddy's a hardshell Baptist and don't allow me to wear no short skirts or* *lipstick.* □ *I used to listen to the Sunday sermon on the radio, but not since they got this hardshell Baptist preacher.*

hardtack hard, dry bread, usually in the form of biscuits. □ *We took hardtack with us as an emergency supply.* □ *That winter, we lived on hardtack and beans.*

hardware a firearm. □ *What kind of hardware you carryin'?* □ *That old Colt is a pretty impressive piece of hardware.*

has more than one string to his fiddle has many talents. □ *Joe has more than one string to his fiddle. He's a good painter, and he also cooks and fixes cars.* □ *This job involves a lot of different duties. We'll need to hire someone who has more than one string to his fiddle.*

has the world by the tail (with a downhill drag) has destiny under control. □ *The young businessman had the world by the tail with a downhill drag. He had made a million dollars before he was twenty-five.* □ *She's got the world by the tail now, but her fame won't last forever.*

hasty pudding corn pudding. □ *We always have hasty pudding on Thanksgiving day.* □ *Maw boiled up some hasty pudding and fed us early and sent us to bed.*

hate someone or something like sin to hate someone or something a great deal. □ *She won't eat brussels sprouts. She hates 'em like sin.* □ *I don't want that man anywhere near me. I hate him like sin.*

have a bad case of the simples to be stupid. □ *That boy has a bad case of the simples. He don't understand anything.* □ *She acts smart enough on the playground, but get her in the classroom and she has a bad case of the simples.*

have a bear by the tail to have a very difficult problem to solve; to be in a dilemma. □ *Mary volunteered to take on that big project at work, and now she has a bear by the tail.* □ *Joe sure has a bear by the tail. How's he going to get the money to pay his gambling debts without telling his wife how he lost the money?*

have a bone to pick with someone to have something to argue about with someone. (See also *have a chicken to pick with someone.*) □ *Jim says he has a bone to pick with me about the way I spoke to his girlfriend.* □ *She's a quarrelsome woman. Always has a bone to pick with someone.*

have a burr under one's saddle to be irritated by something. □ *Joe has a burr under his saddle because Jane's going out with Bill tonight.* □ *Mary must have a burr under her saddle. She's been snapping at me all day.*

have a chicken to pick with someone to have something to argue about with someone. (See also *have a bone to pick with someone.*) □ *I've got a chicken to pick with you. Why did you pull all my washing off the clothesline?* □ *I've got a chicken to pick with Bill on the subject of where he parks his car.*

have a conniption (fit) to become violently upset. □ *Ma about had a conniption fit when she saw the dent I put in the car.* □ *Don't have a conniption just because I had a few drinks.*

have a corncob up one's ass AND **have a poker up one's ass** **1.** to be very stiff. (Use with caution.) □ *How come you're acting so high and mighty with me? Do you have a corncob up your ass?* □ *He was a terrible actor, stiff and wooden. He looked like he had a poker up his ass.* **2.** to be very touchy or irritable. □ *Wow! Old Mr. Webster really has a corncob up his ass this morning. Watch out!* □ *Tom has a poker up his ass and he's looking for you. Better make yourself scarce.*

have a (good) mind to do something have an inclination to do something. □ *I have a good mind to tell him just what I think of him.* □ *She had a mind to go to college, but her folks talked her out of it.*

have a hen on the nest to have work in progress. □ *Joe may not have a 9-to-5 job right now, but he's got plenty of hens on the nest and will be making some money for sure.* □ JANE: *Are you working on anything right now?* TOM: *Well, I've got a hen on the nest, yes.*

have a kick to it to have a strong flavor; to have a high alcohol content. □ *I like that salsa. It has a kick to it.* □ *Tom's moonshine sure has a kick to it—don't drink too much of it, now!*

have a leg up on someone else to have an advantage over someone; to have an edge on someone. (See also *give someone a leg up*.) □ *Jed had a leg up on Tom and managed to get first prize.* □ *It's not fair. Because he is the judge's kid, he has a leg up on the rest of us.*

have a mind as sharp as a steel trap to be very intelligent. (See also *have a mind like a (steel) trap*.) □ *She's a smart kid. Has a mind as sharp as a steel trap.* □ *They say the professor has a mind as sharp as a steel trap, but then why can't he figure out which bus to take in the morning?*

have a mind like a (steel) trap to be intelligent. (See also *have a mind as sharp as a steel trap*. Sometimes used ironically, as in the second example.) □ *She has a mind like a steel trap; she can figure out anything.* □ *I had to spend half an hour explaining to Jim how to turn the radio on. He's got a mind like a trap.*

have a poker up one's ass See *have a corncob up one's ass*.

have a price on one's head to have a reward offered for one's capture. □ *Ever since Slim killed a man, he's had a price on his head.* □ *She had gone from a respected citizen to an infamous bandit with a price on her head.*

have a sticky rope to steal cattle habitually. (Patterned on *have sticky fingers*.) □ TOM: *How'd Jim get all them cattle?* BILL: *He has a sticky rope.* □ *Too many of my cattle have been disappearing. Somebody around here must have a sticky rope.*

have a yellow streak down one's back to be cowardly. (See also *yellow-bellied*.) □ *He's got a yellow streak down his back. He runs away from fights.* □ *She had a yellow streak down her back when it came to challenging her mother-in-law.*

have ants in one's pants to be very restless and impatient. □ *Jimmy had ants in his pants all morning, and constantly demanded,*

"When are we gonna go?" □ *She was squirming around like she had ants in her pants.*

have been through the mill to have been through difficult times. □ *You could tell by the look on his face that he'd been through the mill.* □ *What with their barn burning down and the hail destroying all their crops, that family has been through the mill.*

have callouses from patting one's own back AND **break one's arm patting oneself on the back** to be a braggart. □ *If you haven't heard about Bill's latest achievement, he'd be glad to tell you. He has callouses from patting his own back.* □ JANE: *I did a really wonderful job, if I do say so myself.* TOM: *If you're not careful, you'll break your arm patting yourself on the back.*

have cause to do something to have a justifiable reason to do something. □ *Do you have cause to think that Mary took your money?* □ *He had no cause to yell at me like that.*

have eight acres of Hell in oneself to be very determined. (Usually used to describe women.) □ *Don't ever get in Mary's way. She's got eight acres of Hell in her.* □ *When they tried to take Jane's children from her, they discovered she had eight acres of Hell in her.*

have hell to pay See *have the devil to pay (and no pitch hot).*

have just one oar in the water to not be thinking clearly. □ *Tom has some crazy plan for opening his own restaurant. If you ask me, he has just one oar in the water.* □ *She has just one oar in the water if she thinks Bill is going to pay any attention to her.*

have kittens to get extremely upset. □ *My mother pretty near had kittens when she found out I got fired.* □ *Calm down. Don't have kittens.*

have more luck than sense to be lucky but not intelligent. □ *Jane went driving out into Death Valley without any water. She survived —she has more luck than sense.* □ TOM: *I like to steal statues out of people's lawns. Nobody's ever caught me.* MARY: *You have more luck than sense.*

have no truck with something to have nothing to do with something. □ *After the way Mary treated me, I'll have no truck with her.* □ *We only show good, wholesome movies at this theater. We have no truck with most of that Hollywood trash.*

have one's ass in a sling to be severely punished. (Use with caution. See also *put someone's ass in a sling.*) □ *If I don't get this finished on time, I'll have my ass in a sling.* □ *If I ever catch that no-good thief, I'll put his ass in a sling.*

have one's druthers See *have one's rathers.*

have one's ears pinned back to receive a severe scolding. (See also *pin someone's ears back.*) □ *Jimmy went to the principal's office and had his ears pinned back.* □ *When Jane asked if she could borrow the car, she got her ears pinned back instead.*

have one's lady's time to have one's menstrual period. (See also *Grandma's come; visit from Flo; monthlies; bad time (of the month).*) □ *Mary never slowed down one bit when she was having her lady's time.* □ *She gets a little snippy when she's having her lady's time.*

have one's nose out of joint to have one's feelings hurt; to feel offended. □ *Mary's got her nose out of joint because we didn't ask her to the party.* □ *Joe had his nose out of joint because I forgot his birthday.*

have one's rathers AND **have one's druthers** to have what one prefers; to have one's way. □ *If I had my rathers, we'd go out every Friday night.* □ *I suspicion that if Joe had his druthers, he'd be taking Mary to the dance instead of Jill.*

have one's say See *speak one's piece.*

have oneself something to get, have, or take something. □ *I'll have myself some of that coconut cream pie, if you don't mind.* □ *You just go and have yourself a nice, long nap.*

have someone or something in one's sights to have one's gun aimed at someone or something. □ *The sniper had the soldier in his sights.* □ *I had the deer in my sights. I fired.*

have someone's hide to punish someone severely. (See also *take it out of someone's hide.*) □ *The sheriff swore he'd have the outlaw's hide.* □ *You lousy no-good so-and-so! I'll have your hide!*

have something hung up and salted to know everything about something. (Often used ironically, as in the second example.) □ *The historian sure had Louisiana history hung up and salted.* □ *Jim's sixteen years old, and he thinks he has the opposite sex hung up and salted.*

have sticky fingers to steal habitually. (See also *have a sticky rope.*) □ *I soon found that the store clerk I hired had sticky fingers.* □ *Jim must have sticky fingers. He sure didn't get all that money working as a waiter.*

have the devil to pay (and no pitch hot) AND **have hell to pay** to have to suffer terrible consequences. □ *We're so far in debt that if our crops fail this year, we'll have the devil to pay and no pitch hot.* □ *If the mayor doesn't fulfill her campaign promises, she'll have the devil to pay.*

have the mullygrubs to feel depressed. □ *She had the mullygrubs because her husband was out of town.* □ *Joe had the mullygrubs. We tried to cheer him up.*

have the nerve of a government mule to be overly bold. □ *Joe has the nerve of a government mule! He walked right up and asked me if I would leave my husband and marry him!* □ *She'll do fine in the business world. She's smart and experienced and has the nerve of a government mule.*

hay-burner a horse. (Slang.) □ *Why Sally likes to ride around on them pokey old hay-burners instead of riding in a car, I'll never know.* □ *Blaze was sure a good hay-burner, did good work for me every day of his life.*

hayseed an ignorant country person. (Mildly derogatory. See also *redneck; yahoo.*) □ *The teacher thought he was more cultured than the hayseeds he had to teach.* □ *Don't wear those overalls. They make you look like a hayseed.*

hayshant See *Hessian.*

He wears a ten-dollar hat on a five-cent head. He is stupid but rich. □ *He got the job because he's the boss's son, not because he's smart. He wears a ten-dollar hat on a five-cent head.* □ *He was a frivolous young man who wore a ten-dollar hat on a five-cent head.*

head cheese See *souse meat.*

head for tall timber to flee. □ *When we heard Pa's angry bellow, we headed for tall timber.* □ *The bank robbers headed for tall timber with their loot.*

head for the hills to flee for high ground, as if a dam had burst. (Said in response to some general threat. Usually jocular.) □ *Here comes the sheriff. Head for the hills!* □ *School's out for the year! Head for the hills!*

heap of something a great deal of something. (Usually with the indefinite article *a*.) □ *Tom's got a heap of money, but no one to spend it on.* □ *A teacher has to have a heap of patience as well as a lot of smarts.*

heap sight a lot; very much. □ *This one is a heap sight better than that one.* □ *You got a heap sight more taters than I did.*

hear tell (as) "I heard . . ." □ *I heard tell that Sam Harris is in town. Is it true?* □ *I hear tell as Mary's breaking up with Bill, but I can't say as I believe it.*

heave (Jonah) to vomit. (As if the biblical Jonah were being vomited up by the huge fish that swallowed him. See also *heaves.*) □ *Something I ate made me heave Jonah all night.* □ *Are you sick? Do you need to heave?*

heave to one's feet to stand up. □ *The whole audience heaved to their feet and applauded.* □ *He heaved to his feet to say hello.*

Heavens to Betsy! "My goodness!" (A mild oath.) □ *Heavens to Betsy! What was that noise?* □ *Heavens to Betsy! It's good to hear your voice!*

heaves persistent vomiting. (See also *heave (Jonah).*) □ *Riding down that twisty mountain road gave me the heaves.* □ *He's really sick. He had the heaves all day.*

heist someone or something (up) to lift someone or something. □ *See if you can heist that box onto the top shelf.* □ *Dad heisted me up so I could see over the fence.* Ⓣ *John groaned and heisted up the bale of hay.*

hell-bent for election AND **hell (-bent) for leather** very fast. □ *The report's due tomorrow, so she's typing away at it hell-bent for election.* □ *They speeded down the highway hell for leather.*

hell (-bent) for leather See *hell-bent for election.*

hell on a holiday a big commotion. □ *It was hell on a holiday outside the stadium when the team won the big game.* □ *What's going on down on Main Street? Sounds like hell on a holiday!*

hellacious horrible; severe. □ *His pa gave him a hellacious beating for breaking his brother's tooth.* □ *This has been one hellacious day.*

Hellfire and damnation! "Damn it!" (An oath used to express anger or irritation.) □ *Hellfire and damnation! Turn that radio down!* □ *Hellfire and damnation! This is the second time our picnic's been rained out.*

Hell's bells! "Damn!" (A mild oath, used to express irritation.) □ *Hell's bells! Why can't you ever get here on time?* □ *Hell's bells! That's the second glass I broke today.*

hemp fever a hanging. □ TOM: *How did that famous horse thief die?* MARY: *Hemp fever.* □ *When the ranchers caught up with him, the cattle rustler caught a bad case of hemp fever.*

hen fruit eggs. □ *I had hen fruit and bacon for breakfast.* □ *There's a mess of hen fruit in the icebox.*

hen party a party attended by only women or girls. □ *When our husbands are out of town, we always get together for a little hen party.* □ *No men invited. This is strictly a hen party.*

hen-pecked ruled and abused by a woman, usually the victim's wife. □ *Poor Joe. He's a real hen-pecked husband.* □ *You can tell by the way he says "Yes, dear," that he's hen-pecked.*

hep someone to help someone. □ *Could you hep me with this heavy sack?* □ *She needs somebody to hep her up the stairs.*

her See *she.*

Here's your hat, what's your hurry? "It is time for you to go." (Jocular.) □ *I hate to rush you out the door, but here's your hat, what's your hurry?* □ JANE: *I suppose I'd better be on my way.* CHARLIE: *Here's your hat, what's your hurry?*

hern hers. (See also *hisn; theirn; ourn.*) □ *It's hern. She can do with it what she likes.* □ *My heart is hern forever.*

Hessian AND **hayshant** an unruly child. (*Hessian* refers to mercenary soldiers from Hesse, used by Britain during the Revolutionary War.) □ *My grandchildren came to visit. They were a bunch of Hessians.* □ *Hold on there, you hayshant! Wash them hands before you come to the table.*

het up agitated. (From *heated up.*) □ *Now, Sarah, don't get all het up.* □ *Jed is het up about something. Don't rightly know what.*

Hey. Hello. (Chiefy Southern. Now widespread in the U.S. See also *Howdy!; Howdy-do!*) □ *Hey, Mr. Johnson! How are you today?* □ TOM: *Hey.* BILL: *Hey. How ya doin'?*

hifalutin' fancy and pretentious. □ *Jim thinks I'm stupid just 'cause I don't understand all them hifalutin' words he uses.* □ *Mary wants lots of hifalutin' junk like wine coolers and crystal candy dishes.*

high-and-mighty pretentious. □ *She's a snob, real high-and-mighty.* □ *Nobody likes to be around him because he acts so high-and-mighty.*

high lonesome an episode of extreme drunkenness. □ *She said she wouldn't marry him, so he went off on a high lonesome.* □ *The day she got the job, she went on a high lonesome you'd have to see to believe.*

high-powered fancy; impressive. □ *He was bragging about his high-powered education.* □ *She has all kinds of high-powered friends in town.*

high-tail it to leave quickly; to go quickly. □ *When they saw the police comin', they high-tailed it out of there.* □ *If you hear your ma calling, you'd better high-tail it on home.*

high time about the right time for something. □ *It's high time we were leaving.* □ *It's high time you started thinking about saving for your old age.*

high-toned pretentious; grand. □ *The preacher gave a high-toned speech about what a fine citizen Uncle Fred had been.* □ *We made fun of the radio announcer's high-toned way of talking.*

hike one's tail to leave. □ *I could see they wanted to be alone, so I decided to hike my tail.* □ *Hike your tail on out of here, you hear?*

hind end the rump of someone or some creature. □ *If you say that again, I'll swat you right across the hind end.* □ *The mule slipped and came down right on her hind end.*

hind end of creation a very remote place. □ *I wish I lived in the city. I'm tired of living here in the hind end of creation.* □ *Joe moved out to a little shack at the hind end of creation.*

hindside first backwards. □ *You've got your shirt on hindside first.* □ *The horse came out of the stable hindside first.*

hire something done to hire someone to do something for you. □ *When I was in a wheelchair after my surgery, I couldn't cut the grass myself. I had to hire it done.* □ MARY: *Did you make these curtains?* JANE: *No, I hired it done.*

hisn his. (See also *hern; theirn; ourn.*) □ *Joe's willing to fight for what's hisn.* □ *This piece of cake is yourn, and that one's hisn.*

hisse(l)f himself. □ *He wants to keep the best foal for hisself.* □ *He did it hissef.*

hissy (fit) a tantrum. (Often with *throw*. Probably refers to an angry, hissing cat.) □ *Jane practically has a hissy fit every time she gets a run in her nylons.* □ *The boss is really mad today. It's just one hissy fit after another.*

hit it. (Usually at the beginning of a sentence or a clause.) □ *Hit don't matter.* □ *Hit really don't matter a-tall.*

hit pay dirt to get great riches. □ *After years of poverty, the writer hit pay dirt with his third novel.* □ *Jane's doing well. She really hit pay dirt with her new business.*

hit the hay to go to bed. □ *It's getting late. I'd better hit the hay.* □ *We didn't hit the hay till after midnight.*

hit the trail to leave; to go. □ *It's time for us to hit the trail.* □ *What time do you want to hit the trail tomorrow morning?*

hitched married. □ *Jim and Jane are gonna get hitched.* □ *They've been hitched for three years now.*

hits it's. □ *Hits about time to go home.* □ *Hits later than you think.*

hoe cake a cake of corn bread. (Said to be a basic bread that could be baked on the side of a hoe. See also *johnny cake.*) □ *The* *campers baked some hoe cakes in the skillet.* □ *If you want a snack, there's some cold hoe cake in the cupboard.*

hoe down a community dance with country music, particularly fiddle music. □ *Will you go to the hoe down with me tomorrow night, Jed?* □ *There's going to be a hoe down Saturday night, down in the hollow.*

hoe one's own row to mind one's own business. (See also *chew one's own tobacco.*) □ TOM: *You're cutting up those carrots awful small.* JANE: *Hoe your own row!* □ *He didn't get involved in other people's fights. He just hoed his own row.*

hog-killin' weather cold autumn weather. (The time of year that hogs were slaughtered.) □ *It was hog-killin' weather. Winter would be coming soon.* □ *The leaves were falling. It was hog-killin' weather.*

hog-leg a pistol. □ *He had a hog-leg in his belt.* □ *He oiled up his hog-leg.*

hog wild wild; out of control. □ *I went hog wild at the sale and bought six new pairs of shoes.* □ *There were a dozen different desserts at the picnic. A person who liked sweets could go hog wild.*

hogan a Navajo Indian round house. □ *He built his hogan with the door facing east.* □ *I saw a group of hogans in the distance.*

hogtie to tie an animal's legs together so that it cannot move; to restrain someone or something. □ *We hogtied the calves before we branded them.* □ *Jim threatened to hogtie his kids if they didn't settle down.*

hogwash nonsense. □ TOM: *I heard on the radio that the world is going to end next Thursday.* MARY: *That's hogwash, and you know it.* □ JANE: *This ad says you can lose thirty pounds in a week without dieting.* TOM: *Hogwash.*

hold oneself too high to be overly proud. □ *He holds himself too high to socialize with country folks like us.* □ *Although she was rich and successful, she didn't hold herself too high.*

hold with something to agree with something. □ *I don't hold with these newfangled ideas of child-raising.* □ *Bill doesn't hold with all his wife's political views.*

Hold your horses! AND **Hold your tater!** "Wait." □ TOM: *Let's go! Let's go!* MARY: *Hold your horses.* □ *Hold your tater, now. Where did you say you was going?*

Hold your tater! See *Hold your horses!*

hole up (somewhere) **1.** to take shelter somewhere. □ *During the blizzard, we holed up in a lean-to made of branches.* □ *Looks like bad weather coming. We'd better find a place to hole up.* **2.** to hide somewhere. □ *The police are looking for me. I need somewhere to hole up.* □ *The outlaw holed up in a cave.*

holler **1.** to yell. □ *The little boy hollered when he stubbed his toe.* □ *What are you hollerin' for?* **2.** a yell. □ *He let out a holler that could have been heard in the next county.* □ *Give a holler if you need anything.* **3.** a hollow; an area of lowlands; a valley. □ *Jim's house is down in the holler.* □ *The holler flooded out in the last big rain.*

holler uncle AND **cry uncle; say uncle** to admit defeat. (See also *cry calf rope.*) □ *Joe kept pounding on Jim, trying to get him to holler uncle.* □ *He twisted my arm until I cried uncle.* □ *I won't let you up till you say uncle.*

holy roller a member of a religious sect with a frenzied, energetic style of worship. (Somewhat derogatory.) □ *We're not holy rollers. We're just Baptists.* □ *On Sunday mornings, the holy rollers carry on so you can hear them for blocks around.*

hombre a man. (Spanish. Sometimes a term of address, as in the second example.) □ *Don't mess with that hombre. He'd shoot you as soon as look at you.* □ *What can I do for you, hombre?*

(home) folks one's family. □ *It sure is good to see the home folks again.* □ *Sally went to visit her folks.*

home fries AND **cottage fries** potatoes cut in slices and fried. □ *The restaurant serves chicken and home fries.* □ *Nobody makes cottage fries like my Aunt Louise.*

homebody someone who likes to stay at home. □ *I try to get Jane to come out and do things with me, but she's such a homebody!* □ *I'm a homebody. I don't like to travel.*

homegrown **1.** grown in one's garden at home. □ *Homegrown tomatoes are a hundred times better than what you find in a store.* □ *Try some of our homegrown sweet corn.* **2.** homelike; local. □ *I always liked his homegrown humor.* □ *Jed drank nothing but homegrown whisky that he bought from his cousin.*

homely enough to stop a clock ugly. □ *She's a sweet girl, but homely enough to stop a clock.* □ *No one asks Mary out, and no wonder. She's homely enough to stop a clock.*

(hominy) grits coarsely ground corn, usually boiled and served as a breakfast or side dish. □ *For dinner, Jane served us fried catfish and hominy grits.* □ *Tom likes grits for breakfast.*

hone for someone or something to long for someone or something. □ TOM: *What's wrong with Jane?* MARY: *She's honing for her sweetheart.* □ *Jimmy was honing for the red bicycle in the toy store window.*

honeychile dear; sweetheart. (An endearment.) □ *Come on over here, honeychile. Lord, how you've grown!* □ *Don't worry, honeychile. I'll take care of everything for you.*

honin' a desire; a longing. □ *It's beautiful here, but I feel a honin' for home.* □ *I had a honin' to see your face again.*

hooch hard liquor. □ *I got a bottle of hooch out in the toolshed.* □ *We brew our own hooch down in the holler.*

hoof it to walk. □ *If nobody gives us a ride, we'll have to hoof it.* □ *She hoofed it home from the dance in her high-heeled shoes.*

hook-a-hendum See *thingamajig.*

hoosegow a jail. (From Mexican Spanish *jusgado.*) □ *The sheriff put the outlaw in the hoosegow.* □ *I had to spend ninety days in the hoosegow.*

Hoosier **1.** someone from Indiana. □ *My dad's a Hoosier.* □ TOM: *Indiana's a wonderful place.* JANE: *Spoken like a true Hoosier.* **2.** an ignorant rural person. (Derogatory. Usually not capitalized.) □ *We don't want no hoosiers in this bar.* □ *The last tenants were a bunch of hoosiers who really wrecked the place.*

hootenanny a party at which people sing and make music together. □ *All my cousins play instruments, and most of us sing, so every family reunion turns into a hootenanny.* □ *There's a hootenanny every Friday night in the church basement.*

hootentrankis See *thingamajig.*

hoppergrass a grasshopper. (See also *peckerwood.*) □ *There's a little hoppergrass sitting on your knee.* □ *The hoppergrasses ate up most of our vegetables last year.*

hoppin' John a dish made of rice, beans, bacon, and spices. □ *What does she put in her hoppin' John to make it so tasty?* □ *Every good Carolina cook knows how to make hoppin' John.*

hopping mad very angry. □ *Joe got hopping mad when the sales clerk was rude to him.* □ *The student's practical jokes made the teacher hopping mad.*

hoppytoad See *hoptoad.*

hoptoad AND **hoppytoad** a toad. □ *Don't step on that little hoppytoad!* □ *There is a hoptoad in the sink!*

horn in (on something) to intrude (on something). □ *I wish we could have just one conversation without Charlie horning in.* □ *Bill tried to horn in on our card game.*

hornswoggle to cheat or fool someone. □ *That car dealer hornswoggled me into buying this no-good piece of trash.* □ *The customers were mad when they found out they'd been hornswoggled.*

horse opera AND **hoss opry** a Western movie. □ *We went to see that latest hoss opry last night.* □ *There's nothing on television but sex, violence, and a horse opera.*

horse sense common sense; knowledge of the way the world works. □ *Just use a little horse sense, and you'll be able to tell when someone's trying to cheat you.* □ *He's not an educated man, but he's got plenty of horse sense.*

horsefeathers nonsense. □ *The promises they make in that TV ad are pure horsefeathers.* □ MARY: *I heard you can cure arthritis by wearing a copper bracelet.* JANE: *Horsefeathers! That's just an old wives' tale.*

horseflesh **1.** the horse species. □ *Jane is a good judge of horseflesh. She can tell you if that mare's worth the price.* □ *The blacksmith is selling some horseflesh he got from the sheriff.* **2.** a horse. □ *That little gelding is a nice piece of horseflesh.* □ *When I get me a hunk of horseflesh, I will go out riding with you.*

horsewhip to whip someone with a heavy whip made to whip horses. □ *Joe oughta be horsewhipped for the way he treated Sally.* □ *Bill horsewhipped the man who had cheated him.*

hoss **1.** a horse. □ *Old Paint's a good old hoss.* □ *Who owns that bay hoss with the white stockings?* **2.** a person; a buddy. (A term of address.) □ *Are you coming with us, hoss?* □ *Calm down, there, hoss.*

hoss opry See *horse opera*.

Hot damn! AND **Hot (diggety) dog!** "Wow!"; "Hooray!" (An exclamation of surprise and delight.) □ *Hot damn! I just won a vacation trip to Florida!* □ *Hot diggety dog! Mary said she'd go out with me!*

Hot (diggety) dog! See *Hot damn!*

hot enough to burn a polar bear's butt very hot. (Used to describe weather.) □ *Every day in August was hot enough to burn a polar bear's butt.* □ *Even in October, it was hot enough to burn a polar bear's butt.*

hot-foot it (off to) somewhere to go somewhere as fast as possible. □ *I've got to hot-foot it off to school.* □ *When they heard the police sirens, the thieves hot-footed it to their hideout.* □ *When she saw that dog coming, the cat hot-footed it off to the yard.*

house moss See *curly dirt.*

How bout them apples? "What do you think of that?" (Often used to express admiration, as in the first example.) □ TOM: *I got first prize!* MARY: *Well! How bout them apples?* □ *Joe got a job as a newspaper reporter. How bout them apples?*

Howdy! "Hello!" (See also *Hey.; Howdy-do!*) □ *Howdy! Long time no see!* □ JANE: *Howdy!* MARY: *Hi! How are you?*

howdy and a half a short distance. (See also *two whoops and a holler; tater chunk.*) □ TOM: *Is it far to the dime store?* JANE: *Just a howdy and a half.* □ *Her house was a howdy and a half from the place where I grew up.*

Howdy-do! "Hello, how are you?" (See also *Howdy!; Hey.*) □ *Joe tipped his hat and said, "Howdy-do!"* □ *Howdy-do! Good to see you!*

howsomever however. □ *I like Mary. Howsomever, I don't think she's the best person for the job.* □ *I know the dishwasher is a good buy, howsomever, we just don't have the money.*

humdinger an outstanding person or thing. (See also *rip snorter.*) □ *That show sure was a humdinger!* □ *Jim baked a humdinger of a pecan pie.*

hunker down to squat down. □ *The cat hunkered down, ready to pounce.* □ *I hunkered down behind the car, hoping no one would see me.*

hunker down to something to apply oneself to something, to get started working at something. □ *I hunkered down to my chores, hoping to get them done before noon.* □ *If you want to get a good grade on that report, you'd better hunker down to it.*

hunkydory very good; fine. □ TOM: *How's things?* CHARLIE: *Oh, everything's hunkydory.* □ *If you can come over at five, that'll be hunkydory.*

hurtin' for something in need of something. □ *I went to fetch a bottle of coke. My sick child was hurtin' for it.* □ *Jim was hurting for a new set of tools.*

hurty painful. □ *Jimmy had a hurty finger and put it on ice until it get better.* □ *My back is sort of hurty. Must be my rhumatiz.*

hush puppies small balls of fried cornmeal dough. (Perhaps something that would be tossed to a dog to quiet it.) □ *Would you like hush puppies or home fries with that?* □ *Mary fried up some hush puppies.*

I

I could knock you for a row of brick houses. I feel like hitting you very hard. □ *When Dad saw that we broke the window, he said, "I could knock you for a row of brick houses."* □ *I could knock you for a row of brick houses, but I'm going to let you go —this time.*

I declare (to goodness)! "What a surprise!" (See also *I swan!*) □ *I declare to goodness! You certainly have grown since I saw you.* □ TOM: *Jim and Sally are going to get married.* MARY: *Well, I declare!*

I didn't go to do it! "I did not mean to do it." □ *I'm sorry if I hurt your feelings. I didn't go to do it!* □ MOTHER: *Did you dirty up my clean carpet?* CHILD: *I didn't go to do it!*

I do believe. "I think." □ *Jim's in love with that gal, I do believe.* □ *Jane's store will do well, I do believe.*

I don't mind telling you. "I want you to know." □ TOM: *You have a beautiful garden.* MARY: *Thank you. But I don't mind telling you, it's an awful lot of work.* □ *I don't mind telling you, I was as pleased as Punch when my daughter won the race.*

I don't rightly know. "I do not know." □ TOM: *When will Joe be getting back?* CHARLIE: *I don't rightly know.* □ JANE: *What's the difference between a first cousin and a first cousin once removed?* MARY: *I don't rightly know.*

I felt like a penny waiting for change. I felt worthless or helpless. □ *When I lost the race, I felt like a penny waiting for change.* □

My best girl went off with someone else. I felt like a penny waiting for change.

I kicked the slats out of my cradle laughing at that (joke). See *I knocked the slats out of my cradle laughing at that.*

I knocked the slats out of my cradle laughing at that AND **I kicked the slats out of my cradle laughing at that (joke).** That is an old joke. □ TOM: *How come you didn't laugh at Jim's joke?* JANE: *I knocked the slats out of my cradle laughing at that one, that's why.* □ *How old is that comedian? I kicked the slats out of my cradle laughing at the jokes he told!*

I swan! "What a surprise!" (See also *I declare (to goodness)!*) □ *Well, I swan! I didn't expect to see you here!* □ TOM: *I hear Charlie just won a thousand dollars!* JANE: *I swan!*

I wasn't brought up in the woods to be scared by owls. I am not foolish or easily frightened. □ *His threats don't scare me. I wasn't brought up in the woods to be scared by owls.* □ MARY: *You'll be sorry you ever crossed me.* JANE: *I wasn't brought up in the woods to be scared by owls.*

icebox a chest that holds a block of ice and the food it is meant to keep cold. (Many people still call a refrigerator an icebox.) □ *Put the milk back in the icebox before it sours.* □ *I reckon we need another hundred pounds for the icebox.*

I'd bet a blue stack on it. I am certain. (Refers to a stack of blue poker chips, which have the highest value. See also *I'd bet money (on it).*) □ JANE: *Do you think the governor will resign?* TOM: *I'd bet a blue stack on it.* □ *It'll rain tomorrow. I'd bet a blue stack on it.*

I'd bet money (on it). I am certain. (See also *I'd bet a blue stack on it.*) □ CHARLIE: *Do you think Joe's planning to sell his house?* TOM: *I'd bet money on it.* □ *I'd bet money that Jane will get that job.*

I'd (just) as leave do something I would rather do something. □ TOM: *Do you want to go to Joe's party?* JANE: *We can if you want* *to, but I'd as leave not.* □ *I'd just as leave eat dinner at home tonight.*

I'd (just) as soon as do something I would prefer something. □ TOM: *Why don't you give Joe a call?* JANE: *I'd as soon as you did it.* □ *I'd just as soon as we didn't stay here long.*

idee AND **idy** idea. □ *I had no idee you were so smart!* □ *Where did you get the idy that the Hatfields are lazy?*

idy See *idee.*

If a toady frog had wings, he wouldn't bump his ass. See *If frogs had wheels, they wouldn't bump their butts.*

If frogs had wheels, they wouldn't bump their butts. AND **If a toady frog had wings, he wouldn't bump his ass.** It is useless to wish for impossible things. (Use caution with *ass*.) □ TOM: *If I had two hundred thousand dollars, I could buy that farm.* JANE: *Yeah, and if frogs had wheels, they wouldn't bump their butts.* □ CHARLIE: *If I was rich and famous, I'd make people listen to me.* BILL: *If a toady frog had wings, he wouldn't bump his ass.*

If it ain't chickens, it's feathers. There are always problems.; That is life. □ *Now that I'm finally done with school, I've got to worry about getting a job. If it ain't chickens, it's feathers.* □ *He's got plenty of money now, but he's in such bad health he can't enjoy it. If it ain't chickens, it's feathers.*

If it was a snake it woulda bit you. It was very close to you. □ JANE: *Where's the phone book?* TOM: *Right there! If it was a snake it woulda bit you.* □ BILL: *I can't find my other shoe. I've looked all over the house.* MARY: *It's right behind you. If it was a snake it woulda bit you.*

If that don't beat a pig a-pecking! "That's amazing!" (See also *beat bobtail; Don't that (just) beat all?; that beats something all to pieces.*) □ TOM: *A Republican won the Senate seat!* JANE: *If that don't beat a pig a-pecking!* □ MARY: *Jim lost twenty pounds in one month.* CHARLIE: *If that don't beat a pig a-pecking!*

If that don't beat all! See *Don't that (just) beat all!*

If you get burnt you got to set on the blister. If you get a bad bargain, you must live with it. □ *I'm sorry now I ever bought this no-good used car. Oh, well. If you get burnt you got to set on the blister.* □ *Take a good look at anything before you buy it. If you get burnt you got to set on the blister.*

if you've a mind to do something if you really want to do something. □ *If you've a mind to run for class president, you'd best start making campaign posters.* □ *You can do just about anything if you've a mind to.*

iffen AND **effen** if. □ *Iffen you don't mind, I'd like to turn on the fan.* □ *Effen you like her, tell her so!*

ijit AND **eejit** an idiot. □ *Why are you such an ijit?* □ *Jed is allus acting like an eejit!*

I'll be a suckegg mule! "I am very surprised!" (See also *I'll be!*) □ TOM: *Joe got two hundred thousand for that old house of his.* JANE: *Well, I'll be a suckegg mule! I didn't think he could get more than a hundred and twenty.* □ *Well, I'll be a suckegg mule! My mare had twin foals!*

I'll be! "I am very surprised!" (See also *I'll be a suckegg mule!*) □ CHARLIE: *Joe and Sally got married last weekend.* JANE: *Well, I'll be!* □ *I'll be! Bill got the top score on the test!*

I'll eat my hat. "I will be very surprised." (Used to express strong disbelief in something.) □ *If Joe really joins the Army, I'll eat my hat.* □ *If this car gives you any trouble, I'll eat my hat.*

ill someone to irritate someone. □ *That wheezy laugh of Jane's sure can ill a body.* □ *It ills me when you don't pay attention.*

in a coon's age in a long time. (See also *in an age of years; in dog's years; month of Sundays; since Hector was a pup.*) □ *I ain't seen Joe in a coon's age.* □ *I haven't been roller-skating in a coon's age.*

in a fix in trouble. (See also *fix.*) □ *Jim and Jane are in a fix, all right. She's pregnant, and they're not married.* □ *We were in a fix —lost in the big city with no money, and night coming on.*

In a pig's ass! See *In a pig's eye!*

In a pig's ear! See *In a pig's eye!*

In a pig's eye! AND **In a pig's ass!; In a pig's ear!** "Nonsense!" (Use caution with *ass*.) □ TOM: *I wasn't going to steal it. I was just looking at it.* JANE: *In a pig's eye! I saw you put it in your pocket!* □ MARY: *Bill says he's sorry and he'll never yell at me again if I take him back.* JANE: *In a pig's ass! He's made those promises a hundred times before.* □ TOM: *I thought you said I could keep this.* CHARLIE: *In a pig's ear! I said you could borrow* it.

in a swivet in an angry or upset state. □ *She stomped in all in a swivet, but I got her to quieten down.* □ *Joe was in a swivet when he heard the news.*

in all my born days in my entire life. □ *I've never seen such fireworks in all my born days.* □ *That's the best party I was ever at in all my born days.*

in an age of years in a long time. (See also *in a coon's age; in dog's years; month of Sundays; since Hector was a pup.*) □ *How have you been? I haven't talked to you in an age of years.* □ *Jane hasn't ridden a horse in an age of years.*

in dog's years in a long time. (See also *in a coon's age; in an age of years; month of Sundays; since Hector was a pup.*) □ *I haven't heard this song in dog's years.* □ *Jim hadn't played baseball in dog's years, but he was eager to try.*

in for it in trouble. □ *I knew I was in for it when I saw Dad get out his belt.* □ *If I ever catch that chicken thief, he'll be in for it for sure.*

In God we trust, all others pay cash. You may not buy things on credit here. (Jocular.) □ CUSTOMER: *I'll pay for this next time,*

OK? SALES CLERK: *Nope. In God we trust, all others pay cash.* □ *A sign on the cash register said, "In God we trust, all others pay cash."*

in high cotton doing very well. (See also *shit in tall cotton.*) □ *Jim's in high cotton ever since he got that raise.* □ TOM: *How's your sister?* MARY: *She's in high cotton. Just bought a nice new house.*

in hog heaven very happy; having a wonderful time. □ *Bill's a fan of Clark Gable, so when the movie theater had a Clark Gable movie festival, Bill was in hog heaven.* □ *Jane loves to quilt, so she was in hog heaven when they opened that new store for quilters.*

in low cotton depressed. (Compare to *in high cotton.*) □ *She was in low cotton because her dress got torn.* □ *Jed is in low cotton because his favorite hound is dead.*

in no time flat very quickly. □ *He had the room tidied up in no time flat.* □ *The waiter brought our food in no time flat.*

in special particularly; especially. □ TOM: *I'm going into town. Anything you want me to bring you?* MARY: *Nothing in special.* □ *I wasn't going anywhere in special, just walking around to see what I could see.*

in stitches laughing very hard. □ *Charlie had us in stitches with all his jokes.* □ *The movie sure was funny. I was in stitches!*

in the family way pregnant. □ *My daughter's in the family way.* □ *You should have seen how Tom waited on his wife when she was in the family way.*

in the pink (of health) in very good health. □ *He recovered completely from his surgery and has been in the pink ever since.* □ *She was lively and active and in the pink of health.*

in the rise of her bloom in her young womanhood. □ *That summer, she was in the rise of her bloom, and a dozen young men came to call.* □ *He was very protective of his daughter, who was in the rise of her bloom.*

in these parts around here; in this area. (See also *in those parts.*) □ *There aren't any big hospitals in these parts.* □ *Joe's the richest man in these parts.*

in those parts around there; in that area. (See also *in these parts.*) □ *I've got a cousin who lives in those parts.* □ *We used to spend our vacations in those parts.*

in trouble pregnant and unmarried. (A euphemism.) □ *They had to get married. She was in trouble.* □ *She'll be in trouble before long, if she doesn't quit running around like that.*

Indian corn corn with kernels of different colors. □ *For Thanksgiving, we decorated the house with pumpkins and Indian corn.* □ *He made a beautiful wreath of Indian corn.*

Indian file single file; in line one behind the other. □ *We walked Indian file up the narrow trail.* □ *The teacher had the students line up Indian file.*

Indian giver someone who takes back a gift. (Some people may object to this expression.) □ CHARLIE: *You know that book I gave you? I was wondering if I could have it back.* TOM: *Indian giver!* □ *I'm sorry now that I gave that hat to Jane, but I'm not an Indian giver, so I won't ask for it back.*

infare a party following a wedding. □ *All the bride's cousins from miles around came to the infare.* □ *Her mother and her aunts outdid themselves making food for the infare.*

infernal damned. (A mild expletive.) □ *This is the fourth time that infernal tractor has broken down.* □ *Jim's infernal pride makes it impossible for him to admit he's wrong.*

Injun an American Indian. □ *There's a bunch of Injuns out on the reservation.* □ *I bought this turquoise ring from the Injun who made it.*

innocent as a babe unborn See *innocent as a newborn babe.*

innocent as a newborn babe AND **innocent as a babe unborn** completely innocent. □ *She's thirteen years old, but innocent as a newborn babe.* □ *Joe was the one who broke the window, but he tried to look as innocent as a babe unborn.*

inspect the timber to go to the bathroom in the woods. □ *Excuse me while I go to inspect the timber.* □ *Joe stopped by the side of the road to inspect the timber.*

is all "That is all."; "That is all I meant to say." (Often used to end a sentence.) □ *I'm not mad at you. I'm just disappointed, is all.* □ *Jane's not a bad kid. She's headstrong, is all.*

I'se I'm. (From *I is.*) □ *I'se sure glad you're here!* □ *I'se really tired.*

It don't make (me) no nevermind. It does not matter, I do not care one way or the other. □ TOM: *Should we use the plain dishes or the fancy china?* MARY: *It don't make no nevermind.* □ CHARLIE: *Who's gonna drive, you or me?* SALLY: *It don't make me no nevermind.*

It sure is hell when it's this way, and it's this way now. Things are going very badly. (Jocular.) □ TOM: *I can't believe how bad things are at work.* JANE: *Yep. It sure is hell when it's this way, and it's this way now.* □ *When Joe saw the mess his kids had made of the house on the day he was expecting company to come, he grumbled, "It sure is hell when it's this way, and it's this way now."*

it would take an act of Congress to do something it is almost impossible to do something. □ *It would take an act of Congress to get Bill to wear a necktie.* □ *She's a sour woman. It would take an act of Congress to get her to put a smile on her face.*

It'll all come out in the wash. It does not matter.; No lasting damage has been done. □ TOM: *I feel so bad about what I said to Bill. I don't think he'll ever forgive me.* MARY: *Oh, don't worry. It'll all come out in the wash.* □ JANE: *I'll never forgive myself for losing Mary's book.* CHARLIE: *Just tell her you're sorry, and offer to pay for the book. It'll all come out in the wash.*

it'll be a cold day in Hell when something happens something will never happen. (See also *It'll be a long day in January when something happens.*) ☐ *It'll be a cold day in Hell when the city council agrees on where to build that bridge.* ☐ *It'll be a cold day in Hell when I forgive you.*

it'll be a long day in January when something happens something will never happen. (There are few hours of daylight in January. See also *It'll be a cold day in Hell when something happens.*) ☐ TOM: *Maybe this will be the year that Mama treats herself to a nice vacation.* JANE: *Are you kidding? It'll be a long day in January when she does that!* ☐ *It'll be a long day in January when that car dealer gives an honest price.*

It's for a fact. It is true. ☐ CHARLIE: *I can't believe that Bill's selling his house.* TOM: *It's for a fact!* ☐ *It's for a fact that chocolate is poison to cats.*

it's raining pitchforks (and hammer handles) It is raining very hard. ☐ *Take an umbrella. It's raining pitchforks and hammer handles out there!* ☐ CHARLIE: *Have you looked outside? How's the weather?* MARY: *It's raining pitchforks.*

itsy bitsy See *itty bitty.*

itty bitty AND **itsy bitsy** very small. ☐ *I remember when you was just an itty bitty baby.* ☐ *Gramma sewed with itsy bitsy stitches.*

I've done my do I have done my share. ☐ TOM: *Aren't you going to finish cleaning the kitchen?* JANE: *I've done my do. You can do the rest.* ☐ *I feel I've done my do, and someone else should do the rest.*

I've seen better heads on nickel beers. "This person is stupid." ☐ *Jim's good-looking, but I've seen better heads on nickel beers.* ☐ *My students this term aren't what you'd call bright. I've seen better heads on nickel beers.*

J

jackleg incompetent. □ *The only doctor who would stay in that God-forsaken town was a jackleg sawbones who killed half his patients.* □ *I get so tired of these jackleg politicians, I just want to vote them all out of office.*

jackrabbit a long-eared hare that can jump great distances. □ *My dog was chasing a jackrabbit.* □ *Jim was so excited, he was jumping around like a jackrabbit.*

jambalaya a spicy stew made with rice, tomatoes, sausage, seafood, and other meats. (From Louisiana French.) □ *That restaurant serves a good jambalaya.* □ *Everyone wanted seconds of Bill's jambalaya.*

jaw to talk. □ *The men sat jawing in the parlor while the women washed dishes and gossiped in the kitchen.* □ *Jim can jaw for hours on end.*

jaw-cracker a dentist. □ *Gotta see the jaw-cracker about this fool tooth of mine.* □ *The jaw-cracker says I need a root canal.*

jawrin idle chatter; hurtful talk. □ *Those gossipy women do a right smart of harm with all their jawrin.* □ *She got tired of her husband's jawrin, so she left him.*

JB See *Stetson.*

jedge judge. □ *Good morning, jedge. How are you?* □ *The jedge hammered on his table and people just kept on a-talking.*

jerk a knot in someone's tail See *put a knot in someone's tail.*

jerky strips of dried meat, usually beef. □ *We took jerky with us on the trail, because it keeps well.* □ *I had a stick of beef jerky for a snack.*

jest AND **jist** just. □ *You're jest teasing me!* □ *I jist said you was pretty. I didn't mean anything by it! Honest Injun.*

jim dandy excellent. □ *This is a jim dandy knife. Where'd you get it?* □ TOM: *I'll meet you at six, OK?* CHARLIE: *That'll be jim dandy.*

jimson weed a poisonous weed with white or purple flowers. □ *I need something to kill that jimson weed growing in my south forty.* □ *There's a nasty patch of jimson weed in the middle of my garden.*

jist See *jest.*

joe pye weed a tall weed with purple flowers. □ *Gramma says they used to make some kind of medicine out of joe pye weed.* □ *That stuff growing by the side of the road is joe pye weed.*

John B See *Stetson.*

John B. Stetson See *Stetson.*

John Hancock AND **John Henry** a signature. □ *Wait. I forgot to put my John Hancock on that check.* □ *I put my John Henry on the petition.*

John Henry See *John Hancock.*

johnny cake AND **journey cake** a cake of corn bread. (See also *hoe cake. Johnny* is probably a Northeast pronunciation of *journey*, or *journey* is *johnny* with an excresent *r*.) □ *We had johnny cake for breakfast.* □ *I made a quick meal of journey cake and greens.*

Johnny-come-lately a new person; a recent arrival. □ *Mary is a Johnny-come-lately in our club.* □ *I've lived in this town ten years,* *but I'm a Johnny-come-lately compared to my neighbor, who's been here for fifty.*

Johnny jump-up a violet. ☐ *It's so pretty in the spring, when the Johnny jump-ups bloom.* ☐ *The front yard was full of Johnny jump-ups, blooming purple and white.*

jojos potatoes fried in a spicy batter. ☐ *Let's stop at the snack shop and get some jojos.* ☐ *Would you like some jojos with your sandwich?*

Joshua tree a tall yucca plant. ☐ *The desert was dotted with Joshua trees.* ☐ *The Joshua tree in our front yard must have been growing for twenty or thirty years, it was so tall.*

journey cake See *johnny cake.*

(Judge) Lynch a lynch mob. (Supposedly refers to William Lynch.) ☐ *The case was tried before Judge Lynch, and the prisoner duly hanged.* ☐ *The horse thief preferred staying in jail to coming up before Judge Lynch.*

jug a jail. ☐ *I spent thirty days in the jug.* ☐ *Bill's in the jug again.*

juice a cow to milk a cow. ☐ *Have you ever juiced a cow before?* ☐ *The farmer went to the barn to juice the cow.*

jump a claim to take something claimed by someone else. (See also *claimjumper.*) ☐ *John was going out with Sally, but then his best friend jumped his claim and married her.* ☐ *No one was surprised when Jane took Mary's report and put her own name on it. Jane has often been known to jump a claim.*

jump out of one's skin to jump from fear or startlement. ☐ *He was so nervous, he jumped out of his skin when he heard the door slam.* ☐ *The eerie noise made me jump out of my skin.*

jump over the broomstick to get married. ☐ *Jim and Jane have decided to jump over the broomstick.* ☐ *The happiest day of my life was when your mother said she'd jump over the broomstick with me.*

Jumping Jehosaphat! "Good Lord!" (A mild oath, used to express surprise.) □ *Jumping Jehosaphat! What have you done to my car?* □ *Jumping Jehosaphat! I never seen so many people in one place before!*

just come after a chunk of fire to come for a short visit. (An excuse for a visit, as if to borrow a burning ember to take home and use to start one's fire.) □ *We won't stay long. We just come after a chunk of fire.* □ *They're not staying to dinner. They just come after a chunk of fire.*

just fell off the turnip truck ignorant. □ *He stood there gawking at the buildings in town like he just fell off the turnip truck.* □ *My cousin acts like she just fell off the turnip truck.*

K

keel over to fall over. □ *He was so drunk he keeled over.* □ *Her face went white and she keeled over.*

keel something over to push something over. □ *He leaned on the flimsy wall and keeled it right over.* 🅃 *The high wind keeled over that sorry old fence.*

keep company (with someone) to be courting with someone. □ *Mary and Bill are keeping company.* □ *I heard that Joe is keeping company with Jim Brown's daughter.*

keep one's chair AND **keep one's seat** to stay seated; to not get up. □ *That's all right. Keep your chair. I'll find my own way out.* □ *Please keep your seats until after the question-and-answer period.*

keep one's eyes peeled AND **keep one's eyes skinned** to watch or look carefully; to be watchful and alert. □ *Keep your eyes peeled for a blue Chevy with a white roof.* □ *During tornado season, we keep our eyes skinned for funnel clouds.*

keep one's eyes skinned See *keep one's eyes peeled.*

keep one's seat See *keep one's chair.*

keep the stork busy See *keep the stork flying.*

keep the stork flying AND **keep the stork busy** to have lots of children. □ *Sally's pregnant again, with their sixth. They sure do keep the stork flying!* □ *Gramma and Grampa kept the stork flying. I've got ten aunts and uncles.*

keep your fingers crossed to hope for good luck. □ *I applied for a job today. Keep your fingers crossed for me.* □ TOM: *I hope you do OK on the test.* JANE: *Keep your fingers crossed.*

Keep your hair on. AND **Keep your hat on.; Keep your shirt on.** "Just calm down and wait." □ *Now, now, keep your hair on. It's not so bad as all that.* □ *Keep your hat on. Joe didn't mean nothing by his remark.*

Keep your hat on. See *Keep your hair on.*

Keep your shirt on. See *Keep your hair on.*

ketch catch. (Eye-dialect.) □ *How many fish did you ketch?* □ *We ketched enough bush bacon to last us for a few days.*

ketch-dog a hunting dog. □ *Old Blue was the best ketch-dog I ever had.* □ *Jane sure knows how to train a ketch-dog.*

Key lime pie a pie filled with lime custard and topped with meringue. (A species of lime unique to the Florida Keys is used in the authentic recipe.) □ *Mary brought one of her Key lime pies to the party.* □ *I don't like Key lime pie. It's too tart for me.*

kick like a mule AND **kick like a steer** **1.** to kick very hard. □ *They say that ostriches will kick like a mule if you bother them.* □ *Stay away from the back end of Tom's horse. It will kick like a steer when a stranger comes up.* **2.** to resist. □ *Jim kicks like a mule every time I ask him to put on a coat and tie.* □ *I tried to get Joe to apologize, but he kicked like a steer.*

kick like a steer See *kick like a mule.*

kick over the traces to rebel. (*Traces* are the straps or chains that attach a horse to a cart or wagon.) □ *After thirty years of listening to his wife's nagging, Bill finally kicked over the traces.* □ *Jim's son kicked over the traces by refusing to work in the family business.*

kick the (natural) stuffing out of someone AND **beat the (natural) stuffing out of someone** to kick or beat someone severely. □

Last time I was in a fight with Joe, he kicked the natural stuffing out of me. □ *You do that again and I'll kick the stuffing out of you.* □ *William threatened to beat the natural stuffing out of any no-'count rascal who laid a hand on his sister.* □ *Dad beat the stuffing out of us when we was kids.*

kill a tree to urinate in the woods. □ *Granpappy is out killing a tree. He'll be back soon if the hogs don't get him.* □ *I gotta go kill a tree.*

killin' a murder. □ *There was another killin' down to the saloon last night.* □ *He did his first killin' at the age of fifteen.*

kilt killed; dead. □ *My cousin Walter was kilt by a bear.* □ *The dog lay there in the crick, half kilt, until somebody came along an' fetched him out.*

kin(folks) relatives. □ *I ain't never been to a party with anybody but kinfolks.* □ *Most of my kinfolks live right here in the valley.* □ *You ain't no kin of mine!* □ *My kin don't have no truck with your kin.*

kiss the Bible See *kiss the book.*

kiss the book AND **kiss the Bible** to swear to the truth of something; to take an oath. □ *I'll kiss the book that Joe was with me all night.* □ TOM: *Are you sure?* JANE: *I'd kiss the Bible.*

Kissin' don't last; cookin' do. Cooking is more important to a marriage than sex or romance. (Jocular.) □ *You want to look for a gal who's a good cook, and never mind if she's sexy. Kissin' don't last; cookin' do.* □ *I've been married forty years, and believe me, kissin' don't last; cookin' do.*

kissing cousins relatives who know one another well enough to kiss when they meet; distant relatives. □ *Joe and I are kissing cousins, though we ain't seen one another since we was kids.* □ *Technically, we're second cousins once removed, but I just say we're kissing cousins.*

kit and caboodle equipment or belongings. □ *Whose's kit and caboodle is in the middle of the floor?* □ *Bill packed up his kit and caboodle and left home that same day.*

kiver cover; bedclothes. □ *I wrapped up in the kivers to keep warm.* □ *You keep pulling all the kivers to your side.*

knee baby See *arm baby.*

knee-high by the 4th of July Corn seedlings are supposed to be as high as someone's knee by July 4th. □ *What with this drought, I don't think the crop will be knee-high by the 4th of July.* □ *It's gonna be a good year. Knee-high by the 4th of July.*

knee-high to a grasshopper See *knee-high to a jackrabbit.*

knee-high to a jackrabbit AND **knee-high to a grasshopper** very small. (Usually used to describe children.) □ *I've known you since you were knee-high to a jackrabbit.* □ *My, how you've grown! The last time I saw you, you were knee-high to a grasshopper!*

kneewalking drunk so drunk that one cannot walk. □ *Joe gets kneewalking drunk every Saturday night.* □ *They weren't just a little high. They were kneewalking drunk!*

knock-down-drag-out (fight) a violent fight; a seemingly endless fight. □ *Sounds like the couple upstairs are having another knock-down-drag-out fight.* □ *That saloon's a rough place. There's a knock-down-drag-out in there every fifteen minutes or so.*

knock-head room a room with a low ceiling. □ *She had her own bedroom, a little knock-head room right up under the roof.* □ *They were paying an outrageous rent for two knock-head rooms and a kitchen.*

knock someone or something cat-west AND **knock someone or something galley-west** to beat up someone or something severely. □ *Sheriff Jones knocked the little punk cat-west.* □ *Daddy threatened to knock us galley-west if we did anything to hurt the livestock.*

knock someone or something galley-west See *knock someone or something cat-west.*

knock someone or something sky-winding to beat up someone or something. □ *If Jim finds out you've been courtin' his gal, he'll knock you sky-winding.* □ *When I catch that varmint, I'm gonna knock him sky-winding.*

knock the bejeebers out of someone or something to beat someone or something severely. (See also *beat the bejeebers out of someone or something.*) □ *If I catch you doing that again, I'll knock the bejeebers out of you.* □ *He grabbed the poor dog and just knocked the bejeebers out of it.*

know as much about something as a hog knows about Sunday to have no knowledge of something. □ *Don't let Jim make dessert for the picnic. He knows as much about pies as a hog knows about Sunday.* □ *I had quite a time changing the tire, since I know as much about cars as a hog knows about Sunday.*

know in reason to know; to be certain. □ *I know in reason that Jim would never kill a man.* □ *She knew in reason that land values were going up.*

know no more about something than a frog knows about bed sheets to have no knowledge of something. □ *Don't let Bill fix your car. He knows no more about cars than a frog knows about bed sheets.* □ *When I first started studying French literature, I knew no more about it than a frog knows about bed sheets.*

know someone's hide in a tanyard to know someone very well or intimately. □ CHARLIE: *Do you know Bill?* JANE: *Well, I'd know his hide in a tanyard.* □ *You can try to disguise yourself, but I'd know your hide in a tanyard any day.*

L

lady-broke won over by a woman. ("Broken" by a woman in the way that a *bronco* is broken or busted by a cowboy.) □ *Jim was a fun-loving scoundrel until he got lady-broke. Now he's all fine manners and clean shirt-fronts.* □ *He was a fierce old bachelor. Swore he'd never be lady-broke.*

ladyfingers small, sweet, rectangular cakes. □ *Dessert was ladyfingers and ice cream.* □ *The chef soaked the ladyfingers in rum.*

lagniappe a bonus; something extra; especially an extra gift given by a seller to a buyer. (Pronounced *LAN-yap*. From an Amerindian language via Spanish.) □ *I bought some fish from Joe, and he gave me a basket of crawdads as a lagniappe.* □ *The public TV station offered all kinds of lagniappes, from coffee mugs to videotapes, for people who give a donation.*

laid up sick or injured and unable to go out. □ *Mary's sorry she can't come. She's laid up with the flu.* □ *Bill's two broken legs kept him laid up for a month.*

lamb fries lamb's testicles. □ *The missus served a big plate of lamb fries, and I et every one.* □ *Nothing better than lamb fries at the start of a meal.*

Land o' Goshen! "My goodness gracious!" (A mild oath. *Goshen* was an agricultural region in Egypt occupied by the Israelites before the Exodus.) □ *Land o' Goshen, it's sure good to see you.* □ *Land o' Goshen! Look at that rain come down!*

land-office business a very great deal of business. □ *The ice-cream stand's doing land-office business in this hot weather.* □ *The new grocery store is doing land-office business.*

land so poor it wouldn't even raise a fuss land where nothing will grow. (See also *land too poor to raise a racket on.*) □ *I inherited two hundred acres from my uncle, but it's land so poor it wouldn't even raise a fuss.* □ *The soil's exhausted. That land is so poor it wouldn't even raise a fuss.*

land too poor to raise a racket on land where nothing will grow. (See also *land so poor it wouldn't even raise a fuss; raise a racket.*) □ *Jill can grow a garden anywhere, even on land too poor to raise a racket on.* □ *This land has been farmed for ninety years. It's too poor to raise a racket on.*

land up in a funeral parlor to end up dead. □ *Ma doesn't like me riding the bucking bronc in the rodeo. She's afraid I'll land up in a funeral parlor.* □ *He went out for a joyride and landed up in a funeral parlor.*

land up somewhere to end up somewhere. □ *We drove all day and landed up in Amarillo.* □ *After years of wandering, he landed up in Seattle.*

Land(s) sakes (alive)! AND **Sakes alive!** "My goodness!" (A mild oath.) □ *Lands sakes! I sure am glad to get home!* □ *Sakes alive! Can't you even set the table without making a fuss?*

language that would fry bacon profanity; swearing; curse words. ("Hot" language.) □ *He carried on in language that would fry bacon.* □ *I was shocked when I heard that sweet little girl use language that would fry bacon.*

lap child See *arm baby.*

larapin' very good. (Pronounced *LER-up-pin.*) □ *We had a larapin' time over to the Smiths' party last night.* □ *Doc gave me some larapin' stuff that took care of my cough right away.*

lard-fat very fat. □ *Joe's so lard-fat, I worry about his health.* □ *He ain't lard-fat. That's muscle.*

lard tub a (fat) person's bottom. □ *I fell right down on my lard tub.* □ *You want me to smack you on the lard tub? Behave!*

lariat a rope with a noose, used to catch animals. (From Spanish *la reata*. See also *lasso*.) □ *Arizona Slim twirled his lariat over his head.* □ *I snagged the runaway calf with my lariat.*

larrup syrup; molasses. □ *Please pass the larrup!* □ *Maw, Jimmy's taking all the larrup!*

larruping really good. □ *We had a larruping good time at the hoedown last night.* □ *He is one larruping young man.*

'lasses molasses. □ *Got any more of them 'lasses cookies?* □ *Grandma loved 'lasses on her griddle cakes.*

lasso **1.** a long rope with a noose, used to catch animals. (From Spanish *lazo*. See also *lariat*.) □ *At the rodeo, the cowboys did fancy tricks with their lassos.* □ *The lasso flew through the air and landed on the horse's neck.* **2.** to catch someone or something with a lasso. □ *She lassoed the steer.* □ *For practice, we tried to lasso the fence posts.*

last one in the back row when the faces was handed out an ugly person. □ *Mary was the last one in the back row when the faces was handed out.* □ *He has a beautiful voice, but he sure was the last one in the back row when the faces was handed out.*

lasty lasting; durable. □ *Shoes ain't so lasty as they used to be.* □ *I got the more expensive cloth because I thought it would be more lasty.*

lavish of something a very great deal of something. (Used with the indefinite article *a*.) □ *Jane puts a lavish of time and money into that fancy car of hers.* □ *The restaurant serves up big, juicy burgers with a lavish of homestyle fries.*

law someone to sue someone. ☐ *He's going to law his neighbor over the property rights.* ☐ *She tried to law the man who cheated her.*

lawman a sheriff or police officer. ☐ *The lawman chased the outlaw through three counties.* ☐ *When Jimmy grows up, he wants to be a lawman with a badge and a gun.*

Lawsamercy! AND **Lawsy!** "My goodness!"; "Lord have mercy!" (A mild oath.) ☐ *Lawsamercy! I sure am tired.* ☐ *Lawsy, child, how did you get so dirty?*

Lawsy! See *Lawsamercy!*

lay eyes on someone or something to see someone or something. ☐ *I've never laid eyes on him before.* ☐ *The first time I laid eyes on that car, it was sitting outside the dry goods store.*

lay for someone or something to lie in wait for someone or something. ☐ *The sheriff was laying for the outlaw.* ☐ *Bill was laying for me when I came out of the saloon.*

lay low and sing small to hide; to make oneself inconspicuous. ☐ *After he robbed the bank, the outlaw decided to lay low and sing small awhile.* ☐ *Jane is looking for you, and she sure is angry. You'd best lay low and sing small.*

lay something by AND **put something by** to preserve something; to keep something for the future; put something aside. ☐ *Mary laid her wedding dress by. One day, her daughter might want to use it.* ☐ *I put a hundred dollars by, in case of an emergency.*

layover for meddlers See *layover to catch meddlers.*

layover to catch meddlers AND **layover for meddlers** a trap designed to catch people who meddle. (A *layover* is a pit trap covered with branches. This is used as a reply to questions from curious children.) ☐ CHILD: *What are you making?* FATHER: *A layover to catch meddlers.* ☐ CHILD: *What are they doing out there?* MOTHER: *Making a layover to catch meddlers.*

lazy man's load an overly big load, instead of a number of smaller loads that would require more trips back and forth. □ *She had everything piled up in her arms in a lazy man's load.* □ *Don't carry a lazy man's load like that. You're sure to drop something.*

lead apes in hell to die an unmarried woman. □ *You ought to accept Bill's proposal, if you don't want to lead apes in hell.* □ *Susan's a sweet woman. It'll be a right shame if she ends up leading apes in hell.*

lead poisoning death from being shot. (Jocular.) □ TOM: *What happened to Slim?* BILL: *He died of lead poisoning, trying to escape from the sheriff.* □ *After the shootout, several men were treated for lead poisoning.*

learn to teach someone something. □ *Come here and I'll learn you how to crochet.* □ *The schoolteacher has been learning the kids their alphabet.*

least little thing the smallest possible thing. (Used with the definite article *the*.) □ *He gets upset over the least little thing.* □ *When she was a girl, she would throw a tantrum over the least little thing.*

leastways AND **leastwise** at least. □ *It's not safe in that part of town. Leastways, I wouldn't go there.* □ *I don't think he's famous. Leastways, I've never heard of him.* □ *Bill doesn't have a girlfriend. Leastwise, none that I know of.* □ *It's foolish to try asking Mary any favors. Leastwise, I wouldn't bother.*

leastwise See *leastways*.

leave to allow someone to do something. □ *Ma won't leave us go.* □ *Leave her sit down for a while.*

leg bail escape from prison, rather than posting a cash bond. (Also *give leg bail*, to escape from prison.) □ *When they went to the prisoner's cell, they discovered he had given them leg bail.* □ *Jeb posted leg bail and nobody could find him.*

leg-weary tired from walking. □ *I was leg-weary from the long walk home.* □ *Jim was leg-weary and his feet hurt.*

less time than skinning a badger very little time. □ TOM: *Will it take long?* JANE: *Less time than skinning a badger.* □ *In less time than skinning a badger, she was ready.*

Let every man skin his own skunk. Everyone should do his own job and not interfere with others.; Each person should do his own dirty work. □ *We weren't supposed to help each other with the homework. "Let every man skin his own skunk," the teacher said.* □ *I hate working in committees. Let every man skin his own skunk, I say.*

let off a little steam to release tension. □ *Sally galloped her horse up and down the riverbed to let off a little steam.* □ *The boys may seem rowdy, but they're just letting off a little steam.*

let on (about someone or something) (to someone) to admit someone or something to someone. □ *Did Joe let on about his drinking to his wife?* □ *He was having money troubles, but he never let on about it.* □ *She knew about the surprise party, but she never let on.*

levee **1.** a dike that prevents a river from spilling over its banks. □ *The flood waters broke through the levee and destroyed the town.* □ *Jed sat on the levee, fishing for catfish.* **2.** a pier; a landing place for riverboats. □ *We walked along the levee, looking out at the boats.* □ *Joe built a levee out back of his place.*

Levi's blue jeans. □ *This old pair of Levi's is my favorite pair of pants.* □ *Bill got a rip in his Levi's.*

lick and a promise a hasty bit of work; a quick once-over. (Usually with the indefinite article *a*.) □ *I was pressed for time, so I just gave the housework a lick and a promise.* □ *Mary spent so much time on her history paper that she had to finish her math homework with a lick and a promise.*

lickety split very fast. □ *I'll fix you up some pancakes lickety split.* □ *The cat ran off lickety split.*

licking a beating. □ *Johnny got a licking for sassing his ma.* □ *In the old days, a teacher could give a student a licking.*

lie like a rug to tell lies shamelessly. □ *He says he didn't take the money, but he's lying like a rug.* □ *I don't believe her. She lies like a rug.*

light a rag (for somewhere) AND **light a shuck (for somewhere)** to leave in a hurry (for somewhere). (See also *light out for somewhere; light out for the territories.*) □ *A storm came up. We lit a rag for the nearest shelter.* □ *We'd better light a rag if we want to get there on time!* □ *When Bill saw his wife coming, he lit a shuck.* □ *Is it eleven o'clock already? I better light a shuck for home.*

light a shuck (for somewhere) See *light a rag (for somewhere).*

light bread white bread. □ *We don't much care for that store-bought light bread.* □ *I suppose that city folks eat nothing but light bread.*

light out for somewhere to go somewhere quickly. (See also *light a rag (for somewhere); light out for the territories.*) □ *When folks heard that gold had been discovered, they lit out for California in droves.* □ *After the outlaw robbed the bank, he lit out for the territories.*

light out for the territories to go far away very quickly. (See also *light a rag (for somewhere); light out for somewhere.*) □ *He lit out for the territories when he heard Sue's pa was coming with his shotgun.* □ *The kids lit out for the territories after they broke Mrs. Johnson's window.*

like a bat out of hell very fast. □ *A red car went by like a bat out of hell.* □ *Joe was running down the street like a bat out of hell.*

like a blind dog in a meat market out of control. □ *The drunk staggered out of the saloon like a blind dog in a meat market, firing his six-shooter at any old thing.* □ *The kids tore through the museum like a blind dog in a meat market, touching everything they weren't supposed to touch.*

like a bump on a log very still and silent. □ *Don't just sit there like a bump on a log!* □ *Jim's no help at all. He just sits like a bump on a log.*

like a can of corn very easy. (Like catching a can of corn falling from a high shelf into the grocer's hands.) □ *Whipping up dinner for twelve is like a can of corn, as far as Jane is concerned.* □ *The championship game was like a can of corn for our team.*

like a house afire very fast and with enthusiasm. □ *Their courtship went like a house afire.* □ *The writer was inspired. She wrote like a house afire.*

like a kid with a new toy very pleased; happily playing with something. □ *Every time Bill gets a new gadget for his kitchen, he's like a kid with a new toy.* □ *Jane is absorbed in that computer. Just like a kid with a new toy.*

-like in a particular way. (For instance, *interested-like*: in an interested way.) □ *The children came up all scared-like and asked why I was crying.* □ *The dog sniffed around cautious-like.*

like Coxey's Army in a large, disorderly group. (The original *Coxey's Army* was a group of demonstrators led to Washington, D.C., by Jacob Coxey in 1894 to demand that the government provide work for the unemployed.) □ *The children came stampeding into the house like Coxey's Army.* □ *What gives you-all the right to trample through the backyard like Coxey's Army?*

like enough it is likely; likely enough. □ *Like enough she called you to see if you were home.* □ *He doesn't get home till six, like enough.*

like fighting snakes chaotic; challenging. (Every time one snake is subdued, another one attacks.) □ *It's like fighting snakes to get anything done at this time of year.* □ *Arguing with you is like fighting snakes.*

like flies to manure eagerly gathering in large numbers. (Has unpleasant connotations because of the reference to manure.) □ *Look at all them folks going to the freak show like flies to manure.* □ *The reporters hovered around the movie star like flies to manure.*

like greased lightning very fast. □ *Once I get her tuned up, this old car will go like greased lightning.* □ *He's a fat kid, but he can run like greased lightning.*

like hell and high lightning very fast. □ *The snowmobiles came zooming down the trail like hell and high lightning.* □ *The powerboat sped up the river like hell and high lightning.*

like herding frogs chaotic; disorderly. (Everytime you get a few frogs headed in the right direction, a few more jump any which way.) □ *Trying to get those kids to march into the auditorium is like herding frogs.* □ *Trying to get the puppies down the basement stairs is like herding frogs.*

like it was going out of style rapidly or frequently. □ *I'm worried about Sally. She's taking aspirin like it's going out of style.* □ *The kids have been eating sweet corn like it was going out of style.*

like licking honey off a blackberry vine very difficult. □ *Getting that roof mended was like licking honey off a blackberry vine.* □ *Asking for Joe's forgiveness was like licking honey off a blackberry vine, but I did it.*

like pigs to the slaughter obediently, despairingly, and in large numbers. □ *Look at them kids lining up to take the college exams, like pigs to the slaughter.* □ *The townsfolk allowed themselves to be led into bankruptcy like pigs to the slaughter.*

like shooting fish in a barrel ridiculously easy. □ *Jane's a good mechanic. Changing a tire is like shooting fish in a barrel, for her.* □ *That comedian has an easy job. Making fun of politicians is like shooting fish in a barrel.*

like stealing acorns from a blind pig very easy. □ *Getting Mary to sign the house over to me was like stealing acorns from a blind pig.* □ TOM: *Was it hard to fool so many people?* CHARLIE: *Nope. It was like stealing acorns from a blind pig.*

like there ain't no tomorrow See *like there's no tomorrow.*

like there's no tomorrow AND **like there ain't no tomorrow** eagerly; rapidly; without stopping. □ *You can't go on eating candy bars like there's no tomorrow.* □ *Jim's spending money like there's no tomorrow.*

like to almost. □ *I like to died laughing when I saw Jim come in wearing a dress.* □ *Mary like to passed out when she saw how bad her house was damaged in the storm.*

like tryin' to scratch your ear with your elbow impossible. □ *Getting those kids to settle down is like tryin' to scratch your ear with your elbow.* □ *Fixing all the leaks in that old roof is like tryin' to scratch your ear with your elbow.*

like water off a duck's back passing away easily without causing any ill effect. □ *My good advice rolled right off him like water off a duck's back.* □ *After I wax the car, the rain slides off it like water off a duck's back.*

likker liquor. (Eye-dialect.) □ *Pappy sez he wants some likker.* □ *This likker is powerful stuff.*

listeners ears. □ *Keep your listeners open and let me know what you hear.* □ *Joe's got a good pair of listeners. He can hear a pin drop three rooms away.*

little bitty very little. □ *Can I have just a little bitty piece of that lemon meringue pie?* □ *He was just a little bitty boy.*

little bugger a cute or mischievous child. □ *"Little bugger looks just like me, don't he?" said the proud father, holding up his baby.* □ *The little buggers tore up the house, playing cowboys and Indians.*

little old ordinary; harmless. □ *Aw, honey, I wasn't gambling. I just went to one little old poker game.* □ CHARLIE: *Did you eat that whole chocolate cake that I was saving for the party?* JANE: *Little old me?*

(little) pick-me-up something that makes you feel better, especially an alcoholic drink. □ *She went to the corner saloon for a little pick-me-up.* □ *A visit with Jane is always a pick-me-up.*

little shaver a child; a baby. □ *I think the little shaver needs her diaper changed.* □ *Tom thinks his grandson is the cutest little shaver there ever was.*

(little) short on one end short. □ *You'll recognize Bill right away. He's got red hair, and he's a little short on one end.* □ *He's not small; he's just short on one end.* □ *The barber cut my hair a little short on one end.*

living high off the hog AND **eating high off the hog** living or eating extremely well. □ *Joe's living high off the hog ever since he won the lottery.* □ *All the guests were eating high off the hog at that wedding reception. I never saw such a banquet!*

living right being virtuous. □ *All the traffic lights went my way this morning. I must be living right.* □ *He was a terror when he was a young man, but now he's living right.*

load of hooey a big lie. (*Hooey* is a euphemism for *dung.*) □ *When I asked why he was late getting to work, Joe gave me a load of hooey about his car being broke.* □ *I've seen enough politicians to know that campaign promises are a load of hooey.*

loaded for bear **1.** ready to fight. □ *Look out for Steven. He's loaded for bear.* □ *The scowl on Slim's face showed that he was loaded for bear.* **2.** drunk. □ *Listen to those guys singing in the street. Sounds like they're loaded for bear.* □ *By the time we left the party, we were loaded for bear.*

loblolly a mud puddle. □ *An old car sped through the loblolly and splashed mud all over my clean clothes.* □ *The kids were happily splashing around in the loblolly.*

lock horns (with someone) to oppose (someone); to quarrel (with someone). □ *No one likes to be around when Joe and Bill lock horns.* □ *I've locked horns with my boss many times.*

loco crazy. (Spanish.) □ *Are you loco? That plan would never work!* □ *Jim's been acting loco ever since his wife walked out.*

loco weed **1.** a weed poisonous to livestock. □ *My best horse ate loco weed and died.* □ JANE: *What's wrong with that steer? He sure is walking funny.* TOM: *Loco weed, I'm afraid.* **2.** marijuana. □ *The kids hung out in the parking lot, smoking loco weed.* □ *The cops found loco weed in Bill's car.*

lollygag (around) to loaf; to loiter. □ *How can I get my work done with you lollygagging around?* □ *I spent my vacation just lollygagging.*

Lone Star state Texas. □ *We spent our vacation in the Lone Star state.* □ *Folks from the Lone Star state are proud of their home.*

long in the tooth old. □ *That actor is getting a little long in the tooth to play the romantic lead.* □ *I may be long in the tooth, but I'm not stupid.*

long johns long, winter underwear. □ *Put your long johns on before you go out in that snow.* □ *I got a nice pair of cotton long johns.*

long sweetenin' liquid sweetener, such as molasses or syrup. □ *I make my muffins with long sweetenin' instead of sugar.* □ *The candy recipe calls for two cups of long sweetenin'.*

(long) tall drink of water See *big drink of water.*

Long time no see. "It has been a long time since I saw you." □ *Howdy, there! Long time no see!* □ *Jim nodded at me. "Long time no see," he said.*

look like a saddle on a sow to look ridiculous and out of place. □ TOM: *How do you like my new diamond earring?* JANE: *It looks like a saddle on a sow.* □ *The fancy wheels on that beat-up old car look like a saddle on a sow.*

look like a sheep-killing dog to look embarrassed. □ *Henry looked like a sheep-killing dog when I caught him with his hand in the cookie jar.* □ *She must have done something wrong. If she didn't, how come she looks like a sheep-killing dog?*

lookahere look here; look at this. □ *Why, lookahere! There's a little bitty puppy sittin' outside our door.* □ *Lookahere, Nelly, you can't go spending so much money on fancy clothes.*

lookathere look there; look at that. □ *Lookathere at what Jim's got.* □ *Lookathere. The sun's rising.*

lookayonder look over there. □ *Lookayonder—I think that's Doc's car comin'.* □ *Lookayonder and tell me if you see any clouds on the horizon.*

loose-footed not settled; liking to wander. □ *I was loose-footed when I was young.* □ *Slim was just a loose-footed cowboy.*

Lord almighty See *Lordy.*

(lord) high muck-a-muck a very important person. (Humorous.) □ *Jim's acting like he's some kind of lord high muck-a-muck. What's gotten into him?* □ *Mary got a promotion, so now she's a real high muck-a-muck.*

Lord love a duck! "My goodness!" (An exclamation of surprise.) □ *Lord love a duck! How that rain is coming down!* □ *Lord love a duck! Did you see that cat chasing that dog?*

Lord willing and the creek don't rise See *God willing and the creek don't rise.*

Lordy AND **Lord almighty** "My goodness!" □ *Lordy, it's hot!* □ *Lord almighty, I'm late already.*

love apple a tomato. □ *Jim's got a big patch of love apples in his garden.* □ *For a nice side dish, just slice up some love apples and sprinkle on a little salt.*

low-down evil; mean. □ *You low-down, lying sneak!* □ *That was a low-down way to treat a person.*

lower someone's ears to cut someone's hair. (Jocular. See also *get one's ears set out.*) □ *I asked the barber to lower my ears.* □ *Looks like somebody lowered Joe's ears!*

M

Ma AND **Maw** Mother. □ *Ma taught me how to read.* □ *My Maw cooks bettern yourn.*

Mackerel skies and mares' tails make lofty ships carry low sails. Clusters of small clouds and long wispy clouds mean that strong winds will blow. (See also *mackerel sky.*) □ *There's a big wind coming. Just look at the clouds. Mackerel skies and mares' tails make lofty ships carry low sails.* □ *Grampa did not rely on weather forecasters, but on old sayings like "Mackerel skies and mares' tails make lofty ships carry low sails."*

mackerel sky a sky filled with small clouds in a pattern that looks like fish scales. □ *It's not too sunny out. There's a mackerel sky.* □ *We lay on the hillside, looking up at the mackerel sky.*

mad enough to bite off a drawbar extremely angry. (See also *(as) mad as a (blind) hornet; mad enough to kick a cat.* A *drawbar* is a piece of iron or steel that joins a farm tractor to a plow or some other farm implement that is to be drawn along behind the tractor.) □ *Jim's insults made me mad enough to bite off a drawbar.* □ *What's wrong with Mary? She looks mad enough to bite off a drawbar.*

mad enough to chew nails and spit rivets extremely angry. □ *He stomped in, mad enough to chew nails and spit rivets.* □ *When she saw that we had ruined her work, she was mad enough to chew nails and spit rivets.*

mad enough to kick a cat very angry. (See also *(as) mad as a (blind) hornet; mad enough to bite off a drawbar.*) □ *Stay out* *of my way. I'm mad enough to kick a cat!* □ *The team lost. The coach was mad enough to kick a cat.*

madder than a wet hen See *(as) mad as a wet hen.*

mail-order wife a wife obtained by advertising for one. □ *When Joe bought his ranch, he sent away for a mail-order wife.* □ *She became a mail-order wife because she didn't want to be an old maid.*

make a beeline (for someone or something) to go directly (to someone or something). □ *He made a beeline for the bathroom.* □ *The snowmobile made a beeline across the field.*

make a miration to make a show of admiring something. (From *admiration.*) □ *My folks ignore me, but make a miration over every little thing my sister does.* □ *All the relatives gathered around, making a miration over the new baby.*

make a pile (of money) to make a great deal of money. □ *Jane promised me I could make a pile of money selling encyclopedias.* □ *He made a pile writing movie scripts.*

make oneself scarce [for someone] to become difficult to find; [for someone] to go into hiding. □ *Tom is mad and is looking for you. Better make yourself scarce.* □ *Make yourself scarce! Here comes the sheriff.*

make out like a bandit to make a large profit. □ *Joe's making out like a bandit, selling them fancy cameras.* □ *Mary made out like a bandit, playing twenty-one in Las Vegas.*

make out like something to pretend something. □ *Let's make out like we're cowboys and Indians.* □ *Joe made out like he had a lot of money, and folks believed him.*

make over someone to praise someone excessively; to make a fuss over someone. □ *They aren't paying attention to me. They're too busy making over my sister.* □ *When he came home from college, all his kinfolk came to make over him.*

make (so) bold (as) to do something to dare to do something. □ *Would you care to dance, if I may make so bold as to ask?* □ *She made bold to confront her rival.*

make tracks ((to) somewhere) to go (somewhere) quickly and directly. □ *It's time for us to make tracks to the theater.* □ *It's getting late. We'd better make tracks.*

make water to urinate. □ *She's got some kind of condition where it hurts when she makes water.* □ *Can we stop at this here gas station? I need to make water.*

man-baby a male child. □ *Her first child was a man-baby.* □ *He wanted a man-baby to carry on his name.*

mantilla a lace shawl, often worn covering the head. (Spanish. Pronounced *man-TEE-ya*.) □ *Laura has a beautiful mantilla that belonged to her grandmother.* □ *She fixed her mantilla in place with a carved tortoiseshell comb.*

many (and many)'s the time there have been many times. □ *Many and many's the time I warned him not to go to the swimmin' hole by himself.* □ *Many's the time she's forgiven her husband.*

marble orchard See *bone orchard.*

mare's nest a mess. □ *Jim's room is a mare's nest. He never cleans it.* □ *Mary left the kitchen a mare's nest after cooking the big meal.*

marry up (with someone) to marry (someone). □ *They married up in the spring.* □ *Jane's going to marry up with someone she met at school.*

marryin' a wedding. □ *I guess I'll see you at the marryin' on Saturday.* □ *Everyone in town was invited to the marryin'.*

mash to press. □ *Mash the red button to turn it on.* □ *I mashed the switch, but the light didn't come on.*

Master's call death. (Usually with *the*.) □ *Ma went to the Master's call two years ago, God rest her soul.* □ *After a long illness, he yielded up to the Master's call.*

mauger weak; thin. □ *She was a mauger woman with a bad temper.* □ *I been feeling a little mauger of late.*

maverick **1.** a stray, unbranded calf. □ *I found a maverick out on the range. Guess it's mine now.* □ *We better brand them mavericks.* **2.** an unconventional person. □ *Jim was considered a maverick because he preferred bird-watching to hunting.* □ *The gunslinger was a maverick who roamed from town to town.*

Maw See *Ma.*

meadow muffin a pile of cow or horse manure. (Jocular. See also *cow chip.*) □ *I ruined my new shoes stepping in a meadow muffin.* □ *Joe's old horse ambled down the road, leaving a trail of meadow muffins behind it.*

meaner than a junkyard dog (with fourteen sucking pups) cruel; eager to fight. □ *Don't mess with her. She's meaner than a junkyard dog with fourteen sucking pups.* □ *They say Jim's meaner than a junkyard dog, but really, he's a sweetheart.*

measure someone on the ground to knock someone over. (A threat.) □ *He said he'd measure me on the ground. I said I'd punch his lights out.* □ *If I ever catch that con artist, I'll measure him on the ground.*

meat bee a stinging wasp. (See also *yellow jacket.*) □ *She went hiking in the woods and got stung by a meat bee.* □ *He stepped in a nest of meat bees.*

meddle with someone or something to fool or play with someone or something. □ *Do you aim to ask my sister to marry you? Or are you just meddling with her?* □ *Make him leave my stuff alone. He's always meddling with my things.*

men-folks men. (See also *women-folks.*) □ *The men-folks sat in the parlor and gossiped while the women did the dishes.* □ *When she was a little girl, Mary used to like to go fishing with the men-folks.*

mend to recover from an illness. □ TOM: *How's your mother? I heard she was sick.* MARY: *Mending nicely, thank you.* □ *It took Joe a long time to mend after his heart attack.*

mesa a hill with a flat top and steep sides; a tableland. (Spanish for "table." Pronounced *MAY-sa.*) □ *Acoma Pueblo is built on top of a mesa.* □ *We climbed to the top of the mesa to look at the view.*

mesquite a small, thorny, desert shrub. (From an Amerindian language via Spanish. Pronounced *mes-SKEET.*) □ *We made a fire out of mesquite.* □ *The cowboys wore chaps to protect their legs from the mesquite.*

mess with someone or something to trifle or fool with someone or something. □ *If you mess with Jim, he'll beat the bejeebers out of you.* □ *I caught them kids messing with matches!*

midwarp of the night the middle of the night; midnight. □ *They stayed up drinking and singing till the midwarp of the night.* □ *A sudden noise woke me at the midwarp of the night.*

might as well be hung for a sheep as (for) a lamb might as well commit a large fault as a small one, since the same punishment will result. □ *I'll take the expensive fishing rod. My wife will be mad at me no matter how much I spend, so I might as well be hung for a sheep as for a lamb.* □ *Figuring that they might as well be hung for a sheep as a lamb, the kids ate the whole pie, instead of just sneaking one piece.*

might could might be able to. □ CHARLIE: *Can you come out with me after work?* TOM: *I might could. I'll have to see if my wife has other plans.* □ *I might could help you, if you'll tell me what's the matter.*

mighty very. □ *We had a mighty fine time. Thanks for having us over.* □ *Jim's mighty stubborn.*

might(y) nigh almost. □ *We mighty nigh lost Mary that time she fell through the ice in the river.* □ *That was might nigh the worst night of my life.*

milk teeth baby teeth; the first set of teeth. □ *The baby was just getting her milk teeth.* □ *When he was seven years old, he started losing his milk teeth.*

mind to remember. □ *Do you mind the time we went on a picnic by the lake?* □ *His face looks familiar, but I can't mind his name.*

mind someone to obey someone. □ *Mind your sister while I'm away.* □ *Pa would whip us if we didn't mind him.*

mind the store (for someone) to look after things. □ *The boss left his secretary to mind the store for him when he went out of town.* □ *I have to run an errand. Mind the store, would you?*

mint julep a drink made of whiskey, sugar, and mint. □ *We sat on the shady porch, sipping mint juleps.* □ *My cousin from Mississippi taught me how to make a mint julep.*

misery chronic pain, such as arthritis. □ *I've tried everything to get rid of this misery in my back.* □ *Mrs. Belton keeps up with her knitting and sewing, in spite of all her miseries.*

misremember to forget something; to be uncertain about something. □ *I am afraid that I misremembered to fix the back porch step.* □ *I sort of misremembered when her birthday was. Sure made her mad.*

missus AND **the missus** a wife. □ *Is your missus at home now?* □ *I will ask the missus if there's enough food for you to eat with us.*

mite a very little bit. (Used with the indefinite article *a*.) □ *When Jane was sixteen, she got in a mite of trouble with the law.* □ JANE: *Would you like some more cake?* MARY: *Just a mite.*

Miz Mrs. □ *When you see Miz O'Halloran, tell her I said howdy.* □ *I'd like you to meet Miz Mary Jackson.*

moccasin a poisonous water snake. (Also *water moccasin.*) □ *Don't go in the river over there. It's full of mocassins.* □ *She got bit by a moccasin and died.*

mommick someone or something up to dirty someone or something. ☐ *He walked through a mud puddle in his new shoes and mommicked them up.* 🅃 *It took me three hours to clean the house, and it took Bill twenty minutes to mommick up the whole place.*

month of Sundays a long time. (See also *in a coon's age; in an age of years; in dog's years; since Hector was a pup.*) ☐ *I haven't been to a movie in a month of Sundays.* ☐ *It's been a month of Sundays since we visited your ma.*

monthlies a menstrual period. (See also *Grandma's come; visit from Flo; have one's lady's time; bad time (of the month).*) ☐ *She took it easy during her monthlies.* ☐ *It was past time for her monthlies. She thought she might be pregnant.*

moon-calf a foolish or stupid person. ☐ *Joe's acting like a moon-calf again. He must be in love.* ☐ *The young boy was a genius, but his teacher thought he was a moon-calf.*

moonshine corn liquor. ☐ *Pa had a still out in the woods to make moonshine.* ☐ *I keep a jug of moonshine for medicinal purposes.*

more hopeless than a one-legged man at a (butt-)kickin' contest completely hopeless. (Use caution with the *butt* version.) ☐ *My business will never succeed. It's more hopeless than a one-legged man at a butt-kickin' contest.* ☐ *Joe will never get Sally to go out with him. It's more hopeless than a one-legged man at a kickin' contest.*

more noise than a jackass in a tin barn AND **more noise than a mule in a tin barn** a great deal of noise. ☐ *Hush up! You kids are making more noise than a jackass in a tin barn!* ☐ *What's wrong with the engine? It's making more noise than a mule in a tin barn.*

more noise than a mule in a tin barn See *more noise than a jackass in a tin barn.*

more something than Carter had oats a very great deal of the thing named. (See also *more'n farmers have hay.*) ☐ TOM: *Is*

Bill very rich? JANE: *Rich? He's got more money than Carter had oats!* □ *Mary collects postcards. She has more postcards than Carter had oats.*

more ways than a country man can whip a mule many different ways. □ *Jane knows how to do up her hair more ways than a country man can whip a mule.* □ *All we had to eat was beans. I learned to fix beans more ways than a country man can whip a mule.*

more'n farmers have hay a great deal; to a great extent. (See also *more something than Carter had oats.*) □ *She's got boyfriends more'n farmers have hay.* □ *I hope things start to get better for Tom. He's had trouble more'n farmers have hay.*

mort a large quantity. □ *We've got a mort of tomatoes from the garden this summer. Would you like some to take home?* □ *They had a mort of trouble when they was first married.*

mosey to go at a leisurely pace. □ *Let's mosey on over to Joe's place.* □ *The tenderfoots moseyed down the trail.*

mostest most. □ *I got some but John has the mostest.* □ *Whoever is the fustest with the mostest wins the game.*

mountain canary a burro. □ *We had three mountain canaries to carry our supplies.* □ *In the morning, we were waked by the call of the mountain canary.*

mountain dew corn liquor. □ *My granddaddy made the best mountain dew.* □ *I'll have another glass of that there mountain dew.*

mountain lion a large wildcat. (See also *cougar; catamount; puma.*) □ *We saw a mountain lion's footprints in the snow.* □ *Something's been killing my sheep. I think it's a mountain lion.*

mountain oysters See *Rocky Mountain oysters.*

mourners' bench a bench near the pulpit in a church, where people sit who are supposedly concerned about their sins. (See also *amen corner.)* ☐ *I sat through the service on the mourners' bench, praying for God's grace.* ☐ *Jane sat up on the mourners' bench, crying and carrying on during the sermon.*

mouth organ a harmonica. ☐ *Play us a tune on your mouth organ.* ☐ *Joe played a song on his mouth organ, accompanying himself on the guitar.*

Much obliged! "Thank you!" ☐ TOM: *I'd be glad to help you.* JANE: *Much obliged!* ☐ CHARLIE: *Can I borrow your typewriter?* MARY: *Certainly.* CHARLIE: *Much obliged!*

mudcat a catfish. ☐ TOM: *Catch anything?* JANE: *Just a couple of mudcats.* ☐ *We had the mudcats fried for dinner.*

mule in horse harness a common person dressed in fine clothes or putting on fine manners. ☐ *Joe wore a tuxedo, but everyone could tell he was just a mule in horse harness.* ☐ *The Joneses act so fine, but as far as I'm concerned, they're mules in horse harness.*

mule skinner someone who drives mules. ☐ *Curly was an experienced mule skinner who had been down the Santa Fe trail many times.* ☐ *The mule skinner stopped the wagon to see what was wrong with his team.*

mushmelon a musk melon; a cantaloupe. ☐ *Jane's growing mushmelons and cantaloupes this year.* ☐ *We had a nice juicy mushmelon for dessert.*

mustang a wild horse. ☐ *The cowboy tried to rope the mustang.* ☐ *Joe tried to break the mustang, but it threw him off every time.*

My eye! AND **My foot!** "Nonsense!"; "I do not believe that!" (See also *My granny!*) ☐ TOM: *Joe says to tell you he didn't mean what he said.* JANE: *He didn't mean it, my eye!* ☐ JANE: *I didn't mean to make you ruin your drawing.* CHARLIE: *My foot! You pushed my arm on purpose!*

My foot! See *My eye!*

My granny! "Nonsense!"; "I do not believe it!" (See also *My eye!*) □ *Sally's twenty-five years old, my granny! She's thirty-one if she's a day.* □ JANE: *I feel I should apologize.* TOM: *My granny! You didn't do anything you need to feel sorry for.*

My momma didn't raise no fool(s). AND **My momma didn't raise no stupid child.** I am not stupid. □ *I can tell when a man's trying to cheat me. My mama didn't raise no fools.* □ BILL: *I love you. That other girl was just a fling.* MARY: *Oh, come on. My mama didn't raise no fool.* □ SALESMAN: *If you don't buy it right now, someone else will buy it.* CUSTOMER: *Look, my mama didn't raise no stupid child. I know you're just trying to pressure me.*

My momma didn't raise no stupid child. See *My momma didn't raise no fool(s).*

N

nag a poor horse. (Slang.) □ *I don't have a car. Just this old nag.* □ *I can't believe I put a hundred dollars on that nag to win the race!*

nana AND **naner** a banana. □ *Little Jed ain't never seen a naner before. Let him taste of it.* □ *I like nanas on my cereal.*

naner See *nana.*

narrow between the eyes untrustworthy. □ *I had a feeling he was narrow between the eyes, so I didn't loan him any money.* □ *Don't ever let that cousin of mine near your girlfriend. He's narrow between the eyes.*

narvish nervous. □ *That horse is awful narvish, twitching his ears all the time.* □ *She felt a little narvish as she stepped onto the stage.*

nary not; not any; none. (Compare to *ary.*) □ *None of my friends came to the party. Nary a one.* □ TOM: *Can I borrow an onion?* MARY: *I'd let you, but I ain't got nary.*

near side the left side. (See also *off side.*) □ *There's something wrong with the ox on the near side.* □ *Always mount a horse from the near side.*

necessary an outhouse. (See also *federal building; gardenhouse.*) □ *They don't have an indoor toilet, just a necessary in the back yard.* □ *He's sick with something. He spent the whole day in the necessary.*

neck of the woods an area or vicinity. □ *We haven't seen Joe in this neck of the woods for at least a year.* □ *I'm not too familiar with that neck of the woods.*

necktie frolic See *necktie party.*

necktie party AND **necktie frolic; necktie social** a hanging. □ *We'll have a little necktie party for the horse thief.* □ *The outlaw was invited to a necktie frolic.* □ *The prisoner could hear the good citizens of the town preparing a necktie social just for him.*

necktie social See *necktie party.*

need something like a pig needs a hip pocket to have no need for something. □ *I can't believe Sally's pregnant again. She needs another baby like a pig needs a hip pocket.* □ *Joe ain't much of a scholar. He needs an encyclopedia like a pig needs a hip pocket.*

needle grass a grass with sharp seed heads. □ *We'd better burn that patch of needle grass so the cows won't try to eat it.* □ *We went walking through the prairie and got needle grass stuck in our legs.*

neighbor (someone) round to visit and take care of someone. □ *Jane went neighboring round to see if Tom needed anything.* □ *While Mary was sick, we neighbored her round every day.*

neither hide nor hair nothing; no sign. □ *Joe went out at six o'clock and we've seen neither hide nor hair of him since.* □ *My dog is missing. There's neither hide nor hair of him to show where he went.*

nester a pioneer farmer. □ *The cowboy scorned the nesters who came to settle the land.* □ *Whole families of nesters came West in covered wagons.*

never said pea turkey did not say anything. □ *How was I to know that Mary needed money, when she never said pea turkey?* □ *No one knew that it was Bill's birthday. He never said pea turkey.*

nigh on to do something almost did something. □ *I nigh on to died when I saw her coming across the room to me.* □ *Bill nigh on to killed his best friend in that fight.*

nigh onto almost. □ *It was nigh onto six o'clock.* □ *They earned nigh onto three hundred dollars.*

nip and tuck neck and neck. □ *It was nip and tuck to the end of the race.* □ *The boys ran nip and tuck to the swimming hole.*

nit-brained stupid; foolish. □ *Sometimes she says the most nit-brained things you ever did hear.* □ *I'm tired of putting up with them nit-brained customers at the store.*

no-(ac)count worthless. □ *Mary's husband is a lazy, no-account bum.* □ *John was hanging out with a bunch of no-'count juvenile delinquents.*

no call for something no reason to do something. □ *Why did you make fun of Mary's clothes? There was no call for that!* □ *Now, now, there's no call for you to show off.*

no great shakes nothing important. □ TOM: *I spilled my drink on your carpet. I'm so sorry.* MARY: *Don't worry. It's no great shakes.* □ *Jane said it was the best movie ever made, but I thought it was no great shakes.*

No harm done. "Everything is all right."; "Nothing is hurt." (Often used to respond to an apology, as in the second example.) □ *The car went off the road, but no one was hurt. No harm done.* □ TOM: *I'm so sorry! I didn't mean to shove you.* CHARLIE: *No harm done.*

no rue-back with no trading back. (Used in bargaining.) □ *I gave him my horse for his ox team, no rue-back.* □ *You can have my quilt if I can have them earbobs of yours, no rue-back.*

no-see-ums small, biting insects. □ *Clouds of no-see-ums gathered around us as we walked up the trail.* □ *It's nice up at the lake, except for the mosquitoes and the no-see-ums.*

No-siree! See *No-siree bob(tail)!*

No-siree bob(tail)! AND **No-siree!** "No." (Emphatic.) □ TOM: *Aren't you a Democrat?* JANE: *No-siree bobtail! Everyone in my family is a Republican.* □ *I don't like working with Bill. No-siree bob, I don't!* □ *No-siree! I don't cotton to drinking when I'm meant to be plowing.*

no two ways about it there can be no disagreement. □ FATHER: *Time for you to go to bed.* CHILD: *But—* FATHER: *Bedtime! No two ways about it!* □ *No two ways about it—prices are definitely going up.*

noggin the head or brain. □ *Use your noggin! You'll figure something out.* □ *He gets the queerest ideas in his noggin.*

nohow no way; not in any way. □ *I tried and tried, but I couldn't get the lawn mower to work nohow.* □ *Ain't nohow anybody's going to get past my old watchdog.*

No'm. "No, ma'am." □ MARY: *Can I get you another slice of pie?* TOM: *No'm. I'm full.* □ SALLY: *Did you take the money I left on the desk?* BILL: *No'm.*

not a patch on someone or something nowhere near as good as someone or something. □ *This new truck ain't a patch on my old Ford.* □ *She's not a patch on your first wife, if you don't mind my saying so.*

not about to certainly not going to. □ *It wasn't a very good meal, but I wasn't about to say so to the host.* □ *Jim wasn't about to say what he really thought.*

not dry behind the ears AND **wet behind the ears** inexperienced. □ *From the questions she asked, you could tell she was not dry behind the ears.* □ *I wanted to hire an experienced waiter, but I wound up with this kid who's still wet behind the ears.*

not enough brains to grease a skillet stupid. □ *She has a sweet personality, but not enough brains to grease a skillet.* □ *I don't* *know how he ever passed first grade. He don't have enough brains to grease a skillet.*

not enough meat on him to make a poor man a bowl of soup very thin. □ *When he got out of the army, he didn't have enough meat on him to make a poor man a bowl of soup.* □ *She's too skinny. Not enough meat on her to make a poor man a bowl of soup.*

not enough room to swing a cat very little room. □ *Have you seen Jane's new apartment? Not enough room to swing a cat!* □ *Such little classrooms—not enough room to swing a cat!*

not enough sense to pound sand in a rat hole not enough sense to think clearly. □ *I declare, sometimes I think you don't have enough sense to pound sand in a rat hole!* □ *He's got plenty of book learning, but not enough sense to pound sand in a rat hole.*

not enough to dust a fiddle very little. □ TOM: *How much snow did you get?* JANE: *Not enough to dust a fiddle.* □ *I'll need to borrow some sugar. I don't have enough to dust a fiddle.*

not know someone or something from Adam's housecat AND **not know someone or something from Adam's off ox** not to know someone or something at all. (*Adam's off ox* is Adam's right-hand ox. An elaboration of *not know someone from Adam.*) □ *No, I don't recognize you. I don't know you from Adam's housecat.* □ *He says he went to high school with me, but I don't know him from Adam's off ox.*

not know someone or something from Adam's off ox See *not know someone or something from Adam's housecat.*

not long for this world about to die. □ *Sally's not long for this world, I'm afraid.* □ *The vet knew that the old dog was not long for this world.*

not much for something not good at something; not liking to do something. □ *Daddy wasn't much for romance, but he did bring Mama flowers on her birthday every year.* □ *I never got a letter from Jane, but I didn't worry. I knew she wasn't much for writing.*

not on your Nellie AND **not on your tintype** "No." (Very emphatic.) □ TOM: *Are you going to Joe's party?* JANE: *Not on your Nellie! His parties bore me to death!* □ CHILD: *I'm going to have this last slice of pie, OK?* MOTHER: *Not on your tintype! I'm saving that for your father.*

not on your tintype See *not on your Nellie.*

not playing with a full deck not able to think clearly for any of a variety of reasons. □ *Sometimes I think Bill is not playing with a full deck. Last night I saw him run out into the snow with his bathing suit on.* □ CHARLIE: *Joe says he saw Martians land in front of the courthouse last night.* MARY: *Yeah, but Joe's not playing with a full deck.*

not since the year One not for a long time. □ TOM: *When was the last time you saw Mary?* JANE: *Not since the year One.* □ *Not since the year One have so many people come to the town festival.*

not sure but what something to believe something. □ *I'm not sure but what Joe's in love with Mary.* □ JANE: *Is the interstate the best way to go?* MARY: *I'm not sure but what it is.*

not worth a continental worthless. □ *Most of those "collectibles" aren't worth a continental.* □ *I paid two hundred dollars for that land, and now I find out it's not worth a continental.*

not worth a hill of beans worthless. □ *Bill's promises aren't worth a hill of beans.* □ *This set of collector's coins cost me fifty dollars, and now it's not worth a hill of beans.*

not worth a shovelful of chicken tracks worthless. (See also *wouldn't give (someone) a shovelful of chicken tracks for someone or something.*) □ *Jim thinks his old comic books are worth a lot of money, but they're not worth a shovelful of chicken tracks.* □ *Some of the things at antique shows are valuable, but a lot of them aren't worth a shovelful of chicken tracks.*

nothing to sneeze at something significant. □ TOM: *I only earned a hundred dollars.* JANE: *A hundred dollars is nothing to sneeze at.* □ *He hasn't had a lot of education, but his work experience is nothing to sneeze at.*

(Now) what did you go and do that for? "Why did you do that?" □ *The baby spilled her glass of juice. "Now what did you go and do that for?" her father asked as he cleaned it up.* □ TOM: *I told Bill we're going to give him a surprise party.* MARY: *What did you go and do that for?*

odd jobs all types of jobs; miscellaneous types of work. □ *Joe did odd jobs to make ends meet.* □ *Jane mows lawns in the summer and does odd jobs in the winter.*

of a morning in the morning. □ *Our neighbors often came round of a morning.* □ *I like to have a cup of tea of a morning.*

off ear the right ear. (Compare with *near side.* See also *off ox; off side.*) □ *He's deaf in the off ear.* □ *She wore one earring in her off ear.*

off one's feed not eating as much as one usually does. □ *I'm afraid something's wrong with the cow. She's off her feed.* □ *Bill didn't take that last piece of fried chicken. He must be off his feed.*

off ox the ox on the right side of an ox team. (See also *off ear; off side.*) □ *The off ox stumbled and the plow lurched.* □ *You hitch up the off ox. I'll hitch up the near one.*

off side the right side. (See also *near side.*) □ *The horse threw one of the shoes on his off side.* □ *The cow was limping on her off side.*

offen See *off'n.*

off'n AND **offen** off. □ *I took the books off'n the table.* □ *Get that cat offen my clean clothes.*

Oh, foot! "Oh, darn!" (A mock oath.) □ *Oh, foot! The electricity's out again.* □ *Oh, foot! I made a wrong turn.*

okey-dokey "all right"; "OK." □ TOM: *Come on over.* JANE: *Okey-dokey.* □ *That's okey-dokey with me.*

Okie someone from Oklahoma. (Can be considered insulting.) □ *I'm an Okie born and bred. Grew up in Bartlesville.* □ *Jim thinks we're ignorant Okies just because we're poor.*

Old Dominion the state of Virginia. □ *I can tell by your accent that you hail from the Old Dominion.* □ *There are many historic landmarks in our beloved Old Dominion.*

old hand an experienced person. □ *I don't need you to help me. I'm an old hand at riding horses.* □ *By my fourth baby, I was getting to be an old hand at motherhood.*

old man a husband. (See also *old woman.*) □ *My old man works over at the paper mill.* □ *Jane and her old man went out to pick blueberries.*

Old Man River See *Old Muddy.*

Old Muddy AND **Big Muddy; Old Man River** the Mississippi River. □ *Riverboats still travel up and down Old Muddy.* □ *We crossed the Big Muddy at St. Louis.* □ *They watched the barges floating down Old Man River.*

Old Ned the devil. □ *That mustang's got plenty of the Old Ned in him.* □ *Old Ned tempted me, and I went astray.*

Old Scratch the devil. □ *Sometimes Old Scratch gets the best of me, and I do things I know I shouldn't oughta.* □ *Mary must have made a bargain with Old Scratch, to keep her looking so young.*

old stomping ground(s) a place where one formerly lived, worked, or played. □ *Dad took me up to Chicago to show me his old stomping grounds.* □ *Yes, I'm familiar with Albuquerque. It's my old stomping ground.*

old-time old-fashioned. □ *They had an old-time square dance in the veterans' hall.* □ *I love the old-time hymns like "Bringing in the Sheaves."*

old-timer an old person. □ *The historian talked to the old-timers and wrote down the stories they told.* □ *A couple of old-timers were playing checkers out in front of the general store.*

old-timey old-fashioned. □ *Granny has a real old-timey telephone in her hallway.* □ *These clothes ain't old-timey. They just outlived their time.*

old woman a wife. (See also *old man.*) □ *My old woman still looks pretty good when she gets gussied up.* □ *Come on over, and bring your old woman!*

on account of because; because of. □ *Gramma can't knit anymore on account of her arthritis.* □ *I can't come on account of Mama won't let me.*

on end a period of time without end. □ *She could listen to fiddle music for hours on end.* □ *We waited for hours on end to hear the band.* □ *For days on end, she watched for him to come back.*

on God's footstool on Earth. □ *I was the happiest person on God's footstool.* □ *I think this valley is about the prettiest place on God's footstool.*

on God's green earth on Earth; in the whole world. □ *He thought she was the most wonderful woman on God's green earth.* □ *You won't find a better breed of horses on God's green earth.*

on the dodge fleeing from something; escaping from the law. □ *He had been on the dodge for weeks and hadn't dared to show his face in the daylight.* □ *She escaped from prison. She's on the dodge.*

on the fritz broken; not working. □ *I can't watch my soap opera because my TV's on the fritz.* □ *It sure is hot in here. The air-conditioning must be on the fritz again.*

on the hoof walking around, as a beast with four feet. □ *We didn't think of the cow as a pet. To us, she was milk and cheese on the hoof.* □ *The rich young woman knew that many of the men who courted her saw her as wealth on the hoof.*

on the QT in secret. □ *She told me she was getting married, but she asked me to keep it on the QT.* □ *He slipped me a few dollars on the QT.*

on the ticket on credit. □ *We had to buy our groceries on the ticket that month.* □ *He bought that car on the ticket.*

on the warpath looking for a fight. □ *The boss was on the warpath this morning. We all stayed out of her way.* □ *Joe is on the warpath for the guy who stole his money.*

oncet AND **wunst** once. (Pronounced *WUHNST.*) □ *I been to Atlanta oncet.* □ *Sally had a dress like that wunst.*

one one or the other. (Used at the end of a sentence.) □ *Jim looks awful sick. That, or he's drunk, one.* □ *You'll have to pay the money now, or else pay interest on it, one.*

one-holer an outhouse with one seat. (And, of course, *two-holer, three-holer, four-holer*, etc.) □ *They didn't have an indoor toilet. Just an old one-holer out in the yard.* □ *The kids at camp lined up to use the two-holer in the morning.*

one-horse town a very small town. (Derogatory.) □ *I can't wait to get out of this one-horse town.* □ *The band toured dozens of one-horse towns that summer.*

one jump ahead a little bit ahead of someone or something. □ *Jane always stays one jump ahead of the people she owes money to.* □ *The company was one jump ahead of its competitors.*

one-pipe shotgun a single-barreled shotgun. (See also *two-pipe shotgun.*) □ *Jim got a one-pipe shotgun for his fourteenth birthday.* □ *That two-pipe shotgun ain't no good for rabbits. You want to use a one-pipe shotgun.*

one red cent a single penny. (Used in negative expressions, as in the examples.) □ *I won't pay you one red cent for such shoddy repair work!* □ *The millionaire never gave one red cent to charity.*

one's best bib and tucker one's best clothes. □ *Mary put on her best bib and tucker for the school dance.* □ *It's going to be a fancy dinner, so put on your best bib and tucker.*

one's cake is dough one has lost status. □ *Mary's cake is dough ever since she got drunk at the party.* □ *She used to be the most popular girl in town, but now her cake is dough.*

One's eyes are bigger than one's belly. AND **One's eyes are bigger than one's stomach.** One took more food than one could eat. (Sometimes used to scold children for taking too much food.) □ *Ain't you gonna finish your potatoes? I guess your eyes are bigger than your belly!* □ *Harry left most of his cake on his plate. His eyes were bigger than his stomach.*

One's eyes are bigger than one's stomach. See *One's eyes are bigger than one's belly.*

one's fingers are all thumbs someone's fingers or hands are awkward or unskilled. □ *Joe ain't much of a woodcarver. His fingers are all thumbs.* □ *I never could learn to sew, not even to mend my own clothes. My fingers are all thumbs.*

one's level best the very best one can do. □ *I did my level best, but I couldn't finish my dessert.* □ *Jim vowed to do his level best in school next year.*

one's own self one's self. □ *You stay out of this. I'll do it my own self.* □ *If Sally wants to cook that fancy meal, she's going to have to do it her own self. I ain't helping.*

one's Sunday best one's best clothes. □ *She dressed up in her Sunday best and went to town.* □ *He put on his Sunday best for the big dance.*

onliest only. □ *That old mule was Joe's onliest friend.* □ *Mary is the onliest child her mother has left.*

open one's head to speak. □ *Come on. Open your head. Let's hear your opinion.* □ *Nellie's awful shy. She almost never opens her head.*

Open your mouth and shut your eyes and I'll give you a big surprise. AND **Open your mouth and shut your eyes and I'll give you something to make you wise.** Shut your eyes, and I will give you something to eat. (A children's rhyme.) □ *Bill said, "Open your mouth and shut your eyes, and I'll give you a big surprise." I shut my eyes, and he put a piece of candy in my mouth.* □ JANE: *Open your mouth and shut your eyes, and I'll give you something to make you wise.* CHARLIE: *I'm not going to shut my eyes. You'll put that frog in my mouth.*

Open your mouth and shut your eyes and I'll give you something to make you wise. See *Open your mouth and shut your eyes and I'll give you a big surprise.*

opry opera. (See also *horse opera.*) □ *I don't think I could stay awake at an opry to know whether I liked it or not.* □ *City folks go to a lot of opries and such.*

ornery stubborn; crabby. (Pronounced *OR-nur-rie* or *ON-rie.*) □ *The ornery horse wouldn't go where I wanted him to.* □ *Sally folded her arms and got an ornery look on her face.*

orts scraps and bits of organic material. □ *There was some chicken orts left around after Jed dressed the chicken.* □ *Somebody ought to sweep the floor. There's orts everywhere.*

other side death; the afterlife. □ *He hoped to see his beloved wife again on the other side.* □ *My daddy crossed over to the other side before I was born.*

ourn ours. (See also *hisn; hern; theirn.*) □ *This house is ourn now.* □ *The Guernsey cattle are ourn.*

out of kilter not working; not adjusted properly. (See also *out of whack.*) □ *The air conditioner is out of kilter. It blows hot air instead of cold.* □ *You can't use that telephone. It's out of kilter.*

out of whack not working properly. (See also *out of kilter.*) □ *The TV is all out of whack. The picture is fuzzy and there's no sound.* □ *Jane's stomach is out of whack, so she's on a liquid diet.*

outcoyote someone or something See *outfox someone or something.*

outen See *out'n.*

outfit an organization. □ *The Boy Scouts is a pretty good outfit.* □ *Jim runs some kind of wholesale outfit.*

outfox someone or something AND **outcoyote someone or something** to outsmart someone or something. □ *The horse thief outfoxed the sheriff and got clean away.* □ *Jim thought he could outcoyote me by pretending he wasn't at home.*

outlaw someone who has broken the law; a fugitive. □ *The outlaw hid out in the cave.* □ *The sheriff tracked the outlaw across five counties.*

out'n AND **outen** out of. □ *She took the flour out'n the pantry.* □ *How do you get the honey outen the honeycomb?*

outsider an illegitimate child. (See also *ash-barrel baby; blackberry baby; brush colt; volunteer; woods colt.*) □ *All her kids was outsiders.* □ *She was pregnant before she got married, so her baby was an outsider.*

over my dead body "Never."; "Not while I am alive." (An emphatic refusal.) □ TOM: *Jane and I are getting married.* BILL: *Over my dead body.* □ *My son is getting a motorcycle—over my dead body.*

over to at. (See also *up to.*) □ *There's a party over to the Jones' place.* □ *What's going on over to the newspaper office? All the lights are on.*

overhalls overalls. □ *He wore a clean pair of overhalls.* □ *The children put on their overhalls and went out to pick cotton.*

own-born cousins first cousins. □ *Jim and me is own-born cousins.* □ *Most of my own-born cousins live in this same town.*

own up (to something) to confess to something; to admit having done something. □ *I felt better after I owned up.* □ *Whoever took my wallet had better own up to it!*

oxbow a U-shaped curve in a river. □ *A stand of oak trees grew by the oxbow.* □ *Follow the river to the oxbow, then turn west.*

P

Pa AND **Paw** Father. □ *Pa, can I go out and play?* □ *"Aw, Paw," the child moaned as he did his chores.*

pack a weapon to carry the weapon named. □ *He's dangerous. He always packs a gun.* □ *Jim was packing a switchblade.*

pack of lies a group of lies; a succession of lies. □ *Bill told my friends a pack of lies about me.* □ *Everything the salesman told me about this car was a pack of lies.*

padre a priest. (Spanish.) □ *They needed a padre to perform the wedding ceremony.* □ *We asked the padre to lead us in a prayer.*

paint AND **pinto** a white-and-brown, or white-and-black horse. (*Pinto* is Spanish. See also *Appaloosa; bay; chestnut; palomino; piebald; roan.*) □ *I'll ride the palomino. You ride the paint.* □ *My old pinto Stormy was the best saddle horse I ever had.*

paint one's tonsils to drink whiskey. (Jocular. See also *tonsil paintin'.*) □ *The cowboys went to the saloon to paint their tonsils.* □ *What say we find a bar and paint our tonsils?*

paint the town red to go out and have a wild time. □ *When you come to visit, we'll paint the town red.* □ *The two friends got together and painted the town red.*

painted woman a woman wearing makeup, often considered to be of ill-repute in some communities. (Derogatory in contexts where makeup is considered sinful or the work of a sinful woman.) □ *Why do you want to go to the city and live among them painted women and sinful men?* □ *Sally hid the fact that she used lipstick, lest her neighbors accuse her of being a painted woman.*

painter a panther; a large wildcat. □ *He took his gun in case he ran into a painter.* □ *I heard a painter growl in the distance.*

paisano a country person; a peasant. (Spanish.) □ *The paisanos worked the land for their landlord.* □ *His rough hands and sunburned skin told me he was a paisano.*

palomino a horse with a gold-colored coat and cream-colored mane and tail. (See also *Appaloosa; bay; chestnut; paint; piebald; roan.*) □ *That palomino was beautiful, but the meanest animal on God's green earth.* □ *A woman on a palomino carried the flag at the head of the parade.*

pan out to work out satisfactorily. □ *Bill's hardware store didn't pan out.* □ *They hoped this new venture would pan out.*

pantywaist a weak or effeminate man. (Derogatory.) □ *He talks tough, but he's a real pantywaist.* □ *Stand up and fight like a man, you pantywaist!*

pappy a father. □ *My pappy taught me how to play the mouth organ.* □ *Bill is Jim's pappy.*

pard(ner) friend; partner. (Often used as a form of address.) □ *Say, pardner, let us have a drink from your canteen.* □ *The gambler and his pard roamed from town to town.*

pass muster to be acceptable. □ *Before we went to church on Sunday, we had to pass muster with Ma. She made sure our faces were washed and our clothes were clean.* □ *How's my typing? Will it pass muster?*

pass the time of day to chat. □ *I stopped to pass the time of day with Miz Jones.* □ *It took him a long time to do his shopping, because he passed the time of day with everyone in the store.*

passel a large number. (Usually used with the indefinite article *a*.) □ *When Sally grows up, she wants a house in the country and a passel of kids.* □ *A passel of folks had gathered to hear the man preaching on the street corner.*

Paw See *Pa.*

pay someone any mind to pay attention to someone. (Usually used in negative expressions.) □ CHILD: *Billy's teasing me.* MOTHER: *Well, just you don't pay him any mind.* □ *When Jane starts talking politics, I don't pay her any mind.* □ *Don't pay him no mind. He's just being obnoxious.*

pea green very inexperienced. (See also *green; greenhorn.*) □ *The waiter was pea green. He took forever to get our orders right.* □ *The sergeant had to train the pea green recruits.*

peaked weak; unwell. (Pronounced *PEEK-id.*) □ *I think I'll turn in early. I'm feeling peaked.* □ *Are you OK? You look a little peaked.*

'pears to me it appears to me. □ *'Pears to me that your dog is sick.* □ *Joe's getting to think mighty highly of himself, 'pears to me.*

peart See *pert.*

peck of something a lot of something, usually trouble. □ *You are in a whole peck of trouble now!* □ *We had a whole peck of problems with the icebox.*

peckerwood **1.** a woodpecker. □ *I heard a peckerwood pecking on a tree—tok! tok! tok!* □ *The tree was full of peckerwood holes.* **2.** a poor white person. (Now almost always disparaging.) □ *Those peckerwoods can't even afford shoes!* □ *Some of those pecker-woods walk miles in barefeet to get schooling.*

pecking order a hierarchy; the levels of power in a group. □ *Bill is the first in the pecking order around here. Don't ever make him mad.* □ *I don't understand the pecking order in the women's club at all.*

persnickety fussy; picky. □ *Joe is awful persnickety about his food. He won't eat anything the least bit spicy.* □ *She's so persnickety. She always finds fault with everything.*

pert AND **peart** lively; cheerful; spirited. □ *She was a right pert young girl.* □ *I was poorly last week, but I'm peart today, thank you.*

pert(y)near almost; "pretty near." □ *I pertnear killed that deer when my car hit it.* □ *She slipped and pertynear fell right down.*

pesky bothersome; irritating. □ *These pesky kids keep interrupting me.* □ *There was this one pesky fly kept buzzing in my ear all night.*

peter out to run out. □ *His strength had petered out by the end of the hike.* □ *Her voice petered out as she forgot what she wanted to say.*

piccalilli a spicy relish made of vegetables and peppers. □ *Aunt Beth made two quarts of piccalilli.* □ *Have some of this piccalilli with your catfish.*

pick someone or something off to shoot someone or something. □ *See that blackbird on the telephone wire? I can pick it off at fifty yards.* [T] *The outlaw, up on the cliff, picked off the deputies down in the valley.*

pickin' and singin' country singing accompanied by picking a guitar or banjo. □ *There'll be plenty of pickin' and singin' at the hoedown.* □ *The band did plenty of good old-time pickin' and singin'.*

piddle around to mess around; to waste time. □ *I piddled around with the TV, but I couldn't fix it.* □ *She spent her whole summer just piddling around.*

piddlin' worthless. □ *He gave me some piddlin' excuse about having to stay late at the office.* □ *She thinks she's so great because she got second prize in some piddlin' contest.*

pie plant rhubarb. □ *I like pie plant and strawberry pie.* □ *I picked some pie plant from the garden.*

pie safe a wooden box for storing bread and pies. □ *I got some sweet rolls in the pie safe. Help yourself.* □ *My daddy made that pie safe for my mama.*

piebald a horse with patches of black and white on its coat. (See also *Appaloosa; bay; chestnut; paint; palomino; roan.*) □ *Would you rather ride the piebald or the bay?* □ *Jim's piebald was the fastest horse in the county.*

pike a toll road; a highway; a road. □ *Take the county road till you get to the pike.* □ *The car was going down the pike at about eighty miles an hour.*

pin someone's ears back to scold someone severely. (See also *have one's ears pinned back.*) □ *Ma pinned my ears back for hitting my little sister.* □ *No matter how many times the teacher pinned her ears back, Jane kept giggling in class.*

pinda See *pinder.*

pinder AND **pinda** a peanut. (Probably from Kikongo, a Bantu language of Western Central Africa.) □ *Have some of these roast pinders.* □ *Joe puts pindas in his meat stews.*

pine-straw dried pine needles. □ *The trail was covered with pine-straw.* □ *We sat on the pine-straw under the old pine tree.*

piney-woods **1.** the pine woods of the Southern U.S. □ *I grew up in the piney-woods, and I think it's the most beautiful place on earth.* □ *He was from a little town in the piney-woods.* **2.** from or having to do with the Southern pine woods. □ *She was a piney-woods girl, born and raised.* □ *I still remember those piney-woods afternoons, with the warm breezes carrying the scent of the trees.*

piney-woods rooter a wild hog. □ *Joe shot a piney-woods rooter and brought it home for supper.* □ *We heard a piney-woods rooter crashing around in the brush.*

pinñon a small pine tree that grows in the mountains. (Spanish.) □ *They cut down some pinñons for firewood.* □ *We had roasted pinñon nuts for a snack.*

pinto See *paint.*

piss and moan to complain obnoxiously. (Use with caution.) □ *Jane's always pissin' and moanin' about how she never gets to go into town.* □ *I got tired of listening to Bill piss and moan about his job.*

piss and vinegar AND **spit and vinegar; vim and vinegar** liveliness; high spirits. (Use caution with *piss.*) □ *When we was young we was full of piss and vinegar. We'd do anything for fun.* □ *The kitten was full of spit and vinegar. She'd fight with other cats, strings, and her own tail.* □ *The bully tried to make Joe give him his lunch money, but Joe, who was always full of vim and vinegar, said, "Who's gonna make me?"*

piss poor very poor. (Use with caution.) □ *They're so piss poor they can't afford electric lights.* □ *He was piss poor when he started out, but now he's the richest man in town.* □ *I'll never get into college—my grades are piss poor.*

piss up a rope AND **piss up a tree** get lost; go away and stop bothering me. (Use with caution.) □ *I asked Joe to help me, and he told me to go piss up a rope.* □ TOM: *What about that money you owe me?* BILL: *Go piss up a tree.*

piss up a tree See *piss up a rope.*

pizen poison. □ *Lots of the berries you find in the woods are pizen.* □ *She drank pizen and died.*

pizen vine poison ivy. □ *I brushed against a patch of pizen vine and got a terrible rash.* □ *Look out for that pizen vine when you go camping.*

plague someone to bother someone. □ *Quit plaguing me. I'm trying to think.* □ *The kids plagued their pa till he promised to build them a toy wagon.*

Plague take it! "Damn it!" (A mock oath.) □ *Plague take it! The cat got out and killed all the chicks!* □ *Plague take it! I jest can't get this checkbook to balance.*

plant someone to bury someone (a corpse). □ *I went to Jim's funeral, but I didn't go to the graveyard to see them plant him.* □ *They planted the dead man the day he was shot.*

play it close to the vest to keep one's plans secret. □ JANE: *Is Joe going to sell his land?* TOM: *I don't know. He's playing it close to the vest.* □ *We have no idea who will get the promotion. Our boss is playing it close to the vest.*

play possum to pretend to be dead. □ *I played possum while the grizzly sniffed at me.* □ *Joe played possum, hoping the enemy soldier wouldn't notice him.*

play-pretty a toy. □ *Look, honey! Daddy brought you a play-pretty.* □ *The children sat on the porch with their play-pretties.*

plaza a public square. (Spanish.) □ *There will be speeches in the plaza at noon.* □ *The plaza was filled with people celebrating New Year's Eve.*

plow someone's furrow to have sexual intercourse with someone. (Use with caution.) □ *I hear Joe is plowing Sally's furrow.* □ *Don't you plow that gal's furrow unlessen you intend to marry her.*

plow to the end of the row to finish what one is supposed to do. □ *You can count on Mary. It may take her awhile, but she'll plow to the end of the row.* □ *Bill refused to give up. He was bound and determined to plow to the end of the row.*

plug ugly **1.** very ugly. □ *He was plug ugly even before his nose got broke.* □ *She's plug ugly, with a bad temper to boot.* **2.** a very ugly person. □ *She's not a plug-ugly, but she's not pretty, either.* □ *The postmaster was an old plug-ugly who always smoked a cigar.*

plug(ed) nickel a worthless thing. (Often used in the expressions *wouldn't give a plugged nickel for someone or something* or *someone or something is not worth a plugged nickel,* meaning someone or something is worthless.) □ *That was a good car when Bill bought it, but I wouldn't give a plugged nickel for it now.* □ *That land ain't worth a plug nickel.*

plumb quite; completely. □ *It was plumb stupid of you to leave your keys in the car.* □ *Thanks for the loan. That's plumb decent of you.*

plumb loco completely crazy. □ *Jim gets plumb loco if he drinks too much whiskey.* □ *Mary says she can talk to ghosts. I think she's plumb loco.*

plumgranny a pomegranate. □ *Mary lives in California. She has a plumgranny tree growing in her front yard.* □ *Plumgrannies are my favorite fruit.*

plump someone or something down to set someone or something down firmly. (Someone includes *oneself.*) □ *She plumped herself down in the rocking chair.* 🅃 *Joe plumped down the groceries on the table.*

plunder room a storage room. □ *On rainy days, we'd play up in Grandma's plunder room, going through all the old trunks.* □ *Put the empty boxes in the plunder room. We might need them later.*

Podunk **1.** a small, fictional country town. □ *My company transferred me to Podunk, Idaho.* □ *The movie was popular in the cities, but it was too racy for the folks in Podunk, U.S.A.* **2.** resembling or having to do with a small country town. □ *I hate this little Podunk town.* □ *The educated young man was snubbed by Podunk society.*

point-blank plainly; directly. □ *He point-blank refused to help me.* □ *She was point-blank the meanest woman I ever met.*

poke **1.** a bag; a paper sack. □ *I put the tomatoes in my poke and headed home.* □ *Everything she has in the world is in that poke.* **2.** someone who drives cows. (See also *cow poke.*) □ *I was a poke for thirty years.* □ *They're hiring pokes up at Johnson's Ranch.* **3.** a plant with edible leaves and poisonous berries. □

Get some of that poke for a salad. □ *We found a patch of poke in the woods.*

poker face a facial expression that reveals no emotion. □ *I never know if Bill's joking. He says the most outrageous things with a poker face.* □ *I couldn't tell from her poker face if she was lying or not.*

pokey **1.** a jail. □ *How long is he in the pokey for?* □ *Did you hear that Jane's in the pokey?* **2.** slow. □ *How come you're so pokey this morning?* □ *He could outrun any kid in his class, but he was awfully pokey when it came to walking to school.*

polecat **1.** a skunk. (The *pole* is from the French word for *chicken*. See also *wood pussy.*) □ *A polecat got into our basement and is stinking up the whole place.* □ *My dog chased a polecat yesterday, and now he's sorry.* **2.** a bad person. □ *If I ever catch that low-down polecat, I'm gonna beat the living daylights out of him.* □ *My mother tried to tell me that Jim was a polecat, but I wouldn't listen to her.*

polish the apple to flatter. □ *He got promoted because he knows how to polish the apple.* □ *I get so sick of having to polish the apple for Aunt Josephine just because she's rich.*

poncho a cape that covers the front and back of the wearer. (From an Amerindian language via Spanish.) □ *There were handwoven ponchos for sale in the market.* □ *I wear a waterproof poncho when I bicycle through the rain.*

pone a cake of corn bread. (See also *cornpone.*) □ *She baked the pone on the griddle.* □ *They dipped the pone in milk as they ate it.*

po(or) Joe a great blue heron. □ *There's a poor Joe out fishing upstream, there. See him?* □ *We saw a po' Joe flying overhead.*

poor white (trash) a white person or white people without property. (Derogatory.) □ *She was scared to go down by the river where the poor white trash lived.* □ *Jim was a poor white from Alabama.*

poorly unwell; sick. □ *Is your ma still feeling poorly?* □ *I'm sorry I won't be able to go with you. I'm poorly today.*

poppet a doll. □ *"Mommy, Jimmy ripped the head off my poppet," wailed Jane.* □ *The little children played with their poppets all afternoon.*

portiere a long curtain that hangs over a door. (French.) □ *The drawing room had beautiful red velvet portieres.* □ *She pulled back the portieres and looked out.*

posse a group of people called by the sheriff to look for someone. (Latin. Short for *posse comitatus.*) □ *A posse was formed to look for the missing man.* □ *The posse was determined not to let the bank robbers escape.*

possum an opossum. □ *A possum hung from the tree by her tail.* □ *The dogs were chasing a possum.*

pot liquor cooking juices. □ *We ate the greens, pot liquor and all.* □ *Joe sopped up the pot liquor with his corn bread.*

pot luck a meal made of dishes brought by each guest. □ *There's a pot luck at the church on Thursday night.* □ *We had a pot luck lunch at Jim's.*

pot shot **1.** a random shot. □ *He took pot shots at the pigeons on his neighbor's roof.* □ *The boys was out back taking pot shots at the neighbor's dog with the beebee gun.* **2.** an insulting comment. □ *His insulting remark was a pot shot at Bill.* □ *Jane's pot shot at her husband surprised us all.*

pot someone or something to shoot someone or something. □ TOM: *Did you pot anything?* BILL: *Just a couple of ducks.* □ *The kids were out potting cans with their BB guns.*

power of something a great deal of something. (Often used in the expression *do someone a power of good.*) □ *It does me a power of good just to hear your voice on the telephone.* □ *Mr. Jackson has done folks a power of evil in his day.*

powerful very. □ *Go easy on that moonshine. It's powerful strong.* □ *He's a powerful smart man.*

prairie dog a type of large rodent that lives in burrows. (In the Western states.) □ *There's a prairie dog village up on that hill.* □ *I saw a prairie dog scurry across the road.*

prairie oyster See *Rocky Mountain oyster.*

prairie strawberries See *Arizona strawberries.*

Praise the Lord! "Thank goodness!" (An exclamation of happiness or relief.) □ TOM: *I just got a call from Jane. Her plane landed safely.* MARY: *Praise the Lord!* □ *Praise the Lord! It's a beautiful day.*

praline a candy made of pecans, brown sugar, and butter. □ *Try one of Mary's pralines.* □ *We had pralines and coffee after dinner.*

prayer-bones knees. □ *He staggered and fell down on his prayer-bones.* □ *She's got the arthritis in her prayer-bones.*

prayer-meetin' a religious revival meeting. □ *The prayer-meetin' lasted all Saturday and Sunday.* □ *Jim got religion at the prayer-meetin'.*

preach someone's funeral to scold someone severely. □ *Daddy preached my funeral for sassing Miz Wilcox.* □ *Joe's ma was always preaching his funeral, but he never changed his wicked ways.*

preacher a minister, especially an evangelist minister. (See also *preacher-man.*) □ *Bill went to Bible school to study to be a preacher.* □ *The preacher married the young couple.*

preacher-man an evangelical minister. (Somewhat derogatory. See also *preacher.*) □ *I ain't gonna let no preacher-man tell me what to do.* □ *Every time I turn on the TV, there's some preacher-man telling me to send him my money.*

pretty oneself up to make oneself pretty; to get gussied up. □ *Pretty yourself up, honey. I'm taking you out tonight.* □ *It takes Sally two hours to pretty herself up.*

prickly pear a cactus with oval leaves and long spines, with a pear-shaped fruit. □ *There's a prickly pear growing in our front yard.* □ *There was nothing for the cattle to eat. Just prickly pear and tumbleweeds as far as the eye could see.*

prime the pump to give a little bit in order to get a great deal. □ *I brought Joe a present as a way of priming the pump, since he might be able to give me a job.* □ *Jane tried to prime the pump by flattering Mary all night, hoping that Mary would ask if she needed anything.*

prolly probably. (Eye-dialect.) □ *I'll prolly be there on time.* □ *It'll prolly rain on the picnic. It generally does.*

pronto right away; swiftly. (Spanish.) □ *We'd better get going pronto.* □ *When the boss says call, you'd better call—pronto.*

prospector someone who looks for gold or other precious minerals. □ *The prospector found a big vein of gold up in the hills.* □ *The prospector roamed across California, with only his mule for company.*

pueblo a village, especially a Southwestern Indian village. (Spanish.) □ *The pueblo houses are built of adobe.* □ *The pueblo of San Ildefonso is famous for its pottery.*

puff like a grampus AND **puff like a steam engine** to pant; to breathe heavily. □ *By the time I got to the top of the stairs, I was puffing like a grampus.* □ *He ran doggedly along, puffing like a steam engine.*

puff like a steam engine See *puff like a grampus.*

pug-ugly very ugly. □ *That is one pug-ugly little dog you got there.* □ *Maw! Jimmy called me a pug-ugly monkey!*

puke **1.** to vomit. (Use with caution.) □ *I'm sick. I have to puke.* □ *Gory movies make me want to puke.* **2.** a worthless person. (Use with caution.) □ *That lying puke told me he'd be here at six.* □ *Look, you little puke, I don't want to see your face in this town again.*

pull freight for the tules to flee from the law. (*Tules* is Spanish for bullrushes. See also *pull (one's) freight.*) □ *After Slim killed that deputy, he had to pull freight for the tules.* □ *As soon as the bandits robbed the stagecoach, they pulled freight for the tules.*

pull in one's horns See *draw in one's horns.*

pull (one's) freight to go; to get moving. (See also *pull freight for the tules.*) □ *We'd best pull our freight if we want to get to Dallas on time.* □ *She pulled her freight without even stopping for breakfast.*

pull oneself up by the bootstraps to better oneself by one's own hard work. □ *Nobody helped him. He pulled himself up by the bootstraps.* □ *They started with nothing, pulled themselves up by the bootstraps, and became the wealthiest family in town.*

pull up stakes to leave a place where one had settled; to move to another place. □ *Bill gets transferred a lot, so he and his wife have to pull up stakes every three years or so.* □ *After their first winter in Minnesota, they pulled up stakes and moved south.*

pulleybone a wishbone. □ *Whenever we had chicken, Ma would let us kids have the pulleybone.* □ *Jimmy made a wish on the pulleybone.*

puma a large wildcat. (See also *catamount; cougar; painter.*) □ *A big black puma stalked beneath the trees.* □ *My horse was attacked by a puma.*

puppy a thing. □ *Jane's bicycle wheel was badly bent. "This puppy's gonna need some fixing," she sighed.* □ *Did Jed show show you the truck he fixed up? A lot of work went into that puppy!*

purdy See *purty.*

pure salt good sense. □ *Listen to what Jim's saying. It's pure salt.* □ *Mary's advice is always pure salt.*

purse proud stingy. □ *Seems the richer folks is, the more purse proud they get.* □ *Her husband was purse proud and wouldn't give her a dime for new clothes.*

purty AND **purdy** pretty. □ *You sure look purty with your hair all curled.* □ *That's a purdy little pony, all right.*

put a knot in someone's tail AND **jerk a knot in someone's tail; tie a knot in someone's tail** to keep someone from doing something. □ *Jim's folks put a knot in his tail by grounding him for a month.* □ *If they think they can jerk a knot in my tail by taking away my credit cards, they are sadly mistaken.* □ *We hid the car keys from Mary, to tie a knot in her tail.*

put (great) store by someone or something See *set (great) store by someone or something.*

put on the dog **1.** to show off. □ *There is no point in putting on the dog for Uncle Fred. He knows that we're just folks.* □ *Sarah always puts on the dog when she has folks over for supper.* **2.** to act superior. □ *Mary is always putting on the dog on account of she went to college.* □ *Jim was putting on the dog again, using all kinds of hifalutin' words.*

put on the feed bag to have a meal; to eat. □ *Why don't we stop and put on the feed bag?* □ *By the end of the hike, I sure was ready to put on the feed bag.*

put one's name in the pot to join others for a meal. □ *Why don't you stay and put your name in the pot?* □ *He put his name in the pot for lunch with us.*

put someone in mind of something to remind someone of something. □ *Sally just put me in mind of a joke I heard the other day.* □ *That puts me in mind of the time Joe and I took a picnic down to the lake.*

put someone on a cooling board to kill someone. (Refers to the marble slab on which the dead are prepared for burial.) □ *Doc's got some stranger on the cooling board, wonders if anybody can* *identify him.* □ *Arizona Slim threatened to put Black Bart on the cooling board.*

put someone or something out to pasture to retire someone or something. □ *That mare is getting old. It's time we put her out to pasture.* □ *The boss wants to put Jane out to pasture, but Jane says she wants to keep working.*

put someone up (for the night) to give someone a place to stay (for the night). □ *We've got an extra room. We can put you up for the night.* □ *No need to stay in a hotel. I'm sure Cousin Joe can put you up.*

put someone's ass in a sling to bother someone; to cause someone to be irritatable. □ *She makes me so mad. She puts my ass in a sling every time I talk to her.* □ *What's the matter? Who put your ass in a sling?*

put something by See *lay something by.*

put the fear of God in someone to frighten someone very much. □ *The car accident put the fear of God in Mary. She drives much more carefully now.* □ *The judge aimed to put the fear of God in criminals by giving them the heaviest possible sentences.*

put the Indian sign on someone to put a curse on someone. □ *John must have put the Indian sign on me. Nothing I do has gone right since I saw him last.* □ *The children ran away from the old lady, scared that she would put the Indian sign on them.*

put the quietus on someone or something to kill someone or something. (See also *quietus.*) □ *If I ever catch that armadillo that's been digging up my garden, I'm gonna put the quietus on him.* □ *The bandit had to put the quietus on the stagecoach driver who had seen his face.*

Put up or shut up. Do something, or stop talking about what you are going to do. (To *put up* is to place one's bet in a card game.) □ MARY: *I could see your bet and raise it. On the other hand, maybe I should fold. . . .* TOM: *Put up or shut up.* □ *Jim keeps saying that he's going to give a big donation to the church. I say he should put up or shut up.*

quality high-class people. □ *Mary tried to talk like quality, but she wound up sounding awful funny.* □ *Mr. and Mrs. Green are quality, no doubt about it.*

Queen of the May a very important person. □ *Jane's acting like she's Queen of the May.* □ *When Mary won the spelling bee, she acted like she was Queen of the May.*

quick-like (a bunny) quick. (The *bunny* version is cute.) □ *Get over here right now! Quick-like a bunny!* □ *I'll just wash the dishes right quick-like before we go.*

quick on the trigger quick to attack. □ *Don't be so quick on the trigger. See what John has to say before you give him Hail Columbia.* □ *If the police officer hadn't been so quick on the trigger, she might have been killed.*

quicker than hell could scorch a feather very quickly. □ *I only made one mistake, but I got fired quicker than hell could scorch a feather.* □ *Quicker than hell could scorch a feather, she had ripped up the letter and tossed the pieces into the wind.*

quicker than you can bat an eye very quickly. □ *Quicker than you can bat an eye, his hand whipped out and caught the ball.* □ *She had the flat tire off quicker than you can bat an eye.*

quicker than you can holler howdy very quickly. □ *She had that baby diapered quicker than you can holler howdy.* □ *The race was over, quicker than you can holler howdy.*

quicker than you could count two very quickly. □ *The snowstorm came up quicker than you could count two.* □ *Joe had breakfast on the table quicker than you could count two.*

quieten (down) to become quiet. (See also *quieten someone or something (down).*) □ *The kids were noisy at first, but they quietened down.* □ *The audience quietened as the lights dimmed.*

quieten someone or something (down) to make someone or something quiet. □ *The cowboy quietened his horse down.* □ *I wish I knew what would quieten him.*

quietus death. (Pronounced kway-AY-tus. See also *put the quietus on someone or something.*) □ *After ninety-three years, the old settler finally met his quietus.* □ *The outlaw had brought many men and women to their quietus.*

quilting bee a gathering at which people assemble a quilt. □ *I heard a lot of good gossip at the quilting bee last Saturday.* □ *Let's hold a quilting bee to finish off this quilt.*

quittin' time time to stop working for the day. □ *I can't wait till quittin' time.* □ *How come you're still working? It's quittin' time!*

R

rabbit ranch a poor farm. □ *She gave up trying to get a living out of that rabbit ranch and moved to town.* □ *Joe started out with just a little rabbit ranch, and now he's the wealthiest landowner in the county.*

rag tag and bobtail worthless; unpleasant people. □ *Let's send Junior to a private school. I don't want him mixing with the rag tag and bobtail in the public schools.* □ *Everyone goes to the flea market on Saturday, from the wealthiest families to the rag tag and bobtail.*

rain bull yearlings See *rain bullfrogs.*

rain bullfrogs AND **rain bull yearlings** to rain very hard. □ *It's raining bullfrogs out there! I'm soaked!* □ *One minute the sky was clear, and the next minute it was raining bull yearlings.*

raining as hard as a cow pissing on a flat rock raining very hard. (Use with caution.) □ *It's raining as hard as a cow pissing on a flat rock. So much for our baseball game.* □ *After two months of drought, it was raining as hard as a cow pissing on a flat rock.*

raise a racket See *raise a ruckus.*

raise a ruckus AND **raise a rumpus; raise a racket** to make a lot of noise. (See also *ruckus.*) □ *How can I work with you kids raising a ruckus?* □ *The downstairs neighbors were raising a rumpus all night long.* □ *Some critter is raisin' a racket in the henhouse.*

raise a rumpus See *raise a ruckus.*

raise hell to make a great deal of noise or trouble. □ *If she doesn't get what she wants, she raises hell.* □ *I get tired of them youngsters raising hell all night.*

raise someone up to bring up someone. □ *Sally's parents were killed when she was a baby, so her aunt and uncle raised her up.* 🅃 *Jed and Effie raised up Sally like she was their own.*

raised on a floored pen brought up in great comfort. □ *He was raised on a floored pen, so it was hard for him to get used to poverty.* □ *She was raised on a floored pen, never went to bed hungry in her life.*

raised on prunes and proverbs brought up to be very proper and prudish. □ *He was raised on prunes and proverbs. Nobody ever showed him a good time.* □ *I can tell from the way she purses her mouth that she was raised on prunes and proverbs.*

raised on sour milk bad-tempered; always complaining. □ *You'll never get Joe to say something nice about anything. He was raised on sour milk.* □ *She was a cross lady, raised on sour milk.*

raised someone from a pup to have brought someone up from childhood. □ *My Aunt Nelly raised me from a pup.* □ *How could you be so ungrateful to your sister, when she raised you from a pup?*

raising bee a gathering at which people put up a house or barn. □ *They held a raising bee to build the young couple's new house.* □ *The women brought food to the raising bee.*

rambunctious spirited; causing trouble. □ *I had to take care of my two rambunctious brothers.* □ *The horse was feeling mighty rambunctious and tried to throw me more than once.*

ramspunxious extraordinary; very good. □ *They made a ramspunxious feast to welcome Bill home.* □ *She's a ramspunxious dancer.*

ranch a farm where livestock is raised. □ *John owns a sheep ranch.* □ *The cowboys worked on the O'Connor Ranch all summer.*

ranch (something) out See *wrench (something) out.*

rancher the owner of a ranch. □ *My daddy and his daddy before him were ranchers.* □ *The rancher fenced off his land.*

ranchero the owner of a ranch. (Spanish.) □ *The local rancheros got together to talk about grazing rights.* □ *He was the most powerful ranchero in the valley.*

rarin' to do something very eager to do something. □ *"Hurry up!" Bill shouted. He was rarin' to go.* □ *The kids were rarin' to play baseball after school.*

rat's nest a big tangle of hair, string, yarn, etc. □ *The little girl's hair was full of rat's nests.* □ *I tugged at the rat's nest with my comb.*

rattler a rattlesnake. □ *A big nest of rattlers was sunning themselves on the boulder.* □ *I almost stepped on a rattler.*

rawhide animal skin that has not been tanned. □ *They tied the bundle together with strips of rawhide.* □ *We gave the dog some rawhide to chew on.*

razorback a wild hog. □ *A razorback came charging through the woods.* □ *Jim shot a razorback the other day.*

Reach! "Put your hands up!" □ *"Reach!" said the masked man.* □ *"Reach!" the police officer shouted to the fleeing man.*

read one's plate to bow one's head and say grace at the table. □ *Jimmy, you know you are supposed to read your plate like the rest of us.* □ *When I ate supper over at the Hatfields', they all read their plates and said as how they do it every night.*

ready to roll ready to go; ready to get started. □ *Is everybody ready to roll?* □ *We packed our bags quickly and were ready to roll by six A.M.*

real McCoy the real thing; genuine. □ *This is not a copy of a Grandma Moses painting. It's the real McCoy.* □ *How do I know this signature is the real McCoy?*

reb(el) a Confederate soldier in the U.S. Civil War (1861–1865); someone who still sympathizes with the Confederate cause. □ *Grampa joined the Union Army, figuring he could lick the rebels single-handed.* □ *"The South will rise again," said the old reb.*

rebel yell a loud yell like the battle cry of Confederate soldiers during the U.S. Civil War (1861–1865). □ *The singer started out with a rebel yell.* □ *Joe gave a rebel yell and plunged into the fight.*

reckon to think; to believe; to calculate. □ *I reckon it'll take about an hour to get to Jacksonville.* □ *Let the kids play in the mud. I reckon it won't hurt 'em.*

(recognizing) sense the ability to think and to make good decisions. (Often used in negative expressions.) □ *Sally may have a lot of schoolin', but she doesn't have an ounce of recognizing sense.* □ *Don't you have enough sense to keep from throwing your money away at that casino?*

red-eye cheap whiskey. □ *Bill had a bottle of red-eye in his suitcase.* □ *I bought some red-eye. I wanted to get drunk.*

redneck an ignorant country person. (Derogatory. See also *hayseed; yahoo.*) □ *My cousin's a real redneck—stupid and bigoted.* □ *I don't like to go to that bar. Most of the people who go there are rednecks.*

Remington a rifle. (Named for the Remington company that manufactured it in the 19th century.) □ *I've still got my granddad's Remington.* □ *He carried his Remington across his saddle.*

rench (something) out See *wrench (something) out.*

rest one's features to be quiet. □ *Hush a minute. Rest your features.* □ *I wish you'd get that aunt of yours to rest her features for just one gol dern minute.*

restin' powder a sedative. □ *The Doc gave her a restin' powder to calm her nerves.* □ *He takes a restin' powder to get to sleep at night.*

return thanks to say a prayer before eating. □ *Uncle Bill, will you please return thanks?* □ *They returned thanks before they ate.*

revenoor See *revenuer.*

revenuer AND **revenoor** an agent of the U.S. Treasury who searches for illegal alcohol stills that violate U.S. laws against untaxed liquor. □ *Pappy says a revenuer has been sneaking around the still.* □ *Old Jed thinks that every stranger in the valley is a revenuer.*

rhumatiz rheumatism. □ *My rhumatiz has been acting up to beat the band.* □ *Sarah's rhumatiz has been giving her fits.*

rib someone (about someone or something) to tease someone (about someone or something). □ *Don't get upset. I was just ribbing you.* □ *Bill's friends ribbed him about his new tie.*

ride herd on someone or something to keep someone or something under control. □ *I'm riding herd on my sister's kids tonight.* □ *With Mr. Jackson riding herd on them, you better believe the third-graders will behave.*

ride shank's ponies to walk. (See also *by ankle express; shank's mare.*) □ *My car's in the shop, so I've been riding shank's ponies.* □ *It's not far. We might as well ride shank's ponies.*

ride the gravy train to do very well; to have plenty of everything. □ *The best-selling writer was riding the gravy train.* □ *Once Jim inherits his uncle's money, he'll be riding the gravy train.*

riding a cloud dead. □ *I'm an orphan. Both my folks are riding a cloud.* □ *He felt so weak, he was sure he'd be riding a cloud by sunset.*

rig a truck. □ TOM: *What kind of rig are you driving?* CHARLIE: *An eighteen-wheeler.* □ *On the job, I drive a green government rig.*

Riggin' ain't ridin'. Having fancy clothes and equipment does not mean you can do the job well. □ *Them folks that come to the rodeo with their fancy saddles generally can't compete with plain old cowboys. Riggin' ain't ridin'.* □ JANE: *Look at that woman with the expensive square dance outfit. She's probably a much better dancer than me.* TOM: *Don't be too sure. Riggin' ain't ridin'.*

right very. □ *Thank you. That's right nice of you.* □ BILL: *The folks next door brought us a pie.* MARY: *That was right neighborly.*

right down very; downright. □ *Thank you. That's right down nice of you.* □ *He can be right down stubborn when he wants to be.*

right from the git-go right from the start. (*Git* is eye-dialect for *get*.) □ *Let's get one thing straight right from the git-go. I'm the boss around here.* □ *Anna has been working hard right from the git-go.*

right quick very quickly. □ *When they heard the fire alarm, the people got out of the building right quick.* □ *That aspirin got rid of my headache right quick.*

right smart a fairly large amount. □ *It's going to take a right smart of work to make that house fit to live in.* □ *I've got a right smart of ice cream in the freezer. You want some?*

right smart chance of something a good deal of something. (Used with the indefinite article *a*.) □ *Weatherman says there'll be a right smart chance of rain tonight.* □ *Tom's bound to make it as a musician. He's got talent and a right smart chance of determination to go with it.*

rightchere right here. □ *I left my pencil rightchere. Now it's gone.*

rile someone up to make someone angry. □ *Don't let Jane's foolish talk rile you up.* 🅃 *The TV news always riles up Jim.*

ring-tailed snorter an unpleasant, easily angered person. □ *Bill is such a ring-tailed snorter that nobody invites him anywhere.* □ *Whenever she talks politics, Mary turns into a ring-tailed snorter.*

rip snorter **1.** a remarkable person or thing. (See also *humdinger.*) □ *The dance last night was a real rip snorter.* □ *Jim's a rip snorter when it comes to playing baseball.* **2.** a very funny joke. □ *Jed told a real rip snorter at the end of the meal.* □ *With Sam, it's just one rip snorter after another.*

ripe smelly. □ *The baby's kind of ripe. I think it's time to change him.* □ *Something in the refrigerator is awfully ripe.*

risin' bread yeast bread. □ *I made two loaves of risin' bread.* □ *I can make corn bread, but I never got the hang of risin' bread.*

rising a swelling; a boil. □ *I don't like the looks of that rising on your arm. You'd best see the doctor about it.* □ *She got an enormous rising where the yellow jacket bit her.*

riz rose; risen. □ *The sun riz before I was even out of bed.* □ *He riz up in his chair and opened one eye, then went back to sleep.*

road apple a lump of horse manure in the road. □ *Don't step in the road apples.* □ *The dog sniffed at the road apple.*

roan a horse whose coat is speckled with white. (See also *Appaloosa; bay; chestnut; paint; palomino; piebald.*) □ *The roan mare was twelve years old.* □ *That roan is the gentlest horse I got.*

roasting ear an ear of corn that is good to eat roasted. (See also *boiling ear.*) □ *Jim has some hamburgers, and I've got some roasting ears. Let's have a cookout.* □ *We buried the roasting ears in a pit with hot coals.*

Robin Hood's barn everywhere. □ *We've been all over Robin Hood's barn looking for you.* □ *The high wind scattered the haystacks over Robin Hood's barn.*

Rocky Mountain oysters AND **mountain oysters; prairie oysters** the testicles of a farm animal—such as a pig, calf, or sheep—cooked and served as food. □ *Ever tried Rocky Mountain oysters? I'll cook some up for you.* □ *Why, we consider Rocky Mountain oysters a delicacy.* □ *Effie cooked up a mess of prairie oysters and that's what we had for supper.*

rode hard and put up wet overworked and not taken care of. □ *The deep lines and haggard expression in his face showed that he'd been rode hard and put up wet for many years.* □ *She was plumb worn out, rode hard and put up wet.*

rodeo a contest of cowboy skills, such as roping animals and riding. □ *She won first place at the rodeo for riding the obstacle course.* □ *Charlie rides wild bulls at the rodeo.*

roll up the sidewalks to close all the businesses and cease all activity. □ *Not much night life in this town. They roll up the sidewalks at eight o'clock.* □ *All the restaurants were closed. They had rolled up the sidewalks for Easter Sunday.*

root hog or die to work hard or perish. □ *When I lost all my money in the bank crash, it was root hog or die for me.* □ TOM: *How can we beat our competitors?* MARY: *Root hog or die.*

rotgut bad liquor. □ *I wouldn't drink that rotgut if my life depended on it.* □ *We got drunk on some rotgut of Jim's.*

roughneck a rough, violent person. □ *After hanging out with that gang for a few months, Joe started acting like a roughneck himself.* □ *A bunch of roughnecks came into the store and started making trouble.*

roundup the time when cattle, people, or things are gathered together. □ *After the roundup, we'll load all the cattle onto trucks.* □ *Here's a roundup of the local news.*

roust up to revive. □ *She rousted up when she heard her mother's voice.* □ *He had a fainting fit, but he rousted up when they sprinkled cold water on his face.*

rubberneck to stare at something; to gawk. (Derogatory.) □ *Drivers in the other lane were rubbernecking at the traffic accident.* □ *Hundreds of people came by to rubberneck at the house where the murderer had lived.*

ruckus a great deal of noise. (See also *raise a ruckus.*) □ *What's all that ruckus in the street?* □ *I can't think with the TV making such a ruckus.*

ruination ruin. □ *Going out with that no-'count boy will be your ruination.* □ *Working outdoors has been the ruination of my complexion.*

rule the roost to be in charge at home. □ *There was no doubt that Pa ruled the roost when we were kids.* □ *Bill may be the boss at work, but his wife rules the roost.*

run (just) shy of something AND **be (just) shy of something** to run short of something, to not quite be or have reached something. □ *That year's snowfall ran just shy of three hundred inches.* □ *This year's profits ran shy of last year's.* □ *I was just shy of my seventeenth birthday.* □ *He was shy of seven feet tall.*

run like a scalded dog to run away fast. □ *When Sally started hinting that she wanted to get married, Jim ran like a scalded dog.* □ *Whenever I need help with anything, Jane runs like a scalded dog.*

rustle up some grub to get or cook some food. □ *You build up the fire. I'll rustle up some grub.* □ *When we got back from our hike, Bill rustled up some grub.*

rustler a cattle thief. □ *The rustler had stolen twenty head of cattle.* □ *The ranchers swore they'd get the rustler dead or alive.*

S

sack a paper or cloth bag. □ *Put the groceries in the sack.* □ *The curtains were made out of old flour sacks.*

sage hen a woman. □ *There was a sage hen in a blue dress who looked like she was a good dancer.* □ *Jim set up house with a cute little sage hen from Nebraska.*

sagebrush a small desert shrub. □ *I love the smell of the sagebrush in the afternoon sun.* □ *We used sagebrush to kindle the fire.*

saguaro a large, many-branched cactus. (From Mexican Spanish.) □ *After the rain, the saguaros bloomed.* □ *This bird lives in holes in the saguaro.*

Sakes alive! See *Land(s) sakes (alive)!*

saloon a bar; a place where liquor is sold and drunk. □ *The sheriff walked into the saloon.* □ *Bill owns a saloon down on Third Street.*

salt a mine to put ore in a mine; to put something valuable into something in order to make it more attractive. □ *They salted the mine to get Joe to buy it.* □ *When the potential buyer came to look at their business, they salted the mine by having dozens of their friends call up and pretend to be customers.*

salt something away to stash something away; to keep something, especially money, for the future. □ *He saved some money from every paycheck, and soon he had salted ten thousand dollars away.* 🅃 *He salted away his money in government bonds.*

salt something down to preserve something with salt. □ *We salted the hog meat down.* 🅃 *We ate some of the venison and salted down the rest.*

sang **1.** ginseng. □ *I know where the sang grows in the woods.* □ *We sold two pounds of sang to some health nut from the city.* **2.** to hunt for ginseng. □ *Y'all want to go sangin' with me?* □ *Jane knows a good place to sang.*

sap-risin' time **1.** springtime. □ *The ground was beginning to thaw. It was sap-risin' time.* □ *In sap-risin' time, the kids played happily in the mud.* **2.** youth; adolescence. □ *Sap-risin' time was upon him. He began to get interested in girls.* □ *In sap-risin' time, she had had many admirers. Now that she was older, fewer beaux came to call.*

sarsaparilla See *sassparilla.*

sashay to walk with a gliding step. □ *She sashayed over, a smile on her face.* □ *They sashayed across the dance floor.*

sass sauce. □ *Can I have some applesass?* □ *Put some of that sass on my taters.*

sass someone to speak disrespectfully to someone. □ *Don't you sass me, girl!* □ *Ma gave me a whipping for sassing her.*

sassafrass tea tea made by steeping sassafrass roots. □ *A drink of sassafrass tea will settle your stomach.* □ *Gramma showed us how she makes sassafrass tea.*

sassparilla AND **sarsaparilla** root beer. (From Spanish *zarzaparrilla,* a plant.) □ *Bartender! Give me another sassparilla!* □ *Pappy drank nothing in his whole life but a little sarsaparilla.*

sassy disrespectful. □ *The boys liked her high spirits and her sassy ways.* □ *Grampa spanked me for being sassy.*

savvy **1.** to understand. □ *I'm not coming back here, you savvy?* □ *She savvies a lot more than she lets on.* **2.** knowledgeable; in the know. □ *Jed is a real savvy guy.* □ *Tom ain't too savvy, and he's likely to tell everyone in town the whole truth.*

saw buck a ten-dollar bill; ten dollars. (See also *double saw buck.*) □ *I'm down to my last saw buck.* □ *Can you lend me a saw buck till payday?*

saw gourds to snore. □ *I couldn't sleep with my husband sawing gourds all night.* □ *She sawed gourds so loud you could hear her two rooms away.*

sawbones a doctor; a surgeon. □ *The sawbones came and stitched up the cut on my chin.* □ *Doc Sanders is the only sawbones in town.*

say one's piece See *speak one's piece.*

say uncle See *holler uncle.*

Say what? "What?"; "What did you say?" □ TOM: *I'm going to run for President.* MARY: *Say what?* □ JANE: *The plane tickets will cost a thousand dollars.* CHARLIE: *Say what?*

scairt See *afeard.*

scalawag **1.** a tricky, dishonest person. □ *I can't believe I trusted that scalawag with my money.* □ *He was a scalawag, but women loved him.* **2.** a Southerner who supported the North's Reconstruction program after the U.S. Civil War (1861–1865). □ *We drove Jones out of the neighborhood, on account of he was a scalawag.* □ *The scalawags tried to convince us that Reconstruction was good.*

scare someone out of a year's growth AND **scare someone pea green; scare ten years off someone's span of life; scare the (living) daylights out of someone** to frighten someone very much. □ *When Jim fainted, it scared me out of a year's growth. I had no idea what to do!* □ *The horror movie scared Mary pea green.* □ *Don't you ever run off like that again! You scared ten years off* *my span of life!* □ *Don't sneak up behind me like that! You scared the daylights out of me!* □ *The horror movie scared the living daylights out of Tom.*

scare someone pea green See *scare someone out of a year's growth.*

scare ten years off someone's span of life See *scare someone out of a year's growth.*

scare the (living) daylights out of someone See *scare someone out of a year's growth.*

scared shitless very scared. (Use with caution.) □ *The house was rocking back and forth. I was scared shitless.* □ *Someone was standing outside Joe's window, screaming his name. Joe was scared shitless.*

Scat! "Bless you!" (A polite response to a sneeze.) □ *I sneezed. "Scat!" Joe said.* □ TOM: *Aahh-choo!* BILL: *Scat!*

schoolin' education. (See also *book-learning.*) □ *I ain't had no schoolin', but I know when I am right.* □ *How are you doing with your schoolin', youngun?*

schoolmarm See *schoolteacher.*

schoolteacher AND **schoolmarm** a teacher of elementary or secondary school. (A *schoolmarm* is specifically a female teacher.) □ *Jim was a schoolteacher for fifteen years.* □ *We boarded the schoolmarm at our house.*

scorcher a hot day. □ *"Sure is a scorcher today," Pa said as he wiped his brow.* □ *It was such a scorcher outside, we stayed home with the air conditioner on.*

scratch the skin to only begin to address something. □ *The governor's education proposal will only scratch the skin. There's so* *much more we must do to improve our schools.* □ *The book review just scratched the skin—there's a lot more in the book that isn't mentioned.*

screech owl AND **squinch owl** an owl with a shrill cry. □ *We heard the screech owls coming out at night.* □ *There's an old squinch owl living in our garage.*

scuppernong a large, sweet grape. □ *We ate scuppernongs right off the vine.* □ *I put scuppernongs in my fruit salad.*

sech See *sich.*

see someone home to escort someone home. □ *It's been a pleasure talking to you. May I see you home?* □ *I'll be fine. Jane can see me home.*

see the elephant to see the sights. □ *I thought we'd go to Charleston to see the elephant.* □ *They have a big fair in August. Folks come from miles around to see the elephant.*

see the like of something to see anything like something. □ *Did you ever see the like of that crazy hat with all the feathers on it?* □ *It was the strangest car I ever laid eyes on. I'd never seen the like of it.*

seed seen. (The past participle of *see.*) □ *I think I seed suthin over in the corner.* □ *You look like you seed a ghost.*

seen saw. □ *He seen all there was to see and came home.* □ *I seen the truck coming, but couldn't get out of the way in time.*

sell like hotcakes to sell very rapidly. □ *The band's records were selling like hotcakes.* □ *At the craft fair, Joe's stuffed animals just sat there, while Jane's pot holders sold like hotcakes.*

sell one's saddle to reach a very low point in one's life; to be desperate. □ *Bill had sold his saddle. No one would hire him, and all his friends were gone.* □ *Things may be bad, but you haven't sold your saddle yet.*

sell someone a bill of goods See *sell someone a piece of goods.*

sell someone a piece of goods AND **sell someone a bill of goods** to fool someone; tell someone a lie. □ *Jim swore to me that he had stopped drinking, but I found out that he sold me a piece of goods.* □ *I'm not listening to Mary anymore. Every time I do, she sells me a bill of goods.*

send someone to hell and the devil to punish someone severely. □ *When Daddy found out I had sassed the teacher, he sent me to hell and the devil.* □ *I hope they send that criminal to hell and the devil.*

serape a large shawl. (From Mexican Spanish.) □ *They wrapped their serapes around them as the cold wind blew.* □ *She wove me a beautiful serape.*

set to sit. □ *I need to set awhile.* □ *Pull up a chair. Set a spell.*

set (great) store by someone or something AND **put (great) store by someone or something** to value someone or something a great deal. □ *You know I set great store by your advice.* □ *Gramma put store by camphor oil as a cure for most ills.*

set in [for something, such as pain, illness, cold weather] to begin. □ *I have to get this done before winter sets in.* □ *When the pain sets in, take some pills.*

set one's cap for someone to want to get someone to marry one. (Usually said of girls or women.) □ JANE: *Mary's set her cap for Bill.* CHARLIE: *Bill better look out, then. Mary always gets her way.* □ *Sally set her cap for the richest man in town.*

set one's sights on someone or something to decide to pursue someone or something. □ *She had set her sights on the mayor's office, and no one was going to stop her from getting it.* □ *When it came time to marry, he set his sights on the youngest Wilkins girl.*

set up to someone to court someone. □ *Are you setting up to my daughter?* □ *I hear Jim's setting up to Sally.*

settee AND **divan** a couch; a sofa. □ *We bought a new settee and matching chairs.* □ *Mary bought yellow fabric to reupholster her divan.*

settle someone's hash to stop or restrain someone. □ *I sued him for all he was worth. That ought to settle his hash.* □ *She had gossiped once too often. Her friends decided to settle her hash by never telling her anything again.*

seven-year itch a rash, especially scabies. □ *We were boiling our clothes with bleach to get rid of the seven-year itch that was going around.* □ *The Doc gave me some lotion for my seven-year itch.*

sez says. (Eye-dialect.) □ *It's too cold for man or beast. That's what I always sez.* □ *She sez she'll be right there.*

shack whacky crazy from having to stay indoors too long. (See also *cabin fever.*) □ *If this blizzard lasts one more day, I'm gonna get shack whacky.* □ *It rained the whole time we were up at the cabin. We were all going shack whacky.*

shacking up living together without being married. □ *They're not married. They're just shacking up.* □ *Mary about had a heart attack when she found out her daughter was shacking up with a man.*

shade up to rest in the shade. □ *Let's shade up under this tree for a minute.* □ *It was a hot day. Folks was shading up under the awning in front of the store.*

shake a leg to start moving briskly. □ *Come on! Shake a leg! Let's get going!* □ *We'd better shake a leg if we want to get there on time.*

shake like a holly in a high wind AND **shake like a leaf (in the wind); shake like a willow in the wind** to shake violently. □ *When Sally heard her daddy yelling, she started shaking like a holly in a high wind.* □ *What's the matter? You're shaking like a leaf!* □ *He was so excited he was shaking like a willow in the wind.*

shake like a leaf (in the wind) See *shake like a holly in a high wind.*

shake like a willow in the wind See *shake like a holly in a high wind.*

shakedown a place to sleep. □ *When Joe got to town, he went looking for a shakedown.* □ *Do you have a shakedown for the night?*

shame and a scandal a shameful thing. (Used with the indefinite article *a*.) □ *It's a shame and a scandal, the way young folks carry on today.* □ *The way Joe treats his poor wife is a shame and a scandal.*

shank of the afternoon the late afternoon. (See also *shank of the evening.*) □ *Bill said he'd come by in the shank of the afternoon.* □ *By the time I got home, it was the shank of the afternoon and time to get supper started.*

shank of the evening the early or late part of the evening. (See also *shank of the afternoon.*) □ *We sat on the porch until the shank of the evening.* □ *Round about the shank of the evening, the truck driver started looking for a place to stop for the night.*

shank's mare walking; on foot. (See also *by ankle express; ride shank's ponies.*) □ *We traveled by shank's mare.* □ *Shank's mare was the only form of travel we could afford.*

shanty a hut; a small, rough house. □ *After they lost their houses in the storm, lots of folks were living in shanties.* □ *She tried to brighten up the shanty by hanging calico curtains in the window.*

sharpen someone's hoe to beat someone up. □ *Bill called Joe a scalawag, so Joe sharpened Bill's hoe.* □ *If I ever catch the so-and-so who's been stealing my chickens, I'll sharpen his hoe.*

Sharps a hunting rifle. □ *I took my Sharps when I went deer hunting.* □ *Joe hung a Sharps in the back window of his truck.*

shavetail **1.** a horse with a plucked tail. (See also *broomtail.*) □ *The cowboy rode a shavetail.* □ *Which horse is yours? The shavetail or the broomtail?* **2.** a mule. (See also *hard tail.*) □ *The shavetail hauled the barge.* □ *Jim had a shavetail to carry his pack.*

she AND **her; 'er** it. □ *Help me lift this crate. She's a heavy one.* □ TOM: *Is this picture hanging straight?* JANE: *Move 'er up a little on the left-hand side.*

shell something out to pay something. □ *The shoes cost a hundred dollars. I reluctantly shelled it out.* □ *He shelled fifty dollars out for a ticket to that concert.*

shenanigans antics; pranks. □ *Bill was the class clown. All the other students laughed at his shenanigans.* □ *On Halloween, kids used to push outhouses over and other such shenanigans.*

shiftless lazy; not willing to work. □ *Mary's husband is a shiftless bum.* □ *She'll never amount to anything. She's shiftless.*

shimmy a chemise or slip; a woman's undergarment. □ *She lay around all morning in her shimmy, eating chocolates and reading a magazine.* □ *She had a beautiful shimmy with lace around the hem.*

shindig a lively party. □ *They're having a shindig with square dancing and bluegrass music.* □ *Practically everyone in town came to that shindig.*

shiner a black eye. □ *Where'd you get that shiner?* □ *Joe wore sunglasses to hide his shiner.*

shinny up something to climb up something. □ *She shinnied up the tree.* □ *The lineman shinnied up the telephone pole.*

shirt-tail at half-mast a shirt-tail that is not tucked into the pants. □ *Jim's a slob, always wearing a grubby shirt with the shirt-tail at half-mast.* □ *He looked a sight, with his hair all on end and his shirt-tail at half-mast.*

shit in tall cotton to do very well. (Use with caution. See also *in high cotton.*) □ *I'll be shitting in tall cotton once I sell the old house.* □ *He's shitting in tall cotton ever since he won the lottery.*

shit or get off the pot See *shoot or give up the gun.*

shitepoke **1.** a stork. □ *Did you see that shitepoke flying overhead?* □ *The shitepoke was standing in the shallow water.* **2.** someone with long legs. □ *Bill's a regular shitepoke. He must have a five-foot stride.* □ *Jane's such a shitepoke she has a hard time getting pants to fit.*

shitkicker **1.** a farmer's boot. (Use with caution.) □ *I wore my shitkickers to go hiking.* □ *He bought a good, heavy pair of shitkickers.* **2.** a farmer. (Use with caution.) □ *Bill's son said he didn't want to be no shitkicker when he grew up.* □ *My dad and all my uncles were shitkickers.*

shivaree a noisy serenade for newlywed couples. □ *We found the hotel where Bill and Mary were staying and gave them a shivaree.* □ *It was a custom for boys to give the young couple a shivaree until the bridegroom came out and gave them a bribe to go away.*

sho'nuff sure enough; certainly. □ *I'm sho'nuff planning to go to the fair.* □ *She sho'nuff is pretty.*

shoo-fly pie a pie made with molasses, sugar, and spices. □ *Shoo-fly pie is a favorite dish at my Grampa's house in Pennsylvania.* □ *That shoo-fly pie is awfully rich. Just give me a small slice.*

shoot dozens to curse. □ *He always shoots dozens when he gets drunk.* □ *How dare you! Shooting dozens at your own mama!*

shoot or give up the gun AND **shit or get off the pot** to either take action or decide not to take action. (Use caution with *shit*.) □ *The governor can't delay making a decision forever. She'll have to shoot or give up the gun.* □ *Are you going to call Jim, or aren't you? Shit or get off the pot!*

shoot-out a gunfight. □ *Six men were killed in the shoot-out.* □ *There was a shoot-out between the rival gangs.*

shoot someone full of daylight to shoot someone many times. □ *The outlaw shot the stagecoach driver full of daylight.* □ *Make one move, and I'll shoot you full of daylight.*

shoot someone on sight to shoot someone as soon as the person is seen. □ *He swore to shoot the cattle rustler on sight.* □ *He is armed and dangerous. Shoot him on sight.*

shoot the breeze See *shoot the bull.*

shoot the bull AND **shoot the breeze** to talk aimlessly. □ *Joe and Bill are just shooting the bull.* □ *I met Jim downtown and shot the breeze with him for a little while.*

shoot the works to get everything possible. □ *They really shot the works for this party.* □ *For your wedding, I want you to have everything you ever wanted. Shoot the works.*

shoot-up a gunfight; a fight in which people shoot each other. □ *There was a famous shoot-up at the O.K. Corral.* □ *Slim drew his gun, and the shindig turned into a shoot-up.*

shooting iron a gun. (See also *talking iron.*) □ *I keep my shooting iron handy.* □ *Joe had a shooting iron slung over his shoulder.*

shooting-match an event; an organization; a family. (Often with *whole.*) □ *I got fed up with the whole shooting-match and left that job as soon as I could.* □ *There was a fine shooting-match going on at the church, but I left.*

shore sure. □ *I shore do like Anadama bread.* □ TOM: *Can you come with us?* JANE: *Shore I can!*

short-coat preacher a lay preacher. □ *Brother Samuels ain't a reverend. He's just a short-coat preacher.* □ *Bob felt called to be a short-coat preacher.*

short horse, soon curried a small problem or job that can be easily taken care of. □ TOM: *Uh-oh. We're out of gas.* MARY: *Short horse, soon curried. I see a gas station up at the next corner.* □ *If the baby's sick, that's a problem. But if he's just hungry, that's a short horse, soon curried.*

short sweetening sugar. □ *She sprinkled some short sweetening on her bread and butter.* □ *You didn't put enough short sweetening in this here cake.*

shorthorn a young or inexperienced person. □ *Joe's a shorthorn, so you'll have to show him what to do.* □ *I ain't got time to explain things to a shorthorn.*

shotgun shack a small, poorly built house. □ *Bill and Mary are living in a shotgun shack out back of his pappy's house.* □ *The sign said "House For Rent," but the house looked more like a shotgun shack.*

shotgun wedding a forced wedding (i.e., at gunpoint), especially one at which a woman's relatives force a man to marry her because he made her pregnant. □ *Bill and Mary had a shotgun wedding, but they've stuck together for twenty-five years now.* □ *Jim was careful not to get his girlfriend pregnant. The last thing he wanted was a shotgun wedding.*

Show Me state the state of Missouri. (Missourians supposedly demand proof of a claim by saying, "I'm from Missouri. You'll have to show me.") □ *We drove through the Show Me state on our way to Oklahoma.* □ *I don't take anything on faith. I'm from the Show Me state.*

show one's face to appear in public. □ *He was so embarrassed, he didn't want to show his face at work.* □ *If you ever show your face in this town again, I'll shoot you full of daylight.*

showdown a meeting of opponents that will decide the final winner. □ *The showdown between the outlaw and the sheriff took place at high noon.* □ *If Jane keeps opposing me, we will have to have a showdown.*

shrink of the moon the period of each month during which the moon gets smaller. □ *The shrink of the moon is a good time to plant your turnips.* □ *Every night was a little darker, on account of it was the shrink of the moon.*

shuck someone's corn to have an extramarital affair with someone. □ *I heard tell that Mary's shucking Joe's corn.* □ *His wife threw him out when she found out he was shucking that young girl's corn.*

shuteye sleep. □ *I need to get some shuteye.* □ *He lay back in the rocking chair and got some shuteye.*

si-godlin See *anti-godlin.*

sic someone to attack someone. □ *Joe let his dog loose at the intruders and said, "Sic 'em, Fido! Sic 'em!"* □ *"Them's fightin' words," Slim said to the stranger. Then he sicced him.*

sich AND **sech** such. □ *I ain't never seen sich a mad woman. She threw a real hissy fit.* □ *Please put your coat and sech in the bedroom.*

sick (un)to death of someone or something very tired of someone or something. □ *I'm sick to death of this rotten weather.* □ *Turn off the TV. I'm sick unto death of that comedian.*

side gal a mistress. □ *He's got him a wife and a side gal.* □ *I won't be your side gal. Divorce your wife, and then you can go out with me.*

sidekick the companion of a powerful or important person. □ *Sancho Panza is Don Quixote's sidekick.* □ *I liked Tonto, the Lone Ranger's sidekick, better than I liked the Lone Ranger.*

sidewinder a rattlesnake that moves sideways. □ *I saw a sidewinder's track in the sand.* □ *The horse was spooked by a sidewinder.*

sight for sore eyes someone or something that someone has been wanting to see. □ *Hello! Come in! My, you're a sight for sore eyes.* □ *After my four years in Illinois, the New Mexico landscape was a sight for sore eyes.*

sight of something a good deal of something. (See also *heap sight.* Used with the indefinite article *a*.) □ *You'll have to put a sight of money into that old house to get it fixed up.* □ *With six children in the family, I've got a sight of laundry to do every day.*

sight to behold an amazing thing to see. □ *They cleaned Jim up and dressed him up fancy until he was a sight to behold.* □ *After playing in a mud puddle all afternoon, the kids were a sight to behold.* □ *Come Christmastime, everyone on our block decorates their houses with colored lights. It's truly a sight to behold.*

signify to matter; to be important. □ *Did they get married in 1960 or 1961? Oh well, it don't signify, I suppose.* □ *She spends all her time fussing about things that don't signify, like which fork to use at the dinner table.*

since Hector was a pup in or for a long time. □ *Why, I ain't made caramel apples since Hector was a pup!* □ *I haven't been back to Louisiana since Hector was a pup.*

since the hog et grandma in a long time. (Jocular.) □ *I haven't been to such a nice party since the hog et grandma.* □ *Mary hasn't taken a trip out of town since the hog et grandma.*

singlin's single-distilled corn whiskey. (See also *doublin's*.) □ *Put the singlin's through the still another time, and you get doublin's.* □ *Let's sample these singlin's.*

sink hole a basin or pot-shaped area of erosion or subsidence. □ *The ground gave way in the backyard leaving a big sink hole.* □ *I waded carefully across the river, trying to keep away from the sink holes.*

sinker a biscuit. □ *Hey, Cookie, give us some more of them sinkers.* □ *The cook at the boarding house makes pretty good sinkers.*

sinkin' spell a faint, dizzy feeling. □ *I had one of my sinkin' spells and almost fell down the stairs.* □ *The hot, smoky room gave him a sinkin' spell.*

sit down and take a load off (your feet) to sit down and relax. □ *Come on in, sit down, and take a load off your feet.* □ *Let's stop at my place. We can sit down and take a load off.*

sit tight to sit still and wait. □ *Just sit tight for a few more minutes.* □ *We'd better sit tight till Joe gets here.*

sittin' pretty AND **sittin' purty** doing well. □ *If I get a good price for my land, I'll be sittin' pretty.* □ *She's sittin' purty now that she's got a job in the county government.*

sittin' purty See *sittin' pretty.*

six-gun See *six-shooter.*

six-shooter AND **six-gun** a handgun with six chambers. □ *The sheriff pulled out his six-shooter and fired six shots.* □ *I had a six-gun, but the other guy had an automatic rifle.*

size someone or something up to evaluate someone or something. □ *He looked at the stranger, sizing him up.* □ *Jed sized his opponent up and punched him in the snoot.*

sizzle sozzle a slow rain. □ *The crops could use a good sizzle sozzle.* □ *It's no fun to go out in this sizzle sozzle, but it sure is good for the garden.*

skedaddle to leave quickly. □ *The kids skedaddled when they saw the old man coming.* □ *We'd better skedaddle if we want to get to the movie on time.*

skeeter a mosquito. □ *Look at all them skeeter bites on my leg.* □ *I had bug repellant, but that didn't stop the skeeters up at the lake.*

skin out to leave quickly. □ *What happened? How come Tom skinned out like that?* □ *The burglars heard the police sirens and skinned out of the house.*

skin someone to cheat someone. (See also *skinned.*) □ *The riverboat gambler skinned the traveler.* □ *They skinned me, all right. Sold me this cure-all medicine that turns out to be pure water.*

skin someone alive to punish someone severely. □ *Ma was so mad, she was ready to skin me alive.* □ *If you disobey me again, I'll skin you alive.*

skin the cat to perform an acrobatic stunt, first hanging by one's knees, then swinging up to land on one's feet on the ground. (A children's term.) □ *The other kids watched Sally skin the cat from the horizontal bar.* □ *Jimmy was the best at skinning the cat.*

skinned cheated. (See also *skin someone.*) □ *He got skinned in a poker game.* □ *The more I look at this used car I bought, the more I suspicion that I been skinned.*

skitters diarrhea. □ *It's serious when a little kid gets the skitters.* □ *Something I ate gave me the skitters.*

skookum good. □ *That stew is skookum. Can I have some more?* □ *He was a skookum carpenter.*

skunk a scoundrel; a bad, dishonest person. □ *That dirty rotten no-good skunk!* □ *Word got out that Jim Jamison was a lying skunk.*

skunk egg See *courtin'-apple.*

skunked defeated; deceived and beaten. □ *The other team skunked us but good.* □ *Went fishing and had nary a bite. We was plumb skunked.*

sky-pilot a preacher. (Someone who guides people to heaven.) □ *The sky-pilot preached on loving our neighbor as ourselves.* □ *The sky-pilot came to the lumber camp and tried to convert us.*

slap someone up the side of the head See *slap someone upside the head.*

slap someone upside the head AND **slap someone up the side of the head** to slap someone in the face. □ *Be quiet or I'll slap you upside the head.* □ *He wouldn't stop staring so I slapped him up the side of the head.*

slapjack a pancake. (See also *flapjack.*) □ *I got a good recipe for cornmeal slapjacks.* □ *Mary made a nice stack of slapjacks.*

slaunchways crooked. (See also *anti-godlin; catabias; catawampus; whopper-jawed.*) □ *You got that shelf nailed up slaunchways.* □ *Hold on a minute. Your hat's on slaunchways.*

slave away (at something) to work extremely hard (at something). (See also *work like a beaver; slave over something.*) □ *She slaved away at the housework from morning till night.* □ *He stayed in the office till nine at night, slaving away.*

slave over something to work very hard at something. (See also *work like a beaver; slave away (at something).*) □ *I really slaved over that paper, but I got a bad grade on it.* □ *He slaves over a hot stove at the restaurant all day.*

slew a great deal; a large number. □ *Mary made a whole slew of quilted pot holders for the craft fair.* □ *Bill wants a wife and a whole slew of kids.*

slice off the same bacon a person or thing that is very similar to another person or thing. (Used with the indefinite article *a*.) □ *You can sure tell that Jim is Bill's son. He's a slice off the same bacon.* □ *Mary has very conservative ideas, and Jane's thinking is a slice off the same bacon.*

slickem **1.** butter. □ *Could you please pass the slickem? This here bread is as hard as a rock.* □ *The slickem's gone bad again.* **2.** hair cream. □ *Why don't you rub some slickem into that cowlick?* □ *I bought a jar of slickem and I know it'll get me a girl.*

slicker a raincoat. □ *I got a nice yellow slicker on sale for twenty dollars.* □ *Take your slicker. Looks like rain.*

slicker than calf slobbers very slick and slippery. (See also *(as) slick as owl grease.*) □ *The bathroom floor was slicker than calf slobbers.* □ *There's a big patch of oil on the road there. It's slicker than calf slobbers.*

slim pickings a poor selection. □ *I got to the fruit market late. It was pretty slim pickings by the time I got there.* □ *She's trying to get a teaching job, but it's slim pickings for teachers this year.*

sling hash to serve food, especially for a living. □ *You've got a college degree! You shouldn't be content to sling hash in a road-side diner!* □ *I'm his wife, all right. At least I sling his hash and clean his house.*

slink like a suckegg hound to slink around in an ashamed way. □ *He came in at one A.M., slinking like a suckegg hound.* □ *What did you do? How come you're slinking like a suckegg hound?*

slipper slide a shoehorn. □ *Hand me that slipper slide and I'll see if I can't get this shoe on.* □ *I used the slipper slide, and my foot just slid right into the shoe.*

slough a swamp. (Pronounced *SLEW*.) □ *When it rains, the valley turns into a slough.* □ *We caught some frogs down at the slough.*

slow elk a cow, especially one shot by a hunter. □ TOM: *How was your huntin' trip?* CHARLIE: *Got me a couple of slow elk, is all.* □ *I took a good look at the animal to make sure it was a buck and not a slow elk.*

slum-gullion a dish made of noodles, ground meat, and tomatoes. □ *I didn't have much time to make supper, so I just whipped up some slum-gullion.* □ *I put a little hot sauce in my slum-gullion to spice it up.*

sluts wool See *curly dirt.*

smack dab in the middle right in the middle. □ *The lightning struck smack dab in the middle of our property.* □ *She put a beauty mark smack dab in the middle of her cheek.*

small and yellow and few to the pod worthless; weak. (Refers to small peas. See also *small potatoes and few to the hill.*) □ *Jim wouldn't even help his own mother when she was sick. That man is small and yellow and few to the pod.* □ *Her friends were so small and yellow and few to the pod that they wouldn't stand up for her when she was in trouble.*

small potatoes a small, unimportant thing. □ *Her high school track meets were small potatoes to the young athlete. She was training* *for the Olympics.* ☐ *Jim's life ambition is to own his own store. I say that one little store is small potatoes. He should try to start a chain of stores.*

small potatoes and few to the hill unlikely to do well; not doing well. ☐ TOM: *What do you think of Mary's new business?* JANE: *Small potatoes and few to the hill, I'm afraid.* ☐ *He's so lazy, anything he tries will be small potatoes and few to the hill.*

smidgin a tiny bit. ☐ MARY: *Care for some shoo-fly pie?* JANE: *Just a smidgin, thank you.* ☐ *I put a smidgin of cream cheese on each cracker.*

Smith and Wesson a revolver. (Named for Horace Smith and Daniel B. Wesson, who manufactured it.) ☐ *She kept a loaded Smith and Wesson in her purse.* ☐ *He pulled out his Smith and Wesson and said, "Hold it right there."*

smitten in love. ☐ *I was smitten from the first time I saw you.* ☐ *Just look at Bill's face when he talks about Jane. He's smitten.*

smoke a cigarette. ☐ *Can I borrow a smoke?* ☐ *Joe went to the store for a pack of smokes.*

smoke like a chimney to smoke tobacco a great deal. ☐ *Everyone at work smokes like a chimney. I can barely breathe.* ☐ *In the restaurant's smoking section, the diners were smoking like chimneys.*

snake doctor a dragonfly. ☐ *A snake doctor hovered in the reeds.* ☐ *I saw a snake doctor flash by as I sat on the levee.*

snake oil a fraud, especially a fraudulent medicine. ☐ TOM: *Do you think those weight-loss pills really work?* JANE: *No. I think they're pure snake oil.* ☐ *The fortune-teller sold love potions, hexes, and other such snake oil.*

snake(bite) medicine hard liquor. ☐ *Looks like you could use some snakebite medicine.* ☐ *She kept some snake medicine in the cupboard for special occasions.*

snap-beans green beans. □ *I'm growing snap-beans and tomatoes.* □ *Wash these snap-beans and we'll have them for lunch.*

snappin' turtle a large, biting turtle. □ *Don't go swimming in the pond. A snappin' turtle lives there.* □ *Last time I went swimming in the lake, a big ol' snappin' turtle froze onto my toe.*

snit an offended state; a tantrum. □ *Don't get yourself in such a snit, Effie. There's no point in getting your dander up.* □ *Mrs. Hatfield is in such a snit! Nobody liked her gooseberry pie at the fair.*

snollygoster a clever, dishonest, self-serving person. □ *He's a low-down snollygoster with no sense of decency.* □ *I hate to see that snollygoster succeed at the expense of honest people.*

snoot the nose. (From *snout.*) □ *Get your goldurned snoot out of my business!* □ *Don't you ever blow your snoot at the table again!*

snoreifferous state sleep. (Humorous. Akin to *somniferous.*) □ *I was in the snoreifferous state the instant my head hit the pillow.* □ TOM: *Is Joe awake?* JANE: *Nope. He appears to be in the snoreifferous state.*

snorf See *curly dirt.*

snuck sneaked. □ *I snuck into the movie theater through the back door.* □ *He snuck a piece of cake while his ma wasn't looking.*

so broke he couldn't even pay attention completely without money. (Jocular.) □ *Jim can't pay me back now. He's so broke he couldn't even pay attention.* □ *After the business failed, she was so broke she couldn't even pay attention.*

so crooked he has to screw on his socks very dishonest. (Jocular.) □ *Don't trust him. He's so crooked he has to screw on his socks.* □ *The banker was well-known to be so crooked he had to screw on his socks.*

so dark all the bats stayed home very dark. (Jocular.) □ *It was a cloudy night, so dark all the bats stayed home.* □ *Last night was the new moon. It was so dark all the bats stayed home.*

so dark you couldn't find your nose with both hands very dark. □ *I went down in the cellar. It was so dark you couldn't find your nose with both hands.* □ *They stumbled through the forest, which was so dark you couldn't find your nose with both hands.*

so dry the trees were chasing the dogs very dry. (Jocular. Used to describe weather.) □ *That summer was so dry the trees were chasing the dogs.* □ *That was the big drought of '87. It was so dry the trees were chasing the dogs.*

so dumb he couldn't teach a hen to cluck very stupid. □ *I can't believe they let Joe teach school. He's so dumb he couldn't teach a hen to cluck.* □ *She'll never figure out how to do her own income tax. She's so dumb she couldn't teach a hen to cluck.*

so low you could sit on a newspaper and swing your legs AND **so low you could sit on the curb and swing your legs** very dishonest; tricky; immoral. (Humorously insulting.) □ *What a rotten trick! I declare, you're so low you could sit on a newspaper and swing your legs.* □ *I found out you asked another girl on a date. You're so low you could sit on the curb and swing your legs.*

so low you could sit on the curb and swing your legs See *so low you could sit on a newspaper and swing your legs.*

so old it's got whiskers very old. (Usually used to describe old jokes.) □ *That joke is so old it's got whiskers!* □ *Jim was all excited about a new joke he had learned, but it's not a new joke at all. It's so old it's got whiskers.*

so to speak in a manner of speaking. □ *He's a bit under the weather, so to speak.* □ *He don't know his sitting down place from a hole in the ground, so to speak.*

sockdologer an extraordinary thing. (Pronounced *SOCK-DOLL-uh-jur.*) □ *That November blizzard was a sockdologer.* □ *Whenever Jim gives a party, it's a sockdologer.*

soft soap **1.** homemade soap made of lye and animal fat. □ *The house smelled something awful when Grandma made a batch of soft soap.* □ *None of your modern cleansers can beat old-fashioned soft soap when it comes to getting out a stain.* **2.** to flatter someone. □ *The salesman was an expert at soft soaping his customers.* □ *You can soft soap me all you want, I'm still not going to let you use my car.*

sombrero a hat with a wide, round brim. (Spanish.) □ *The waiters at the Mexican restaurant all wear sombreros.* □ *The sombrero kept the sun off my face.*

some kind of something **1.** a very good something. □ *Jane has turned out to be some kind of teacher.* □ *We really need some kind of help.* **2.** a very bad something. □ *He's some kind of fiddle player, all right. Don't let him bring his fiddle.* □ *This ackenpucky is some kind of dinner!* **3.** very much something. □ *That kid is some kind of smart.* □ *It was some kind of fun.*

some pumpkins an extraordinary person or thing. □ *Jim sure thinks his girlfriend is some pumpkins.* □ *Have you seen my new tractor? It's some pumpkins!*

someone ain't worth the powder and lead it would take to shoot someone someone is worthless. □ *Mary's low-down boyfriend ain't worth the powder and lead it would take to shoot him.* □ JANE: *Sometimes I'd like to kill Tom.* MARY: *Oh, he ain't worth the powder and lead it would take to shoot him.*

someone knows where the bear shits someone knows how things are. (Use with caution.) □ *Bill's a good woodsman. He knows where the bear shits.* □ *Listen to what she's telling you. She knows where the bear shits.*

someone's ears are burning someone is being talked about. (According to this superstition, one's ears feel hot when one is being talked about.) □ *My ears are burning. Are y'all talking about me?* □ *Joe's ears were burning. He felt sure everyone was gossiping about him.*

someone's game is up someone is about to die. □ *Sounds like Bill ain't doing too good. I think his game is up.* □ *This is it, dear. My game is up.*

someone's oil doesn't reach the dipstick someone is unable to think clearly. □ *Tom has such strange ideas, I sometimes think his oil doesn't reach the dipstick.* □ *It'll be hard for her to get a job. Any employer can see that her oil doesn't reach the dipstick.*

someone's shit don't stink someone is perfect. (Usually used ironically. Use with caution.) □ *Mary's a lousy worker, but she flatters the boss, so he thinks her shit don't stink.* □ *How come you're going out with Jim instead of me? Jim's shit don't stink, is that it?*

someone's tongue wags at both ends someone is very talkative. □ *She's quiet as a church mouse around grown-ups, but when she's with other kids, her tongue wags at both ends.* □ *When he gets going on country music, his tongue wags at both ends.*

something awful AND **something terrible** a very great deal. □ *Sally brags about her kids something awful.* □ *The traffic was jammed up something terrible.*

something old, something new, something borrowed, and something blue things worn by the bride on her wedding day. (According to this superstition, a bride should wear one of each of these four kinds of things.) □ *On my wedding day, I had my mother's old dress, new shoes, and a blue ribbon in my hair. Jane lent me a handkerchief, so I could have something old, something new, something borrowed, and something blue.* □ *"My dear, are you all ready?" asked the mother of the bride. "Something old, something new, something borrowed, and something blue?"*

something on a stick very special. □ *Mary sure is a snob. She really thinks she's something on a stick.* □ *To Jim, that old pickup truck is something on a stick.*

something scandalous in a scandalous way. □ *Mary and Jim have been carrying on something scandalous, and her a married woman!* □ *At the party, the young folks got drunk something scandalous.*

something terrible See *something awful.*

somewheres somewhere. □ *I can't find my glasses. I must have left them somewheres.* □ *I think there's a grocery store somewheres around here.*

sooey AND **sooie; sui** the sound used to call pigs and hogs. □ *Mary took the hog feed out to the yard and called, "Sooey!"* □ *Sooie! Here, pig, pig, pig!* □ *As a joke, Bill called us in to dinner with a cry of "Sui!"*

soogan AND **sugan** a blanket. □ *The cowboy wrapped himself up in his soogan and went to sleep.* □ *The kids slept on a sugan on the floor.*

sooie See *sooey.*

sooky See *suky.*

Sooner someone from Oklahoma. □ *Jim is a Sooner from Tulsa.* □ *I was born in Missouri, but I've lived in Oklahoma City most of my life, so I consider myself a Sooner.*

sopaipilla a square of light, fried dough. (From Spanish. Pronounced *soe-pee-a-PEE-a.*) □ *Dessert was sopaipillas with honey.* □ *They have good stuffed sopaipillas at that restaurant.*

sorry(-lookin') pitiful in appearance; bad-looking. □ *I ain't gonna give you two hundred dollars for that sorry-lookin' horse.* □ *Jim was a sorry sight, with his shirt in tatters and mud all over him.*

soul-case the rib cage. □ *Someone stuck a knife in his soul-case.* □ *Her soul-case was bruised when she fell off the horse.*

sourdough **1.** a bread made with fermented batter. □ *Jim makes good sourdough.* □ *I have a recipe for sourdough rye bread.* **2.** a cook. □ *Don't make the sourdough mad, unless you want burned biscuits for dinner.* □ *He'd been a sourdough on the ranch for twenty years.*

souse meat AND **head cheese** the meat from a pig's head, pressed and preserved. □ *Grandma knew how to make souse meat.* □ *We ate head cheese all winter.*

Southern fried chicken chicken pieces deep-fried in batter. □ *Bill makes the best Southern fried chicken you'll ever taste.* □ *After two years up North, I missed the taste of real Southern fried chicken.*

Southern gentleman a well-mannered, chivalrous man from the Southern U.S. □ *Joe prides himself on being a Southern gentleman.* □ *He opened the door for the ladies and tipped his hat like a real Southern gentleman.*

Southern hospitality generous, gracious treatment of guests, which is supposed to be typical of the Southern U.S. □ *My Georgia cousins showed us real Southern hospitality during our visit.* □ *Our hosts offered us the best of everything they had, with true Southern hospitality.*

spang in the middle exactly in the middle. (Emphatic.) □ *She hit the target spang in the middle.* □ *The ball came down spang in the middle of the playing field.*

Spanish moss a kind of moss that grows in tree branches and hangs down in long stringy masses. (This kind of moss is common in parts of the Southern United States.) □ *The drive was lined with old trees covered in Spanish moss.* □ *The Spanish moss in the trees was our first sign that we had arrived in the South.*

spark to court. □ *Jane went out sparkin' with her young man.* □ *He came over on Friday nights to spark.*

sparrow grass asparagus. □ *The sparrow grass in our garden came up early in the spring.* □ *Let me cook you up some fresh sparrow grass.*

speak now or forever hold your peace make your objections now, or do not make any in the future. (From the marriage service in the *Book of Common Prayer*.) □ *Is this movie OK with you?*

Speak now or forever hold your peace. □ *The preacher said to speak now or forever hold your peace, but he didn't stop long enough for me to speak.*

speak one's mind See *speak one's piece.*

speak one's piece AND **have one's say; speak one's mind; say one's piece** to say what one wishes to say. □ *You haven't asked me for advice, but I feel I need to speak my piece.* □ *Having said his piece, he sat down and was silent for the rest of the night.* □ *She had her say. Now she's happy.*

(speak softly and) carry a big stick do not boast or threaten, but be well-prepared to fight. □ *If you want others to respect you, speak softly and carry a big stick.* □ *Don't mess with John. He carries a big stick.*

speechify to make a speech. (See also *speechifying.*) □ *There's no need to speechify. Just say what you think.* □ *At the school board meeting, folks speechified for hours.*

speechifying making speeches. (See also *speechify.*) □ *All this speechifying is putting me to sleep.* □ *I listened to the candidates' speechifying on the radio.*

spell **1.** a fit. □ *Sally had one of her fainting spells, but she's better now.* □ *Joe's an epileptic. He's prone to spells every now and then.* **2.** a while. (Used with the indefinite article *a.*) □ *Come on in and set a spell.* □ *If you're feeling faint, you'd better lie down for a spell.*

spell someone (for a while) to take one's turn at something. □ *If you get tired of driving, I can spell you for a while.* □ *Somebody better spell him before he falls asleep on the job.*

spelling bee a spelling contest. □ *I won first prize in the spelling bee.* □ *The schoolchildren had a spelling bee every Friday.*

spit and vinegar See *piss and vinegar.*

spit cotton to be extremely thirsty. □ *Could I have a glass of water? It's ninety degrees out here and I'm spitting cotton.* □ *After biking for an hour in the sun, they were spitting cotton.*

spittin' image someone who resembles someone else very closely. □ *He's the spittin' image of his pa.* □ *You're the spittin' image of Cary Grant!*

spittoon a cuspidor. □ *A brass spittoon sat in the corner of the barroom.* □ *Poor old Jed just kept missing the spittoon, time after time.*

splendiferous wonderful; great; splendid. □ *They threw a splendiferous party.* □ *We had some splendiferous fireworks for the Fourth of July.*

spook to scare someone or something. □ *A sudden movement in the bushes spooked the horse, and it bolted.* □ *Sally went out to the barn and got spooked by an old barn owl.*

spoon bread AND **batter bread** a baked cornmeal pudding. □ *The spoon bread was smooth and tasty.* □ *I poured some gravy on my batter bread.*

S'posing I do? "What if I do?" □ TOM: *You're not going to watch that TV program, are you?* JANE: *S'posing I do?* □ MARY: *Do you really want to cut the legs off that pair of pants?* CHARLIE: *S'posing I do?*

spraddle (out) to spread out. □ *The dog lay spraddled out on the ground.* □ *He stood with his legs spraddled.*

Spread that on the grass to make it green. "That is nonsense." (The *that* is manure = nonsense.) □ TOM: *But I love you!* JANE: *Spread that on the grass to make it green.* □ SALLY: *This car gets two hundred miles to the gallon.* CHARLIE: *Spread that on the grass to make it green.*

spring chicken a young person. (Usually used in the negative.) □ *I can't walk as fast as you young folks. I'm no spring chicken, you know!* □ *That actress still looks awful good, though she's no spring chicken.*

squat See *diddly(-squat).*

squaw a woman, especially an American Indian woman. (Offensive to some people.) □ *Joe married a squaw and had a bunch of half-breed kids.* □ *You ought to get a squaw to do the cooking around here.*

squeal like a stuck pig to squeal loudly; to give sharp piercing cries. (See also *bleed like a stuck pig.*) □ *When I tickled Mary, she squealed like a stuck pig.* □ *Bill squealed like a stuck pig while I tried to get the splinter out of his foot.*

squeezings See *(corn) squeezings.*

squinch owl See *screech owl.*

stack cake a layer cake. □ *She made a fancy stack cake for Bill's birthday.* □ *It was a stack cake, with raspberry preserves between the layers.*

stake (out) one's claim to mark out what one is claiming (land, for example). □ *The settlers staked out their claims near the river.* □ *The scientist staked her claim in her area of research.*

stakeout a police activity that involves watching or waiting for a suspect. □ *The officer went on the stakeout.* □ *They needed more officers for the stakeout at the suspect's house.*

stampede an uncontrollable rush of animals or people. (Literal and figurative uses.) □ *The cowboys were almost crushed in the cattle stampede.* □ *On the day of the big sale, there was a stampede of customers.*

standin' in need of something needing something. □ *How are you doing? Are you standin' in need of anything?* □ *You could tell from the look on his face, he was standin' in need of a kind word.*

Stars and Bars the Confederate flag used during the U.S. Civil War (1861–1865). □ *Bill has the Stars and Bars painted on the side of his pickup truck.* □ *They took the Union flag down and hauled the Stars and Bars aloft.*

steal away like a thief in the night to leave secretly. □ *He sneaked in through the window to his sweetheart's room and then stole away like a thief in the night.* □ *The outlaw tried to steal away like a thief in the night.*

steeper than a cow's face See *(as) steep as a cow's face.*

step around to have an extramarital affair. □ *Mary left Bill. She found out he was stepping around.* □ *He suspicioned that his wife was stepping around.*

step off the carpet to get married. □ *You and Jane have been going out a long time. When are you going to step off the carpet?* □ *The happiest day of his life was when he and Mary stepped off the carpet.*

step on someone's corns See *tread on someone's toes.*

Stetson AND **John B. Stetson; JB; John B** a cowboy hat, named for John B. Stetson, a maker of cowboy hats. □ *He put on his Stetson and mounted his horse.* □ *I bought a new John B. Stetson at the Western wear store.* □ *He wore a funny-looking JB about two sizes bigger than his head.* □ *The rain ran off the sides of my John B and on down my back.*

stewed to the gills very drunk. □ *You won't get any sense out of her. She's stewed to the gills.* □ *Don't let him drive—he's stewed to the gills!*

stick in someone's craw to bother someone; to be hard for someone to accept. □ *The results of the election stuck in Bill's craw.* □ *Laura's decision stuck in my craw. I couldn't believe she was really going to leave her job.*

stick-to-it-iveness determination; perseverance. □ *Don't give up when things get hard. Have a little stick-to-it-iveness.* □ *Jim had good luck, but he also had stick-to-it-iveness, and that's why he succeeded.*

stick (to someone) like white on rice See *be on someone like white on rice.*

stick to someone's ribs to fill someone's stomach; to satisfy someone's hunger. □ *That barbecued chicken sure sticks to my ribs.* □ *They cooked a good, old-fashioned breakfast, the kind that really sticks to your ribs.*

stick to your guns to be persistent, to defend one's point of view. □ *Don't let them talk you out of it. Stick to your guns.* □ *Jim stuck to his guns, and in the end, he got his way.*

stick-up a robbery at gunpoint. □ *The masked man said, "This is a stick-up."* □ *The traveler was the victim of a stick-up.*

still have some snap left in one's garters to still be energetic. (Said of old people.) □ *Gramma's eighty years old, but she still has some snap left in her garters. Why, she went out dancing just last night!* □ *He may look like a prim old man, but he still has some snap left in his garters.*

stir one's stumps to get ready to go. □ *We'd better stir our stumps if we want to get there on time.* □ *Come on! Get out of bed and stir your stumps!*

stogie a cigar. □ *He had a big, fat stogie sticking out of his mouth.* □ *Jim smokes cheap stogies that smell awful.*

stomp to stamp. □ *He stomped in, bellowing, "What's for dinner?"* □ *She stomped on the cockroach.*

stomp the bejeebers out of someone or something to stamp or kick someone or something severely. (See also *beat the bejeebers out of someone or something; knock the bejeebers out of someone or something.*) □ *The bandits stomped the bejeebers out of the poor cowboy.* □ *You could really stomp the bejeebers out of somebody with them big heavy boots.*

stone cold very cold. □ *The food was stone cold.* □ *By the time they found the body, it was stone cold.*

stone-cold sober not at all drunk; very sober. □ JANE: *Are you drunk?* TOM: *No! I'm stone-cold sober!* □ *The shocking news turned us stone-cold sober in an instant.*

stone dead dead. (Emphatic.) □ *He fell over, stone dead.* □ *They found her huddled in the snowbank, stone dead.*

stone deaf completely deaf. □ *She can't hear you. She's stone deaf.* □ *How could Beethoven write music when he was stone deaf?*

Stone the crows! "What a surprise!" □ *Well, stone the crows! I sure didn't expect to see you here!* □ *Stone the crows! Joe was right—it* is *snowing!*

stone's throw a short distance. (Used with the indefinite article *a*.) □ *The Smiths' place is just a stone's throw from here.* □ *Once you get to the courthouse, the city hall is just a stone's throw away.*

store-bought(en) bought at a store. □ *My missus said she sure would like a nice store-bought hat.* □ *This store-boughten bread ain't much good.*

straight shooter someone who speaks very directly and frankly. □ *Mary's a straight shooter. You can believe what she tells you.* □ *Tom never beats around the bush. He's a real straight shooter.*

stranger someone you do not know. (Used as a form of address. "Howdy, stranger!" is sometimes used humorously, to greet a friend one has not seen in a long time.) □ *What can I do for you, stranger?* □ *Howdy, stranger! I haven't seen you since the big football game!*

straw boss an overseer; someone who supervises workers for the owner of a business. □ *The straw boss told the ranch hands to brand the cattle.* □ *Joe is the straw boss on this project.*

stretch someone's neck to hang someone. □ *They took the cattle rustler out to the big oak tree and stretched his neck.* □ *The lynch mob wanted to stretch the prisoner's neck.*

stretch the blanket See *throw the hatchet.*

strike it rich to become rich. □ *The author struck it rich with his last novel.* □ *Lots of folks come to the big city to try to strike it rich.*

string someone up to hang someone. □ *When they caught the cattle thief, they strung him up.* 🅃 *The townsfolk wanted to string up the murderer.*

study on something to think carefully about something. □ *Study on it for a while before you make a decision.* □ *I sat up late, studying on what I could do to help Joe.*

stump to travel from place to place, giving campaign speeches. (See also *stump speech.*) □ *The candidate spent months stumping in the Midwest.* □ *The mayoral candidates stumped at grocery stores, at shopping malls, at public schools, and in the town square.*

stump liquor illicit liquor, bought by leaving money in a tree stump. □ *I got a pint of some real good stump liquor.* □ *He took me out in the woods to a place where I could get some stump liquor.*

stump speech a campaign speech. (See also *stump.*) □ *Our news broadcast will include excerpts from the Democratic candidate's stump speech.* □ *Both candidates gave stump speeches in our town.*

Such is life in the West, and the further west you go, the sucher it is. Life is like that. (Humorous.) □ TOM: *Every time I get a little extra money, seems some emergency comes along and I have to spend it.* BILL: *Such is life in the West, and the further west you go, the sucher it is.* □ CHARLIE: *Driving cattle is really hard work.* TOM: *Such is life in the West.* BILL: *And the further west you go, the sucher it is.*

suchlike and so on; and such things. □ *Have you been going to a lot of parties and dances and suchlike?* □ *He likes expensive food, champagne and caviar, and suchlike.*

suck the hind teat to get the smaller portion; to get an unfairly small amount. □ *My sister always gets the best of everything around here. I'm tired of sucking the hind teat.* □ *Seems to me the government policy gives the old folks everything they want, while little children are left to suck the hind teat.*

Sucker someone from Illinois. □ *He was a Sucker from Carbondale.* □ *I'm proud to say I'm a Sucker, born and bred in Peoria.*

sucker-bait a lure for foolish people. □ *The ad was sucker-bait, promising a thousand dollars a week for stuffing envelopes.* □ TOM: *That school says they'll train you for a lucrative career in just six months.* JANE: *Oh, come on, Tom. That's sucker-bait. They just want your tuition money.*

sugan See *soogan.*

sugar dear; darling. (A term of endearment.) □ *Hey, sugar, you look awful cute in that new dress.* □ *"Hello, sugar," Gramma said, giving me a big hug.*

sugar peas a type of pea that can be eaten with the pod. □ *My tomatoes aren't doing so well, but my sugar peas are coming up real nice.* □ *I boiled up some sugar peas for a vegetable at dinner.*

sui See *sooey.*

suit someone's fancy to please someone. □ *We can go biking, driving, boating—whatever suits your fancy.* □ *It was a funny little hat, but it suited my fancy.*

suky AND **sooky** a generic name for a cow. □ *Suky stood still while I milked her.* □ *Easy there, Sooky. Good girl.*

sumbitch son of a bitch. (Use with caution.) □ *That old sumbitch wouldn't give me my money back.* □ *You sumbitch! Get your damn car out of my way!*

summer and winter all year long. □ *She complains about the weather summer and winter.* □ *A farmer has to work hard summer and winter.*

sumpin AND **suthin** something. □ *He always brings home sumpin for his kids when he goes away on a trip.* □ *Iffen there's suthin you want, jest ask for it.*

Sunday go-to-meeting fine; formal. (Usually used to describe clothes.) □ *They put on their Sunday go-to-meeting clothes for the church social.* □ *Her outfit had a Sunday go-to-meeting look about it.*

sunny-side up [for eggs to be] fried with the uncooked yolks on top. (See also *bright-eyed.*) □ *I'll have two eggs, sunny-side up.* □ WAITRESS: *How do you want those eggs?* DINER: *Sunny-side up.*

survigrous very vigorous. (Pronounced *sir-VIG-russ.*) □ *The squash vines in the garden are looking survigrous.* □ *He was a sickly baby, but a survigrous child.*

suspicion to suspect. □ *I suspicion Tom's not happy at home.* □ *She's going to quit her job, I suspicion.*

suthin See *sumpin.*

swallow something hook, line, and sinker to believe or accept something wholeheartedly. (Like an unsuspecting fish.) □ *The ad said that the pills had no side effects, and people swallowed it hook, line, and sinker.* □ *He said that this time he was really going to stop drinking once and for all. She swallowed it hook, line, and sinker.*

swear on a stack of Bibles to swear to the truth of something; to take a solemn oath. □ *She swears on a stack of Bibles it wasn't Bill she saw.* □ *All her friends were prepared to swear on a stack of Bibles that she didn't steal the money.*

sweat something out to endure something. □ *It was a difficult school year, but he sweated it out.* □ *The shopkeeper had no choice but to sweat the hard times out.*

sweet-mouth someone to flatter someone. □ *After I sweet-mouthed her, she started to get friendly.* □ *I don't believe a word you say. You're just trying to sweet-mouth me.*

sweet on someone in love with someone. □ *How come Bill's sending Sally all those presents? Is he sweet on her or something?* □ *I was sweet on Jimmy all through fifth grade, but I didn't dare tell him.*

sweet potato pie a pie made with a spiced sweet potato custard. □ *We had sweet potato pie with whipped cream on top.* □ *I like a little nutmeg and cloves in my sweet potato pie.*

sweet tooth a strong liking for sweets. □ *This sweet tooth of mine makes it hard for me to lose weight.* □ *Charlie sure has a sweet tooth. Dessert is his favorite part of any meal.*

swell like a bullfrog to swell up enormously. □ *He's so proud he's swelling like a bullfrog.* □ *Her ankle was swelling like a bullfrog.*

swell up like a poisoned pup to swell a lot. □ *When Jim got those bee stings, he swelled up like a poisoned pup.* □ *Last time I was pregnant, my legs were swelled up like a poisoned pup.*

swig a swallow of liquid. □ *Gimme a swig of that rotgut.* □ TOM: *Have a taste of this lemonade.* CHARLIE: *OK, I'll take a swig.*

swimmin' hole a small natural body of water used for swimming. □ *We're going down to the swimmin' hole. You coming?* □ *The kids spent the whole afternoon at the swimmin' hole.*

swing a wide loop to travel a great deal. □ *He was a traveling salesman. He swung a wide loop in his day.* □ *She had swung a wide loop, and had plenty of snapshots to prove it.*

swink and tote to work very hard. □ *She swinked and toted from dawn till dusk while her Ma was sick.* □ *Her husband swinks and totes while she stays at home and gossips.*

swoll up swollen. □ *Something's wrong with my ankle. It's all swoll up.* □ *She looked terrible. Her eyes were red and her face was swoll up.*

swum swam. □ *He swum all the way across the pond.* □ *We swum for a while and then went back to school.*

T

table-muscle a big belly. □ *After Bill got married, he developed a table-muscle.* □ *Joe's got a good-size table-muscle on him.*

tail up and stinger out ready for action. (Like a scorpion.) □ *She came into the room tail up and stinger out, just spoiling for a fight.* □ *The boxer swaggered into the ring, tail up and stinger out.*

take a gander to take a look. □ *Come over here and take a gander at this.* □ *Doc Jones took a gander at my sore throat.*

take a look-see to take a look. □ TOM: *My foot hurts.* JANE: *Let me take a look-see. Maybe you've got a splinter.* □ *Something's making a funny noise in my car engine. Could you take a look-see?*

take a notion to do something to decide to do something; to want to do something. □ *Bill took a notion to climb that big tree in the holler.* □ *After seeing the commercial for flight school, Mary took a notion to become a pilot.*

take a shine to someone to take a liking to someone. □ *For some reason, Uncle Jim really took a shine to me.* □ *She took a shine to her best friend's brother.*

take ill See *take sick.*

take it on the chin to receive a great injury; to lose terribly. □ *He really took it on the chin in that fight.* □ *Her little grocery store took it on the chin when they built that new supermarket.*

take it out of someone's hide to punish someone severely. (See also *have someone's hide.*) □ *When I catch the guy who stole my money, I'll take it out of his hide.* □ *If I was to go spray-painting my name around town, my daddy would take it out of my hide!*

take on (so) to be overly dramatic. (See also *carry on (so).*) □ *Hush now. Don't take on so.* □ *She took on for half an hour when she heard the news.*

take on wood AND **wood up** to have a drink together. □ *Will you take on wood with me before you head home?* □ *The two friends would wood up every Friday night.*

take one's Bible oath to swear to the truth of something; to take a solemn oath. □ *I'd take my Bible oath that Jane didn't steal the money.* □ *Would you take your Bible oath on that?*

take out after someone or something to chase after someone or something. □ *I took out after my brother, Jed, and caught him and walloped him good.* □ *The bees took out after me and might have stung me to death, iffen I hadn't jumped in the crick.*

take sick AND **take ill** to become sick. □ *When did Jill take sick?* □ *He took ill suddenly.*

take someone down a notch (or two) See *take someone down a peg (or two).*

take someone down a peg (or two) AND **take someone down a notch (or two)** to make someone less boastful; to shame someone who is overly proud. □ *Bill always went around saying he was the best runner in the whole school. Then Joe beat him in a race. That took him down a peg or two.* □ *She's awfully full of herself. I wish somebody would take her down a peg.* □ *It sure took Andy down a notch or two, to have his mother scold him in front of his friends.* □ *After bragging about what a great actress she was, Sally forgot her lines onstage. That took her down a notch for sure.*

take someone out to the woodshed to punish someone. □ *The boss is going to find out the people responsible for this failure and* *take them out to the woodshed.* □ *If you don't settle down, I'm going to have the principal take you out to the woodshed.*

take someone's word (on something) to believe what someone says (about something). □ *All right. I'll take your word on it.* □ *You can take my word that it's true.*

take the big jump to die. □ *I've lived a good, long life. I reckon it's about time for me to take the big jump.* □ *Sometimes I'm so depressed I just want to take the big jump.*

take to someone or something to like someone or something. □ *They took to each other the first time they met.* □ *She took to Oregon so much that she decided to move there.*

take up with someone to start a romantic relationship with someone. □ *He took up with a woman he met at work.* □ *We were surprised to hear that Jim took up with Mary.*

taking harp lessons dead. (Jocular.) □ *When I get through with you, you'll be taking harp lessons.* □ CHARLIE: *How's your husband?* JANE: *He's taking harp lessons. I've been a widow for three years.*

talk a blue streak to talk very fast and a very great deal. (See also *cuss a blue streak.*) □ *Every time the two friends got together, they talked a blue streak.* □ *Don't get him going about cameras, or he'll talk a blue streak.*

talk box one's mouth. (See also *think box.*) □ *Shut your talk box for one cotton-picking minute.* □ *The ball hit him right in the talk box.*

talk like a cotton gin in pickin' time to talk fast and a great deal. □ *The two sisters hadn't seen each other in a year. They were talking like a cotton gin in pickin' time.* □ *She talks like a cotton gin in pickin' time. You can't shut her up.*

talk one's head off to talk at length. □ *She talked her head off the whole time she was here.* □ *There's Jim and Joe, talking their heads off.*

talk some sense into someone to try to make someone be reasonable and do the right thing. □ *I've tried and tried to make Joe understand that he can't drop out of school. Maybe you can talk some sense into him.* □ *Jane's parents and friends tried to talk some sense into her, but she was determined to go on the Antarctic expedition.*

talk someone's arm off AND **talk someone's ear off** to talk to someone at great length. □ *Ask him about his latest land deal, and he'll talk your arm off.* □ *Go and rescue Jane. That old bore is talking her ear off.*

talk someone's ear off See *talk someone's arm off.*

talk trash (about someone) to gossip (about someone); to say bad things (about someone). □ *Jim just loves to talk trash about me to all my friends.* □ *If you don't quit talking trash, I'm gonna whup you but good.*

talk turkey to speak plainly about the business at hand. □ *I couldn't get that salesman to talk turkey.* □ *OK. Enough beating around the bush. Let's talk turkey.*

talking iron a gun. (See also *shooting iron.*) □ *When I've got my talking iron, folks generally don't argue with me.* □ *He says it's his land, and he's got a talking iron to back him up.*

tall tale a fanciful, exaggerated story. □ *There are many tall tales about the legendary hero, Paul Bunyan.* □ *Grampa loved to tell us kids tall tales about his life in the logging camp.*

tamale a dish made of spicy meat and cornmeal, wrapped in a corn husk and steamed. (From an Amerindian language via Spanish.) □ *The street vendor sold tamales and ears of sweet corn.* □ *Mama made tamales for dinner.*

tan someone's hide to beat someone as punishment. □ *Ma tanned our hides if we misbehaved.* □ *Don't run in the house, or I'll tan your hide.*

tangle with someone or something to oppose or interfere with someone or something. □ *Everyone warned me not to tangle with Tom.* □ *The puppy soon learned not to tangle with spiders.*

Tar Heel someone from North Carolina. □ *The museum in Charlotte had exhibits about several famous Tar Heels.* □ *My grandpa was a Tar Heel from Durham, North Carolina.*

tarnation damnation. (A mock oath or epithet.) □ *Tarnation! Who left that window open during the rain?* □ *What in tarnation are you doing?*

tarp a large piece of waterproof material. □ *Spread a tarp over the firewood so it won't get rained on.* □ *It was raining. The cowboy covered himself with his tarp.*

taste of something to take a taste of something. □ *Here, taste of this candy.* □ *Soon as I tasted of it, I knew I'd want more.*

tater a potato. □ *I dug up some taters from the garden.* □ *Slice them taters thin.*

tater chunk a short distance. (See also *howdy and a half; two whoops and a holler.*) □ *His farm was just a tater chunk from ours.* □ *It was just a tater chunk from the school to the grocery store.*

teepee a conical tent, especially one used by Plains Indians. □ *They decorated their teepees with painted designs.* □ *The kids built a teepee in the backyard.*

tejano a Texan of Hispanic origin. (From Spanish.) □ *Luis is a tejano.* □ *The tejanos were proud of their Mexican heritage.*

tell a story to lie. □ *I suspicioned he was telling a story.* □ *When I asked where she'd been, she told me a story.*

Tell it to a sailor on horseback. I do not believe you. □ TOM: *I'm sorry I was late. There was a terrible traffic accident—* MARY: *Tell it to a sailor on horseback. You're late because you're always late.*

□ JANE: *I wasn't going to eat that piece of cake. I was just going to smell it.* TOM: *Tell it to a sailor on horseback.*

tell the truth and shame the devil to tell the truth, even though it may hurt the teller. □ *Who broke that window, Mary? Come on—tell the truth and shame the devil.* □ *I've got to tell the truth and shame the devil. I was the one who took the money.*

tell t'other from which to tell one from another. □ *The twins looked so much alike, you couldn't tell t'other from which.* □ *Is this your coat or mine? I can't tell t'other from which.*

ten-gallon hat a large cowboy hat. □ *That must be Jim a'comin'. I'd recognize his big black ten-gallon hat anywhere.* □ *I bought a ten-gallon hat with a fancy feather hatband.*

tend to your own ball of yarn See *tend to your own knitting.*

tend to your own knitting AND **tend to your own ball of yarn** mind your own business. □ TOM: *What are you doing with that screwdriver?* JANE: *Tend to your own knitting.* □ CHARLIE: *Did you ask Mary to the dance?* TOM: *Tend to your own ball of yarn.*

tenderfoot a novice; someone who is new to something. □ *He's such a tenderfoot he doesn't even know how to ride horseback.* □ *Can you help me with this? I'm kind of a tenderfoot in the kitchen.*

Tennessee toothpick a raccoon bone used as a toothpick. □ *Bill has a Tennessee toothpick set in a fancy handle he carved himself.* □ *He picked his teeth with a Tennessee toothpick.*

tequila liquor made from the mescal plant. (Spanish.) □ *He ordered a shot of tequila.* □ *I bought a bottle of tequila.*

tetched (in the head) crazy. (From *touched.*) □ *The professor's students thought he was a little tetched in the head.* □ *Don't pay her any mind. She's tetched.*

tetchy irritable; touchy. □ *What makes you so tetchy today?* □ *The baby's acting awful tetchy.*

thank God for small favors Be thankful that something good has happened in a bad situation. □ CHARLIE: *We're out of gas, but I think I see a gas station up ahead.* TOM: *Thank God for small favors.* □ *He had a heart attack, but it was right there in the doctor's office, so they could take care of him right away. Thank God for small favors.*

thank you kindly thank you very much. □ TOM: *May I give you a lift?* JANE: *Why, yes. Thank you kindly.* □ MARY: *That's a nice suit, and you wear it well.* CHARLIE: *Thank you kindly, ma'am.*

thankee See *thanky.*

thanky AND **thankee** thank you. (From *thank ye* = thank you.) □ *Thanky very much for your help.* □ *I'm glad of your present. Thankee.*

that ain't no lie what was said is true. □ TOM: *Sure is hot today.* JANE: *That ain't no lie.* □ *I'm plumb exhausted, and that ain't no lie.*

that beats something all to pieces that is much better than the person or thing named. (See also *beat bobtail; Don't that beat all?; If that don't beat a pig a-pecking!*) □ *Mary's layer cake beats mine all to pieces.* □ *I say the book beats the movie all to pieces.*

That (old) dog won't hunt. "The excuse given is unbelievable or unacceptable." □ STUDENT: *My homework paper got lost.* TEACHER: *That old dog won't hunt. You've "lost" three papers already this year.* □ TOM: *I wasn't flirting with that girl. I was just asking her where she got her necklace, so I could get one for you.* MARY: *That dog won't hunt.*

that there that. (See also *this here.*) □ *Gimme that there can of nails.* □ *That there car is an old Pontiac.*

that very thing exactly that. □ *Why, I was just looking for that very thing!* □ *You know, I was just about to say that very thing.*

thataway that way. (Indicates direction. See also *thisaway.*) □ *The highway's over thataway.* □ TOM: *Which way did he go?* CHARLIE: *Thataway!*

That's a fine how-do-you-do. That is a terrible situation. □ *Well, that's a fine how-do-you-do! I tried to call Mary, and her number is disconnected!* □ *That's a fine how-do-you-do. I come home and find the kids are playing catch with my best crystal bowl.*

That's all she wrote. That is all.; That is everything. □ TOM: *Have we done everything we were supposed to do?* JANE: *Yep. That's all she wrote.* □ *At the end of his lecture, the speaker said, "That's all she wrote. Any questions?"*

That's for dang sure! "That is quite certain!" (The formulaic response to *That's for sure!* The accent is always on the *dang*.) □ TOM: *That's for sure!* JANE: *That's for dang sure!* □ SALLY: *We'll be there and that's for sure!* BILL: *Yup! That's for dang sure!*

That's the ticket. That is right.; That is a good idea. □ TOM: *What will we tell Ma when she asks where we've been?* CHARLIE: *We could say we was visiting a sick friend.* TOM: *That's the ticket!* □ JANE: *We could nail these boards together, or we could use glue.* BILL: *Glue! That's the ticket.*

That's the tune the old cow died on. That tune is badly played. □ *All morning long, I can hear my neighbor's son practicing the same song on his violin. That's the tune the old cow died on.* □ TOM: *What did you think of that song?* CHARLIE: *That's the tune the old cow died on.*

That's the way the hog bladder bounces. Life is like that.; That is the way things go. □ TOM: *I didn't get the job.* JANE: *Oh, well. That's the way the hog bladder bounces.* □ *I just found out I failed that class. That's the way the hog bladder bounces, I guess.*

The bigger the mouth, the better it looks closed. One should not talk too much. □ *She flapped her gums all night. Someone should tell her that the bigger the mouth, the better it looks closed.* □ *You talk too much. The bigger the mouth, the better it looks closed.*

The devil's beatin' his wife. Warm rain is falling while the sun is shining. □ *Sure is funny weather we're having. The devil's beatin' his wife.* □ *It was a summer afternoon, and the devil was beatin' his wife.*

The fat is in the fire. Terrible trouble is certain to come. □ *Bill's wife found out that he spent all their savings. The fat's in the fire now.* □ *The fat's in the fire. I told Joe I'd have his car fixed today, and there's no way I can do it.*

the Good Book the Bible. □ *I read some in the Good Book every day.* □ *Sally's always quoting from the Good Book.*

the great beyond death. □ *The fortune-teller claimed to get messages from the great beyond.* □ *I often think of my loved ones in the great beyond, and long for the day I will see them again.*

The latch string is always out. "You are always welcome." □ *Come by anytime. The latch string is always out.* □ *No need to call before you come over. For you folks, the latch string is always out.*

(the) Lord only knows No one but God knows. □ *The Lord only knows if John's marriage will be a happy one.* □ *How Mary can stay so cheerful through her terrible illness, the Lord only knows.*

the Lord's Day Sunday; the Christian day of worship. □ *She never got a moment's rest, not even on the Lord's Day.* □ *He believed that all businesses should close on the Lord's Day.*

the Missis the wife. □ *I think we can come over on Sunday. Let me ask the Missis.* □ *The Missis made me promise not to drink.* □ *What's the matter, Jim? Having trouble with the Missis?*

the missus See *missus.*

The old woman's picking her geese. It is snowing. □ TOM: *How's your weather out there?* JANE: *The old woman's picking her geese.* □ *Yesterday it was sunny and warm, but today, the old woman's picking her geese.*

The same dog bit me. I think the same thing. □ CHARLIE: *I suspicion Jim's drunk.* TOM: *The same dog bit me.* □ JANE: *Is it just me, or is the food at this restaurant really awful?* MARY: *It ain't just you. The same dog bit me.*

the well at wit's end inspiration that comes from desperation. □ *The deadline was coming fast. I needed some help from the well at wit's end.* □ *After a sleepless night trying to find a solution, the well at wit's end finally came.*

theirn theirs. (See also *hisn; hern; ourn.*) □ *That was a clever idea of theirn.* □ *My brother's family says the land is theirn.*

theirselves themselves. □ *They want to do it theirselves.* □ *They sat all by theirselves.*

them those. □ *Where'd you get them nice-lookin' peaches?* □ *It's gonna be one of them hot and sticky summer days.*

Them as has, gits. Rich people can always get more. □ *The millionaire keeps making more and more money, because he has lots of money to invest. Them as has, gits.* □ TOM: *Bill already owns half the property in town, and here the court went and awarded him that vacant lot.* JANE: *You know how it is—them as has, gits.*

Them's fighting words! What you just said will lead to a fight. (Said as a threat.) □ *I heard what you said about my brother, and them's fighting words.* □ *Put up your dukes. Them's fighting words!*

(there ain't) nothin' to it It is easy. □ MARY: *How do you keep your car so shiny?* TOM: *There ain't nothin' to it. I just wax it once a week.* □ *It took Jane just two minutes to sew up the hole in my shirt. "See?" she said. "Nothin' to it!"*

thereabouts in that area; a rough estimate. □ TOM: *How many head of cattle do you have?* MARY: *A hundred and fifty or thereabouts.* □ *The racetrack is in Dansville or thereabouts.*

there's more down (in the) cellar in a teacup "There is plenty of food, please have a second helping." □ *Have some more gumbo.*

There's more down in the cellar in a teacup. □ CHARLIE: *I hate to take the last helping of your batter bread.* MARY: *Go on, go on! There's more down cellar in a teacup.*

There's no flies on someone. someone is full of energy and drive. □ *Joe's started stocking the newest computers in his store. There's no flies on him.* □ *There's no flies on Jane. She's up at five every morning, training for the big race.*

There's no fool like an old fool. When old people are foolish, they are very foolish indeed. □ *Great-uncle Roger thinks that pretty girl is really in love with him. There's no fool like an old fool.* □ *Grandma sure looks a sight, trying to do them newfangled dances. There's no fool like an old fool.*

They ate before they said grace. AND **They planted the corn before they built the fence.** An unmarried couple is going to have a baby. □ *Jane's not just fat, she's pregnant. She and Jim ate before they said grace.* □ *Jim and his wife planted the corn before they built the fence, but they got married right before the baby came.*

They planted the corn before they built the fence. See *They ate before they said grace.*

they's they are. (From *they is*.) □ *Move your feet. They's in the way.* □ *They's late for dinner again.*

thicker than boll weevils AND **thicker than fleas on a fat pup** thickly; in a dense crowd. □ *The crowd was thicker than boll weevils.* □ *Seems like troubles have come down on Mary thicker than fleas on a fat pup.*

thicker than fleas on a fat pup See *thicker than boll weevils.*

thingamabob See *thingamajig.*

thingamajig AND **ditty; do-fotchet; doohickey; doorinckus; hook-a-hendum; hootentrankis; thingamabob; whangdoodle** an unknown thing or device. (See also *contraption; doodad; whatchamacallit.*) □ *They had one of those thingamajigs that* *makes milk shakes.* □ *I bought this ditty that peels and cores an apple all at once.* □ *Jane's sewing machine has all kinds of fancy do-fotchets on it.* □ *The doohickey that keeps the drawer shut is broken.* □ *Joe's always buying some new doorinckus for his computer.* □ *What do you do with this hook-a-hendum here?* □ *He's selling some kind of hootentrankis that attaches to your vacuum cleaner.* □ *The hotel door locked with a thingamabob that takes a card instead of a key.* □ *They had a whangdoodle on the gas pump to make it stop automatically.*

think a heap of someone or something to regard someone or something highly. □ *I'm glad you like Bill. I think a heap of him, myself.* □ *Mary thinks a heap of the quilts them Amish women make.*

think box a brain or mind. (See also *talk box.*) □ *She has a mighty powerful think box. She can solve any problem.* □ *There's something wrong with his think box. He's a little bit crazy.*

think someone hung the moon (and stars) AND **think someone is God's own cousin** to think someone is perfect. □ *Joe won't listen to any complaints about Mary. He thinks she hung the moon and stars.* □ *Jim is awful stuck-up. He thinks he's God's own cousin.*

think someone is God's own cousin See *think someone hung the moon (and stars).*

think the sun rises and sets on someone to think someone is the most important person in the world. (See also *think someone hung the moon (and stars).*) □ *Her daddy just thinks the sun rises and sets on her.* □ *She worships that boyfriend of hers. She thinks the sun rises and sets on him.*

thinks the sun comes up to hear him crow seems boastful or conceited. □ *He's awful conceited. He thinks the sun comes up to hear him crow.* □ *Since she got elected class president, she thinks the sun comes up to hear her crow.*

this a-way and that a-way first one way and then the other. □ *She was craning her neck this a-way and that a-way, looking for him.* □ *The dogs were running this a-way and that a-way.*

this child I or me. □ *This child ain't eating no Mexican food. I've had my tongue burned off once too often, thank you.* □ *Don't you try to sweet-mouth this child.*

this here this. (See also *that there.*) □ *Just let me fix this here chair leg.* □ *This here picture was painted by my Aunt Lena.*

thisaway this way. (Indicates direction. See also *thataway.*) □ *It's Joe, and he's headed thisaway.* □ *Look over thisaway. Can you see it now?*

thousand-legger a centipede; a many-legged bug. □ *Yuck! There's a thousand-legger crawling up your leg!* □ *The tree's leaves were covered with thousand-leggers.*

'thout(en) **1.** without. □ *Drat it, I've come out 'thouten my spectacles.* □ *He left her 'thout any money.* **2.** unless. □ *I won't go 'thouten Joe goes too.* □ *Jim can't pay you 'thout Jane pays him.*

thrash to beat or whip someone or something. □ *I thrashed him pretty good.* □ *Sass me one more time, boy, and I'll thrash you.*

three-cornered pants diapers. □ *I've known you since you were in three-cornered pants.* □ *Who's the little feller in the three-cornered pants?*

throddy chubby. □ *He was a throddy little boy, but grew up into a tall, slender man.* □ *Good cooks tend to be throddy from eating their own food.*

throw in with someone to become partners with someone. □ *Henry needed a partner to help run his business, so I threw in with him.* □ *She threw in with her friend from college, who was opening a hardware store.*

throw the hatchet AND **stretch the blanket** to exaggerate. □ *Jim is always throwing the hatchet about the size of the fish he caught.* □ *Maybe I did stretch the blanket a little when I was telling you about our town.*

Thunder ain't rain. Talking about doing something is not the same as doing it. □ BILL: *Joe says he's going to take me to court!* MARY: *Don't worry about it yet. Thunder ain't rain.* □ *Joe keeps boasting about how he's gonna win this race, but thunder ain't rain.*

thunder berries beans. (From the wind they raise.) □ *I had thunder berries for dinner. They gave me gas all night.* □ *Dish me up some of them thunder berries.*

thunderation "Damnation." (A mock oath.) □ *Thunderation! Who's been messing with my tools?* □ *"Thunderation!" Bill swore as the wind blew his tent away.*

thunderjug a chamber pot. □ *While Jane was sick abed, she had to use the thunderjug.* □ *On cold nights, I don't go all the way out to the outhouse. I use the thunderjug.*

thunk thought. (The past tense and past participle form of *think.*) □ *He thunk awhile and finally gave his answer.* □ *He thunk about it for a second. Then he just went and did it.*

ticker the heart. □ *Joe takes pills for some kind of problem with his ticker.* □ *By the time I got to the top of the stairs, my ticker was going a mile a minute.*

tie a knot in someone's tail See *put a knot in someone's tail.*

till the cows come home for a very long time; until very late at night. □ *Those kids could dance and drink till the cows come home.* □ *Mary wanted to party till the cows came home.*

till yet until now; to this day. □ *They were fighting on their wedding day. They've been married thirty years, and they're fighting till yet.* □ *Their family secret remains a secret till yet.*

time's a-wastin' Time is running out.; It is getting late. □ *Hurry up! Time's a-wastin'!* □ *How come you're still in bed? Time's a-wastin'!*

tinhorn a pretentious, showy person. (See also *tinhorn gambler.*) □ *He was a tinhorn with a flashy suit and a smooth way of talking.* □ *Who invited the tinhorn with all the diamond rings?*

tinhorn gambler a pretentious, showy gambler. (See also *tinhorn.*) □ *Miss Bessie won't ride the riverboats. She says they're full of loose women and tinhorn gamblers.* □ *He says he's a speculator, but I say he's just a tinhorn gambler.*

tip one's hand to show one's resources to one's opponents. □ *He tipped his hand when he let on that he had hired a private detective.* □ TOM: *Don't tell Joe that you have proof he's been cheating.* JANE: *Don't worry. I won't tip my hand.*

tipsy cake a cake soaked in liquor. □ *I have Grandma Peters' recipe for tipsy cake.* □ *She puts so much whiskey in her tipsy cake, it could make you high as a Georgia pine.*

tizzy a confused, upset state. □ *Ma was in a tizzy when she heard that my sister was pregnant.* □ *Sally's awfully flighty. The least little thing will send her into a tizzy.*

to at; in. □ *John is over to Effie's house.* □ *Granpappy is out to the Chick Sale.*

to beat the band to do something very energetically; to do something with enthusiasm. □ *They were laughing to beat the band.* □ *Those two could dance to beat the band.*

to boot as well; in addition. □ *I learned a lot at my summer job, and made good money to boot.* □ *For a hundred dollars, I'll sell you the hog and half a dozen chickens to boot.*

to hell and gone See *all over creation.*

to oncet at once; right away. (See also *oncet.*) □ *I'd better do it to oncet.* □ *When Ma called, we came running to oncet.*

to one's harm to one's disadvantage; causing harm to oneself. □ *She married him, to her harm.* □ *He rode his bicycle into the city, to his harm.*

to-rectly See *two-rectly.*

to speak of of any importance. □ TOM: *Did he have any friends?* JANE: *None to speak of.* □ *Mama and Daddy only ever had one fight to speak of.*

toadsticker See *frogsticker.*

tobacco chaw See *chaw (of tobacco).*

tolerable quite; rather. □ *It's a tolerable hot day.* □ *We had a tolerable pleasant time at the party.*

tol(er)able (well) pretty well; OK. □ TOM: *How are you feeling?* JANE: *Tolerable well.* □ CHARLIE: *How's the work coming?* TOM: *Tolable well.* □ MARY: *How's your aunt after her surgery?* JANE: *She's getting along tolable.*

tomahawk AND **tommyhawk** a hatchet. □ *They had a contest to see who could throw a tomahawk the furthest.* □ *The handle of the tommyhawk was decorated with beads.*

tomcatting **1.** going from place to place having fun. □ *He did a fair amount of tomcatting when he was young.* □ *The children were plumb tuckered out after a long day of tomcatting.* **2.** to be enjoying the company of many different women. □ *If you want me to take you back, you'll have to quit your dadburned tomcatting.* □ *John got caught tomcatting and his girlfriend dumped him.*

tomfool foolish. □ *Joe gets all these tomfool notions about "modern agriculture" from those hifalutin' books he reads.* □ *When we was kids, we was always playing all sorts of tomfool pranks.*

tomfoolery nonsense; antics. □ *Joe likes to play practical jokes and indulge in other such tomfoolery.* □ *Bill put on a monster mask, sneaked up behind Mary, and said, "Boo!" She looked at him calmly and said, "Quit your tomfoolery."*

tommyhawk See *tomahawk.*

tonsil paintin' drinking whiskey. (Jocular. See also *paint one's tonsils.*) □ *Too much tonsil paintin' killed him in the end.* □ *They got together on Friday nights for tonsil paintin' and playin' poker.*

too big for one's britches overly proud. □ *Ever since she won the race, she's been too big for her britches.* □ *We thought that Bill was getting too big for his britches. It was time to take him down a peg.*

too clever by half too smart. □ *They tried to trick her, but she was too clever by half.* □ *The outlaw was too clever by half. The sheriff's men never caught up with him.*

too many pigs for the tits too many people needing something and not enough to go around. (Use with caution.) □ *The company had to fire some workers. There were too many pigs for the tits.* □ *I can't take on another project. I've got too many pigs for the tits as it is.*

too poor to paint and too proud to whitewash poor; but proud. □ *They're from a fine old family, but too poor to paint and too proud to whitewash.* □ *Too poor to paint and too proud to whitewash, they hid their poverty from their neighbors as long as they could.*

toot one's own horn See *blow one's own horn.*

tooth-dentist a dentist. (See also *jaw-cracker.*) □ *You best go see the tooth-dentist about that toothache of yourn.* □ *The tooth-dentist says I got to have a filling.*

torn-down rough and wild. □ *He'll grow up a criminal if he hangs out with them torn-down lowlifes out in the parking lot.* □ *She was a mean, torn-down woman, and no mistake.*

tortilla a thin pancake of corn or wheat. (Spanish. Pronounced *tor-TEE-ya.*) □ *We had beans and tortillas for lunch.* □ *The chile rellenos come with corn tortillas on the side.*

tote one's own skillet to be independent; to do one's own work. □ *He's been toting his own skillet since he was fifteen.* □ *She wasn't afraid of toting her own skillet. In fact, she was eager to leave home.*

tote someone or something to carry someone or something. □ *Let me tote your bags for you.* □ *She toted the big box up the stairs.* □ *He was toting a Smith and Wesson in his shoulder holster.*

t'other the other. □ *I crossed to t'other side of the road.* □ *She couldn't decide between one and t'other.*

touch-me-not **1.** a haughty person. □ *Have you met the new schoolteacher? She's a real touch-me-not!* □ *He's a touch-me-not, puts on airs.* **2.** a weed with reddish flowers. □ *There was a patch of touch-me-not growing in the yard.* □ *The touch-me-not was in bloom.*

tough customer a rough, difficult, violent person. □ *Look out for Jim. He's one tough customer.* □ *I could tell from the cold look in his eyes that he was a tough customer.*

tough it out to be strong and endure. □ *He had a hard time in boot camp, but he toughed it out.* □ *She thought about quitting her job, but then she decided to tough it out.*

tough row to hoe a difficult situation to face. (Used with the indefinite article *a*.) □ *Ever since her husband died, Mary has had to provide for her six children. That's a tough row to hoe.* □ *John's got a tough row to hoe, holding down two jobs to pay for his schooling.*

tough sledding See *hard sledding.*

tow sack a bag made of burlap. (See also *gunny sack.*) □ *I had a tow sack full of dried barley.* □ *She wrapped tow sacks around her feet to keep them warm in the winter.*

towhead someone with very pale blond hair. □ *I was a towhead when I was little, but now my hair is dark.* □ *My mama's dark, but my dad is a towhead.*

trading post a place where Indians trade with whites. □ *Smith ran a trading post up in Dakota country.* □ *We bought a beautiful Navajo rug at the trading post.*

traipse (around) to go aimlessly from place to place. □ *I'm tired of traipsing around. I'm ready to settle down.* □ *They traipsed all over the country.*

traipse (over) to go carelessly or thoughtlessly. □ *He traipsed over and invited himself in.* □ *She came traipsing in at about midnight.*

tread on someone's toes AND **step on someone's corns** to clumsily offend or anger someone. □ *Jim somehow manages to say the wrong thing at the wrong time and generally tread on everyone's toes.* □ *I think I stepped on Charlie's corns when I mentioned the property tax, because he got red in the face and left the room right then.*

tree someone or something to trap or corner someone or something. (Literal and figurative uses.) □ *The dogs treed the possum.* □ *The lawyer's shrewd questions treed the witness.*

triple-distilled to the highest degree. □ *He's a triple-distilled fool for trusting Bill with his money.* □ *She's a right down mean woman, triple-distilled.*

trouble one's (little) head about something to worry about something. (See also *don't worry your (pretty little) head about it.*) □ *Don't you trouble your little head about that. I'll take care of it.* □ *You shouldn't trouble your head about it. Everything will turn out fine.*

(true) grit the will to keep working or fighting until you succeed. □ *Our team has true grit. They were behind fourteen points at halftime, but they came back in the second half to win the game!* □ *The runner kept going even after she hurt her knee. Everyone admired her grit.*

truth to tell "truthfully"; "to tell the truth." □ *Truth to tell, I'm worried about Jim.* □ *You should be more polite to Mrs. Green, though, truth to tell, I don't like her either.*

tuckered out exhausted. □ *You go on without me. I'm plumb tuckered out.* □ *We best rest awhile. Joe looks tuckered out.*

tumbleweed a spiky weed that grows in the southwestern U.S. (So called because it tumbles along in the wind when dry.) □ *The ditch was full of tumbleweeds.* □ *The dog chased the tumbleweed.*

turkey bumps AND **goose bumps** gooseflesh; small bumps that appear on the skin when one is cold or frightened. □ *It's chilly out. I've got turkey bumps.* □ *The ghost story gave me goose bumps.*

(turkey-)gobbler a turkey. □ *I don't keep much livestock anymore, just a cow and a couple of turkey-gobblers.* □ *The yard was full of gobblers. What a noise they made!*

turkey shoot an easy task. □ *Don't worry. This'll be a turkey shoot.* □ *"It wasn't a battle," the soldier said. "It was a turkey shoot."*

turkey-tail to fan out; to spread out. □ *The highway turkey-tails into five or six little roads about a mile from here.* □ *The book fell open and the pages turkey-tailed out.*

turkey's nest See *dust bunny.*

turn belly up AND **go belly up** **1.** to die. □ *The cattle were turning belly up by the score.* □ *Jimmy's goldfish went belly up during the night.* **2.** to fail. □ *Johnson's store went belly up when the new supermarket opened.* □ *The bank predicted the business would go belly up before the end of the year.*

twicet twice. (Pronounced *TWAIST.*) □ *I've been to San Francisco oncet or twicet.* □ *I've had to tell you twicet already.*

twister a tornado. □ *The twister took the roofs off all the houses on our block.* □ *Get down in the basement. There's a twister coming.*

two bits twenty-five cents. □ *Pay phones used to cost twenty cents, and now they cost two bits.* □ *I need two bits for the toll booth.*

two jumps ahead of someone a good way ahead of someone. □ *Her market research kept her two jumps ahead of her competitors.* □ *I was just starting to think of vacation plans, not realizing that my wife was two jumps ahead of me. She had already made hotel reservations.*

two-pipe shotgun a double-barreled shotgun. (See also *one-pipe shotgun.*) □ *Dad always used a two-pipe shotgun for duck hunting.* □ *That two-pipe shotgun ain't no good for rabbits. You want to use a one-pipe shotgun.*

two-rectly AND **to-rectly** directly. (Possibly from the meaning of "two" that is associated with *di-*.) □ *Keep your shirt on. I'll be with you two-rectly.* □ *You are supposed to go over to Granny's place to-rectly.*

two shakes of a lamb's tail a very short time. □ *I'll be ready in two shakes of a lamb's tail.* □ *It will only take her two shakes of a lamb's tail.*

two whoops and a holler a short distance. □ *Lexington? That's just two whoops and a holler from here.* □ *We're just two whoops and a holler from the downtown.*

U

Uff da! Goodness! (Norwegian. Used to express irritation.) □ *Uff da! I walked two miles to the store—and they were closed!* □ *There's just no reasoning with Bill. Uff da!*

ugly enough to gag a maggot very ugly. □ *That hoss is ugly enough to gag a maggot.* □ *He was ugly enough to gag a maggot, but good-tempered and polite.*

uncommon very; quite. □ *Thank you. That's uncommon kind of you.* □ *Joe is uncommon handy with tools.*

ungodly extremely. □ *This weather has been ungodly cold.* □ *They had an ungodly hard time driving through the heavy rain.*

(un)lessen unless. □ *Don't come botherin' me while I'm on the phone, unlessen you want your bottom smacked!* □ *Not much to do around here, lessen you like to go fishing.*

unreconstructed referring to a Southerner still opposed to the North. (The Reconstruction was the period during which the North controlled the Southern states following the Civil War (1861–1865).) □ *Granddad is an unreconstructed Southerner. He hates the "damn Yankees."* □ *The unreconstructed rebels met and discussed making war on the North.*

up a storm energetically; with the fury of a storm. □ *When I left them, they were talking up a storm.* □ *The quilters sat there sewing up a storm.*

up a stump puzzled and upset; not knowing what to do. □ *This problem has me up a stump.* □ *Her mother wanted her to stay, and her father wanted her to go. She was up a stump.*

up a tree stymied; baffled. □ *I am up a tree and I just can't figure this out.* □ *Well, you got me up a tree. I don't know how to answer you.*

up and at 'em up and taking action. □ *Dad woke me at seven, saying, "Up and at 'em!"* □ *It's six-thirty. Time for us to be up and at 'em.*

up and did something did something suddenly. □ *That summer, she up and died.* □ *He had lived here for twenty years, and then one day, he up and left for good.*

up one side and down the other thoroughly. □ *She scolded him up one side and down the other.* □ *They shopped the whole downtown up one side and down the other.*

up the creek without a paddle in trouble and having no way out. □ *If we run out of gas we're up the creek without a paddle because there isn't a gas station for miles.* □ *Lost in a strange town, and now robbed of her wallet, she was up the creek without a paddle.*

up to at. (See also *over to.*) □ *There's something going on up to Jim's place.* □ *Are you going to the party up to the Browns'?*

upchuck to vomit. □ *She got motion-sick and had to upchuck.* □ *The gory movie made me want to upchuck.*

uppity openly disrespectful. □ *The uppity waiter insisted that I had ordered enchiladas, when I told him I had ordered tostadas.* □ *That uppity secretary is always sassing people on the phone.*

upscuddle a quarrel. □ *She and her sister had some kind of upscuddle, and now they're not talking.* □ *Their neighbors got tired of hearing all their upscuddles.*

use your head for more than a hatrack AND **use your head for more than something to keep your ears apart** to think. □ *How are we going to solve this problem? Come on, use your head for more than a hatrack.* □ *Instead of whining about it, why don't you use your head for more than something to keep your ears apart?*

use your head for more than something to keep your ears apart See *use your head for more than a hatrack.*

V

vamoose to leave quickly. (Spanish. Pronounced *va-MOOSE.*) □ *We'd better vamoose.* □ *The crooks vamoosed when they saw the cops coming.*

vanity cake a fried, puffed pastry. □ *Her vanity cakes were light and delicious.* □ *We made vanity cakes for the tea party.*

vaquero a cowboy. (Spanish.) □ *He had been a vaquero for thirty years.* □ *The vaqueros drove the cattle across the river.*

varmint a bothersome creature or person. □ *In this town, we shoot varmints like you.* □ *This spray kills roaches, ants, mice, and other varmints.*

veranda a porch. □ *The veranda was cool in the evening breeze.* □ *A screened veranda ran around two sides of the house.*

vigilante a citizen who punishes criminals, without legal authority. (From Spanish.) □ *A group of vigilantes caught the thief and beat the daylights out of him.* □ *The vigilantes resented the interference of the police.*

vim and vinegar See *piss and vinegar.*

vinegar pie a pie with a filling of butter, eggs, sugar, spices, and vinegar to give it a tart flavor. □ *Instead of lemon pie, the pioneer families made vinegar pie.* □ *There was every kind of pie at the picnic, from pumpkin pie and apple pie to vinegar pie and shoo-fly pie.*

visit from Flo a menstrual period. (See also *Grandma's come; have one's lady's time; monthlies; bad time (of the month).*) □ TOM: *Are you sick?* MARY: *No, just having a visit from Flo.* □ *I had my first visit from Flo when I was twelve years old.*

vittles food. □ *Stay for dinner. We've got plenty of vittles.* □ *Jim cooked us up some nice vittles.*

volunteer **1.** a crop plant that grows outside of a field or garden; a plant that grows where nothing was planted. □ *A whole bunch of corn volunteers were growing in the ditch.* □ *I didn't plant those beans. They're volunteers.* **2.** an illegitimate child. (See also *ash-barrel baby; blackberry baby; brush colt; outsider; woods colt.*) □ *Jim was a volunteer, but his mother got married later, and her husband raised Jim as his own.* □ *Bill and his wife don't have any children, but there are plenty of volunteers that look just like Bill.*

W

wag one's chin to talk. (See also *chin music.*) □ *She loves to visit. She'll wag her chin for hours.* □ *He was on the phone, wagging his chin to his buddy.*

waist baby See *arm baby.*

Wait an hour for the weather to change. The weather changes very quickly here. □ *You know what New Mexico is like in the summer. Wait an hour for the weather to change.* □ *It's raining now, but wait an hour for the weather to change.*

wait on someone to court someone. □ *Jane has several fellows waiting on her.* □ *Bill is waiting on Joe Brown's daughter.*

walk on egg(shell)s to be extremely careful. □ *Jane's so sensitive, you have to walk on eggshells when you talk to her.* □ *Jim's awfully fussy about his house. His visitors have to walk on eggs to keep from dirtying anything.*

walk uphill to be pregnant. (A euphemism.) □ *Just a month after she got married, Sally was walking uphill.* □ TOM: *Mary looks awfully tired.* JANE: *Well, she's walking uphill, you know.*

wallop to strike someone or something. □ *Jane walloped her brother right smart.* □ *Jed walloped Tom with one hand while Toby held Tom tight.*

war paint makeup. □ *It took her half an hour to put on her war paint.* □ *She had so much war paint on, I thought her face would crack.*

warbag a bag for carrying one's belongings. □ *He put all his things in his warbag and hit the trail.* □ *My warbag busted open and scattered all my stuff on the ground.*

warsh See *worsh.*

wash a dry riverbed. □ *They rode their horses down the wash.* □ *During the spring flooding season, that wash turns into a river.*

wasn't hurt a hair unharmed. □ *The baby was crying up a storm, but he wasn't hurt a hair.* □ *It looked like a terrible car wreck, but the people in the cars weren't hurt a hair.*

water shy dirty, not liking to wash or bathe. □ *Kids is just naturally water shy.* □ *He smells because he's water shy.*

weak north of the ears stupid. □ *She's a little weak north of the ears, but real kind-hearted.* □ *His teachers thought he was weak north of the ears because of the dumb things he said in class.*

wear out one's welcome to stay too long. □ *I'll be getting along home now. I don't want to wear out my welcome.* □ *They stayed five days and had worn out their welcome by the third day.*

wear someone out to whip or beat someone severely. □ *I'll wear you out if you so much as touch my electric saw again.* □ *Pa didn't just spank us. He wore us out.*

wear someone to a frazzle to exhaust someone. □ *Her work wears her to a frazzle.* □ *Taking care of them kids must wear you to a frazzle.*

wear the britches (in the family) AND **wear the pants (in the family)** to be in charge in the family. □ *Jane bosses her husband around something scandalous. It's clear that she wears the britches in the family.* □ *I don't intend to let my wife wear the pants in the family.* □ *Mary's a strong-minded woman, but her husband still wears the britches.*

wear the britches off someone to whip someone. □ *If your Pa finds out you did that, he'll wear the britches off you.* □ *Ma would wear the britches off us for cussing.*

wear the pants (in the family) See *wear the britches (in the family).*

Well, bust my buttons! "What a surprise!" □ *Well, bust my buttons! It's good to see you!* □ *Well, bust my buttons! You did all the dishes!*

well-fixed rich. □ *Joe must be pretty well-fixed. He buys himself a new car every year.* □ *She's well-fixed, but she won't give to charity.*

well-heeled rich. □ *He was a well-heeled businessman from the city.* □ *They lived very simply, although they were quite well-heeled.*

Well, shut my mouth! I am very surprised! □ *Well, shut my mouth! I didn't know you were in town!* □ TOM: *The Governor's on the phone and wants to talk to you.* JANE: *Well, shut my mouth!*

We're swingin' on the same gate. We are in agreement. □ CHARLIE: *I think Bill should quit drinking so much.* TOM: *We're swingin' on the same gate.* □ *Your Pa and I are swingin' on the same gate. We don't think you should marry that young man.*

we's we are. (From *we is.*) □ *We's happy the way we is.* □ *When we's at Granny's house, can I climb her front tree?*

wet behind the ears See *not dry behind the ears.*

wet one's whistle to take a drink. □ *He stopped at the bar to wet his whistle.* □ *I don't need a big glass of water. Just enough to wet my whistle.*

we'uns we. □ *We'uns ain't going nowhere with you'uns.*

whale into someone to beat someone. □ *Jim insulted Joe's girlfriend, so Joe whaled into him.* □ *He'll whale into you for no reason at all.*

wham bam thank you ma'am a bump in the road. (See also *excuse me ma'am*. Most known now for sexual connotations.) □ *We hit a wham bam thank you ma'am and lost one of our hubcaps.* □ *Watch out for the wham bam thank you ma'am at the corner of Third Street.*

whang on someone or something to beat or hit someone or something. □ *He's out there whanging on the car bumper, trying to straighten out the dent.* □ *I whanged on the mule's sides, but it wouldn't move.*

whangdoodle See *thingamajig*.

what-all what. □ *What-all did you bring with you?* □ *He built the barn, the toolshed, the storm cellar, and I don't know what-all else.*

What do you know (about that)? That is very interesting. □ TOM: *I heard that Jim and Mary are getting married.* JANE: *Well! What do you know about that?* □ *What do you know? Bill finally sold his house!*

What the Sam Hill? What? (A mock oath. *Sam Hill* is hell.) □ *What the Sam Hill are you doing?* □ *What the Sam Hill do you mean by that?*

whatchamacallit an unknown thing; something whose name you cannot remember. (See also *contraption; doodad; thingamajig.*) □ *Can't you use the whatchamacallit? The vacuum cleaner?* □ *My car's in the shop. They're fixing the whatchamacallit that injects the fuel into the engine.*

What's that? "What did you say?" □ TOM: *We're leaving tomorrow.* JANE: *What's that?* □ *What's that? Did you say "Iowa" or "Idaho"?*

whip the devil around the stump See *beat the devil around the stump*.

whippersnapper a presumptuous person; an upstart. □ *That young whippersnapper says he wants to marry my daughter!* □ *There's always some whippersnapper in the audience who likes to make smart remarks.*

whistle-pig a groundhog. □ *How'm I gonna get that whistle-pig out of my garden?* □ *We saw a whistle-pig come out of his burrow.*

whistle up a gum tree to waste time. □ *Trying to get Joe to help is whistling up a gum tree. He never helps out.* □ *The inventor spent several years whistling up a gum tree before coming up with a successful design.*

white lightning corn whiskey. □ *Grampa distilled his own white lightning.* □ *One sip of that white lightning could get you knee-walking drunk.*

who-all who. □ *Who-all's coming to dinner?* □ *Who-all did you invite?*

Who put a nickel in your slot? Why are you talking so much? □ *You're awfully talkative today. Who put a nickel in your slot?* □ *You're usually so shy. Who put a nickel in your slot?*

Whoa, Nellie! Wait! Stop! □ TOM: *When I get that money, I'm gonna get me my own place, and then you and I can get married, and—* JANE: *Whoa, Nellie! When did I say I was going to marry you?* □ *Whoa, Nellie! Did you measure them boards before you started cuttin' 'em?*

whole heap more a great deal more. □ *I think a whole heap more of Joe than I do of his brother.* □ *Don't quit now. There's a whole heap more work to be done.*

whole kit and caboodle a group of equipment or belongings. (Often with the definite article *the*.) □ *When I bought Jane's dairy farm, she left me the milking machine,the cream separator—the whole kit and caboodle.* □ *The salesman managed to sell John the whole kit and cabbodle.*

(whole) mess of someone or something a lot of someone or something. (Used with the indefinite article *a*.) □ *We went out on the lake and caught a whole mess of bluegill.* □ *I cooked up a mess of chili and had all my friends over to eat it.*

whole shebang AND **whole shooting match** everything; the whole thing. □ *Mary's all set to give a fancy dinner party. She's got a fine tablecloth, good crystal, and silverware, the whole shebang.* □ *How much do you want for the whole shooting match?*

whole shooting match See *whole shebang.*

whoop **1.** a yell. □ *He gave a whoop that you could hear five miles away.* □ *The team gave a whoop of victory.* **2.** to yell. □ *"Glory be!" he whooped.* □ *The audience whooped when the singer came onstage.*

whoop it up to celebrate with great energy. □ *They really whooped it up at Jane and Joe's wedding reception.* □ *After the game, the winning team went out and whooped it up.*

whopper a big lie. □ *Jim told a whopper about being the richest man in the county.* □ *When they came back from fishing, they told a bunch of whoppers about the ones that got away.*

whopper-jawed crooked. (See also *anti-godlin; catabias; catawampus; slaunchways.*) □ *The board was whopper-jawed. We had to cut it straight.* □ *The seam was sewed all whopper-jawed, so the coat didn't fit.*

whup someone or something to whip someone or something. □ *Ma whupped us with a leather strap.* □ *I'll whup you on your bird dog if you sass me again.*

widder-man a widower. (See also *widder(-woman).*) □ *His wife died and left him a widder-man.* □ *The widder-man refused to leave the house where he had lived with his wife.*

widder(-woman) a widow. (See also *widder-man.*) □ *He married a widder-woman from out Springfield way.* □ *The widder was tired of wearing black.*

will do to ride the river with is very trustworthy. (See also *would go to the well with someone.*) □ *I'd trust Jane with my life. She'll do to ride the river with, all right.* □ *He's been my best friend for fifteen years. I'd say he'll do to ride the river with.*

Winchester a repeating rifle. (Named for Oliver Winchester, who manufactured it.) □ *The cowboy kept his Winchester close at hand.* □ *He fired his Winchester at the fleeing man.*

windmill someone who talks a great deal. □ *He's such a windmill, he bores everybody to death.* □ *She was so happy to see her friends, she was a regular windmill.*

wing-ding a big party. □ *They're holding a wing-ding on Saturday night.* □ *It was a regular wing-ding with music and dancing and the biggest spread of food you ever saw.*

wish book a mail-order catalog. □ *She pored over the pages of the wish book, trying to decide what to buy.* □ *He found exactly the gun he wanted in the wish book, but he knew he could never afford it.*

with a vengeance a very great deal; very energetically. □ *When she got out of that strict school, she started drinking, smoking, and dancing with a vengeance.* □ *He cooked and cleaned with a vengeance, determined to show that he could get along without his wife.*

with blood in one's eye looking very angry and ready to fight. □ *The outlaw stared at the sheriff with blood in his eye.* □ *His rival came toward him with blood in his eye.*

with one's bare face hanging out looking stupid or helpless. □ *I told him the news, and he just stood there with his bare face hanging out.* □ *Don't just sit there with your bare face hanging out! Say something!*

within spittin' distance very close. □ *We're within spittin' distance of town.* □ *The school was within spittin' distance of the church.*

without half trying effortlessly. □ *He was so strong, he could bend an iron bar without half trying.* □ *I wish I had his ability to cook. He makes the most delicious dishes without half trying.*

without let or leave without permission. □ *He came barging in without let or leave.* □ *She borrowed my wagon without let or leave.*

withouten without. □ *I didn't leave home withouten my shoes! I ain't got no shoes!* □ *It's hard to get around these mountains withouten a car.*

wobble like a newborn calf to wobble; to be very unsteady. □ *He was so drunk he wobbled like a newborn calf.* □ *The sick woman had been in bed for weeks. When she finally got up, she was wobbling like a newborn calf.*

women-folks women. (See also *men-folks.*) □ *Jim grew up surrounded by women-folks. He had four sisters, but no brothers.* □ *At the party, the men-folks sat on the porch, while the women-folks gathered in the kitchen.*

wonderment wonder; awe. □ *"Is it really you?" she asked with wonderment on her face.* □ *The children looked at the shooting stars. You could see the wonderment in their eyes.*

wood pussy a skunk. (See also *polecat.*) □ *There's a wood pussy outside the house. I can smell it.* □ *The dog soon learned not to tangle with a wood pussy.*

wood up See *take on wood.*

wooden overcoat a coffin. □ *I want to keep on learning new things and meeting new folks till the day they put me away in a wooden overcoat.* □ *Tom felt so sick, he was sure he'd soon be needing a wooden overcoat.*

woods colt an illegitimate child. (See also *ash-barrel baby; blackberry baby; brush colt; outsider; volunteer.*) □ *John's a woods colt. His mother raised him on her own.* □ *Joe's sired a number of woods colts in his day.*

woolgathering daydreaming; letting one's mind wander. □ *Jane was woolgathering in class again.* □ *Tom never pays attention. He's always woolgathering.*

work like a beaver AND **work like a mule; work like a slave** to work very hard. □ *She has an important deadline coming up, so* *she's been working like a beaver.* □ *I had to work like a mule to get the yard work done.* □ *You need a vacation. You work like a slave in that kitchen.*

work like a mule See *work like a beaver.*

work like a slave See *work like a beaver.*

worser worse. □ *He just gets worser and worser every day.* □ *It's worser than it was before.*

worsh AND **warsh** to wash (someone or something). □ *Who is gonna worsh the dishes tonight?* □ *Did you warsh behind your ears?*

would as soon do something as look at you would be eager to do something. □ *He was a mean so-and-so who would as soon shoot you as look at you.* □ *He'd as soon pick a fight as look at you.*

would go to the well with someone would certainly trust someone a great deal. (See also *will do to ride the river with.*) □ *I'll never believe Joe did such an awful thing. I would go to the well with him.* □ *I would go to the well with Sally. You won't find a finer person anywhere.*

would make a cat laugh is very funny. □ *I declare, this TV program would make a cat laugh.* □ *The expression on your face would make a cat laugh.*

would skin a louse for his hide and tallow See *would skin an ant for its tallow.*

would skin an ant for its tallow AND **would skin a louse for his hide and tallow** is very stingy; hates to spend money. □ *Don't ask him to contribute to charity. He'd skin an ant for its tallow.* □ *His wife saves all their money and won't give him a cent to spend. She would skin a louse for his hide and tallow.*

would spit in a wildcat's eye is very wild. □ *When I was your age, I would spit in a wildcat's eye. Nobody messed with me.* □ *Arizona*

Slim was the meanest torn-down gunslinger in the West. He would spit in a wildcat's eye—he would fight a circle saw and it a-runnin'.

would steal the dime off a dead man's eyes would steal anything; is very dishonest. □ *Jim is a no-'count scalawag who would steal the dime off a dead man's eyes.* □ *Don't ever trust her with anything. She'd steal the dime off a dead man's eyes.*

wouldn't give (someone) a shovelful of chicken tracks for someone or something to think someone or something is worthless. (See also *not worth a shovelful of chicken tracks.*) □ TOM: *Bill's asking three hundred for his old pickup.* JANE: *I wouldn't give him a shovelful of chicken tracks for it.* □ *I wouldn't give a shovelful of chicken tracks for most of that "designer clothing."*

wouldn't hurt nobody none would not hurt anyone. (Note the triple negative.) □ *Having a drink now and then wouldn't hurt nobody none.* □ *He looks rough, but he wouldn't hurt nobody none.*

wouldn't miss something for a farm in Texas does or do not want to miss something. □ *We could tell that Jim was about to get his comeuppance. We wouldn't miss that for a farm in Texas.* □ JANE: *Will you be able to come to my wedding?* MARY: *Will I be able? Honey, I wouldn't miss your wedding for a farm in Texas!*

wouldn't trust him as far as you could throw a bull by the tail See *wouldn't trust him as far as you could throw him.*

wouldn't trust him as far as you could throw him AND **wouldn't trust him as far as you could throw a bull by the tail** would not trust the person named at all. □ TOM: *Is Joe trustworthy?* JANE: *No. I wouldn't trust him as far as you could throw him.* □ *I know he promised not to drink, but I wouldn't trust him as far as you could throw a bull by the tail.*

wouldn't want to be in someone's shoes would not trade places with someone who is in a bad situation. □ *Now Jim has to explain to his wife how he wrecked their car. I wouldn't want to be in his shoes.* □ *She may be rich, but I wouldn't want to be in her shoes. Everyone in her family hates her.*

wrack and ruin complete destruction or ruin. □ *They went back after the fire and saw the wrack and ruin that used to be their house.* □ *Drinking brought him nothing but wrack and ruin.*

wrang wrung. □ *I wrang out the rag and laid it out to dry.* □ *Who wrang these shirts out?*

wrench (something) out AND **rench (something) out; ranch (something) out** to rinse. □ *She wrenched her clothes in the river.* □ *Let me wrench out this cup before you drink from it.*

wunst See *oncet.*

wuz was. (Eye-dialect.) □ *Where wuz you when I needed you?* □ *I wuz out slopping the hogs.*

Y

yahoo an ignorant country person. (Very derogatory. See also *hayseed; redneck.*) □ *A truckload of yahoos followed me all the way to town.* □ *On the bus, I wound up next to some yahoo who kept spitting tobacco out the window.*

y'all you (plural or singular). □ *"When did y'all get into town?" she asked me.* □ *"Where do y'all hail from?" we asked the tourists.*

yamp to steal something. □ *He yamped a knife out of Joe's bed-roll.* □ *She was always yamping my spare change.*

yarb an herb. □ *Jane makes a good yarb tea.* □ *Jim went out in the woods looking for some yarbs.*

yarn **1.** an exaggerated story; a tall tale. □ *Grampa told us a yarn about an old plow horse he used to have. He said it could pull a whole house!* □ *Don't believe Joe's yarns.* **2.** to tell tall tales. □ *The guys are yarning about all the fish they almost caught.* □ *She could yarn for hours about what hifalutin' folks her family used to be.*

yaws a contagious disease that causes skin ulcers. □ *Bill had the yaws. No one wanted to sit next to him.* □ *The whole family caught the yaws.*

Ye gods (and little fishes)! "What a surprising thing!" □ *Ye gods and little fishes! Someone covered my car with broken eggs!* □ *Ye gods! What a rainstorm!*

yearling a one-year-old animal. □ *The horse was a yearling.* □ *We sold all the yearling bulls.*

yellow-bellied cowardly. (See also *have a yellow streak down one's back.*) □ *He hated to fight. He was yellow-bellied.* □ *She accused him of being a yellow-bellied no-'count.*

yellow jacket a wasp that gives a painful sting. □ *A cloud of yellow jackets rose up when I stepped on their nest.* □ *His arm swelled up where the yellow jacket bit him.*

Yep. "Yes." □ CHARLIE: *Are you coming to the meeting?* JANE: *Yep.* □ MARY: *Did you make that yourself?* TOM: *Yep.*

Yes indeed(y (do))! "Definitely yes!" (Emphatic.) □ TOM: *Will you marry me?* JANE: *Yes indeedy do, I will!* □ CHARLIE: *Did your horse win the race?* BILL: *Yes indeedy!*

yonder there. □ *Look over yonder. See that pine tree?* □ *Who's that standing on the hill out yonder?* □ *Up yonder them folks is having a picnic.* □ *We left the broken-down car back yonder and walked up the road.*

you ain't just whistlin' Dixie you are right. □ TOM: *Sure is hot today.* BILL: *Yeah, you ain't just whistlin' Dixie. It's a scorcher.* □ CHARLIE: *That was a good movie.* JANE: *You ain't just whistlin' Dixie. It was the best I've ever seen.*

You bet! 1. "Yes." □ TOM: *Are you coming to the party?* JANE: *You bet!* □ CHARLIE: *May I borrow your hammer?* MARY: *You bet!* **2.** "You're welcome." □ TOM: *Thank you.* JANE: *You bet.* □ SALLY: *I appreciate it.* MARY: *You bet.*

You can bet the farm (on someone or something). you can be certain (of someone or something). □ *This is a good investment. You can bet the farm on it.* □ *You can bet the farm that Joe is gonna get that job.*

You can't hitch a horse up with a coyote. You should not put mismatched things together. □ *I don't think that marriage will work* *out. You can't hitch a horse up with a coyote.* □ *Don't make those two work on the same project. You can't hitch a horse up with a coyote.*

(You) hear? "Do you understand?" (Used to emphasize a command or an invitation.) □ *You stay away from that barbed wire, you hear?* □ *Come back real soon, hear?*

you-know-what something that cannot or should not be mentioned. □ *She kicked him right in his you-know-what.* □ *Joe and Jane were planning a surprise party for Bill. "What time is the you-know-what?" Joe asked Jane, when he saw that Bill was listening.*

You make a better door than you do a window. I cannot see through you, move aside. □ *Joe was just standing in front of the TV. "Hey," I said, "you make a better door than you do a window."* □ CHARLIE: *Isn't this a great view?* JANE: *You make a better door than you do a window. Let me see.*

you may hang me for a chipmunk if . . . I do not believe that the event named will happen. □ *You may hang me for a chipmunk if Joe ever pays that money back.* □ *You may hang me for a chipmunk if this horse loses the race.*

you-uns you. (Plural.) □ *We'd like to have you-uns over for dinner.* □ *How many of you-uns can come?*

youngun a child; a young person. □ *She's got three younguns.* □ *When I was a youngun, I wanted to be a cowboy.*

yourn yours. (See also *hisn; hern; theirn; ourn.*) □ *This here is mine. That there is yourn.* □ *That's yourn. You keep it.*

PHRASE-FINDER INDEX

Use this index to find the form of a phrase that you want to look up in the Dictionary. First, pick out any major word in the phrase you are seeking. Second, look that word up in this index to find the form of the phrase used in the Dictionary. Third, look up the phrase in the Dictionary. The expressions are grouped according to word form, not meaning.

Some of the words occurring in the Dictionary entries do not occur as entries in this index. Entries that are only single words are not indexed here. Grammar words—articles, pronouns, conjunctions, verbal auxiliaries, and the verbs *do* and *be* are not indexed. Look up the simplest form of a major word in the expression.

all the farther □ all the faster □ all the higher □ all the livelong day □ all the more □ all thumbs □ all tore up about something □ all vine and no taters □ all wool and a yard wide □ all wool and no shoddy □ all-fired □ all-overs □ as something as all get-out □ beat someone or something all hollow □ Better the gravy than no grease at all. □ Don't that (just) beat all? □ everything an' all □ If that don't beat all! □ in all my born days □ In God we trust, all others pay cash. □ is all □ It'll all come out in the wash. □ one's fingers are all thumbs □ so dark all the bats stayed home □ that beats something all to pieces □ That's all she wrote. □ what-all □ who-all

ALMIGHTY
Lord almighty

ALONG
(a)long about

ALWAYS
The latch string is always out.

AMEN
amen corner □ amen pew

AMOUNT
amount to much □ amount to something □ don't amount to a bucket of spit

ANADAMA
Anadama bread

ANKLE
by ankle express

ANNIE
(as) strong as Annie Christmas

ANSWER
answer (someone) back □ answer for something

ANT
emmet (ant) □ have ants in one's pants □ would skin an ant for its tallow

ANTI
anti-fogmatic □ anti-godlin □ anti-sigodlin

ANTY
anty-over

ANXIOUS
anxious seat

ANY
any fool thing □ Don't take any wooden nickels. □ pay someone any mind

APART
use your head for more than something to keep your ears apart

APE
lead apes in hell

APPLE
(as) sure as God made little green apples □ apple of someone's eye □ apple pandowdy □ courtin'-apple □ How bout them apples? □ love apple □ polish the apple □ road apple

ARGUFY
argufy (with someone)

ARIZONA
(as) happy as ducks in Arizona □ Arizona strawberries □ Arizona tenor

ARKANSAS
Arkansas toothpick □ Arkansas wedding cake

ARM
(as) busy as a one-armed paper-hanger □ arm baby □ armed to the teeth □ break one's arm patting oneself on the back □ talk someone's arm off

ARMY
like Coxey's Army

AROUND
(as) big around as a molasses barrel □ beat the devil around the stump □ cooter around □ faunch around □ gad around □ gallivant (around) □ get around □ green around the gills □ lollygag (around) □ piddle around □ step around □ traipse (around) □ whip the devil around the stump

ASH
ash-barrel baby

ASLEEP
asleep at the switch

ASS
(as) cold as a welldigger's ass (in January) □ ass-over-teakettle □ ass-over-tit □ couldn't hit a bull in the ass with a bass fiddle □ doesn't know his ass from a hole in the ground □ have a corncob up one's ass □ have a poker up one's ass □ have one's ass in a sling □ If a toady frog had wings, he wouldn't bump his ass. □ In a pig's ass! □ put someone's ass in a sling

ATE
They ate before they said grace.

ATTENTION
so broke he couldn't even pay attention

AWAY
fritter something away □ salt something away □ slave away (at something) □ steal away like a thief in the night

AWFUL
something awful

AWKWARD
(as) awkward as a cow on a crutch □ (as) awkward as a cow on roller skates

AWKWARDNESS
by main strength and awkwardness

AXE
(as) dull as a meat axe □ battle-axe

BABE
innocent as a babe unborn □ innocent as a newborn babe

BABY
(as) slick as a baby's bottom □ arm baby □ ash-barrel baby □ blackberry baby □ breast baby □ doll baby □ floor baby □ gran(d)-baby □ innocent as a babe unborn □ innocent as a newborn babe □ knee baby □ man-baby □ waist baby

BACK
(a)back of □ (as) helpless as a turtle on his back □ (as) high as the hair on a cat's back □ answer (someone) back □ back and forth □ back door trots □ back East □ be (back) in harness □ beans that talk behind your back □ break one's arm patting oneself on the back □ go for wool and come back shorn □ harder than the back of God's head □ have a yellow streak down one's back □ have callouses from patting one's own back □ have one's ears pinned back □ last one in the back row when the faces was handed out □ like water off a duck's back □ no rue-back □ pin someone's ears back

BACKWARDS
(as) slow as coal tar running uphill backwards

BACON
bring home the bacon □ bush bacon □ language that would fry bacon □ slice off the same bacon

BAD
bad as I hate to do it □ bad blood □ bad man □ bad medicine □ bad off □ bad place □ bad time (of the month) □ bad-mouth someone □ have a bad case of the simples

BADGER
less time than skinning a badger

BAG
put on the feed bag

BAIL
leg bail

BAIT
(as) sorry as owl bait □ buzzard bait □ crow bait □ sucker-bait

BAKE
baker's dozen □ half-baked

BALEFUL
(as) baleful as death

BALL
ball the jack □ Great balls of fire! □ tend to your own ball of yarn

BAM
wham bam thank you ma'am

BAND
to beat the band

BANDIT
make out like a bandit

BANGER
Bible-banger

BANKER
emptier than a banker's heart

BAPTIST
hardshell Baptist

BAR
bar none □ bar-dog □ Stars and Bars

BARBED
barb(ed) wire

BARBER
(as) conceited as a barber's cat

BARE
bare-faced lie □ with one's bare face hanging out

BAREFOOT
as often as a goose goes barefoot

BARK
bark up the wrong tree

BARN
(as) broad as a barn door □ barn-burner □ Chick Sale (barn) □ more noise than a jackass in a tin barn □ more noise than a mule in a tin barn □ Robin Hood's barn

BARREL
(as) big around as a molasses barrel □ (as) crooked as a barrel of fish hooks □ (as) sound as a barrel □ ash-barrel baby □ cash on the barrel-head □ grin like a barrel of possum heads □ like shooting fish in a barrel

BARRELHEAD
cash on the barrelhead

BASKET
can't carry a tune in a bushel basket

BASS
couldn't hit a bull in the ass with a bass fiddle

BAT
like a bat out of hell □ quicker than you can bat an eye □ so dark all the bats stayed home

BATTER
batter bread

BATTLE
battle-axe

BATTLING
battlin' board □ battlin' stick

BEAD
draw a bead on someone or something

BEAN
beans that talk behind your back □ butter bean □ doesn't know beans □ down to chili and beans □ full of beans □ not worth a hill of beans □ snap-beans

BEANPOLE
(as) skinny as a (bean)pole

BEAR
(as) busy as a hibernating bear □ (as) hungry as a bear □ (as) slick as bear grease □ bear grass □ have a bear by the tail □ hot enough to burn a polar bear's butt □ loaded for bear □ someone knows where the bear shits

BEAT
all beat out □ beat bobtail □ beat someone or something all hollow □ beat someone till his hide won't hold shucks □ beat the (natural) stuffing out of someone □ beat the bejeebers out of someone or something □ beat the bejesus out of someone or something □ beat the daylights out of someone or something □ beat the devil and carry a rail □ beat the devil around the stump □ beat the tar out of someone □ beaten biscuit □ Don't that (just) beat all? □ If that don't beat a pig a-pecking! □ If that don't beat all! □ that beats something all to pieces □ The devil's beatin' his wife. □ to beat the band

BEAVER
(as) busy as a beaver (building a new dam) □ eager beaver □ work like a beaver
BECK
at someone's beck and call
BED
bed down □ bed someone down □ go to bed with the chickens □ go to bed with the sun □ know no more about something than a frog knows about bed sheets
BEE
bee-gum □ meat bee □ quilting bee □ raising bee □ spelling bee
BEEF
(as) dead as a beef □ (as) dead as a tin of corned beef
BEELINE
make a beeline (for someone or something)
BEER
I've seen better heads on nickel beers.
BEERSHEBA
from Dan to Beersheba
BEET
(as) red as a beet
BEFORE
They ate before they said grace. □ They planted the corn before they built the fence.
BEGGAR
beggar-lice
BEHIND
beans that talk behind your back □ behind the door when the brains were passed out □ not dry behind the ears □ wet behind the ears
BEHOLD
beholden (to someone) □ sight to behold
BEJEEBERS
beat the bejeebers out of someone or something □ knock the bejeebers out of someone or something □ stomp the bejeebers out of someone or something
BEJESUS
beat the bejesus out of someone or something
BELIEVE
believe you me □ I do believe.
BELL
(as) clear as a bell □ bell-tail □ doesn't have enough sense to bell a cat □ Hell's bells!
BELLOW
bellow like an ox
BELLY
(as) dark as the inside of a cow's belly □ (as) low as a snake's belly □ belly button □ belly up □ belly up to something □ belly-ache □ belly-buster □ belly-flop □ darker than the inside of a cow's belly □ go belly up □ One's eyes are bigger than one's belly. □ turn belly up □ yellow-bellied
BELT
belt and suspenders
BENCH
mourners' bench
BEND
above one's bend
BENT
bent out of shape □ hell (-bent) for leather □ hell-bent for election
BERRY
(as) busy as a cranberry merchant □ above one's huckleberry □ Arizona strawberries □ blackberry baby □ like licking honey off a blackberry vine □ prairie strawberries □ thunder berries
BEST
(had) best do something □ one's best bib and tucker □ one's level best □ one's Sunday best
BET
bet one's bottom dollar □ I'd bet a blue stack on it. □ I'd bet money (on

it). □ You bet! □ You can bet the farm (on someone or something).

BETSY
(as) crazy as a betsy bug □ Heavens to Betsy!

BETTER
(damn) sight better □ better had (do something) □ better than a poke in the eye with a sharp stick □ Better the gravy than no grease at all. □ I've seen better heads on nickel beers. □ The bigger the mouth, the better it looks closed. □ You make a better door than you do a window.

BETWEEN
between a rock and a hard place □ between hay and grass □ between whiles □ narrow between the eyes

BEULAH
Beulah land

BEYOND
the great beyond

BIB
one's best bib and tucker

BIBLE
Bible-banger □ Bible-thumper □ kiss the Bible □ swear on a stack of Bibles □ take one's Bible oath

BIG
(as) big around as a molasses barrel □ (as) big as a house □ (as) big as all outdoors □ (as) big as life, and twice as natural □ (as) big as life, and twice as ugly □ (speak softly and) carry a big stick □ big dog □ big drink of water □ big dude □ big enough to choke a cow □ big enough to choke a hog □ big enough to shade an elephant □ big honker □ Big Muddy □ big time □ big-doins □ big-eye(d) □ biggest duck in the puddle □ biggest frog in the pond □ give someone the big eye □ One's eyes are bigger than one's belly. □ One's eyes are bigger than one's stomach. □ Open your mouth and shut your eyes and I'll give you a big surprise. □ take the big jump □ The bigger the mouth, the better it looks closed. □ too big for one's britches

BIGHORN
bighorn (sheep)

BILED
(as) drunk as a biled owl

BILL
fill the bill □ sell someone a bill of goods

BIRD
bird dog □ bird-dog someone or something

BISCUIT
beaten biscuit □ biscuit-bread □ cathead biscuit

BIT
every little bit helps □ hair of the dog (that bit you) □ If it was a snake it woulda bit you. □ The same dog bit me. □ two bits

BITE
(as) yeller as mustard but without the bite □ bite to eat □ don't make two bites of a cherry □ hair of the dog (that bit you) □ If it was a snake it woulda bit you. □ mad enough to bite off a drawbar □ snake(bite) medicine □ The same dog bit me.

BITSY
itsy bitsy

BITTER
bitter pill (to swallow)

BITTY
itty bitty □ little bitty

BLACK
(as) black as a skillet □ (as) black as a stack of black cats □ (as) black as the ace of spades □ black sheep (of the family) □ black-eyed pea □ black-eyed Susan □ Bless your little black heart.

BLACKBERRY
blackberry baby □ like licking honey off a blackberry vine

BLACK-EYED
black-eyed pea □ black-eyed Susan
BLADDER
That's the way the hog bladder bounces.
BLANK
blankety-blank □ point-blank
BLANKET
eyes like two burnt holes in a blanket □ stretch the blanket
BLANKETY
blankety-blank
BLAZES
Damn it to blue blazes!
BLEED
bleed like a stuck pig
BLESS
bless my soul □ bless my time of day □ Bless your heart. □ Bless your little black heart.
BLIND
(as) mad as a (blind) hornet □ blind pig □ blind staggers □ booze blind □ doesn't know whether to shit or go blind □ don't kiss by the garden gate; love is blind but neighbors ain't □ don't make love by the garden gate; love is blind but neighbors ain't □ like a blind dog in a meat market □ like stealing acorns from a blind pig
BLISTER
Brains in the head saves blisters on the feet. □ If you get burnt you got to set on the blister.
BLOCK
choppin' block
BLOOD
bad blood □ bloody flux □ cut the blood out of someone □ with blood in one's eye
BLOOM
in the rise of her bloom
BLOW
blow a fuse □ blow one's own horn □ blow over □ blown up like a toad
BLUE
blue devils □ blue john □ blue-tick hound □ Bonny Blue Flag □ cuss a blue streak □ Damn it to blue blazes! □ I'd bet a blue stack on it. □ something old, something new, something borrowed, and something blue □ talk a blue streak
BLUEGRASS
bluegrass (music)
BOAR
(as) crazy as a peach-orchard boar □ (as) useless as tits on a boar
BOARD
battlin' board □ put someone on a cooling board
BOARDINGHOUSE
boardinghouse reach
BOBTAIL
beat bobtail □ No-siree bob(tail)! □ rag tag and bobtail
BODY
over my dead body
BOG
chicken bog
BOIL
(as) drunk as a boiled owl □ (as) homely as a boil □ boiled shirt □ boiling corn □ boiling ear □ couldn't boil water (without scorching it) □ couldn't boil water without burning it
BOLD
make (so) bold (as) to do something
BOLL
boll weevil □ thicker than boll weevils
BOLLIX
bollixed up
BONE
bone orchard □ crazy bone □ funny bone □ have a bone to pick with someone □ prayer-bones
BONNY
Bonny Blue Flag
BOO
can't say boo to a goose

BOOK
book-learning □ kiss the book □ the Good Book □ wish book
BOOT
couldn't pour water out of a boot (if there was instructions on the heel) □ to boot
BOOTSTRAP
pull oneself up by the bootstraps
BOOZE
booze blind
BORN
born on crazy creek □ born short and slapped down flat □ born tired and raised lazy □ born with a silver spoon in one's mouth □ in all my born days □ own-born cousins
BORROW
something old, something new, something borrowed, and something blue
BOSS
straw boss □ bossy
BOTH
can't find one's butt with both hands (in broad daylight) □ so dark you couldn't find your nose with both hands □ someone's tongue wags at both ends
BOTHER
don't bother me none
BOTTLE
bottle fever □ cork high and bottle deep
BOTTOM
(as) slick as a baby's bottom □ bet one's bottom dollar □ deal from the bottom (of the deck)
BOUGHT
store-bought(en)
BOUNCE
That's the way the hog bladder bounces.
BOUND
all oak and iron bound □ bound and determined □ bound to do something □ bounden duty
BOUT
How bout them apples?
BOWIE
bowie knife
BOWL
not enough meat on him to make a poor man a bowl of soup
BOX
(as) smart as a box of rocks □ talk box □ think box
BOY
Boy, howdy! □ go at something like a boy killing snakes □ good ole boy
BRAG
brag someone or something up
BRAIN
ain't got the brains God gave a squirrel □ behind the door when the brains were passed out □ Brains in the head saves blisters on the feet. □ nit-brained □ not enough brains to grease a skillet
BRANCH
branch water
BRAND
brand-spanking new
BRASS
(as) hot as the seven brass hinges of hell □ get down to brass tacks
BREAD
Anadama bread □ batter bread □ biscuit-bread □ break bread (with someone) □ cracklin' bread □ egg bread □ greatest thing since sliced bread □ light bread □ risin' bread □ spoon bread
BREAK
break a horse □ break bread (with someone) □ break one's arm patting oneself on the back □ break someone of something
BREAKFAST
from hell to breakfast
BREAST
breast baby
BREATHE
breathe one's horse

BUMP
goose bumps □ If a toady frog had wings, he wouldn't bump his ass. □ If frogs had wheels, they wouldn't bump their butts. □ like a bump on a log □ turkey bumps

BUNG
bung someone or something up □ bunged up

BUNNY
dust bunny □ quick-like (a bunny)

BURN
barn-burner □ couldn't boil water without burning it □ eyes like two burnt holes in a blanket □ hay-burner □ hot enough to burn a polar bear's butt □ If you get burnt you got to set on the blister. □ someone's ears are burning

BURR
have a burr under one's saddle

BURY
bury the hatchet

BUSH
bright-eyed and bushy-tailed □ bush bacon □ bush-whacker □ go to the bushes

BUSHEL
bushel and a peck (and some in a gourd) □ can't carry a tune in a bushel basket

BUSINESS
land-office business

BUST
belly-buster □ bronco buster □ bust a bronco □ bust out laughing □ bust someone wide open □ bust something □ flat busted □ Well, bust my buttons!

BUSY
(as) busy as a beaver (building a new dam) □ (as) busy as a cranberry merchant □ (as) busy as a fish peddler in Lent □ (as) busy as a hibernating bear □ (as) busy as a one-armed paperhanger □ (as) busy as popcorn on a skillet □ keep the stork busy

BUTT
butt naked □ can't find one's butt with both hands (in broad daylight) □ hot enough to burn a polar bear's butt □ If frogs had wheels, they wouldn't bump their butts. □ more hopeless than a one-legged man at a (butt-)kickin' contest

BUTTER
(as) easy as lickin' butter off(en) a knife □ (butter and) egg money □ butter bean

BUTTON
belly button □ dad fetch my buttons □ Well, bust my buttons!

BUY
buy a pig in a poke □ buy something on time □ store-bought(en)

BUZZARD
buzzard bait

CABIN
cabin fever

CABOODLE
kit and caboodle □ whole kit and caboodle

CACTUS
(as) crooked as a rattler in a cactus patch

CAKE
Arkansas wedding cake □ griddle cake □ hoe cake □ johnny cake □ journey cake □ one's cake is dough □ stack cake □ tipsy cake □ vanity cake

CALF
calf slobber(s) □ cry calf rope □ moon-calf □ slicker than calf slobbers □ wobble like a newborn calf

CALL
(from) so far south they call people from Georgia Yankees □ ain't got no call (to do something) □ at someone's beck and call □ call hogs □ call on someone □ call something to mind □ call the dog □ called to

straw □ can't call one's soul one's own □ Master's call □ no call for something

CALLOUS

have callouses from patting one's own back

CALM

(as) calm as a toad in the sun

CAMEL

(as) plain as the hump on a camel

CAMP

camp meeting

CANARY

mountain canary

CANDIDATE

candidate for a pair of wings

CANDLE

can't hold a candle to someone or something

CANDY

drop one's candy

CAP

set one's cap for someone

CAPER

cut capers

CARE

didn't care a whit □ didn't care too hard □ doesn't care who knows it □ don't care if I do

CARESS

(as) cold as a witch's caress

CARPET

step off the carpet

CARRY

(speak softly and) carry a big stick □ beat the devil and carry a rail □ can't carry a tune in a bucket □ can't carry a tune in a bushel basket □ can't carry a tune in a paper sack □ carry on (so) □ carry someone somewhere □ carry weight (with someone) □ Mackerel skies and mares' tails make lofty ships carry low sails

CARTER

more something than Carter had oats

CASE

case of the stiff neck □ case-knife □ have a bad case of the simples □ soul-case

CASH

cash in one's chips □ cash money □ cash on the barrelhead □ In God we trust, all others pay cash.

CAT

(as) black as a stack of black cats □ (as) conceited as a barber's cat □ (as) high as the hair on a cat's back □ (as) nervous as a long-tailed cat in a room full of rocking chairs □ (as) weak as a cat □ as much chance (of something) as a wax cat in hell □ cathead biscuit □ dead cat on the line □ doesn't have enough sense to bell a cat □ Dog my cats! □ knock someone or something cat-west □ mad enough to kick a cat □ not enough room to swing a cat □ not know someone or something from Adam's housecat □ skin the cat □ would make a cat laugh

CATCH

catch hell (about someone or something) □ catch one's death (of cold) □ catching flies □ caught short □ layover to catch meddlers

CATFISH

catfish hole

CATHEAD

cathead biscuit

CATTLE

all hat and no cattle □ cattle guard □ don't rush the cattle

CAUGHT

caught short

CAUSE

have cause to do something

CELLAR

there's more down (in the) cellar in a teacup

CENT

He wears a ten-dollar hat on a five-cent head. □ one red cent

CERTAIN
certain sure □ dead certain
CHAIR
(as) nervous as a long-tailed cat in a room full of rocking chairs □ keep one's chair
CHANCE
as much chance (of something) as a wax cat in hell □ right smart chance of something
CHANGE
change one's tune □ I felt like a penny waiting for change. □ Wait an hour for the weather to change.
CHARGE
charge it to the dust and let the rain settle it
CHARLIE
creeping Charlie
CHASING
so dry the trees were chasing the dogs
CHAW
chaw (of tobacco) □ chaw (something) □ tobacco chaw
CHEESE
head cheese
CHERRY
don't make two bites of a cherry
CHESS
chess pie
CHEW
chew one's own tobacco □ chew the fat □ close chewer and a tight spitter □ mad enough to chew nails and spit rivets
CHICK
Chick Sale (barn)
CHICKEN
chicken bog □ go to bed with the chickens □ have a chicken to pick with someone □ If it ain't chickens, it's feathers. □ not worth a shovelful of chicken tracks □ Southern fried chicken □ spring chicken □ wouldn't give (someone) a shovelful of chicken tracks for someone or something
CHILD
lap child □ My momma didn't raise no stupid child. □ this child
CHILI
down to chili and beans
CHIMNEY
smoke like a chimney
CHIN
chin music □ take it on the chin □ wag one's chin
CHIP
buffalo chip □ cash in one's chips □ cow chip
CHIPMUNK
you may hang me for a chipmunk if . . .
CHOKE
big enough to choke a cow □ big enough to choke a hog □ choke-rag
CHOP
choppin' block
CHRISTMAS
(as) strong as Annie Christmas
CHUCK
chuck wagon
CHUCKLE
chuckle-head □ chuckle-headed
CHUNK
chunk something □ just come after a chunk of fire □ tater chunk
CHURCH
Church ain't out till they quit singing. □ church key
CINCH
(dead) cinch
CIRCLE
could fight a circle-saw (and it a-runnin')
CITY
(city) slicker
CLAIM
jump a claim □ stake (out) one's claim
CLAM
(as) happy as a clam
CLAP
clap-hand

CLEAN
clean someone's plow □ clean up one's duty
CLEAR
(as) clear as a bell
CLEVER
too clever by half
CLOCK
homely enough to stop a clock
CLOSE
(as) close as two coats of paint □ bring-'em close glass □ close chewer and a tight spitter □ close enough to use the same toothpick □ close only counts in horseshoes (and hand grenades) □ close shave □ play it close to the vest □ The bigger the mouth, the better it looks closed.
CLOUD
coming up a cloud □ riding a cloud
CLUCK
so dumb he couldn't teach a hen to cluck
COAL
(as) slow as coal tar running uphill backwards
COAT
(as) close as two coats of paint □ short-coat preacher
COCK
(as) cocky as the king of spades □ cock-and-bull story □ cold cock someone □ go off half-cocked
COFFEE
Confederate coffee
COFFIN
coffin nail □ coffin varnish
COLD
(as) cold as a welldigger's ass (in January) □ (as) cold as a well-digger's ears (in January) □ (as) cold as a welldigger's feet (in January) □ (as) cold as a witch's caress □ (as) cold as a witch's tit □ catch one's death (of cold) □ cold cock someone □ cold feet □ colder than a mother-in-law's kiss □ colder than a pawnbroker's smile □ it'll be a cold day in Hell when something happens □ stone cold □ stone-cold sober
COLLAR
(as) proud as a pup with a new collar □ collar-and-tie men
COLLARD
collard (green)s
COLT
brush colt □ woods colt
COLUMBIA
give someone Hail Columbia
COME
Come 'n get it! □ Come again? □ come Monday □ come out the little end of the horn □ come to a pretty pass □ come up a storm □ coming up a cloud □ doesn't have enough sense to come in out of the rain □ go for wool and come back shorn □ Grandma's come □ It'll all come out in the wash. □ Johnny-come-lately □ just come after a chunk of fire □ thinks the sun comes up to hear him crow □ till the cows come home
COMEUPPANCE
get one's comeuppance
COMMENCE
commence (something)
COMMON
(as) common as an old shoe □ as good as common
COMPANY
keep company (with someone)
CONCEIT
(as) conceited as a barber's cat
CONFEDERATE
Confederate coffee
CONGRESS
it would take an act of Congress to do something
CONNIPTION
have a conniption (fit)
CONSARN
Consarn it!

CONTEST
more hopeless than a one-legged man at a (butt-)kickin' contest
CONTINENTAL
don't give a continental □ not worth a continental
COOK
all hands and the cook □ Kissin' don't last; cookin' do.
COOL
put someone on a cooling board
COON
Coon my dogs! □ in a coon's age
COOT
(as) drunk as a coot
COOTER
(as) drunk as Cooter Brown □ cooter around
CORK
cork high and bottle deep
CORN
(as) dead as a tin of corned beef □ (corn) squeezings □ acknowledge the corn □ boiling corn □ corn dodgers □ corn juice □ Indian corn □ like a can of corn □ shuck someone's corn □ step on someone's corns □ They planted the corn before they built the fence.
CORNCOB
(as) rough as a corncob □ have a corncob up one's ass
CORNER
amen corner □ three-cornered pants
CORRAL
corral someone or something
COST
cost a pretty penny
COTTAGE
cottage fries
COTTON
cotton to someone or something □ cotton-picking □ in high cotton □ in low cotton □ shit in tall cotton □ spit cotton □ talk like a cotton gin in pickin' time
COUNT
close only counts in horseshoes (and hand grenades) □ no-(ac)count □ quicker than you could count two
COUNTRY
country mile □ more ways than a country man can whip a mule
COURT
courtin'-apple
COURTHOUSE
(as) old as the courthouse
COUSIN
Cousin Jack □ kissing cousins □ own-born cousins □ think someone is God's own cousin
COW
(as) awkward as a cow on a crutch □ (as) awkward as a cow on roller skates □ (as) dark as the inside of a cow's belly □ (as) steep as a cow's face □ big enough to choke a cow □ cow chip □ cow flop □ cow juice □ cow paste □ cow patty □ cow pie □ cow poke □ cow puncher □ cow-critter □ darker than the inside of a cow's belly □ juice a cow □ raining as hard as a cow pissing on a flat rock □ steeper than a cow's face □ That's the tune the old cow died on. □ till the cows come home
COWBOY
cowboy pencil
COXEY
like Coxey's Army
COYOTE
coyote round □ You can't hitch a horse up with a coyote.
CRACK
by cracky □ crack (open) the door □ crack (open) the window □ crack a smile □ crack of dawn □ crack one's sides □ cracker-jack □ get cracking □ jaw-cracker
CRACKLE
cracklin' bread
CRADLE
I kicked the slats out of my cradle

laughing at that (joke). □ I knocked the slats out of my cradle laughing at that

CRANBERRY
(as) busy as a cranberry merchant

CRAVE
crave to do something

CRAW
stick in someone's craw

CRAWDAD
crawdad hole

CRAZY
(as) crazy as a betsy bug □ (as) crazy as a peach-orchard boar □ born on crazy creek □ crazy bone □ crazy in the head

CREATION
all over creation □ hind end of creation

CREEK
born on crazy creek □ God willing and the creek don't rise □ Lord willing and the creek don't rise □ up the creek without a paddle

CREEP
creeping Charlie

CRITTER
cow-critter

CROCUS
crocus sack

CROKER
croker sack

CROOKED
(as) crooked as a barrel of fish hooks □ (as) crooked as a dog's hind leg □ (as) crooked as a fish hook □ (as) crooked as a rail fence □ (as) crooked as a rattler in a cactus patch □ so crooked he has to screw on his socks

CROSS
cross over □ cross someone □ get one's wires crossed □ keep your fingers crossed

CROW
as the crow flies □ crow bait □ eat crow □ Stone the crows! □ thinks the sun comes up to hear him crow

CROWDER
crowder pea

CRUTCH
(as) awkward as a cow on a crutch □ (as) funny as a crutch

CRY
cry calf rope □ cry uncle □ for crying out loud

CURB
so low you could sit on the curb and swing your legs

CURLY
curly dirt

CURRIED
short horse, soon curried

CUSS
cuss a blue streak □ cuss someone out

CUSTOMER
tough customer

CUT
cut a rusty □ cut capers □ cut dog has no pups □ cut one's eyes at someone or something □ cut one's eyeteeth on something □ cut out for something □ cut out for somewhere □ cut the blood out of someone □ cut the mustard □ cut up □ cut your peaches □ don't cut no ice (with someone) □ don't cut no squares (with someone)

CUTE
(as) cute as a bug's ear

CYMLIN
cymlin head

DAB
smack dab in the middle

DAD
dad fetch my buttons

DADGUM
dadgum it

DAFT
(as) daft as a brush

DAGNAB
dagnab it

DAM
(as) busy as a beaver (building a new dam)

DAMN
(damn) sight better □ as someone damn well pleases □ Damn it to blue blazes! □ Hot damn!

DAMNATION
Hellfire and damnation!

DAN
from Dan to Beersheba

DANDER
get someone's dander up

DANDY
fine and dandy □ jim dandy

DANG
gol dang □ That's for dang sure!

DARK
(as) dark as the inside of a cow's belly □ darker than the inside of a cow's belly □ so dark all the bats stayed home □ so dark you couldn't find your nose with both hands

DAWN
crack of dawn

DAY
all the livelong day □ bless my time of day □ dog days □ Great day (in the morning)! □ in all my born days □ it'll be a cold day in Hell when something happens □ it'll be a long day in January when something happens □ pass the time of day □ the Lord's Day

DAYLIGHT
beat the daylights out of someone or something □ can't find one's butt with both hands (in broad daylight) □ scare the (living) daylights out of someone □ scare the daylights out of someone □ shoot someone full of daylight

DEAD
(as) dead as a beef □ (as) dead as a tin of corned beef □ (dead) cinch □ dead cat on the line □ dead certain □ dead duck □ dead man's hand □ dead serious □ dead set against something □ dead-eye □ over my dead body □ stone dead □ would steal the dime off a dead man's eyes

DEAF
stone deaf

DEAL
deal from the bottom (of the deck)

DEATH
(as) baleful as death □ catch one's death (of cold) □ sick (un)to death of someone or something

DECK
deal from the bottom (of the deck) □ not playing with a full deck

DECLARE
I declare (to goodness)!

DEEP
cork high and bottle deep

DENTIST
tooth-dentist

DEPOT
built like a depot stove

DERN
gol dern

DESERT
desert rat

DETERMINE
bound and determined

DEVIL
beat the devil and carry a rail □ beat the devil around the stump □ blue devils □ dust devil □ have the devil to pay (and no pitch hot) □ send someone to hell and the devil □ tell the truth and shame the devil □ The devil's beatin' his wife. □ whip the devil around the stump

DEW
mountain dew

DIAMOND
diamond in the rough

DIE
die of throat trouble □ root hog or die □ That's the tune the old cow died on.

DIG
dig up one's tommyhawk
DIGGETY
Hot (diggety) dog!
DIME
would steal the dime off a dead man's eyes
DING
wing-ding
DIP
dip snuff
DIPSTICK
someone's oil doesn't reach the dipstick
DIRT
curly dirt □ dirty someone or something up □ do someone dirt(y) □ hit pay dirt
DISFURNISH
disfurnish someone
DISH
(as) quick as a dog can lick a dish
DISREMEMBER
disremember (someone or something)
DISTANCE
within spittin' distance
DISTILL
triple-distilled
DITHER
(all) in a dither
DITTY
ditty
DIXIE
you ain't just whistlin' Dixie
DOCTOR
snake doctor
DODGE
corn dodgers □ on the dodge
DOG
(as) crooked as a dog's hind leg □ (as) quick as a dog can lick a dish □ (as) sad as a hound dog's eye □ (as) sick as a dog □ bar-dog □ big dog □ bird dog □ bird-dog someone or something □ call the dog □ Coon my dogs! □ cut dog has no pups □ dog days □ dog drunk □ Dog my cats! □ dog trot □ dog-faced liar □ go to see a man about a dog □ hair of the dog (that bit you) □ Hot (diggety) dog! □ in dog's years □ ketch-dog □ like a blind dog in a meat market □ look like a sheep-killing dog □ meaner than a junk-yard dog (with fourteen sucking pups) □ prairie dog □ put on the dog □ run like a scalded dog □ so dry the trees were chasing the dogs □ That (old) dog won't hunt. □ The same dog bit me.
DOGHOUSE
(as) happy as a flea in a doghouse
DOINGS
big-doins
DOKEY
okey-dokey
DOLL
doll baby
DOLLAR
(as) sound as a dollar □ bet one's bottom dollar □ He wears a ten-dollar hat on a five-cent head.
DOMINION
Old Dominion
DOODLE
doodle bug
DOODLY
doodly(-squat)
DOOHICKEY
doohickey
DOOR
(as) broad as a barn door □ back door trots □ behind the door when the brains were passed out □ crack (open) the door □ You make a better door than you do a window.
DOUBLE
double saw buck
DOUGH
dough-god □ one's cake is dough
DOWNHILL
has the world by the tail (with a downhill drag)

DOZEN
baker's dozen □ shoot dozens

DRAG
has the world by the tail (with a downhill drag) □ knock-down-drag-out (fight)

DRAW
draw a bead on someone or something □ draw in one's horns □ draw up □ get the draw on someone

DRAWBAR
mad enough to bite off a drawbar

DRESS
dressed (up) fit to kill □ dressed eggs

DRINK
(long) tall drink of water □ big drink of water

DROP
drop off □ drop one's candy □ get the drop on someone

DROWN
goose-drownder

DRUNK
(as) drunk as a biled owl □ (as) drunk as a boiled owl □ (as) drunk as a coot □ (as) drunk as Cooter Brown □ (as) drunk as who shot John □ dog drunk □ drunker than who shot John □ kneewalking drunk

DRUTHERS
have one's druthers

DRY
dry gulch someone □ dry spell □ got the dry grins □ not dry behind the ears □ so dry the trees were chasing the dogs

DUCK
(as) happy as ducks in Arizona □ be on someone like a duck on a June bug □ biggest duck in the puddle □ dead duck □ like water off a duck's back □ Lord love a duck!

DUDE
big dude □ dude ranch □ duded up

DULL
(as) dull as a meat axe

DUMB
(as) dumb as a shovel □ so dumb he couldn't teach a hen to cluck

DUST
charge it to the dust and let the rain settle it □ dust bunny □ dust devil □ dust kitten □ not enough to dust a fiddle

DUTCH
Dutch oven

DUTY
bounden duty □ clean up one's duty

EAGER
eager beaver

EAR
(as) cold as a welldigger's ears (in January) □ (as) cute as a bug's ear □ boiling ear □ get one's ears set out □ have one's ears pinned back □ In a pig's ear! □ like tryin' to scratch your ear with your elbow □ lower someone's ears □ not dry behind the ears □ off ear □ pin someone's ears back □ roasting ear □ someone's ears are burning □ talk someone's ear off □ use your head for more than something to keep your ears apart □ weak north of the ears □ wet behind the ears

EARLY
gotta get up pretty early in the morning to do something

EARN
earn one's spurs

EARTH
on God's green earth

EAST
back East

EASY
(as) easy as lickin' butter off(en) a knife □ Easy, there!

EAT
bite to eat □ did everything he could 'cept eat us □ don't know whether to eat it or rub it on □ eat

crow □ eat good □ eat someone out of house and home □ eat someone's salt □ eat(en) up with something □ eating high off the hog □ fire-eater □ go to grass (and eat hay) □ grin like a mule eating briars □ I'll eat my hat. □ since the hog et grandma □ They ate before they said grace.

EGG
(as) freckled as a turkey egg □ (butter and) egg money □ dressed eggs □ egg bread □ egg toast □ I'll be a suckegg mule! □ skunk egg □ slink like a suckegg hound

EGGSHELLS
walk on egg(shell)s

EIGHT
have eight acres of Hell in oneself

ELBOW
elbow grease □ like tryin' to scratch your ear with your elbow

ELECTION
hell-bent for election

ELEGANT
elegant sufficiency

ELEPHANT
big enough to shade an elephant □ see the elephant

ELK
slow elk

ELSE
have a leg up on someone else

EMMET
emmet (ant)

EMPTY
emptier than a banker's heart

END
(little) short on one end □ come out the little end of the horn □ hind end □ hind end of creation □ on end □ plow to the end of the row □ someone's tongue wags at both ends □ the well at wit's end

ENGINE
puff like a steam engine

ENOUGH
big enough to choke a cow □ big enough to choke a hog □ big enough to shade an elephant □ close enough to use the same toothpick □ doesn't have enough sense to bell a cat □ doesn't have enough sense to come in out of the rain □ enough and some to spare □ enough of something to plague a saint □ homely enough to stop a clock □ hot enough to burn a polar bear's butt □ like enough □ mad enough to bite off a drawbar □ mad enough to chew nails and spit rivets □ mad enough to kick a cat □ not enough brains to grease a skillet □ not enough meat on him to make a poor man a bowl of soup □ not enough room to swing a cat □ not enough sense to pound sand in a rat hole □ not enough to dust a fiddle □ ugly enough to gag a maggot

ET
since the hog et grandma

EUCHRED
get euchred out of something

EVEN
land so poor it wouldn't even raise a fuss □ so broke he couldn't even pay attention

EVENING
shank of the evening

EVERY
ever(y) which way □ every fool thing □ every little bit helps □ every mother's son of them □ Let every man skin his own skunk.

EVERYBODY
everybody and his brother □ everybody and his uncle

EVERYTHING
did everything he could 'cept eat us □ everything an' all

EXCUSE
excuse me ma'am

EXERCISE
exercised about something

EXPRESS
by ankle express

EYE
(as) sad as a hound dog's eye □ apple of someone's eye □ better than a poke in the eye with a sharp stick □ big-eye(d) □ black-eyed Susan □ bright-eyed □ bright-eyed and bushy-tailed □ cut one's eyes at someone or something □ dead-eye □ eyes like two burnt holes in a blanket □ give someone the big eye □ In a pig's eye! □ keep one's eyes peeled □ keep one's eyes skinned □ lay eyes on someone or something □ My eye! □ narrow between the eyes □ One's eyes are bigger than one's belly. □ One's eyes are bigger than one's stomach. □ Open your mouth and shut your eyes and I'll give you a big surprise. □ Open your mouth and shut your eyes and I'll give you something to make you wise. □ quicker than you can bat an eye □ red-eye □ sight for sore eyes □ with blood in one's eye □ would spit in a wildcat's eye □ would steal the dime off a dead man's eyes

EYEBALL
(as) sensitive as an eyeball

EYEBROW
down to a gnat's eyebrow

EYEFUL
get an eyeful

EYETEETH
cut one's eyeteeth on something

FACE
(as) steep as a cow's face □ bare-faced lie □ dog-faced liar □ feed one's face □ last one in the back row when the faces was handed out □ poker face □ show one's face □ steeper than a cow's face □ with one's bare face hanging out

FACT
and that's a fact □ It's for a fact.

FAIR
fair to middlin' □ fair up

FALL
fall off □ fall out □ just fell off the turnip truck

FAMILY
black sheep (of the family) □ in the family way □ wear the britches (in the family) □ wear the pants (in the family)

FANCY
fancy woman □ suit someone's fancy

FAR
(from) so far south they call people from Georgia Yankees □ wouldn't trust him as far as you could throw a bull by the tail □ wouldn't trust him as far as you could throw him

FARM
wouldn't miss something for a farm in Texas □ You can bet the farm (on someone or something).

FARMER
more'n farmers have hay

FARTHER
all the farther

FASTER
all the faster

FAT
chew the fat □ fat and sassy □ lard-fat □ The fat is in the fire. □ thicker than fleas on a fat pup

FAULT
fault someone

FAUNCH
faunch around

FAVOR
favor someone □ hard-favored □ thank God for small favors

FEAR
put the fear of God in someone

FEATHER
feather into someone □ fuss and feathers □ If it ain't chickens, it's feathers. □ quicker than hell could scorch a feather

FEATURE
rest one's features
FEDERAL
federal building
FEED
feed lot □ feed off someone's range □ feed one's face □ good feed □ off one's feed □ put on the feed bag
FEEL
feel for someone □ feel one's oats □ feeling puny □ I felt like a penny waiting for change.
FEET
(as) cold as a welldigger's feet (in January) □ Brains in the head saves blisters on the feet. □ cold feet □ heave to one's feet □ I felt like a penny waiting for change. □ sit down and take a load off (your feet)
FELL
just fell off the turnip truck
FELT
I felt like a penny waiting for change.
FENCE
(as) crooked as a rail fence □ (as) homely as a mud fence □ fence-lifter □ They planted the corn before they built the fence.
FER
fer why
FESS
fess up
FETCH
dad fetch my buttons
FEVER
bottle fever □ cabin fever □ hemp fever
FEW
few bricks short of a load □ small and yellow and few to the pod □ small potatoes and few to the hill
FIDDLE
(as) slack as fiddle strings □ couldn't hit a bull in the ass with a bass fiddle □ has more than one string to his fiddle □ not enough to dust a fiddle
FIFTH
fifth wheel
FIGGER
figger something up
FIGHT
could fight a circle-saw (and it a-runnin') □ fighting mad □ knock-down-drag-out (fight) □ like fighting snakes □ Them's fighting words!
FIGURE
figger something up
FILE
Indian file
FILL
fill someone full of lead □ fill the bill
FIND
can't find one's butt with both hands (in broad daylight) □ so dark you couldn't find your nose with both hands
FINE
(as) fine as frog hair □ fine and dandy □ fine how do you do □ That's a fine how-do-you-do.
FINGER
have sticky fingers □ keep your fingers crossed □ one's fingers are all thumbs
FIRE
all-fired □ fire-eater □ Great balls of fire! □ just come after a chunk of fire □ The fat is in the fire.
FIRST
hindside first
FISH
(as) busy as a fish peddler in Lent □ (as) crooked as a barrel of fish hooks □ (as) crooked as a fish hook □ fish fry □ gone fishin' □ like shooting fish in a barrel □ Ye gods (and little fishes)!
FIST
hand over fist
FIT
ain't fittin' □ ain't fittin' to roll with a pig □ dressed (up) fit to kill □ fit

to be tied ☐ fit to kill ☐ give someone fits ☐ have a conniption (fit) ☐ hissy (fit)

FIVE

fifth wheel ☐ forty-five ☐ He wears a ten-dollar hat on a five-cent head.

FIX

(all the) fixin's ☐ be fixing to do something ☐ in a fix ☐ well-fixed

FLAG

Bonny Blue Flag

FLAP

flap one's gums ☐ flap one's jaws

FLASH

flash in the pan

FLAT

born short and slapped down flat ☐ flat busted ☐ flat-out ☐ in no time flat ☐ raining as hard as a cow pissing on a flat rock

FLEA

(as) happy as a flea in a doghouse ☐ thicker than fleas on a fat pup

FLO

visit from Flo

FLOAT

float someone a raft of shit

FLOOR

floor baby ☐ raised on a floored pen

FLOP

belly-flop ☐ cow flop

FLUX

bloody flux

FLY

(as) happy as a fly in a pie ☐ as the crow flies ☐ catching flies ☐ keep the stork flying ☐ like flies to manure ☐ shoo-fly pie ☐ There's no flies on someone.

FOAM

foam at the mouth

FOGMATIC

anti-fogmatic

FOLD

folding money

FOLK

(home) folks ☐ men-folks ☐ women-folks

FOOL

any fool thing ☐ be a fool about something ☐ be a fool for something ☐ every fool thing ☐ My momma didn't raise no fool(s). ☐ There's no fool like an old fool.

FOOT

(as) cold as a welldigger's feet (in January) ☐ as often as a goose goes barefoot ☐ Brains in the head saves blisters on the feet. ☐ cold feet ☐ doesn't know B from bull's foot ☐ heave to one's feet ☐ hot-foot it (off to) somewhere ☐ I felt like a penny waiting for change. ☐ loose-footed ☐ My foot! ☐ Oh, foot! ☐ sit down and take a load off (your feet)

FOOTSTOOL

on God's footstool

FOREVER

speak now or forever hold your peace

FORK

fork something over ☐ it's raining pitchforks (and hammer handles)

FORTH

back and forth

FORTY

forty-five ☐ forty-four ☐ forty-niner

FOTCHET

do-fotchet

FOURTEEN

meaner than a junkyard dog (with fourteen sucking pups)

FRAIL

frail someone

FRAZZLE

wear someone to a frazzle

FRECKLE

(as) freckled as a turkey egg

FREEZE

freeze one's tail off

FREIGHT

pull (one's) freight ☐ pull freight for the tules

FRESH

fresh out (of something)

FRITTER
fritter something away
FRITZ
on the fritz
FROG
(as) fine as frog hair □ biggest frog in the pond □ If a toady frog had wings, he wouldn't bump his ass. □ If frogs had wheels, they wouldn't bump their butts. □ know no more about something than a frog knows about bed sheets □ like herding frogs
FROLIC
necktie frolic
FRONT
front name
FRUIT
hen fruit
FRY
cottage fries □ fish fry □ home fries □ lamb fries □ language that would fry bacon □ Southern fried chicken
FULL
(as) full as a tick □ (as) nervous as a long-tailed cat in a room full of rocking chairs □ (as) smart as a tree full of owls □ fill someone full of lead □ full of beans □ full of prunes □ full sixteen hands high □ full up □ not playing with a full deck □ shoot someone full of daylight
FUNERAL
land up in a funeral parlor □ preach someone's funeral
FUNNY
(as) funny as a crutch □ funny bone □ funny paper
FUR
fur piece
FURROW
plow someone's furrow
FURTHER
Such is life in the West, and the further west you go, the sucher it is.
FUSE
blow a fuse
FUSS
fuss and feathers □ land so poor it wouldn't even raise a fuss
GAD
gad about □ gad around
GAG
ugly enough to gag a maggot
GAL
doney(-gal) □ side gal
GALLEY
knock someone or something galley-west
GALLIVANT
gallivant (around)
GALLON
ten-gallon hat
GAMBLER
tinhorn gambler
GAME
someone's game is up
GANDER
take a gander
GARDEN
don't kiss by the garden gate; love is blind but neighbors ain't □ don't make love by the garden gate; love is blind but neighbors ain't □ garden-sass
GARTER
still have some snap left in one's garters
GATE
don't kiss by the garden gate; love is blind but neighbors ain't □ don't make love by the garden gate; love is blind but neighbors ain't □ We're swingin' on the same gate.
GAVE
ain't got the brains God gave a squirrel
GEESE
ain't got the sense God gave geese □ The old woman is picking her geese.
GENTLE
gentle someone or something
GENTLEMAN
Southern gentleman

GEORGIA
(as) high as a Georgia pine □ (from) so far south they call people from Georgia Yankees □ all over hell and half of Georgia

GET
as something as all get-out □ be gettin' on (in years) □ Come 'n get it! □ get a rise from someone or something □ get a rise out of someone or something □ get a skinful □ get about □ get an eyeful □ get around □ get cracking □ get down to brass tacks □ get euchred out of something □ get on with your rat-killin' □ get one's comeuppance □ get one's ears set out □ get one's wires crossed □ get oneself up □ get religion □ get shed of someone or something □ get shet of someone or something □ get shut of someone or something □ get someone's dander up □ get someone's goat □ get sore □ get the draw on someone □ get the drop on someone □ get the kinks (ironed) out □ get wind of something □ get-up □ gotta get up pretty early in the morning to do something □ If you get burnt you got to set on the blister. □ right from the git-go □ shit or get off the pot □ Them as has, gits.

GHOST
ghost town

GIFT
God's gift (to women)

GILL
green around the gills □ stewed to the gills

GIN
talk like a cotton gin in pickin' time

GIT
right from the git-go □ Them as has, gits.

GIVE
ain't got the brains God gave a squirrel □ ain't got the sense God gave geese □ don't give a continental □ don't give a hoot in hell's hollow □ give out something □ give someone a leg up □ give someone down the road □ give someone fits □ give someone Hail Columbia □ give someone some lip □ give someone some sugar □ give someone the big eye □ give someone the go-by □ give someone the high sign □ give someone what-for □ Indian giver □ Open your mouth and shut your eyes and I'll give you a big surprise. □ Open your mouth and shut your eyes and I'll give you something to make you wise. □ shoot or give up the gun □ wouldn't give (someone) a shovelful of chicken tracks for someone or something

GLASS
bring-'em close glass

GLUTTON
glutton for punishment

GNAT
down to a gnat's eyebrow

GOAT
get someone's goat

GOBBLER
(turkey-)gobbler

GOD
(as) safe as in God's pocket □ (as) sure as God made little green apples □ ain't got the brains God gave a squirrel □ ain't got the sense God gave geese □ dough-god □ God willing and the creek don't rise □ God's gift (to women) □ God's honest truth □ God's nightgown! □ harder than the back of God's head □ In God we trust, all others pay cash. □ on God's footstool □ on God's green earth □ put the fear of God in someone □ thank God for small favors □ think someone is God's own cousin □ Ye gods (and little fishes)!

GODFREY
by godfrey
GODLIN
anti-godlin □ si-godlin
GOL
gol dang □ gol dern
GOLLY
by guess and by golly
GOOD
as good as common □ but good □ do someone a power of good □ eat good □ good and something □ good feed □ good for what ails you □ Good grief! □ good many □ good ole boy □ have a (good) mind to do something □ sell someone a bill of goods □ sell someone a piece of goods □ the Good Book
GOODNESS
I declare (to goodness)!
GOOSE
(as) slick as goose grease □ ain't got the sense God gave geese □ as often as a goose goes barefoot □ can't say boo to a goose □ goose bumps □ goose hangs high □ goose honks high □ goose-drownder □ the old woman's picking her geese.
GOPHER
(as) mad as a stunned gopher
GORM
gorm something
GOSH
by guess and by gosh
GOSHEN
Land o' Goshen!
GOSLING
gone gosling
GOSPEL
gospel truth
GOSSIP
gossip-trot
GOT
ain't got a grain of sense □ ain't got a lick of sense □ ain't got no call (to do something) □ ain't got the brains God gave a squirrel □ ain't got the sense God gave geese □ got the dry grins □ gotta get up pretty early in the morning to do something □ If you get burnt you got to set on the blister. □ so old it's got whiskers
GOUGE
gouge someone
GOURD
(as) green as a gourd □ bushel and a peck (and some in a gourd) □ saw gourds
GOVERNMENT
have the nerve of a government mule
GRAB
grab a root
GRACE
They ate before they said grace.
GRACIOUS
gracious plenty
GRAIN
ain't got a grain of sense
GRAMPUS
puff like a grampus
GRAND
gran(d)-baby
GRANDDADDY
(grand)daddy longlegs
GRANDMA
Grandma's come □ since the hog et grandma
GRANNY
granny woman □ My granny!
GRASS
bear grass □ between hay and grass □ buffalo grass □ go to grass (and eat hay) □ grass widow □ grass-roots □ needle grass □ sparrow grass □ Spread that on the grass to make it green.
GRASSHOPPER
knee-high to a grasshopper
GRAVE
(as) still as time in a grave □ grave rock
GRAVEYARD
graveyard widow

GRAVY
Better the gravy than no grease at all. □ ride the gravy train

GREASE
(as) slick as bear grease □ (as) slick as goose grease □ (as) slick as owl grease □ Better the gravy than no grease at all. □ elbow grease □ like greased lightning □ not enough brains to grease a skillet

GREAT
go great guns □ Great balls of fire! □ Great day (in the morning)! □ Great Rebellion □ great unwashed □ greatest thing sincc indoor plumbing □ greatest thing since sliced bread □ no great shakes □ put (great) store by someone or something □ set (great) store by someone or something □ the great beyond

GREEN
(as) green as a gourd □ (as) sure as God made little green apples □ collard (green)s □ green around the gills □ on God's green earth □ pea green □ scare someone pea green □ Spread that on the grass to make it green.

GRENADE
close only counts in horseshoes (and hand grenades)

GRIDDLE
griddle cake

GRIEF
Good grief!

GRIN
got the dry grins □ grin like a barrel of possum heads □ grin like a mule eating briars

GRIT
(hominy) grits □ (true) grit

GROUND
doesn't know his ass from a hole in the ground □ happy hunting ground □ measure someone on the ground □ old stomping ground(s)

GROW
grow like Topsy □ scare someone out of a year's growth

GRUB
grub-slinger □ rustle up some grub

GUARD
cattle guard

GUESS
by guess and by golly □ by guess and by gosh

GULCH
dry gulch someone

GULLION
slum-gullion

GULLY
gully washer

GUM
bee-gum □ by gum □ flap one's gums □ whistle up a gum tree

GUN
go great guns □ gun-shy □ gunning for someone □ shoot or give up the gun □ six-gun □ stick to your guns

GUNNY
gunny sack

GUNPOWDER
(as) slow as wet gunpowder □ didn't invent gunpowder

GURGLE
all gurgle and no guts

GUSSY
gussied up

GUT
all gurgle and no guts

HACK
can't hack it □ hack someone

HAIL
give someone Hail Columbia □ hail from somewhere

HAIR
(as) fine as frog hair □ (as) high as the hair on a cat's back □ by a hair □ hair and hide(, horns and tallow) □ hair of the dog (that bit you) □ Keep your hair on. □ neither hide nor hair □ wasn't hurt a hair

HALF
all over hell and half of Georgia □ go off half-cocked □ half the time □ half-baked □ half-breed □ howdy and a half □ shirt-tail at half-mast □ too clever by half □ without half trying

HALTER
bucking at the halter

HAMMER
hammer and tongs □ it's raining pitchforks (and hammer handles)

HANCOCK
John Hancock

HAND
all hands and the cook □ can't find one's butt with both hands (in broad daylight) □ clap-hand □ close only counts in horseshoes (and hand grenades) □ dead man's hand □ full sixteen hands high □ hand over fist □ last one in the back row when the faces was handed out □ old hand □ so dark you couldn't find your nose with both hands □ tip one's hand

HANDBASKET
go to hell in a handbasket

HANDLES
it's raining pitchforks (and hammer handles)

HANDY
(as) handy as a pocket in a shirt

HANG
(as) busy as a one-armed paperhanger □ goose hangs high □ hangin' judge □ with one's bare face hanging out □ you may hang me for a chipmunk if . . .

HANKER
hanker after someone or something

HAPPEN
it'll be a cold day in Hell when something happens □ it'll be a long day in January when something happens

HAPPY
(as) happy as a clam □ (as) happy as a flea in a doghouse □ (as) happy as a fly in a pie □ (as) happy as a pig in mud □ (as) happy as ducks in Arizona □ (as) happy as pigs in mud □ happy hunting ground

HARD
between a rock and a hard place □ didn't care too hard □ hard put □ hard sledding □ hard tail □ hard-favored □ harder than the back of God's head □ raining as hard as a cow pissing on a flat rock □ rode hard and put up wet

HARDSHELL
hardshell Baptist

HARM
(as) harmless as a pet rabbit □ No harm done. □ to one's harm

HARNESS
be (back) in harness □ mule in horse harness

HARP
taking harp lessons

HASH
settle someone's hash □ sling hash

HASTY
hasty pudding

HAT
all hat and no cattle □ He wears a ten-dollar hat on a five-cent head. □ Here's your hat, what's your hurry? □ I'll eat my hat. □ Keep your hat on. □ ten-gallon hat

HATCHET
bury the hatchet □ throw the hatchet

HATE
bad as I hate to do it □ hate someone or something like sin

HATRACK
use your head for more than a hatrack

HAY
between hay and grass □ go to grass (and eat hay) □ hay-burner □ hit the hay □ more'n farmers have hay

HAYWIRE
go haywire

HEAD
Brains in the head saves blisters on the feet. □ cash on the barrelhead □ cathead biscuit □ chuckle-head □ chuckle-headed □ crazy in the head □ cymlin head □ don't worry your (pretty little) head about it □ grin like a barrel of possum heads □ harder than the back of God's head □ have a price on one's head □ He wears a ten-dollar hat on a five-cent head. □ head cheese □ head for tall timber □ head for the hills □ I've seen better heads on nickel beers. □ knock-head room □ open one's head □ slap someone up the side of the head □ slap someone upside the head □ talk one's head off □ tetched (in the head) □ trouble one's (little) head about something □ use your head for more than a hatrack □ use your head for more than something to keep your ears apart

HEALTH
in the pink (of health)

HEAP
heap of something □ heap sight □ think a heap of someone or something □ whole heap more

HEAR
(You) hear? □ hear tell (as) □ thinks the sun comes up to hear him crow

HEART
Bless your heart. □ Bless your little black heart. □ emptier than a banker's heart

HEAT
(all) het up □ het up

HEAVE
heave (Jonah) □ heave to one's feet

HEAVEN
Heavens to Betsy! □ in hog heaven

HECTOR
since Hector was a pup

HEEL
couldn't pour water out of a boot (if there was instructions on the heel) □ Tar Heel □ well-heeled

HEIST
heist someone or something (up)

HELL
(as) hot as the hobs of hell □ (as) hot as the seven brass hinges of hell □ all over hell and gone □ all over hell and half of Georgia □ as much chance (of something) as a wax cat in hell □ catch hell (about someone or something) □ don't give a hoot in hell's hollow □ from hell to breakfast □ go to hell in a bucket □ go to hell in a handbasket □ have eight acres of Hell in oneself □ have hell to pay □ hell (-bent) for leather □ hell on a holiday □ Hell's bells! □ hell-bent for election □ It sure is hell when it's this way, and it's this way now. □ it'll be a cold day in Hell when something happens □ lead apes in hell □ like a bat out of hell □ like hell and high lightning □ quicker than hell could scorch a feather □ raise hell □ send someone to hell and the devil □ to hell and gone

HELLFIRE
Hellfire and damnation!

HELP
(as) helpless as a turtle on his back □ every little bit helps □ hep someone

HEMP
hemp fever

HEN
(as) mad as a wet hen □ have a hen on the nest □ hen fruit □ hen party □ hen-pecked □ madder than a wet hen □ sage hen □ so dumb he couldn't teach a hen to cluck

HENRY
John Henry

HEP
hep someone

HERD
like herding frogs □ ride herd on someone or something

HERE
(as) sure as I'm sitting here □ (as) sure as I'm standing here □ from here till next Tuesday □ Here's your hat, what's your hurry? □ this here

HET
(all) het up □ het up

HIBERNATING
(as) busy as a hibernating bear

HIDE
beat someone till his hide won't hold shucks □ hair and hide(, horns and tallow) □ have someone's hide □ know someone's hide in a tanyard □ neither hide nor hair □ take it out of someone's hide □ tan someone's hide □ would skin a louse for his hide and tallow

HIGH
(as) high as a Georgia pine □ (as) high as the hair on a cat's back □ (lord) high muck-a-muck □ all the higher □ cork high and bottle deep □ eating high off the hog □ full sixteen hands high □ give someone the high sign □ goose hangs high □ goose honks high □ high lonesome □ high time □ high-and-mighty □ high-powered □ high-tail it □ high-toned □ hold oneself too high □ in high cotton □ knee-high by the 4th of July □ knee-high to a grass-hopper □ knee-high to a jackrabbit □ like hell and high lightning □ living high off the hog □ shake like a holly in a high wind

HIKE
hike one's tail

HILL
head for the hills □ not worth a hill of beans □ small potatoes and few to the hill □ What the Sam Hill?

HIND
(as) crooked as a dog's hind leg □ hind end □ hind end of creation □ suck the hind teat

HINDSIDE
hindside first

HINGE
(as) hot as the seven brass hinges of hell

HIP
need something like a pig needs a hip pocket

HIRE
hire something done

HISSY
hissy (fit)

HIT
couldn't hit a bull in the ass with a bass fiddle □ hit pay dirt □ hit the hay □ hit the trail

HITCH
You can't hitch a horse up with a coyote.

HOB
(as) hot as the hobs of hell

HOE
hoe cake □ hoe one's own row □ hoe down □ sharpen someone's hoe □ tough row to hoe

HOG
big enough to choke a hog □ call hogs □ eating high off the hog □ go whole hog □ hog wild □ hog-killin' weather □ hog-leg □ in hog heaven □ know as much about something as a hog knows about Sunday □ living high off the hog □ root hog or die □ since the hog et grandma □ That's the way the hog bladder bounces.

HOLD
beat someone till his hide won't hold shucks □ can't hold a candle to someone or something □ can't hold a light for someone □ hold oneself too high □ hold with something □ Hold your horses! □ Hold your tater! □ speak now or forever hold your peace

HOLE
ace in the hole □ can't see a hole in a ladder □ catfish hole □ crawdad hole □ doesn't know his ass from a hole in the ground □ eyes like two burnt holes in a blanket □ hole up (somewhere) □ not enough sense to pound sand in a rat hole □ one-holer □ sink hole □ swimmin' hole

HOLIDAY
hell on a holiday

HOLLER
holler uncle □ quicker than you can holler howdy □ two whoops and a holler

HOLLOW
beat someone or something all hollow □ don't give a hoot in hell's hollow

HOLLY
shake like a holly in a high wind

HOLY
holy roller

HOME
(as) ugly as home-made soap □ (home) folks □ bring home the bacon □ bring someone's saddle home □ down-home □ eat someone out of house and home □ home fries □ see someone home □ so dark all the bats stayed home □ till the cows come home

HOMELY
(as) homely as a boil □ (as) homely as a mud fence □ homely enough to stop a clock

HOMINY
(hominy) grits

HONE
hone for someone or something

HONEST
(as) honest as (old) Abe □ God's honest truth

HONEY
like licking honey off a blackberry vine

HONK
big honker □ goose honks high

HOOD
Robin Hood's barn

HOOEY
load of hooey

HOOF
hoof it □ on the hoof

HOOK
(as) crooked as a barrel of fish hooks □ (as) crooked as a fish hook □ hook-a-hendum □ swallow something hook, line, and sinker

HOOT
don't give a hoot in hell's hollow

HOP
(as) thick as hops □ hoppin' John □ hopping mad

HOPELESS
more hopeless than a one-legged man at a (butt-)kickin' contest

HORN
all horns and rattles □ blow one's own horn □ come out the little end of the horn □ draw in one's horns □ hair and hide(, horns and tallow) □ horn in (on something) □ lock horns (with someone) □ pull in one's horns □ toot one's own horn

HORNET
(as) mad as a (blind) hornet

HORSE
break a horse □ breathe one's horse □ Hold your horses! □ horse opera □ horse sense □ hoss opry □ mule in horse harness □ one-horse town □ short horse, soon curried □ You can't hitch a horse up with a coyote.

HORSEBACK
Tell it to a sailor on horseback.

HORSESHOES
close only counts in horseshoes (and hand grenades)

HOSPITALITY
Southern hospitality

HOSS
hoss opry

HOT
(as) hot as the hobs of hell □ (as) hot as the seven brass hinges of hell □ have the devil to pay (and no pitch hot) □ Hot (diggety) dog! □ Hot damn! □ hot enough to burn a polar bear's butt □ hot-foot it (off to) somewhere

HOTCAKE
sell like hotcakes

HOUND
(as) sad as a hound dog's eye □ blue-tick hound □ slink like a suckegg hound

HOUR
Wait an hour for the weather to change.

HOUSE
(as) big as a house □ eat someone out of house and home □ house moss □ I could knock you for a row of brick houses. □ like a house afire

HOUSECAT
not know someone or something from Adam's housecat

HOW
as how □ fine how do you do □ How bout them apples? □ That's a fine how-do-you-do.

HOWDY
Boy, howdy! □ howdy and a half □ Howdy-do! □ quicker than you can holler howdy

HUCKLEBERRY
above one's huckleberry

HUMP
(as) plain as the hump on a camel

HUNG
have something hung up and salted □ might as well be hung for a sheep as (for) a lamb □ think someone hung the moon (and stars)

HUNGRY
(as) hungry as a bear

HUNKER
hunker down □ hunker down to something

HUNT
happy hunting ground □ That (old) dog won't hunt.

HURRY
Here's your hat, what's your hurry?

HURT
hurtin' for something □ wasn't hurt a hair □ wouldn't hurt nobody none

HUSH
hush puppies

ICE
don't cut no ice (with someone)

IF
couldn't pour water out of a boot (if there was instructions on the heel)□ don't care if I do □ don't mind if I do □ If a toady frog had wings, he wouldn't bump his ass. □ If frogs had wheels, they wouldn't bump their butts. □ If it ain't chickens, it's feathers. □ If it was a snake it woulda bit you. □ If that don't beat a pig a-pecking! □ If that don't beat all! □ If you get burnt you got to set on the blister. □ if you've a mind to do something □ you may hang me for a chipmunk if . . .

ILL
ill someone □ take ill

IMAGE
spittin' image

INDEED
Yes indeed(y (do))!

INDIAN
Indian corn □ Indian file □ Indian giver □ put the Indian sign on someone

INDOOR
greatest thing since indoor plumbing

INNOCENT
innocent as a babe unborn □ innocent as a newborn babe

INSIDE
(as) dark as the inside of a cow's belly □ darker than the inside of a cow's belly

INSPECT
inspect the timber
INSTRUCTIONS
couldn't pour water out of a boot (if there was instructions on the heel)
INTO
feather into someone □ talk some sense into someone □ whale into someone
INVENT
didn't invent gunpowder
IRON
all oak and iron bound □ get the kinks (ironed) out □ shooting iron □ talking iron
ITCH
seven-year itch
ITSY
itsy bitsy
ITTY
itty bitty
JACK
ball the jack □ Cousin Jack □ cracker-jack
JACKASS
more noise than a jackass in a tin barn
JACKRABBIT
knee-high to a jackrabbit
JANUARY
(as) cold as a welldigger's ass (in January) □ (as) cold as a welldigger's ears (in January) □ (as) cold as a welldigger's feet (in January) □ (as) slow as molasses in January □ it'll be a long day in January when something happens
JAW
flap one's jaws □ jaw-cracker □ whopper-jawed
JAYBIRD
(as) naked as a jaybird
JEHOSAPHAT
Jumping Jehosaphat!
JERK
jerk a knot in someone's tail
JIM
jim dandy
JIMSON
jimson weed
JINGO
by jingo
JOB
(as) poor as Job's turkey □ odd jobs
JOE
joe pye weed □ po(or) Joe
JOHN
(as) drunk as who shot John □ blue john □ drunker than who shot John □ hoppin' John □ John B □ John B. Stetson □ John Hancock □ John Henry □ long johns
JOHNNY
johnny cake □ Johnny jump-up □ Johnny-come-lately
JOINT
have one's nose out of joint
JOKE
I kicked the slats out of my cradle laughing at that (joke).
JONAH
heave (Jonah)
JOSHUA
Joshua tree
JOURNEY
journey cake
JUDGE
(Judge) Lynch □ hangin' judge
JUICE
corn juice □ cow juice □ juice a cow
JULEP
mint julep
JULY
knee-high by the 4th of July
JUMP
Johnny jump-up □ jump a claim □ jump out of one's skin □ jump over the broomstick □ Jumping Jehosaphat! □ one jump ahead □ take the big jump □ two jumps ahead of someone

JUNE
be on someone like a duck on a June bug

JUNKYARD
meaner than a junkyard dog (with fourteen sucking pups)

JUST
be (just) shy of something □ can (just) whistle for something □ Don't that (just) beat all! □ go to one's (just) reward □ have just one oar in the water □ I'd (just) as leave do something □ I'd (just) as soon as do something □ just come after a chunk of fire □ just fell off the turnip truck □ run (just) shy of something □ you ain't just whistlin' Dixie

KEEL
keel over □ keel something over

KEEP
keep company (with someone) □ keep one's chair □ keep one's eyes peeled □ keep one's eyes skinned □ keep one's seat □ keep the stork busy □ keep the stork flying □ keep your fingers crossed □ Keep your hair on. □ Keep your hat on. □ Keep your shirt on. □ use your head for more than something to keep your ears apart

KETCH
ketch-dog

KEY
church key □ Key lime pie

KICK
alive and kicking □ have a kick to it □ I kicked the slats out of my cradle laughing at that (joke). □ kick like a mule □ kick like a steer □ kick over the traces □ kick the (natural) stuffing out of someone □ mad enough to kick a cat □ more hopeless than a one-legged man at a (butt-)kickin' contest

KID
like a kid with a new toy

KILL
dressed (up) fit to kill □ fit to kill □ get on with your rat-killin' □ go at something like a boy killing snakes □ hog-killin' weather □ kill a tree □ look like a sheep-killing dog

KILTER
out of kilter

KIND
some kind of something □ thank you kindly

KING
(as) cocky as the king of spades

KINK
get the kinks (ironed) out

KISS
colder than a mother-in-law's kiss □ don't kiss by the garden gate; love is blind but neighbors ain't □ kiss the Bible □ kiss the book □ Kissin' don't last; cookin' do. □ kissing cousins

KIT
kit and caboodle □ whole kit and caboodle

KITTEN
(as) weak as a kitten □ dust kitten □ have kittens

KNEE
knee baby □ knee-high by the 4th of July □ knee-high to a grasshopper □ knee-high to a jackrabbit □ knee-walking drunk

KNIFE
(as) easy as lickin' butter off(en) a knife □ bowie knife □ case-knife

KNIT
tend to your own knitting

KNOCK
I could knock you for a row of brick houses. □ I knocked the slats out of my cradle laughing at that □ knock someone or something cat-west □ knock someone or something galley-west □ knock someone or something sky-winding □ knock the bejeebers out of someone or something □

knock-down-drag-out (fight) □ knock-head room

KNOT

jerk a knot in someone's tail □ put a knot in someone's tail □ tie a knot in someone's tail

KNOW

(the) Lord only knows □ can't say, not knowing □ doesn't care who knows it □ doesn't know B from bull's foot □ doesn't know beans □ doesn't know his ass from a hole in the ground □ doesn't know whether to shit or go blind □ don't know whether to eat it or rub it on □ I don't rightly know. □ know as much about something as a hog knows about Sunday □ know in reason □ know no more about something than a frog knows about bed sheets □ know someone's hide in a tanyard □ not know someone or something from Adam's housecat □ not know someone or something from Adam's off ox □ someone knows where the bear shits □ What do you know (about that)? □ you-know-what

LADDER

can't see a hole in a ladder

LADY

have one's lady's time □ lady-broke

LAID

laid up

LAMB

lamb fries □ might as well be hung for a sheep as (for) a lamb □ two shakes of a lamb's tail

LAND

Beulah land □ Land o' Goshen! □ land so poor it wouldn't even raise a fuss □ land too poor to raise a racket on □ land up in a funeral parlor □ land up somewhere □ Land(s) sakes (alive)! □ land-office business

LANGUAGE

language that would fry bacon

LAP

lap child

LARD

lard tub □ lard-fat

LAST

Kissin' don't last; cookin' do. □ last one in the back row when the faces was handed out

LATCH

The latch string is always out.

LATELY

Johnny-come-lately

LAUGH

bust out laughing □ I kicked the slats out of my cradle laughing at that (joke). □ I knocked the slats out of my cradle laughing at that □ would make a cat laugh

LAVISH

lavish of something

LAW

colder than a mother-in-law's kiss □ law someone

LAY

lay eyes on someone or something □ lay for someone or something □ lay low and sing small □ lay something by

LAYOVER

layover for meddlers □ layover to catch meddlers

LAZY

born tired and raised lazy □ lazy man's load

LEAD

fill someone full of lead □ lead apes in hell □ lead poisoning □ someone ain't worth the powder and lead it would take to shoot someone

LEAF

shake like a leaf (in the wind)

LEARN

book-learning

LEAST

least little thing

LEATHER

hell (-bent) for leather

LEAVE
I'd (just) as leave do something □ without let or leave

LEFT
still have some snap left in one's garters

LEG
(as) crooked as a dog's hind leg □ (grand)daddy longlegs □ give someone a leg up □ have a leg up on someone else □ hog-leg □ leg bail □ leg-weary □ more hopeless than a one-legged man at a (butt-)kickin' contest □ shake a leg □ so low you could sit on a newspaper and swing your legs □ so low you could sit on the curb and swing your legs □ thousand-legger

LENT
(as) busy as a fish peddler in Lent

LESS
less time than skinning a badger

LESSON
taking harp lessons

LET
charge it to the dust and let the rain settle it □ Let every man skin his own skunk. □ let off a little steam □ let on (about someone or something) (to someone) □ without let or leave

LEVEL
one's level best

LIAR
dog-faced liar

LICE
beggar-lice

LICK
(as) easy as lickin' butter off(en) a knife □ (as) quick as a dog can lick a dish □ ain't got a lick of sense □ lick and a promise □ like licking honey off a blackberry vine

LICKETY
lickety split

LIE
bare-faced lie □ dog-faced liar □ lie like a rug □ pack of lies □ that ain't no lie

LIFE
(as) big as life, and twice as natural □ (as) big as life, and twice as ugly □ for the life of me □ scare ten years off someone's span of life □ Such is life in the West, and the further west you go, the sucher it is.

LIFTER
fence-lifter

LIGHT
can't hold a light for someone □ light a rag (for somewhere) □ light a shuck (for somewhere) □ light bread □ light out for somewhere □ light out for the territories

LIGHTNING
like greased lightning □ like hell and high lightning □ white lightning

LIKE
(as) like as two peas (in a pod) □ -like □ be on someone like a duck on a June bug □ be on someone like white on rice □ bellow like an ox □ bleed like a stuck pig □ blown up like a toad □ built like a brick outhouse □ built like a brick shithouse □ built like a depot stove □ eyes like two burnt holes in a blanket □ go at something like a boy killing snakes □ grin like a barrel of possum heads □ grin like a mule eating briars □ grow like Topsy □ hate someone or something like sin □ have a mind like a (steel) trap □ I felt like a penny waiting for change. □ kick like a mule □ kick like a steer □ lie like a rug □ like a bat out of hell □ like a blind dog in a meat market □ like a bump on a log □ like a can of corn □ like a house afire □ like a kid with a new toy □ like Coxey's Army □ like enough □ like fighting snakes □ like flies to manure □ like greased lightning □ like hell and high lightning □ like herding frogs □ like it

was going out of style □ like licking honey off a blackberry vine □ like pigs to the slaughter □ like shooting fish in a barrel □ like stealing acorns from a blind pig □ like there ain't no tomorrow □ like there's no tomorrow □ like to □ like tryin' to scratch your ear with your elbow □ like water off a duck's back □ look like a saddle on a sow □ look like a sheep-killing dog □ make out like a bandit □ make out like something □ need something like a pig needs a hip pocket □ puff like a grampus □ puff like a steam engine □ quick-like (a bunny) □ run like a scalded dog □ see the like of something □ sell like hotcakes □ shake like a holly in a high wind □ shake like a leaf (in the wind) □ shake like a willow in the wind □ slink like a suckegg hound □ smoke like a chimney □ squeal like a stuck pig □ steal away like a thief in the night □ stick (to someone) like white on rice □ swell like a bullfrog □ swell up like a poisoned pup □ talk like a cotton gin in pickin' time □ There's no fool like an old fool. □ wobble like a newborn calf □ work like a beaver □ work like a mule □ work like a slave

LIME
Key lime pie

LIMP
(as) limp as a rag

LINE
dead cat on the line □ swallow something hook, line, and sinker

LION
mountain lion

LIP
give someone some lip

LIQUOR
pot liquor □ stump liquor

LITTLE
(as) sure as God made little green apples □ (little) pick-me-up □ (little) short on one end □ Bless your little black heart. □ come out the little end of the horn □ don't worry your (pretty little) head about it □ every little bit helps □ least little thing □ let off a little steam □ little bitty □ little bugger □ little old □ little shaver □ trouble one's (little) head about something □ Ye gods (and little fishes)!

LIVE
living high off the hog □ living right □ scare the (living) daylights out of someone

LIVELONG
all the livelong day

LOAD
few bricks short of a load □ lazy man's load □ load of hooey □ loaded for bear □ sit down and take a load off (your feet)

LOCK
lock horns (with someone)

LOCO
loco weed □ plumb loco

LOFTY
Mackerel skies and mares' tails make lofty ships carry low sails.

LOG
like a bump on a log

LOLLYGAG
lollygag (around)

LONE
Lone Star state

LONESOME
all by one's lonesome □ high lonesome

LONG
(a)long about □ (as) nervous as a long-tailed cat in a room full of rocking chairs □ (grand)daddy longlegs □ (long) tall drink of water □ it'll be a long day in January when something happens □ long in the tooth □ long johns □ long sweetenin' □ Long time no see. □ not long for this world

LONGLEGS
(grand)daddy longlegs
LOOK
look like a saddle on a sow □ look like a sheep-killing dog □ sorry (-lookin') □ take a look-see □ The bigger the mouth, the better it looks closed. □ would as soon do something as look at you
LOOP
swing a wide loop
LOOSE
loose-footed
LORD
(lord) high muck-a-muck □ (the) Lord only knows □ Lord almighty □ Lord love a duck! □ Lord willing and the creek don't rise □ Praise the Lord! □ the Lord's Day
LOT
across lots □ feed lot
LOUD
for crying out loud
LOUSE
would skin a louse for his hide and tallow
LOVE
don't kiss by the garden gate; love is blind but neighbors ain't □ don't make love by the garden gate; love is blind but neighbors ain't □ Lord love a duck! □ love apple
LOW
(as) low as a snake's belly □ (as) low-down as a snake in a wagon track □ in low cotton □ lay low and sing small □ low-down □ lower someone's ears □ Mackerel skies and mares' tails make lofty ships carry low sails. □ so low you could sit on a newspaper and swing your legs □ so low you could sit on the curb and swing your legs
LUCIFER
(as) proud as Lucifer
LUCK
have more luck than sense □ pot luck
LUNG
air one's lungs
LYNCH
(Judge) Lynch
MA'AM
excuse me ma'am □ wham bam thank you ma'am
MACKEREL
Mackerel skies and mares' tails make lofty ships carry low sails. □ mackerel sky
MAD
(as) mad as a (blind) hornet □ (as) mad as a stunned gopher □ (as) mad as a wet hen □ fighting mad □ hopping mad □ mad enough to bite off a drawbar □ mad enough to chew nails and spit rivets □ mad enough to kick a cat □ madder than a wet hen
MADE
(as) sure as God made little green apples □ (as) ugly as home-made soap
MAGGOT
ugly enough to gag a maggot
MAIL
mail-order wife
MAIN
by main strength and awkwardness
MAKE
(as) sure as God made little green apples □ (as) ugly as home-made soap □ don't make love by the garden gate; love is blind but neighbors ain't □ don't make two bites of a cherry □ It don't make (me) no nevermind. □ Mackerel skies and mares' tails make lofty ships carry low sails. □ make (so) bold (as) to do something □ make a beeline (for someone or something) □ make a miration □ make a pile (of money) □ make oneself scarce □ make out like a bandit □ make out like something □ make over someone □ make tracks ((to) somewhere) □ make water □ not enough meat on him to

make a poor man a bowl of soup □ Open your mouth and shut your eyes and I'll give you something to make you wise. □ Spread that on the grass to make it green. □ would make a cat laugh □ You make a better door than you do a window.

MAN

bad man □ collar-and-tie men □ dead man's hand □ go to see a man about a dog □ lazy man's load □ Let every man skin his own skunk. □ man-baby □ men-folks □ more hopeless than a one-legged man at a (butt-)kickin' contest □ more ways than a country man can whip a mule □ not enough meat on him to make a poor man a bowl of soup □ old man □ Old Man River □ preacher-man □ widder-man □ would steal the dime off a dead man's eyes

MANURE

like flies to manure

MANY

good many □ many (and many)'s the time □ too many pigs for the tits

MARBLE

marble orchard

MARE

Mackerel skies and mares' tails make lofty ships carry low sails. □ mare's nest □ shank's mare

MARKET

like a blind dog in a meat market

MARRY

marry up (with someone)

MAST

shirt-tail at half-mast

MASTER

Master's call

MATCH

shooting-match □ whole shooting match

MAY

Queen of the May □ you may hang me for a chipmunk if . . .

MCCOY

real McCoy

MEADOW

meadow muffin

MEAN

(as) mean as a stuck snake □ meaner than a junkyard dog (with fourteen sucking pups)

MEASURE

measure someone on the ground

MEAT

(as) dull as a meat axe □ like a blind dog in a meat market □ meat bee □ not enough meat on him to make a poor man a bowl of soup □ souse meat

MEDDLE

layover for meddlers □ layover to catch meddlers □ meddle with someone or something

MEDICINE

bad medicine □ snake(bite) medicine

MEETING

camp meeting □ prayer-meetin' □ Sunday go-to-meeting

MEN

collar-and-tie men □ men-folks

MERCHANT

(as) busy as a cranberry merchant

MESS

(whole) mess of someone or something □ mess with someone or something

MIDDLE

smack dab in the middle □ spang in the middle

MIDDLING

fair to middlin'

MIDWARP

midwarp of the night

MIGHTY

high-and-mighty □ might(y) nigh

MILE

country mile

MILK

milk teeth □ raised on sour milk

MILL
have been through the mill

MIND
call something to mind □ don't mind if I do □ have a (good) mind to do something □ have a mind as sharp as a steel trap □ have a mind like a (steel) trap □ I don't mind telling you. □ if you've a mind to do something □ mind someone □ mind the store (for someone) □ pay someone any mind □ put someone in mind of something □ speak one's mind

MINE
salt a mine

MINT
mint julep

MIRATION
make a miration

MISS
wouldn't miss something for a farm in Texas

MOAN
piss and moan

MOLASSES
(as) big around as a molasses barrel □ (as) slow as molasses in January

MOMMA
My momma didn't raise no fool(s). □ My momma didn't raise no stupid child.

MOMMICK
mommick someone or something up

MONDAY
come Monday

MONEY
(butter and) egg money □ cash money □ folding money □ for my money □ I'd bet money (on it). □ make a pile (of money)

MONTH
bad time (of the month) □ month of Sundays

MOON
moon-calf □ shrink of the moon □ think someone hung the moon (and stars)

MORE
all the more □ has more than one string to his fiddle □ have more luck than sense □ know no more about something than a frog knows about bed sheets □ more hopeless than a one-legged man at a (butt-)kickin' contest □ more noise than a jackass in a tin barn □ more noise than a mule in a tin barn □ more something than Carter had oats □ more ways than a country man can whip a mule □ more'n farmers have hay □ there's more down (in the) cellar in a teacup □ use your head for more than a hatrack □ use your head for more than something to keep your ears apart □ whole heap more

MORNING
gotta get up pretty early in the morning to do something □ Great day (in the morning)! □ of a morning

MOSS
house moss □ Spanish moss

MOTHER
colder than a mother-in-law's kiss □ every mother's son of them

MOUNTAIN
mountain canary □ mountain dew □ mountain lion □ mountain oysters □ Rocky Mountain oysters

MOURN
mourners' bench

MOUTH
bad-mouth someone □ born with a silver spoon in one's mouth □ foam at the mouth □ mouth organ □ Open your mouth and shut your eyes and I'll give you a big surprise. □ Open your mouth and shut your eyes and I'll give you something to make you wise. □ sweet-mouth someone □ The bigger the mouth, the better it looks closed. □ Well, shut my mouth!

MUCH
amount to much □ as much chance

(of something) as a wax cat in hell □ know as much about something as a hog knows about Sunday □ Much obliged! □ not much for something

MUCK

(lord) high muck-a-muck

MUD

(as) happy as a pig in mud □ (as) happy as pigs in mud □ (as) homely as a mud fence

MUDDY

Big Muddy □ Old Muddy

MUFFIN

meadow muffin

MULE

grin like a mule eating briars □ have the nerve of a government mule □ I'll be a suckegg mule! □ kick like a mule □ more noise than a mule in a tin barn □ more ways than a country man can whip a mule □ mule in horse harness □ mule skinner □ work like a mule

MULLYGRUBS

have the mullygrubs

MUSCLE

table-muscle

MUSIC

bluegrass (music) □ chin music

MUSTARD

(as) yeller as mustard but without the bite □ cut the mustard

MUSTER

pass muster

MUTTON

(as) simple as mutton

NAIL

coffin nail □ mad enough to chew nails and spit rivets

NAKED

(as) naked as a jaybird □ butt naked

NAME

front name □ put one's name in the pot

NARROW

narrow between the eyes

NATURAL

(as) big as life, and twice as natural □ beat the (natural) stuffing out of someone □ kick the (natural) stuffing out of someone

NEAR

near side

NECK

(as) shy as a ring-necked pheasant □ case of the stiff neck □ neck of the woods □ stretch someone's neck

NECKTIE

necktie frolic □ necktie party □ necktie social

NED

Old Ned

NEED

need something like a pig needs a hip pocket □ standin' in need of something

NEEDLE

needle grass

NEIGHBOR

don't kiss by the garden gate; love is blind but neighbors ain't □ don't make love by the garden gate; love is blind but neighbors ain't □ neighbor (someone) round

NELLIE

not on your Nellie □ Whoa, Nellie!

NERVE

have the nerve of a government mule

NERVOUS

(as) nervous as a long-tailed cat in a room full of rocking chairs

NEST

have a hen on the nest □ mare's nest □ rat's nest □ turkey's nest

NEVER

never said pea turkey

NEVERMIND

It don't make (me) no nevermind.

NEW

(as) busy as a beaver (building a new dam) □ (as) proud as a pup with a new collar □ brand-spanking new □ like a kid with a new toy □

something old, something new, something borrowed, and something blue

NEWBORN

innocent as a newborn babe □ wobble like a newborn calf

NEWSPAPER

so low you could sit on a newspaper and swing your legs

NEXT

from here till next Tuesday

NICKEL

Don't take any wooden nickels. □ I've seen better heads on nickel beers. □ plug(ed) nickel □ Who put a nickel in your slot?

NIGH

might(y) nigh □ nigh on to do something □ nigh onto

NIGHT

midwarp of the night □ put someone up (for the night) □ steal away like a thief in the night

NIGHTGOWN

God's nightgown!

NINE

forty-niner

NIP

nip and tuck

NIT

nit-brained

NO

ain't got no call (to do something) □ all gurgle and no guts □ all hat and no cattle □ all show and no go □ all vine and no taters □ all wool and no shoddy □ Better the gravy than no grease at all. □ cut dog has no pups □ don't cut no ice (with someone) □ don't cut no squares (with someone) □ have no truck with something □ have the devil to pay (and no pitch hot) □ in no time flat □ It don't make (me) no nevermind. □ know no more about something than a frog knows about bed sheets □ like there ain't no tomorrow □ like there's no tomorrow □ Long time no see. □ My momma didn't raise no fool(s). □ My momma didn't raise no stupid child. □ no call for something □ no great shakes □ No harm done. □ no rue-back □ no two ways about it □ no-(ac)count □ no-see-ums □ No-siree bob(tail)! □ No-siree! □ that ain't no lie □ There's no flies on someone. □ There's no fool like an old fool.

NOBODY

wouldn't hurt nobody none

NOISE

more noise than a jackass in a tin barn □ more noise than a mule in a tin barn

NONE

bar none □ don't bother me none □ wouldn't hurt nobody none

NOR

neither hide nor hair

NORTH

weak north of the ears

NOSE

have one's nose out of joint □ so dark you couldn't find your nose with both hands

NOT

can't say, not knowing □ not a patch on someone or something □ not about to □ not dry behind the ears □ not enough brains to grease a skillet □ not enough meat on him to make a poor man a bowl of soup □ not enough room to swing a cat □ not enough sense to pound sand in a rat hole □ not enough to dust a fiddle □ not know someone or something from Adam's housecat □ not know someone or something from Adam's off ox □ not long for this world □ not much for something □ not on your Nellie □ not on your tintype □ not playing with a full deck □ not since the year One □ not sure but what something □ not worth a continental □ not worth a hill of beans □ not worth a shovelful of chicken tracks □ touch-me-not

NOTCH
take someone down a notch (or two)

NOTHING
(there ain't) nothin' to it □ nothing to sneeze at

NOTION
take a notion to do something

NOW
(Now) what did you go and do that for? □ It sure is hell when it's this way, and it's this way now. □ speak now or forever hold your peace

NUN
buck nun

OAK
all oak and iron bound

OAR
have just one oar in the water

OAT
feel one's oats □ more something than Carter had oats

OATH
take one's Bible oath

OBLIGE
Much obliged!

ODD
odd jobs

OFFICE
land-office business

OFTEN
as often as a goose goes barefoot

OIL
snake oil □ someone's oil doesn't reach the dipstick

OKEY
okey-dokey

OLD
(as) common as an old shoe □ (as) honest as (old) Abe □ (as) old as the courthouse □ little old □ Old Dominion □ old hand □ old man □ Old Man River □ Old Muddy □ Old Ned □ Old Scratch □ old stomping ground(s) □ old woman □ old-time □ old-timer □ old-timey □ so old it's got whiskers □ something old, something new, something borrowed, and something blue □ That (old) dog won't hunt. □ That's the tune the old cow died on. □ The old woman's picking her geese. □ There's no fool like an old fool.

OLE
good ole boy

ONE
(as) busy as a one-armed paperhanger □ (little) short on one end □ has more than one string to his fiddle □ have just one oar in the water □ last one in the back row when the faces was handed out □ more hopeless than a one-legged man at a (butt-)kickin' contest □ not since the year One □ one jump ahead □ one red cent □ one-holer □ one-horse town □ one-pipe shotgun □ up one side and down the other

ONION
(as) slick as a peeled onion

ONLY
(the) Lord only knows □ close only counts in horseshoes (and hand grenades)

ONTO
nigh onto

OPEN
bust someone wide open □ crack (open) the door □ crack (open) the window □ open one's head □ Open your mouth and shut your eyes and I'll give you a big surprise. □ Open your mouth and shut your eyes and I'll give you something to make you wise.

OPERA
horse opera

OPRY
hoss opry

ORCHARD
(as) crazy as a peach-orchard boar □ bone orchard □ marble orchard

ORDER
mail-order wife □ pecking order
ORGAN
mouth organ
OTHER
In God we trust, all others pay cash. □ other side □ tell t'other from which □ up one side and down the other
OUGHT
hadn't oughta
OUTCOYOTE
outcoyote someone or something
OUTDOOR
(as) big as all outdoors
OUTFOX
outfox someone or something
OUTHOUSE
built like a brick outhouse
OVEN
Dutch oven
OVER
all over creation □ all over hell and gone □ all over hell and half of Georgia □ all-overs □ anty-over □ ass-over-teakettle □ ass-over-tit □ blow over □ cross over □ fork something over □ hand over fist □ jump over the broomstick □ keel over □ keel something over □ kick over the traces □ make over someone □ over my dead body □ over to □ slave over something □ traipse (over)
OVERCOAT
wooden overcoat
OWL
(as) drunk as a biled owl □ (as) drunk as a boiled owl □ (as) slick as owl grease □ (as) smart as a tree full of owls □ (as) sorry as owl bait □ I wasn't brought up in the woods to be scared by owls. □ screech owl □ squinch owl
OWN
blow one's own horn □ can't call one's soul one's own □ chew one's own tobacco □ have callouses from patting one's own back □ hoe one's own row □ Let every man skin his own skunk. □ one's own self □ own up (to something) □ own-born cousins □ tend to your own ball of yarn □ tend to your own knitting □ think someone is God's own cousin □ toot one's own horn □ tote one's own skillet
OX
bellow like an ox □ not know someone or something from Adam's off ox □ off ox
OYSTER
mountain oysters □ prairie oysters □ Rocky Mountain oysters
PACK
pack a weapon □ pack of lies
PADDLE
up the creek without a paddle
PAINT
(as) close as two coats of paint □ paint one's tonsils □ paint the town red □ painted woman □ tonsil paintin' □ too poor to paint and too proud to whitewash □ war paint
PAIR
candidate for a pair of wings
PAN
flash in the pan □ pan out
PANDOWDY
apple pandowdy
PANTS
have ants in one's pants □ three-cornered pants □ wear the pants (in the family)
PAPER
(as) busy as a one-armed paper-hanger □ can't carry a tune in a paper sack □ funny paper
PAPERHANGER
(as) busy as a one-armed paper-hanger
PARLOR
land up in a funeral parlor
PART
in these parts □ in those parts

PARTICULAR
ain't particular
PARTY
hen party □ necktie party
PASS
behind the door when the brains were passed out □ come to a pretty pass □ pass muster □ pass the time of day
PASTE
cow paste
PASTURE
put someone or something out to pasture
PAT
break one's arm patting oneself on the back □ have callouses from patting one's own back
PATCH
(as) crooked as a rattler in a cactus patch □ not a patch on someone or something
PATTY
cow patty
PAUNCH
air one's paunch
PAWN
colder than a pawnbroker's smile
PAY
have hell to pay □ have the devil to pay (and no pitch hot) □ hit pay dirt □ In God we trust, all others pay cash. □ pay someone any mind □ so broke he couldn't even pay attention
PEA
(as) like as two peas (in a pod) □ black-eyed pea □ crowder pea □ never said pea turkey □ pea-green □ scare someone pea green □ sugar peas
PEACE
speak now or forever hold your peace
PEACH
(as) crazy as a peach-orchard boar □ cut your peaches
PEAR
prickly pear
PECK
bushel and a peck (and some in a gourd) □ hen-pecked □ If that don't beat a pig a-pecking! □ peck of something □ pecking order
PEDDLER
(as) busy as a fish peddler in Lent
PEEL
(as) slick as a peeled onion □ keep one's eyes peeled
PEG
take someone down a peg (or two)
PEN
raised on a floored pen
PENCIL
cowboy pencil
PENNY
cost a pretty penny □ I felt like a penny waiting for change.
PEOPLE
(from) so far south they call people from Georgia Yankees
PET
(as) harmless as a pet rabbit
PETER
peter out
PEW
amen pew
PHEASANT
(as) shy as a ring-necked pheasant
PICK
(little) pick-me-up □ cotton-picking □ have a bone to pick with someone □ have a chicken to pick with someone □ pick someone or something off □ pickin' and singin' □ slim pickings □ talk like a cotton gin in pickin' time □ The old woman's picking her geese.
PICTURE
(as) pretty as a picture
PIDDLE
piddle around
PIE
(as) happy as a fly in a pie □ chess

pie □ cow pie □ Key lime pie □ pie plant □ pie safe □ shoo-fly pie □ sweet potato pie □ vinegar pie

PIECE

down the road a piece □ fur piece □ say one's piece □ sell someone a piece of goods □ speak one's piece □ that beats something all to pieces

PIG

(as) happy as a pig in mud □ (as) happy as pigs in mud □ ain't fittin' to roll with a pig □ bleed like a stuck pig □ blind pig □ buy a pig in a poke □ If that don't beat a pig a-pecking! □ In a pig's ass! □ In a pig's ear! □ In a pig's eye! □ like pigs to the slaughter □ like stealing acorns from a blind pig □ need something like a pig needs a hip pocket □ squeal like a stuck pig □ too many pigs for the tits □ whistle-pig

PIKE

down the road a pike

PILE

make a pile (of money)

PILL

bitter pill (to swallow)

PILLAR

from pillar to post

PILOT

sky-pilot

PIN

have one's ears pinned back □ pin someone's ears back

PINE

(as) high as a Georgia pine □ pine-straw □ piney-woods □ piney-woods rooter

PINK

in the pink (of health)

PIPE

one-pipe shotgun □ two-pipe shotgun

PISS

don't have a pot to piss in (or a window to throw it out of) □ piss and moan □ piss and vinegar □ piss poor □ piss up a rope □ piss up a tree □ raining as hard as a cow pissing on a flat rock

PITCH

have the devil to pay (and no pitch hot)

PITCHFORK

it's raining pitchforks (and hammer handles)

PITY

for pity('s) sake(s)

PIZEN

pizen vine

PLACE

bad place □ between a rock and a hard place

PLAGUE

enough of something to plague a saint □ plague someone □ Plague take it!

PLAIN

(as) plain as the hump on a camel

PLANT

pie plant □ plant someone □ They planted the corn before they built the fence.

PLATE

read one's plate

PLAY

not playing with a full deck □ play it close to the vest □ play possum □ play-pretty

PLEASE

(as) something as you please □ as someone damn well pleases

PLENTY

gracious plenty

PLOW

clean someone's plow □ plow someone's furrow □ plow to the end of the row

PLUG

plug ugly □ plug(ed) nickel

PLUMB

plumb loco

PLUMBING

greatest thing since indoor plumbing

PLUMP
plump someone or something down
PLUNDER
plunder room
POCKET
(as) handy as a pocket in a shirt □ (as) safe as in God's pocket □ need something like a pig needs a hip pocket
POD
(as) like as two peas (in a pod) □ small and yellow and few to the pod
POINT
point-blank
POISON
lead poisoning □ pizen vine □ swell up like a poisoned pup
POKE
better than a poke in the eye with a sharp stick □ buy a pig in a poke □ cow poke
POKER
have a poker up one's ass □ poker face
POLAR
hot enough to burn a polar bear's butt
POLE
(as) skinny as a (bean)pole
POLISH
polish the apple
POND
(as) weak as pond water □ biggest frog in the pond
PONY
ride shank's ponies
POOR
(as) poor as Job's turkey □ land so poor it wouldn't even raise a fuss □ land too poor to raise a racket on □ not enough meat on him to make a poor man a bowl of soup □ piss poor □ po(or) Joe □ poor white (trash) □ too poor to paint and too proud to whitewash
POPCORN
(as) busy as popcorn on a skillet
POSSUM
grin like a barrel of possum heads □ play possum
POST
from pillar to post □ trading post
POT
don't have a pot to piss in (or a window to throw it out of) □ go to pot □ pot liquor □ pot luck □ pot shot □ pot someone or something □ put one's name in the pot □ shit or get off the pot
POTATO
small potatoes □ small potatoes and few to the hill □ sweet potato pie
POUND
not enough sense to pound sand in a rat hole
POUR
couldn't pour water out of a boot (if there was instructions on the heel)
POWDER
restin' powder □ someone ain't worth the powder and lead it would take to shoot someone
POWER
do someone a power of good □ high-powered □ power of something
PRAIRIE
prairie dog □ prairie oysters □ prairie strawberries
PRAISE
Praise the Lord!
PRAYER
prayer-bones □ prayer-meetin'
PREACH
preach someone's funeral
PREACHER
preacher-man □ short-coat preacher
PRETTY
(as) pretty as a picture □ (as) pretty as a speckled pup □ come to a pretty pass □ cost a pretty penny □ don't worry your (pretty little) head about it □ gotta get up pretty early in the morning to do something □

play-pretty □ pretty oneself up □ sittin' pretty

PRICE
have a price on one's head

PRICKLY
prickly pear

PRIME
prime the pump

PROMISE
lick and a promise

PROUD
(as) proud as a pup with a new collar □ (as) proud as Lucifer □ (as) proud as Satan □ (as) proud as sin □ do someone proud □ purse proud □ too poor to paint and too proud to whitewash

PROVERB
raised on prunes and proverbs

PRUNE
full of prunes □ raised on prunes and proverbs

PUDDING
hasty pudding

PUDDLE
biggest duck in the puddle

PUFF
puff like a grampus □ puff like a steam engine

PUG
pug-ugly

PULL
pull (one's) freight □ pull freight for the tules □ pull in one's horns □ pull oneself up by the bootstraps □ pull up stakes

PUMP
(as) straight as a yard of pump water □ prime the pump

PUMPKIN
some pumpkins

PUNCHER
cow puncher

PUNISHMENT
glutton for punishment

PUNY
feeling puny

PUP
(as) pretty as a speckled pup □ (as) proud as a pup with a new collar □ cut dog has no pups □ hush puppies □ meaner than a junkyard dog (with fourteen sucking pups) □ raised someone from a pup □ since Hector was a pup □ swell up like a poisoned pup □ thicker than fleas on a fat pup

PURE
pure salt

PURSE
purse proud

PURTY
sittin' purty

PUSSY
wood pussy

PUT
(as) tough as puttin' socks on a rooster □ hard put □ put (great) store by someone or something □ put a knot in someone's tail □ put on the dog □ put on the feed bag □ put one's name in the pot □ put someone in mind of something □ put someone on a cooling board □ put someone or something out to pasture □ put someone up (for the night) □ put someone's ass in a sling □ put something by □ put the fear of God in someone □ put the Indian sign on someone □ put the quietus on someone or something □ Put up or shut up. □ rode hard and put up wet □ Who put a nickel in your slot?

PYE
joe pye weed

QT
on the QT

QUEEN
Queen of the May

QUICK
(as) quick as a dog can lick a dish □ quick on the trigger □ quick-like (a bunny) □ quicker than hell could scorch a feather □ quicker than you can bat an eye □ quicker than you

can holler howdy □ quicker than you could count two □ right quick

QUIET

quieten (down) □ quieten someone or something (down)

QUIETUS

put the quietus on someone or something

QUILT

quilting bee

QUIT

Church ain't out till they quit singing. □ quittin' time

RABBIT

(as) harmless as a pet rabbit □ rabbit ranch

RACKET

land too poor to raise a racket on □ raise a racket

RAFT

float someone a raft of shit

RAG

(as) limp as a rag □ bull(y)-rag someone □ choke-rag □ light a rag (for somewhere) □ rag tag and bobtail

RAIL

(as) crooked as a rail fence □ (as) skinny as a rail □ beat the devil and carry a rail

RAIN

charge it to the dust and let the rain settle it □ doesn't have enough sense to come in out of the rain □ it's raining pitchforks (and hammer handles) □ rain bull yearlings □ rain bullfrogs □ raining as hard as a cow pissing on a flat rock □ Thunder ain't rain.

RAISE

born tired and raised lazy □ land so poor it wouldn't even raise a fuss □ land too poor to raise a racket on □ My momma didn't raise no fool(s). □ My momma didn't raise no stupid child. □ raise a racket □ raise a ruckus □ raise a rumpus □ raise hell □ raise someone up □ raised on a floored pen □ raised on prunes and proverbs □ raised on sour milk □ raised someone from a pup □ raising bee

RANCH

dude ranch □ rabbit ranch □ ranch (something) out

RANGE

feed off someone's range

RARING

rarin' to do something

RAT

desert rat □ get on with your rat-killin' □ not enough sense to pound sand in a rat hole □ rat's nest

RATHER

have one's rathers

RATTLE

all horns and rattles

RATTLER

(as) crooked as a rattler in a cactus patch

REACH

boardinghouse reach □ someone's oil doesn't reach the dipstick

READ

read one's plate

READY

ready to roll

REAL

real McCoy

REASON

know in reason

REBEL

rebel yell

REBELLION

Great Rebellion

RECOGNIZE

(recognizing) sense

RED

(as) red as a beet □ one red cent □ paint the town red □ red-eye

RELIGION

get religion

RENCH

rench (something) out

REST

rest one's features □ restin' powder

RETURN
return thanks
REWARD
go to one's (just) reward
RIB
rib someone (about someone or something) □ stick to someone's ribs
RICE
be on someone like white on rice □ stick (to someone) like white on rice
RICH
strike it rich
RIDE
ride herd on someone or something □ ride shank's ponies □ ride the gravy train □ riding a cloud □ Riggin' ain't ridin'. □ will do to ride the river with
RIG
Riggin' ain't ridin'.
RIGHT
all righty □ I don't rightly know. □ living right □ right down □ right from the git-go □ right quick □ right smart □ right smart chance of something
RILE
rile someone up
RING
(as) shy as a ring-necked pheasant □ ring-tailed snorter
RIP
rip snorter
RISE
get a rise from someone or something □ get a rise out of someone or something □ God willing and the creek don't rise □ in the rise of her bloom □ Lord willing and the creek don't rise □ risin' bread □ sap-risin' time □ think the sun rises and sets on someone
RIVER
Old Man River □ will do to ride the river with
RIVET
mad enough to chew nails and spit rivets
ROAD
down the road a piece □ down the road a pike □ down the road a stretch □ give someone down the road □ road apple
ROAST
roasting ear
ROBIN
Robin Hood's barn
ROCK
(as) nervous as a long-tailed cat in a room full of rocking chairs □ (as) smart as a box of rocks □ (as) smart as a rock □ (as) steady as a rock □ between a rock and a hard place □ grave rock □ raining as hard as a cow pissing on a flat rock
ROCKY
Rocky Mountain oysters
RODE
rode hard and put up wet
ROLL
(as) awkward as a cow on roller skates □ ain't fittin' to roll with a pig □ holy roller □ ready to roll □ roll up the sidewalks
ROOM
(as) nervous as a long-tailed cat in a room full of rocking chairs □ knock-head room □ not enough room to swing a cat □ plunder room
ROOST
rule the roost
ROOSTER
(as) tough as puttin' socks on a rooster
ROOT
grab a root □ grass-roots □ piney-woods rooter □ root hog or die
ROPE
cry calf rope □ have a sticky rope □ piss up a rope
ROUGH
(as) rough as a corncob □ diamond in the rough
ROUND
coyote round □ neighbor (someone) round

ROUST
roust up
ROW
hoe one's own row □ I could knock you for a row of brick houses. □ last one in the back row when the faces was handed out □ plow to the end of the row □ tough row to hoe
RUB
don't know whether to eat it or rub it on
RUCKUS
raise a ruckus
RUE
no rue-back
RUG
lie like a rug
RUIN
wrack and ruin
RULE
rule the roost
RUMPUS
raise a rumpus
RUN
(as) slow as coal tar running uphill backwards □ could fight a circle-saw (and it a-runnin') □ run (just) shy of something □ run like a scalded dog
RUSH
don't rush the cattle
RUSTLE
rustle up some grub
RUSTY
cut a rusty
SACK
can't carry a tune in a paper sack □ crocus sack □ croker sack □ go-way sack □ gunny sack □ tow sack
SAD
(as) sad as a hound dog's eye
SADDLE
bring someone's saddle home □ have a burr under one's saddle □ look like a saddle on a sow □ sell one's saddle
SAFE
(as) safe as in God's pocket □ pie safe
SAGE
sage hen
SAID
never said pea turkey □ They ate before they said grace.
SAIL
Mackerel skies and mares' tails make lofty ships carry low sails.
SAILOR
Tell it to a sailor on horseback.
SAINT
enough of something to plague a saint
SAKE
for pity('s) sake(s) □ Land(s) sakes (alive)! □ Sakes alive!
SALE
Chick Sale (barn)
SALT
be worth one's salt □ eat someone's salt □ have something hung up and salted □ pure salt □ salt a mine □ salt something away □ salt something down
SAM
What the Sam Hill?
SAME
close enough to use the same toothpick □ slice off the same bacon □ The same dog bit me. □ We're swingin' on the same gate.
SAND
not enough sense to pound sand in a rat hole
SAP
sap-risin' time
SASS
fat and sassy □ garden-sass □ sass someone
SASSAFRASS
sassafrass tea
SATAN
(as) proud as Satan
SAVE
Brains in the head saves blisters on the feet.
SAW
could fight a circle-saw (and it a-

runnin') □ double saw buck □ saw buck □ saw gourds

SAY

can't say (a)s I do, (can't say (a)s I don't) □ can't say boo to a goose □ can't say for sure □ can't say, not knowing □ have one's say □ never said pea turkey □ say one's piece □ say uncle □ Say what? □ They ate before they said grace.

SCALD

run like a scalded dog

SCANDAL

shame and a scandal □ something scandalous

SCARCE

make oneself scarce

SCARE

I wasn't brought up in the woods to be scared by owls. □ scare someone out of a year's growth □ scare someone pea green □ scare ten years off someone's span of life □ scare the (living) daylights out of someone □ scare the daylights out of someone □ scared shitless

SCORCH

couldn't boil water (without scorching it) □ quicker than hell could scorch a feather

SCRATCH

like tryin' to scratch your ear with your elbow □ Old Scratch □ scratch the skin

SCREECH

screech owl

SCREW

so crooked he has to screw on his socks

SEAT

anxious seat □ keep one's seat

SEE

can see □ can't see a hole in a ladder □ can't-see time □ couldn't see straight □ go to see a man about a dog □ I've seen better heads on nickel beers. □ Long time no see. □ no-see-ums □ see someone home □ see the elephant □ see the like of something □ take a look-see

SELF

one's own self

SELL

sell like hotcakes □ sell one's saddle □ sell someone a bill of goods □ sell someone a piece of goods

SEND

send someone to hell and the devil

SENSE

(recognizing) sense □ ain't got a grain of sense □ ain't got a lick of sense □ ain't got the sense God gave geese □ doesn't have enough sense to bell a cat □ doesn't have enough sense to come in out of the rain □ have more luck than sense □ horse sense □ not enough sense to pound sand in a rat hole □ talk some sense into someone

SENSITIVE

(as) sensitive as an eyeball

SERIOUS

dead serious

SET

dead set against something □ get one's ears set out □ If you get burnt you got to set on the blister. □ set (great) store by someone or something □ set in □ set one's cap for someone □ set one's sights on someone or something □ set up to someone □ think the sun rises and sets on someone

SETTLE

charge it to the dust and let the rain settle it □ settle someone's hash

SEVEN

(as) hot as the seven brass hinges of hell □ seven-year itch

SHACK

shack whacky □ shacking up □ shotgun shack

SHADE
big enough to shade an elephant □ shade up

SHAKE
no great shakes □ shake a leg □ shake like a holly in a high wind □ shake like a leaf (in the wind) □ shake like a willow in the wind □ two shakes of a lamb's tail

SHAME
shame and a scandal □ tell the truth and shame the devil

SHANK
ride shank's ponies □ shank of the afternoon □ shank of the evening □ shank's mare

SHAPE
bent out of shape

SHARE
go shares in something

SHARP
(as) sharp as a briar □ (as) sharp as a tack □ better than a poke in the eye with a sharp stick □ have a mind as sharp as a steel trap □ sharpen someone's hoe

SHAVE
close shave □ little shaver

SHEBANG
whole shebang

SHED
get shed of someone or something □ take someone out to the woodshed

SHEEP
bighorn (sheep) □ black sheep (of the family) □ look like a sheep-killing dog □ might as well be hung for a sheep as (for) a lamb

SHEET
know no more about something than a frog knows about bed sheets

SHELL
shell something out

SHET
get shet of someone or something

SHINE
take a shine to someone

SHINNY
shinny up something

SHIP
Mackerel skies and mares' tails make lofty ships carry low sails.

SHIRT
(as) handy as a pocket in a shirt □ boiled shirt □ Keep your shirt on. □ shirt-tail at half-mast

SHIT
built like a brick shithouse □ doesn't know whether to shit or go blind □ float someone a raft of shit □ shit in tall cotton □ shit or get off the pot □ someone knows where the bear shits □ someone's shit don't stink

SHITHOUSE
built like a brick shithouse

SHITLESS
scared shitless

SHODDY
all wool and no shoddy

SHOE
(as) common as an old shoe □ wouldn't want to be in someone's shoes

SHOO
shoo-fly pie

SHOOT
(Ah) shoot! □ (as) sure as shootin' □ like shooting fish in a barrel □ shoot dozens □ shoot or give up the gun □ shoot someone full of daylight □ shoot someone on sight □ shoot the breeze □ shoot the bull □ shoot the works □ shoot-out □ shoot-up □ shooting iron □ shooting-match □ six-shooter □ someone ain't worth the powder and lead it would take to shoot someone □ straight shooter □ turkey shoot □ whole shooting match

SHORN
go for wool and come back shorn

SHORT
(little) short on one end □ born short and slapped down flat □ caught

short ☐ few bricks short of a load ☐ short horse, soon curried ☐ short sweetening ☐ short-coat preacher

SHOT
(as) drunk as who shot John ☐ drunker than who shot John ☐ pot shot

SHOTGUN
one-pipe shotgun ☐ shotgun shack ☐ shotgun wedding ☐ two-pipe shot gun

SHOVEL
(as) dumb as a shovel

SHOVELFUL
not worth a shovelful of chicken tracks ☐ wouldn't give (someone) a shovelful of chicken tracks for someone or something

SHOW
all show and no go ☐ Show Me state ☐ show one's face

SHRINK
shrink of the moon

SHUCK
(Ah) shucks! ☐ beat someone till his hide won't hold shucks ☐ light a shuck (for somewhere) ☐ shuck someone's corn

SHUT
get shet of someone or something ☐ get shut of someone or something ☐ Open your mouth and shut your eyes and I'll give you a big surprise. ☐ Open your mouth and shut your eyes and I'll give you something to make you wise. ☐ Put up or shut up. ☐ Well, shut my mouth!

SHY
(as) shy as a ring-necked pheasant ☐ be (just) shy of something ☐ gun-shy ☐ run (just) shy of something ☐ water shy

SIC
sic someone

SICK
(as) sick as a dog ☐ sick (un)to death of someone or something ☐ take sick

SIDE
crack one's sides ☐ near side ☐ off side ☐ other side ☐ side gal ☐ slap someone up the side of the head ☐ sunny-side up ☐ up one side and down the other

SIDEWALK
roll up the sidewalks

SIGHT
(damn) sight better ☐ have someone or something in one's sights ☐ heap sight ☐ set one's sights on someone or something ☐ shoot someone on sight ☐ sight for sore eyes ☐ sight of something ☐ sight to behold

SIGN
give someone the high sign ☐ put the Indian sign on someone

SIGODLIN
anti-sigodlin ☐ si-godlin

SILVER
born with a silver spoon in one's mouth

SIMPLE
(as) simple as mutton ☐ have a bad case of the simples

SIN
(as) proud as sin ☐ hate someone or something like sin

SINCE
greatest thing since indoor plumbing ☐ greatest thing since sliced bread ☐ not since the year One ☐ since Hector was a pup ☐ since the hog et grandma

SING
Church ain't out till they quit singing. ☐ lay low and sing small ☐ pickin' and singin'

SINK
sink hole ☐ sinkin' spell ☐ swallow something hook, line, and sinker

SIREE
No-siree bob(tail)! ☐ No-siree!

SIT
(as) sure as I'm sitting here ☐ sit down and take a load off (your feet)

□ sit tight □ sittin' pretty □ sittin' purty □ so low you could sit on a newspaper and swing your legs □ so low you could sit on the curb and swing your legs

SIX
six-gun □ six-shooter

SIXTEEN
full sixteen hands high

SIZE
all of a size □ size someone or something up

SIZZLE
sizzle sozzle

SKATE
(as) awkward as a cow on roller skates

SKILLET
(as) black as a skillet □ (as) busy as popcorn on a skillet □ not enough brains to grease a skillet □ tote one's own skillet

SKIN
jump out of one's skin □ keep one's eyes skinned □ less time than skinning a badger □ Let every man skin his own skunk. □ mule skinner □ scratch the skin □ skin out □ skin someone □ skin someone alive □ skin the cat □ would skin a louse for his hide and tallow □ would skin an ant for its tallow

SKINFUL
get a skinful

SKINNY
(as) skinny as a (bean)pole □ (as) skinny as a rail

SKUNK
Let every man skin his own skunk. □ skunk egg

SKY
knock someone or something skywinding □ Mackerel skies and mares' tails make lofty ships carry low sails. □ mackerel sky □ sky-pilot

SLACK
(as) slack as fiddle strings

SLAP
born short and slapped down flat □ slap someone up the side of the head □ slap someone upside the head

SLAT
I kicked the slats out of my cradle laughing at that (joke). □ I knocked the slats out of my cradle laughing at that

SLAUGHTER
like pigs to the slaughter

SLAVE
slave away (at something) □ slave over something □ work like a slave

SLED
hard sledding □ tough sledding

SLICE
greatest thing since sliced bread □ slice off the same bacon

SLICK
(as) slick as a baby's bottom □ (as) slick as a peeled onion □ (as) slick as bear grease □ (as) slick as goose grease □ (as) slick as owl grease □ (as) slick as snot □ (city) slicker □ slicker than calf slobbers

SLIDE
slipper slide

SLIM
slim pickings

SLING
grub-slinger □ have one's ass in a sling □ put someone's ass in a sling □ sling hash

SLINK
slink like a suckegg hound

SLIP
slipper slide

SLOBBER
calf slobber(s) □ slicker than calf slobbers

SLOT
Who put a nickel in your slot?

SLOW
(as) slow as coal tar running uphill backwards □ (as) slow as molasses

in January □ (as) slow as wet gunpowder □ slow elk

SLUM

slum-gullion

SLUT

sluts wool

SMACK

smack dab in the middle

SMALL

lay low and sing small □ small and yellow and few to the pod □ small potatoes □ small potatoes and few to the hill □ thank God for small favors

SMART

(as) smart as a box of rocks □ (as) smart as a rock □ (as) smart as a tree full of owls □ (as) smart as a whip □ right smart □ right smart chance of something

SMILE

colder than a pawnbroker's smile □ crack a smile

SMITH

Smith and Wesson

SMOKE

smoke like a chimney

SNAKE

(as) low as a snake's belly □ (as) low-down as a snake in a wagon track □ (as) mean as a stuck snake □ go at something like a boy killing snakes □ If it was a snake it woulda bit you. □ like fighting snakes □ snake doctor □ snake oil

SNAKEBITE

snake(bite) medicine

SNAP

snap-beans □ snappin' turtle □ still have some snap left in one's garters

SNEEZE

nothing to sneeze at

SNOREIFFEROUS

snoreifferous state

SNORT

ring-tailed snorter □ rip snorter

SNOT

(as) slick as snot

SNUFF

dip snuff

SO

(from) so far south they call people from Georgia Yankees □ carry on (so) □ land so poor it wouldn't even raise a fuss □ make (so) bold (as) to do something □ so broke he couldn't even pay attention □ so crooked he has to screw on his socks □ so dark all the bats stayed home □ so dark you couldn't find your nose with both hands □ so dry the trees were chasing the dogs □ so dumb he couldn't teach a hen to cluck □ so low you could sit on a newspaper and swing your legs □ so low you could sit on the curb and swing your legs □ so old it's got whiskers □ so to speak □ take on (so)

SOAP

(as) solemn as soap □ (as) ugly as home-made soap □ soft soap

SOBER

stone-cold sober

SOCIAL

necktie social

SOCKS

(as) tough as puttin' socks on a rooster □ so crooked he has to screw on his socks

SOFT

(speak softly and) carry a big stick □ soft soap

SOLEMN

(as) solemn as soap

SOME

and then some □ bushel and a peck (and some in a gourd) □ enough and some to spare □ give someone some lip □ give someone some sugar □ rustle up some grub □ some kind of something □ some pumpkins □ still have some snap left in one's garters □ talk some sense into someone

SON

every mother's son of them

SOON
I'd (just) as soon as do something □ short horse, soon curried □ would as soon do something as look at you
SORE
get sore □ sight for sore eyes
SORRY
(as) sorry as owl bait □ sorry (-lookin')
SOUL
bless my soul □ can't call one's soul one's own □ soul-case
SOUND
(as) sound as a barrel □ (as) sound as a barrel □ (as) sound as a dollar
SOUP
not enough meat on him to make a poor man a bowl of soup
SOUR
raised on sour milk
SOUSE
souse meat
SOUTH
(from) so far south they call people from Georgia Yankees □ go south □ Southern fried chicken □ Southern gentleman □ Southern hospitality
SOW
look like a saddle on a sow
SOZZLE
sizzle sozzle
SPADE
(as) black as the ace of spades □ (as) cocky as the king of spades
SPAN
scare ten years off someone's span of life
SPANG
spang in the middle
SPANISH
Spanish moss
SPANK
brand-spanking new
SPARE
enough and some to spare
SPARROW
sparrow grass
SPEAK
(speak softly and) carry a big stick □ so to speak □ speak now or forever hold your peace □ speak one's mind □ speak one's piece □ to speak of
SPECIAL
in special
SPECKLE
(as) pretty as a speckled pup
SPEECH
stump speech
SPELL
dry spell □ sinkin' spell □ spell somconc (for a while) □ spelling bee
SPIT
close chewer and a tight spitter □ don't amount to a bucket of spit □ mad enough to chew nails and spit rivets □ spit and vinegar □ spit cotton □ spittin' image □ within spittin' distance □ would spit in a wildcat's eye
SPLIT
lickety split
SPOON
born with a silver spoon in one's mouth □ spoon bread
SPRADDLE
spraddle (out)
SPREAD
Spread that on the grass to make it green.
SPRING
spring chicken
SPUR
earn one's spurs
SQUARE
don't cut no squares (with someone)
SQUAT
diddly(-squat) □ doodly(-squat)
SQUEAL
squeal like a stuck pig
SQUEEZE
(corn) squeezings
SQUINCH
squinch owl

SQUIRREL
ain't got the brains God gave a squirrel
STACK
(as) black as a stack of black cats □ I'd bet a blue stack on it. □ stack cake □ swear on a stack of Bibles
STAGGER
blind staggers
STAKE
pull up stakes □ stake (out) one's claim
STAND
(as) sure as I'm standing here □ standin' in need of something
STAR
Lone Star state □ Stars and Bars □ think someone hung the moon (and stars)
STATE
Buckeye State □ Lone Star state □ Show Me state □ snoreifferous state
STAY
so dark all the bats stayed home
STEADY
(as) steady as a rock
STEAL
like stealing acorns from a blind pig □ steal away like a thief in the night □ would steal the dime off a dead man's eyes
STEAM
let off a little steam □ puff like a steam engine
STEEL
have a mind as sharp as a steel trap □ have a mind like a (steel) trap
STEEP
(as) steep as a cow's face □ steeper than a cow's face
STEER
kick like a steer
STEP
step around □ step off the carpet □ step on someone's corns
STETSON
John B. Stetson
STEW
stewed to the gills
STICK
(speak softly and) carry a big stick □ battlin' stick □ better than a poke in the eye with a sharp stick □ something on a stick □ stick (to someone) like white on rice □ stick in someone's craw □ stick to someone's ribs □ stick to your guns □ stick-to-it-iveness □ stick-up
STICKY
have a sticky rope □ have sticky fingers
STIFF
case of the stiff neck
STILL
(as) still as time in a grave □ still have some snap left in one's garters
STING
tail up and stinger out
STINK
someone's shit don't stink
STIR
stir one's stumps
STITCH
in stitches
STOMACH
One's eyes are bigger than one's stomach.
STOMP
old stomping ground(s) □ stomp the bejeebers out of someone or something
STONE
stone cold □ stone dead □ stone deaf □ Stone the crows! □ stone's throw □ stone-cold sober
STOP
homely enough to stop a clock
STORE
mind the store (for someone) □ put (great) store by someone or something □ set (great) store by someone or something □ store-bought(en)
STORK
keep the stork busy □ keep the stork flying

STORM
come up a storm □ up a storm
STORY
cock-and-bull story □ tell a story
STOVE
built like a depot stove
STRAIGHT
(as) straight as a yard of pump water □ couldn't see straight □ straight shooter
STRAW
called to straw □ pine-straw □ straw boss
STRAWBERRY
Arizona strawberries □ prairie strawberries
STREAK
cuss a blue streak □ have a yellow streak down one's back □ talk a blue streak
STRENGTH
by main strength and awkwardness
STRETCH
down the road a stretch □ stretch someone's neck □ stretch the blanket
STRIKE
strike it rich
STRING
(as) slack as fiddle strings □ has more than one string to his fiddle □ string someone up □ The latch string is always out.
STRONG
(as) strong as Annie Christmas
STUCK
(as) mean as a stuck snake □ bleed like a stuck pig □ squeal like a stuck pig
STUDY
study on something
STUFF
beat the (natural) stuffing out of someone □ kick the (natural) stuffing out of someone
STUMP
beat the devil around the stump □ stir one's stumps □ stump liquor □ stump speech □ up a stump □ whip the devil around the stump
STUN
(as) mad as a stunned gopher
STUPID
My momma didn't raise no stupid child.
STYLE
like it was going out of style
SUCH
Such is life in the West, and the further west you go, the sucher it is.
SUCK
meaner than a junkyard dog (with fourteen sucking pups) □ suck the hind teat □ sucker-bait
SUCKEGG
I'll be a suckegg mule! □ slink like a suckegg hound
SUFFICIENCY
elegant sufficiency
SUGAR
give someone some sugar □ sugar peas
SUIT
suit someone's fancy
SUMMER
summer and winter
SUN
(as) calm as a toad in the sun □ go to bed with the sun □ think the sun rises and sets on someone □ thinks the sun comes up to hear him crow
SUNDAY
know as much about something as a hog knows about Sunday □ month of Sundays □ one's Sunday best □ Sunday go-to-meeting
SUNDRY
all and sundry
SUNNY
sunny-side up
SUPPOSE
S'posing I do?
SURE
(as) sure as God made little green apples □ (as) sure as I'm sitting here □ (as) sure as I'm standing here □

(as) sure as shootin' □ can't say for sure □ certain sure □ It sure is hell when it's this way, and it's this way now. □ not sure but what something □ That's for dang sure!

SURPRISE
Open your mouth and shut your eyes and I'll give you a big surprise.

SUSAN
black-eyed Susan

SUSPENDERS
belt and suspenders

SWALLOW
bitter pill (to swallow) □ swallow something hook, line, and sinker

SWAN
I swan!

SWEAR
swear on a stack of Bibles

SWEAT
sweat something out

SWEET
long sweetenin' □ short sweetening □ sweet mouth someone □ sweet on someone □ sweet potato pie □ sweet tooth

SWELL
swell like a bullfrog □ swell up like a poisoned pup

SWIM
swimmin' hole

SWING
not enough room to swing a cat □ so low you could sit on a newspaper and swing your legs □ so low you could sit on the curb and swing your legs □ swing a wide loop □ We're swingin' on the same gate.

SWINK
swink and tote

SWITCH
asleep at the switch

SWIVET
in a swivet

SWOLL
swoll up

TABLE
table-muscle

TACK
(as) sharp as a tack □ get down to brass tacks

TAG
rag tag and bobtail

TAIL
(as) nervous as a long-tailed cat in a room full of rocking chairs □ bell-tail □ bright-eyed and bushy-tailed □ freeze one's tail off □ hard tail □ has the world by the tail (with a downhill drag) □ have a bear by the tail □ high-tail it □ hike one's tail □ jerk a knot in someone's tail □ Mackerel skies and mares' tails make lofty ships carry low sails. □ put a knot in someone's tail □ ring-tailed snorter □ shirt-tail at half-mast □ tail up and stinger out □ tie a knot in someone's tail □ turkey-tail □ two shakes of a lamb's tail □ wouldn't trust him as far as you could throw a bull by the tail

TAKE
Don't take any wooden nickels. □ it would take an act of Congress to do something □ Plague take it! □ sit down and take a load off (your feet) □ someone ain't worth the powder and lead it would take to shoot someone □ take a gander □ take a look-see □ take a notion to do something □ take a shine to someone □ take ill □ take it on the chin □ take it out of someone's hide □ take on (so) □ take on wood □ take one's Bible oath □ take out after someone or something □ take sick □ take someone down a notch (or two) □ take someone down a peg (or two) □ take someone out to the woodshed □ take someone's word (on something) □ take the big jump □ take to someone or something □ take up with someone □ taking harp lessons

TALE
tall tale

TALK
beans that talk behind your back □ talk a blue streak □ talk box □ talk like a cotton gin in pickin' time □ talk one's head off □ talk some sense into someone □ talk someone's arm off □ talk someone's ear off □ talk trash (about someone) □ talk turkey □ talking iron

TALL
(long) tall drink of water □ a-tall □ head for tall timber □ shit in tall cotton □ tall tale

TALLOW
hair and hide(, horns and tallow) □ would skin a louse for his hide and tallow □ would skin an ant for its tallow

TAN
tan someone's hide

TANGLE
tangle with someone or something

TANYARD
know someone's hide in a tanyard

TAR
(as) slow as coal tar running uphill backwards □ (as) ugly as a tar-bucket □ beat the tar out of someone □ Tar Heel

TASTE
taste of something

TATER
all vine and no taters □ Hold your tater! □ tater chunk

TEA
sassafrass tea

TEACH
so dumb he couldn't teach a hen to cluck

TEACUP
there's more down (in the) cellar in a teacup

TEAKETTLE
ass-over-teakettle

TEAR
torn-down

TEAT
suck the hind teat

TEETH
armed to the teeth □ milk teeth

TELL
done told you □ hear tell (as) □ I don't mind telling you. □ tell a story □ Tell it to a sailor on horseback. □ tell t'other from which □ tell the truth and shame the devil □ truth to tell

TEN
He wears a ten-dollar hat on a five-cent head. □ scare ten years off someone's span of life □ ten-gallon hat

TEND
tend to your own ball of yarn □ tend to your own knitting

TENNESSEE
Tennessee toothpick

TENOR
Arizona tenor

TERRIBLE
something terrible

TERRITORY
light out for the territories

TETCH
tetched (in the head)

TEXAS
gone to Texas □ wouldn't miss something for a farm in Texas

THAN
better than a poke in the eye with a sharp stick □ Better the gravy than no grease at all. □ colder than a mother-in-law's kiss □ colder than a pawnbroker's smile □ darker than the inside of a cow's belly □ drunker than who shot John □ emptier than a banker's heart □ harder than the back of God's head □ has more than one string to his fiddle □ have more luck than sense □ know no more about something than a frog knows

about bed sheets □ less time than skinning a badger □ madder than a wet hen □ meaner than a junkyard dog (with fourteen sucking pups) □ more hopeless than a one-legged man at a (butt-)kickin' contest □ more noise than a jackass in a tin barn □ more noise than a mule in a tin barn □ more something than Carter had oats □ more ways than a country man can whip a mule □ One's eyes are bigger than one's belly. □ One's eyes are bigger than one's stomach. □ quicker than hell could scorch a feather □ quicker than you can bat an eye □ quicker than you can holler howdy □ quicker than you could count two □ slicker than calf slobbers □ steeper than a cow's face □ thicker than boll weevils □ thicker than fleas on a fat pup □ use your head for more than a hatrack □ use your head for more than something to keep your ears apart □ You make a better door than you do a window.

THANK
return thanks □ thank God for small favors □ thank you kindly □ wham bam thank you ma'am

THICK
(as) thick as hops □ thicker than boll weevils □ thicker than fleas on a fat pup

THIEF
steal away like a thief in the night

THING
any fool thing □ every fool thing □ greatest thing since indoor plumbing □ greatest thing since sliced bread □ least little thing □ that very thing

THINK
think a heap of someone or something □ think box □ think someone hung the moon (and stars) □ think someone is God's own cousin □ think the sun rises and sets on someone □ thinks the sun comes up to hear him crow

THOUSAND
thousand-legger

THREE
three-cornered pants

THROAT
die of throat trouble

THROUGH
have been through the mill

THROW
don't have a pot to piss in (or a window to throw it out of) □ stone's throw □ throw in with someone □ throw the hatchet □ wouldn't trust him as far as you could throw a bull by the tail □ wouldn't trust him as far as you could throw him

THUMB
all thumbs □ one's fingers are all thumbs

THUMPER
Bible-thumper

THUNDER
Thunder ain't rain. □ thunder berries

TICK
(as) full as a tick □ blue-tick hound

TICKET
on the ticket □ That's the ticket.

TIE
collar-and-tie men □ fit to be tied □ tie a knot in someone's tail

TIGHT
close chewer and a tight spitter □ sit tight

TILL
beat someone till his hide won't hold shucks □ Church ain't out till they quit singing. □ from here till next Tuesday □ till the cows come home □ till yet

TIMBER
head for tall timber □ inspect the timber

TIME
(as) still as time in a grave □ bad

time (of the month) □ big time □ bless my time of day □ buy something on time □ can't-see time □ half the time □ have one's lady's time □ high time □ in no time flat □ less time than skinning a badger □ Long time no see. □ many (and many)'s the time □ old-time □ old-timer □ old-timey □ pass the time of day □ quittin' time □ sap-risin' time □ talk like a cotton gin in pickin' time □ time's a-wastin'

TIN
(as) dead as a tin of corned beef □ more noise than a jackass in a tin barn □ more noise than a mule in a tin barn

TINHORN
tinhorn gambler

TINTYPE
not on your tintype

TIP
tip one's hand

TIPSY
tipsy cake

TIRED
born tired and raised lazy

TIT
(as) cold as a witch's tit □ (as) useless as tits on a boar □ (as) useless as tits on a bull □ ass-over-tit □ too many pigs for the tits

TOAD
(as) calm as a toad in the sun □ blown up like a toad □ If a toady frog had wings, he wouldn't bump his ass.

TOAST
egg toast

TOBACCO
chaw (of tobacco) □ chew one's own tobacco □ tobacco chaw

TOE
tread on someone's toes

TOLD
done told you

TOLERABLE
tol(er)able (well)

TOMMYHAWK
dig up one's tommyhawk

TOMORROW
like there ain't no tomorrow □ like there's no tomorrow

TONED
high-toned

TONG
hammer and tongs

TONGUE
someone's tongue wags at both ends

TONSIL
paint one's tonsils □ tonsil paintin'

TOO
didn't care too hard □ hold oneself too high □ land too poor to raise a racket on □ too big for one's britches □ too clever by half □ too many pigs for the tits □ too poor to paint and too proud to whitewash

TOOT
toot one's own horn

TOOTH
armed to the teeth □ long in the tooth □ milk teeth □ sweet tooth □ tooth-dentist

TOOTHPICK
Arkansas toothpick □ close enough to use the same toothpick □ Tennessee toothpick

TOPSY
grow like Topsy

TORE
all tore up about something

TORN
torn-down

TOTE
swink and tote □ tote one's own skillet □ tote someone or something

TOUCH
tetched (in the head) □ touch-me-not

TOUGH
(as) tough as puttin' socks on a rooster □ tough customer □ tough

it out □ tough row to hoe □ tough sledding

TOW
tow sack

TOWN
ghost town □ one-horse town □ paint the town red

TOY
like a kid with a new toy

TRACE
kick over the traces

TRACK
(as) low-down as a snake in a wagon track □ make tracks ((to) somewhere) □ not worth a shovelful of chicken tracks □ wouldn't give (someone) a shovelful of chicken tracks for someone or something

TRADE
trading post

TRAIL
hit the trail

TRAIN
ride the gravy train

TRAIPSE
traipse (around) □ traipse (over)

TRAP
have a mind as sharp as a steel trap □ have a mind like a (steel) trap

TRASH
poor white (trash) □ talk trash (about someone)

TREAD
tread on someone's toes

TREE
(as) smart as a tree full of owls □ bark up the wrong tree □ be up a tree □ Joshua tree □ kill a tree □ piss up a tree □ so dry the trees were chasing the dogs □ tree someone or something □ up a tree □ whistle up a gum tree

TRIGGER
quick on the trigger

TRIPLE
triple-distilled

TROT
back door trots □ dog trot □ gossip-trot

TROUBLE
die of throat trouble □ in trouble □ trouble one's (little) head about something

TRUCK
have no truck with something □ just fell off the turnip truck

TRUE
(true) grit

TRUST
In God we trust, all others pay cash. □ wouldn't trust him as far as you could throw a bull by the tail □ wouldn't trust him as far as you could throw him

TRUTH
Ain't it the truth? □ God's honest truth □ gospel truth □ tell the truth and shame the devil □ truth to tell

TRY
like tryin' to scratch your ear with your elbow □ without half trying

TUB
lard tub

TUCK
nip and tuck

TUCKER
one's best bib and tucker □ tuckered out

TUESDAY
from here till next Tuesday

TUNE
can't carry a tune in a bucket □ can't carry a tune in a bushel basket □ can't carry a tune in a paper sack □ change one's tune □ That's the tune the old cow died on.

TURKEY
(as) freckled as a turkey egg □ (as) poor as Job's turkey □ (turkey-)gobbler □ never said pea turkey □ talk turkey □ turkey bumps □ turkey shoot □ turkey's nest □ turkey-tail

TURN
turn belly up
TURNIP
just fell off the turnip truck
TURTLE
(as) helpless as a turtle on his back □ snappin' turtle
TWICE
(as) big as life, and twice as natural □ (as) big as life, and twice as ugly
TWINE
gone where the woodbine twineth
TWO
(as) close as two coats of paint □ (as) like as two peas (in a pod) □ don't make two bites of a cherry □ eyes like two burnt holes in a blanket □ no two ways about it □ quicker than you could count two □ take someone down a notch (or two) □ take someone down a peg (or two) □ two bits □ two jumps ahead of someone □ two shakes of a lamb's tail □ two whoops and a holler □ two-pipe shotgun □ two-rectly
UGLY
(as) big as life, and twice as ugly □ (as) ugly as a tar-bucket □ (as) ugly as home-made soap □ plug ugly □ pug-ugly □ ugly enough to gag a maggot
UNBORN
innocent as a babe unborn
UNCLE
cry uncle □ everybody and his uncle □ holler uncle □ say uncle
UNDER
have a burr under one's saddle
UNS
you-uns
UNTO
sick (un)to death of someone or something
UNWASHED
great unwashed
UPHILL
(as) slow as coal tar running uphill backwards □ walk uphill
UPSIDE
slap someone upside the head
USE
close enough to use the same toothpick □ use your head for more than a hatrack □ use your head for more than something to keep your ears apart
USELESS
(as) useless as tits on a boar □ (as) useless as tits on a bull
VANITY
vanity cake
VARNISH
coffin varnish
VENGEANCE
with a vengeance
VERY
that very thing
VEST
play it close to the vest
VIM
vim and vinegar
VINE
all vine and no taters □ like licking honey off a blackberry vine □ pizen vine
VINEGAR
piss and vinegar □ spit and vinegar □ vim and vinegar □ vinegar pie
VISIT
visit from Flo
WAG
someone's tongue wags at both ends □ wag one's chin
WAGON
(as) low-down as a snake in a wagon track □ chuck wagon
WAIST
waist baby
WAIT
I felt like a penny waiting for change.

□ Wait an hour for the weather to change. □ wait on someone

WALK
kneewalking drunk □ walk on egg (shell)s □ walk uphill

WANT
wouldn't want to be in someone's shoes

WAR
war paint

WARPATH
on the warpath

WASH
gully washer □ It'll all come out in the wash.

WASTE
time's a-wastin'

WATER
(as) straight as a yard of pump water □ (as) weak as pond water □ (long) tall drink of water □ big drink of water □ branch water □ couldn't boil water (without scorching it) □ couldn't boil water without burning it □ couldn't pour water out of a boot (if there was instructions on the heel) □ have just one oar in the water □ like water off a duck's back □ make water □ water shy

WAX
as much chance (of something) as a wax cat in hell

WAY
a ways □ ever(y) which way □ go-way sack □ in the family way □ It sure is hell when it's this way, and it's this way now. □ more ways than a country man can whip a mule □ no two ways about it □ That's the way the hog bladder bounces. □ this a-way and that a-way

WEAK
(as) weak as a cat □ (as) weak as a kitten □ (as) weak as pond water □ weak north of the ears

WEAPON
pack a weapon

WEAR
He wears a ten-dollar hat on a five-cent head. □ wear out one's welcome □ wear someone out □ wear someone to a frazzle □ wear the britches (in the family) □ wear the britches off someone □ wear the pants (in the family)

WEARY
leg-weary

WEATHER
hog-killin' weather □ Wait an hour for the weather to change.

WEDDING
Arkansas wedding cake □ shotgun wedding

WEED
jimson weed □ joe pye weed □ loco weed

WEEVIL
boll weevil □ thicker than boll weevils

WEIGHT
carry weight (with someone)

WELCOME
wear out one's welcome

WELL
as someone damn well pleases □ might as well be hung for a sheep as (for) a lamb □ the well at wit's end □ tol(er)able (well) □ Well, bust my buttons! □ Well, shut my mouth! □ well-fixed □ well-heeled □ would go to the well with someone

WELLDIGGER
(as) cold as a welldigger's ass (in January) □ (as) cold as a welldigger's ears (in January) □ (as) cold as a welldigger's feet (in January)

WESSON
Smith and Wesson

WEST
knock someone or something cat-west □ knock someone or something galley-west □ Such is life in the

West, and the further west you go, the sucher it is.

WET
(as) mad as a wet hen □ (as) slow as wet gunpowder □ madder than a wet hen □ rode hard and put up wet □ wet behind the ears □ wet one's whistle

WHACK
bush-whacker □ out of whack

WHACKY
shack whacky

WHALE
whale into someone

WHAM
wham bam thank you ma'am

WHANG
whang on someone or something

WHAT
(Now) what did you go and do that for? □ Do what? □ give someone what-for □ good for what ails you □ Here's your hat, what's your hurry? □ not sure but what something □ Say what? □ What do you know (about that)? □ What the Sam Hill? □ What's that? □ what-all □ you-know-what

WHEEL
fifth wheel □ If frogs had wheels, they wouldn't bump their butts.

WHEN
behind the door when the brains were passed out □ It sure is hell when it's this way, and it's this way now. □ it'll be a cold day in Hell when something happens □ it'll be a long day in January when something happens □ last one in the back row when the faces was handed out

WHERE
gone where the woodbine twineth □ someone knows where the bear shits

WHETHER
doesn't know whether to shit or go blind □ don't know whether to eat it or rub it on

WHICH
ever(y) which way □ tell t'other from which

WHILE
between whiles □ spell someone (for a while)

WHIP
(as) smart as a whip □ more ways than a country man can whip a mule □ whip the devil around the stump

WHISKER
by a whisker □ so old it's got whiskers

WHISTLE
can (just) whistle for something □ wet one's whistle □ whistle up a gum tree □ whistle-pig □ you ain't just whistlin' Dixie

WHIT
didn't care a whit

WHITE
be on someone like white on rice □ poor white (trash) □ stick (to someone) like white on rice □ white lightning

WHITEWASH
too poor to paint and too proud to whitewash

WHOA
Whoa, Nellie!

WHOLE
(whole) mess of someone or something □ go whole hog □ whole heap more □ whole kit and caboodle □ whole shebang □ whole shooting match

WHOOP
two whoops and a holler □ whoop it up

WHOPPER
whopper-jawed

WHUP
whup someone or something

WHY
fer why

WIDDER
widder(-woman) □ widder-man

WIDE
all wool and a yard wide □ bust someone wide open □ swing a wide loop

WIDOW
grass widow □ graveyard widow □ widder(-woman) □ widder-man

WIFE
mail-order wife □ The devil's beatin' his wife.

WILD
hog wild

WILDCAT
would spit in a wildcat's eye

WILLING
God willing and the creek don't rise □ Lord willing and the creek don't rise

WILLOW
shake like a willow in the wind

WIND
get wind of something □ knock someone or something sky-winding □ shake like a holly in a high wind □ shake like a leaf (in the wind) □ shake like a willow in the wind

WINDOW
crack (open) the window □ don't have a pot to piss in (or a window to throw it out of) □ You make a better door than you do a window.

WING
candidate for a pair of wings □ If a toady frog had wings, he wouldn't bump his ass. □ wing-ding

WINTER
summer and winter

WIRE
barb(ed) wire □ get one's wires crossed

WISE
Open your mouth and shut your eyes and I'll give you something to make you wise.

WISH
wish book

WIT
the well at wit's end

WITCH
(as) cold as a witch's caress □ (as) cold as a witch's tit

WITHIN
within spittin' distance

WITHOUT
(as) yeller as mustard but without the bite □ couldn't boil water (without scorching it) □ couldn't boil water without burning it □ up the creek without a paddle □ without half trying □ without let or leave

WOBBLE
wobble like a newborn calf

WOMAN
fancy woman □ granny woman □ old woman □ painted woman □ The old woman's picking her geese. □ widder(-woman)

WOMEN
God's gift (to women) □ womenfolks

WOOD
Don't take any wooden nickels. □ I wasn't brought up in the woods to be scared by owls. □ neck of the woods □ piney-woods □ piney-woods rooter □ take on wood □ wood pussy □ wood up □ wooden overcoat □ woods colt

WOODBINE
gone where the woodbine twineth

WOODSHED
take someone out to the woodshed

WOOL
all wool and a yard wide □ all wool and no shoddy □ go for wool and come back shorn □ sluts wool

WORD
take someone's word (on something) □ Them's fighting words!

WORK
shoot the works □ work like a bea-

ver □ work like a mule □ work like a slave

WORLD

has the world by the tail (with a downhill drag) □ not long for this world

WORRY

don't worry your (pretty little) head about it

WORTH

be worth one's salt □ not worth a continental □ not worth a hill of beans □ not worth a shovelful of chicken tracks □ someone ain't worth the powder and lead it would take to shoot someone

WRACK

wrack and ruin

WRENCH

wrench (something) out

WRITE

That's all she wrote.

WRONG

bark up the wrong tree

WROTE

That's all she wrote.

YANKEE

(from) so far south they call people from Georgia Yankees

YARD

(as) straight as a yard of pump water □ all wool and a yard wide

YARN

tend to your own ball of yarn

YE

Ye gods (and little fishes)!

YEAR

be gettin' on (in years) □ in an age of years □ in dog's years □ not since the year One □ scare someone out of a year's growth □ scare ten years off someone's span of life □ seven-year itch

YEARLING

rain bull yearlings

YELL

rebel yell

YELLER

(as) yeller as mustard but without the bite

YELLOW

(as) yeller as mustard but without the bite □ have a yellow streak down one's back □ small and yellow and few to the pod □ yellow-bellied □ yellow jacket

YES

Yes indeed(y (do))!

YET

till yet

About the Author

Anne Bertram holds an M.A. in Linguistics from Northwestern University and is a published playwright and poet. She is the author of *NTC's Thesaurus of Everyday American English* and *NTC's Dictionary of Proverbs and Clichés*.